Public Relations Campaigns

Public Relations Campaigns

An Integrated Approach

Second Edition

Regina M. Luttrell

Syracuse University, New York

Luke W. Capizzo

James Madison University, Virginia

Los Angeles | London | New Delhi
Singapore | Washington DC | Melbourne

FOR INFORMATION:

SAGE Publications, Inc.
2455 Teller Road
Thousand Oaks, California 91320
E-mail: order@sagepub.com

SAGE Publications Ltd.
1 Oliver's Yard
55 City Road
London EC1Y 1SP
United Kingdom

SAGE Publications India Pvt. Ltd.
B 1/I 1 Mohan Cooperative Industrial Area
Mathura Road, New Delhi 110 044
India

SAGE Publications Asia-Pacific Pte. Ltd.
18 Cross Street #10-10/11/12
China Square Central
Singapore 048423

Acquisitions Editor: Lily Norton
Associate Editor: Alissa Nance
Editorial Assistant: Sam Diaz
Production Editor: Preethi Agenes Thomas
Copy Editor: Christobel Colleen Hopman
Typesetter: TNQ Technologies
Proofreader: Benny Willy Stephen
Indexer: TNQ Technologies
Cover Designer: Lysa Becker
Marketing Manager: Victoria Velasquez

Printed in Canada

ISBN 978-1-5443-8558-7

This book is printed on acid-free paper.

21 22 23 24 25 10 9 8 7 6 5 4 3 2 1

Brief Contents

Detailed Contents

Foreword

The world of public relations has never been more exciting! When I began my career (back when we walked uphill both ways to school… in the snow and barefoot), there were a handful of things communicators did: media relations, events, reputation management, crisis communications, internal/employee communications, and public and investor affairs.

Today, nearly everything an organization does to communicate with its stakeholders is considered public relations—from Facebook ads and influencer relations to content marketing and search engine optimization. It's so prevalent, in fact, that many marketers are strengthening their communications skills so they can keep up. The best part about that is they have to keep up—we're already there.

There are search engine specialists learning how to pitch journalists and bloggers to *earn* the precious link back to their websites. There are product marketers learning how to write so they can create *owned* content that is interesting and valuable to an audience. And there are social media experts who have been thrown headfirst into a crisis and have had to figure out *how to communicate* their way out.

To boot, we *finally* have a way to show the effectiveness of a public relations program through data. Call it Big Data, small data, or attribution, a communicator has the tools at his or her disposal to prove we are an investment, rather than an expense—as has so long been the case.

It is our time to shine, and we have to make the most of it.

But we aren't quite there yet. I have a friend who is an executive at a Global 500 company. She recently said to me, "You know what's wrong with the PR industry? Most don't know what a strategy is or how to develop one."

That's a real challenge. As an industry, we tend to focus on the tactics and start there versus starting with the end (and the organization's goals) in mind.

The only way to change the perception people have of the PR industry—that we don't do only media relations, that we can develop a strategy, that we can measure our work—is to do things differently. And that begins with strategy development that has measurable goals and more than earned media—or media relations—included.

You can do that when you implement the ROSTIR and PESO models. You'll learn more about these, and how they work, in *Public Relations Campaigns: An Integrated Approach*.

What you will know how to do, by the time you finish reading, is how to do research (R) to help you develop your goals, create your objectives (O) and strategies (S), build a list of tactics (T), figure out your implementation (I) and timeline, and then design your report (R) and do your evaluation.

In between that type of planning is where the PESO Model comes in—paid, earned, shared, and owned media.

Paid media is advertising. Not just Super Bowl–type advertising, but the kind that you can use to amplify your messages online, such as Facebook advertising or pay-per-click.

Earned media is what most people know as publicity—or media relations. You are earning the coverage or mention or interview or story with journalists, bloggers, and influencers.

Shared media is social media. It's more than just posting on your networks, though. It's being strategic about what you're sharing, engaging in conversation, and building community.

And owned media is content marketing. Though it started out as blogging, it's evolved to website content, contributed content for publications and blogs, podcasts, videos, livestreaming, and more.

There also are things to consider including in your plan and implementation where the media types overlap—marketing communications, influencer marketing, email marketing, lead generation, distribution and promotion, and more.

When you combine these models, you effectively create reputation—both online and off. You become a search engine optimization master and you build expertise for the organization and the people who work inside it.

I am often asked which is the most important of the four media types. While they're of equal importance, particularly in an integrated campaign, I am preferential to owned media. You cannot have P, E, or S without O. You need content to share on social media. You need content to amplify through paid media. And you need content to share with journalists and bloggers to prove you have a unique perspective and can string together some sentences intelligently. Content sits at the middle of the model. Get that right—and I mean really right—and you'll win every time.

What's more, the combination of the two models require you to take a Diversity-First Approach considering all aspects of diversity, equity, and inclusion at the start of every initiative. The Diversity & Inclusion Wheel, which you'll learn more about in this book, has six core spokes that you should consider when you're developing any campaign. This means you should consider all six when you're crafting your communications plans and when you're launching a new product or service. It's up to every one of us to be certain that no professor anywhere in the world holds up our work and says to their students, "Who approved this?"

You'll learn more about these gaffes as you continue to read and you'll begin to understand why it's up to you that brands do better when it comes to diversity, equality, and inclusion.

Regina Luttrell and Luke Capizzo will help you get there. If you are a student or a seasoned professional, the case studies, tips, "Think Ahead" points, and the "Think Critically" questions included in this book will help you make the most of your future in communications.

The world, as they say, is our oyster right now. Let's not let marketing or search engine specialists or advertisers take what belongs to us. It's time to stand up and prove we can do more than media relations. Build programs that are strategic. Measure our effectiveness (and tweak, as necessary). And take the lead with public relations. I hope you'll join Regina, Luke, and me in showing every organization in the world that public relations is where they should start and end.

—Gini Dietrich, CEO of Arment Dietrich and
author and founder of *Spin Sucks*

Preface

WHY INTEGRATED CAMPAIGNS? WHY NOW?

The U.S. Bureau of Labor Statistics predicts the employment of public relations (PR) specialists will grow by 7 percent between 2019 and 2029.[1] Growth is being driven by the need for organizations to maintain their public image and build relationships with critical stakeholders and publics. Students are graduating and moving into a communications work environment that is fully integrated: PR, social media, marketing, and advertising are all part of the equation at many organizations. In fact, the 2020 Relevancy Report, an annual research project from the USC Annenberg Center for Public Relations, states that disruption in the profession will continue and the convergence in marketing and PR will deepen.[2] What is evident is that the profession of PR is shifting. Central to success in this changing environment is a strategic approach to strategic PR planning that balances paid, earned, shared, and owned media.

Our book—designed for an upper-level PR campaigns class—integrates PR best practices, marketing approaches, and new media opportunities. Readers will learn about how today's practitioners implement award-winning campaigns and the research-driven, strategic choices that underscore that success. In the second edition of *Public Relations Campaigns: An Integrated Approach*, we lead with PR but also provide broad coverage of the rapidly changing skills and tactics students and practitioners need to thrive in the field of PR. The book is rooted in PR principles that emphasize a practical approach to developing successful integrated PR campaigns. It provides students with the framework and **theory**-based knowledge to begin their work not just as tacticians but as counselors who provide research, perspective, and insights that help organizations communicate more effectively, understand complex environments, build relationships, and add strategic value and insights.

In this second edition, we introduce our diversity-first approach to PR planning and execution, which means that PR practitioners must be intentional with each campaign element. Diversity and inclusion must be considered in all aspects of the campaign process including research, development, planning, and execution. We believe that true diversity and inclusion initiatives require ongoing commitment. Because PR practitioners have a seat at the management table we must help lead the decisions that impact organizations and their internal and external stakeholders. We introduce students to the Diversity & Inclusion Wheel, a tool to use when developing and implementing campaigns. Our hope is that students will understand diversity, equity, and inclusion starting from the earliest phases of campaign planning.

While practical in nature, the pedagogical approach to this textbook is student-centered, inquiry-based learning. Readers have the opportunity to first examine the essential elements of PR planning, then analyze various PR case studies, and also develop the skills and perspective to plan an integrated campaign of their own with the information they have learned.

A variety of features reinforce this approach, providing tips, structure, examples, and context. Each chapter is organized with clear learning objectives ("Think Ahead" points to begin each chapter) and "Think Critically" questions to reinforce and practice key elements. *Public Relations Campaigns: An Integrated Approach* is geared toward the many PR students each year enrolling in "campaigns" classes, with the goal of providing learners with a robust and realistic framework for understanding, developing, and executing integrated PR campaigns. We designed this book to be a guide and reference point for readers by including a series of real-world examples that give context and insight into the world of PR today.

ORGANIZATION OF THE BOOK

Leveraging practical applications of each theory or model of interest, this book provides numerous case studies to aid in a deeper understanding of the underlying principles. The first three chapters introduce readers to the theories behind PR and the process of PR planning, placing particular importance on the ROSTIR model for PR planning: Research/Diagnosis, Objectives, Strategy, Tactics, Implementation, and Reporting/Evaluation as well as the PESO model—paid media, earned media, shared/social media, and owned media. For an advanced course on campaign development, this model moves beyond traditional R.O.P.E. or R.A.C.E. planning models to focus students on each step of the strategic planning process. And finally, we introduce the Diversity & Inclusion Wheel, which helps students understand how to create truly diverse campaigns at each stage in the process.

Chapters 4–10 delve deeper into each individual component of both ROSTIR and PESO models so that students are exposed to a richer discussion of each step of the planning process of an integrated campaign, including how PR practitioners are aligning strategies to achieve client objectives. Key definitions are provided to help in mastering the language of PR professionals. A wide variety of strategies and tactics are introduced to expose students to the many paid, earned, shared, and owned media approaches available to them. It also showcases the ways in which these approaches can combine to support achieving organizational and communication goals and objectives.

The final chapter provides a variety of tools and templates to help students and professionals create campaign plans and execute successful projects.

Introduction **Campaigns in the Professional Public Relations Context**

This section provides an introduction to some of the most commonly used PR models, theories, and principles in the practice of PR.

Part I Strategic Public Relations Planning

Chapter 1 Introduction to Integrated Campaigns

Real-world campaigns are challenged by time, budgets, personnel, personalities, and internal barriers. But talented practitioners can use the tools of PR and integrated communication to develop comprehensive, cohesive, results-driven strategic campaigns. Students begin to understand the impact of campaigns while learning the strategy behind integrated planning and the importance of diversity and inclusion throughout the process.

Case Study: Ambev Wants You to "Dirnk Repsnosilby"

Chapter 2 Strategic Communication Campaign Fundamentals

This chapter hones in on why PR practitioners plan, expands on the elements of a strategic plan, and explores the ROSTIR framework for campaign development and the inclusion of the Diversity Wheel.

Case Study: [unlabeled]™

Chapter 3 Understanding PESO

The key to mastering integrated PR is to recognize the importance of the PESO model and formulate strategic plans based on weaving together paid, earned, shared, and owned media. This chapter explains what PESO is and introduces how each approach can be used to form a strategic, holistic campaign.

Case Study: The Tampon Book

Part II Discovering ROSTIR

Chapter 4 Research, Part I: Diagnosis and Developmental Research

Research is the first step in the PR planning process. This chapter centers on understanding your organization's industry and community environment, crafting research questions, and selecting research methods for integrated PR campaigns while implementing the diversity-first approach.

Case Study: A New Dawn Breaks for Barbie

Chapter 5 Research, Part II: Goals

Understanding an organization and its goals helps PR practitioners define key audiences, stakeholders, and publics. This chapter provides insights to help apply organizational goals to communication- and campaign-focused goals.

Case Study: Burger King—Be Your Way

Chapter 6 Objectives

In this chapter, readers begin to identify what constitutes high-value objectives. Readers will be able to differentiate between various types of objectives, recognize and craft S.M.A.R.T objectives, and learn to focus objectives toward key audiences.

Case Study: HeForShe—Shining a New Light on The HeForShe Movement and Gender Equality

Chapter 7 Strategies

Choosing the right channels can be challenging. Chapter 7 summarizes how best to integrate strategies into PR campaigns by assessing the right approach for an organization's target audience, leveraging an organization's strengths and resources, and examining the competitive landscape.

Case Study: Long-lasting Positive Change: Washington University in St. Louis

Chapter 8 Tactics

Defining the right tools and tactics is critical for the success of any campaign. This chapter classifies the various types of paid, earned, shared, and owned tactics and illustrates how they are strategically used in PR planning.

Case Study: PEEPS® Counts Down to a Sweet New Year

Chapter 9 Implementation

This chapter demystifies the processes behind implementation, including implications surrounding the components of the campaign such as creating timelines, dividing tasks among a team, setting deadlines, setting clear expectations, working with other people outside of the field of PR, building relationships with the media, prioritizing, and the importance of awareness and self-evaluation.

Case Study: Innovation Generates Leaders—Community-wide Girl Scout Cookie Sales Event

Chapter 10 Reporting and Evaluation

This chapter focuses on connecting measurement and evaluation to the overall objectives, how to tell if objectives are achievable, and the best path to prioritize information based on their value to the decision-making process.

Case Study: HP's Continued Commitment to Global Wellness

Part III Campaigns in Action

Chapter 11 Formulating an Integrated Campaign

This final chapter includes a variety of foundational guides and templates that students can use to help reinforce ideas introduced in the book including the ROSTIR PR Planning Guide, the PRSA Independent Practitioners Alliance (IPA) proposal template, an example client report, an audience persona guide, and a crisis communication plan.

Student Learning Resources

This book leads with PR but offers an integrated approach that encompasses aspects of social media, marketing, advertising, and client management, for a broader view of the campaign planning process. This text is offered in 11 chapters, making the content easy to digest within a one-semester course.

Think Ahead: Learning objectives appear at the beginning of each chapter to engage students, encouraging them to think about the material before they connect with the text.

Think Critically: These end-of-chapter questions challenge students to reflect on and apply the material they have learned.

Diversity- & Inclusion-First Approach: To promote effective communication and growth of an organization, students learn to use the Diversity & Inclusion Wheel to think D&I at the inception of any assignment throughout the strategic planning process to evaluation and measurement. The goal is for students to learn to integrate a cross-cultural, multicultural approach to PR aligned under one strategy. Every case study includes a summary of how the campaign employed diversity initiatives.

Case Studies: Numerous case studies demonstrate the proven ROSTIR (research/diagnosis, objectives, strategies, tactics, implementation, reporting/evaluation) and PESO (paid, earned, shared, owned) campaign processes from research to reporting, illustrating exactly how PR campaigns function in the professional world.

Concept Case: At the conclusion of each chapter, readers are introduced to a series of exercises where they can apply the takeaways from each topic to the operational activities of a fictitious client, a national chain of yoga studios. Community Flow Yoga, which is a new start-up chain, is designed to offer a high standard of quality and consistency but also give back to the communities where it does business like a local studio.

PRo Tips: Call-out boxes highlight tips from PR professionals and educators.

Key Terms: Highlighted vocabulary is used as a study guide with complete definitions in the glossary.

Appendix: The appendix includes additional reading material that accompanies and adds additional depth to chapters from the text, particularly in the areas of research, strategy, and tactics.

Acknowledgments

We would like to express our deepest appreciation to those who reviewed drafts of the manuscript and made truly insightful suggestions that we have done our best to incorporate into this book:

Gregg Feistman, *Temple University*
Brenda K. Foster, *American University*
Jessica Block Nerren, *California State University: San Bernardino*
Peggy M. Rupprecht, *North Dakota State University*
Natalie Tindall, *Lamar University*
Justin Walden, *Creighton University*

We give special thanks to Lily Norton and Alissa Nance, our editors at SAGE. We relied upon your expertise as we navigated updating our book to the second edition. Your direction, guidance, thoughtfulness, and patience resulted in a book beyond our expectations. A special note of gratitude to Sam Diaz for facilitating the details.

We would be remiss if we did not thank Ghazal Kawar and Raiah Brown, research assistants from Syracuse University who contributed case studies to the second edition, for their meticulous efforts in pulling together the ancillary materials. We appreciate your experience and wisdom.

Without the countless public relations professionals and public relations educators, this book would not be possible. In particular, Gini Dietrich and her deep knowledge of and evangelism for the PESO model and integrated public relations approaches is a leader in demonstrating its power and practicality. To all, please accept our sincere gratitude.

About the Authors

Regina M. Luttrell, Ph.D., is currently the associate dean of research and creative activity and the director of the W20 Emerging Insights Lab at the S.I. Newhouse School of Public Communications at Syracuse University. A contributor to *PR Tactics* and *PR News*, as well as peer-reviewed journals, she is a noted speaker where she frequently presents at national and international conferences and business events on topics related to the current social media revolution, the ongoing public relations evolution, and millennials within the classroom and workplace. She is the (co)author of the following books: *Social Media: How to Engage, Share, and Connect*; *The Millennial Mindset: Unraveling Fact from Fiction*; *Brew Your Business: The Ultimate Craft Beer Playbook*; *The PR Agency Handbook*; and *A Practical Guide to Ethics in Public Relations*. Prior to entering the educational field, she spent the first portion of her career in corporate public relations and marketing. Her extensive background includes strategic development and implementation of public relations and social media, advertising, marketing, and corporate communications. She has led multiple rebranding campaigns, designed numerous websites, managed high-level crisis situations, and garnered media coverage that included hits with the *New York Times*, the CBS Evening News, and the Associated Press.

Luke W. Capizzo (PhD, APR) is an assistant professor at James Madison University, specializing in public relations. He is the coauthor (with Regina Luttrell) of *The PR Agency Handbook* and has published scholarly work in such outlets as *Public Relations Review*. His research interests include social issues management, corporate social responsibility, public relations and civil society, and public relations education. Prior to attending the University of Maryland to earn his PhD, he practiced public relations for eight years with a focus on media relations in the financial services, commercial real estate, manufacturing, retail, and technology industries, serving in both agency and in-house roles. Working with a wide variety of clients—from the Fortune 500 to small businesses and nonprofits—he garnered media coverage in top national outlets and trade publications, secured and prepared clients for national cable news interviews, and led projects to improve agency-wide media training, staff onboarding, and client evaluation and reporting metrics. He is an Arthur W. Page Center Legacy Scholar (2020) and has earned the APR (Accreditation in Public Relations) designation through the Public Relations Society of America.

Introduction

CAMPAIGNS IN THE PROFESSIONAL PUBLIC RELATIONS CONTEXT

iStock.com/monkeybusinessimages

THINK AHEAD

0.1 Describe relevant theories of communication and explain how they relate to the practice of public relations.

0.2 Grasp different approaches to public relations campaign planning using both communication theory and public relations planning models.

0.3 Identify the five objectives a communicator employs that provide a clear set of potential outcomes for strategic campaigns.

Theories exist to provide a framework for public relations practitioners to develop their decision-making processes and for planning integrated campaigns. Numerous books are available regarding the topic of **communication theory** and how it relates to public relations. This is not one of those books. What you will find within these initial pages is an introduction to some of the most prominent theories and planning models in the practice of public relations. This introduction should be used as an overarching summary of the theories and planning models employed in public relations campaign planning.

This book is intentionally organized with the many theories and principles of public relations introduced first to provide readers with a better sense of the "why" behind the

PRo Tip

CRITERIA FOR EVALUATING THEORY

Scholars Marianne Dainton and Elaine D. Zelley developed a means by which scholarly theories of communication can be evaluated.[1] These include accuracy, practicality, succinctness, consistency, and acuity.

Accuracy	Has research supported that the theory works the way it says it does?
Practicality	Have real-world applications been found for the theory?
Succinctness	Has the theory been formulated with the appropriate number (fewest possible) of concepts or steps?
Consistency	Does the theory demonstrate coherence within its own premises and with other theories?
Acuity	To what extent does the theory make clear an otherwise complex experience?

Source: Marianne Dainton and Elaine D. Zelley, *Applying Communication Theory for Professional Life: A Practical Introduction* (Thousand Oaks, CA: SAGE Publications, 2015).

"how" of planning. **Public relations** theories, principles, and goals are fostered from the ideologies found within the study of communication. Therefore, it is the job of the practitioner to consider the appropriate theories and models when making decisions and building successful relationships with stakeholders. Properly understanding the theory can help explain how to best develop public relations plans that are most effective in practice for the clients that we represent.

PUBLIC RELATIONS THEORIES AND PRINCIPLES

A **theory** is an idea or set of ideas that is intended to explain related facts or events.[2] The public relations industry is built upon various theories, mainly due to the fact that there is no single theory that is able to fulfill every plan or proposal that a practitioner must organize and execute. Practitioners, therefore, must consider which theory and model is appropriate for their specific planning situations. An obvious place to begin is by examining some of the most widely used theories in the practice and planning of public relations.

Excellence Theory

Considered a monumental study in public relations, the Excellence Study and resulting **excellence theory** can be seen as an integration of strategic management theories of public relations into a greater whole.[3] Led by James E. Grunig, the excellence theory is the culmination of a fifteen-year study (1985–2000), funded by the International Association of Business Communicators (IABC), that focused on unveiling the best practices in communication management. Grunig reasoned that the ideal role for public relations is in a strategic management function. By being part of the management team, practitioners encourage leadership to share power through symmetrical two-way communication between an organization and its publics. Rather than using persuasion or one-way "press agentry" approaches, Grunig concluded that providing and receiving information is the most effective and ethical approach to achieving long-term organizational goals, improved relationships with publics, and mutual understanding.[4] The premise behind the excellence theory expressed that the value of public relations lies in the importance of the relationship between an organization and its publics. The development of sound relationships with strategic publics is a critical component for organizations to properly define and achieve goals desired by both the organization and its publics, reduce costs of negative publicity, and increase revenue by providing products and services needed by stakeholders.[5] It is the responsibility of public relations practitioners to identify key publics and cultivate long-term relationships with them using open two-way symmetrical communication. Grunig and his team identified three particular areas of importance to consider:[6]

- Senior management: Involvement in strategic leadership is a critical characteristic of excellent public relations. Public relations executives play a strategic managerial role by having access to key organizational decision makers.
- Organization of communication: The public relations function loses its unique role in strategic management if it is redirected through marketing or other management channels. Therefore, it is essential that the public relations department is headed not by a technician but by a manager who has the ability to conceptualize and direct public relations functions.
- Diversity in public relations: Research illustrates that organizations with excellent public relations value women as much as men within these strategic roles and develop programs to empower women throughout the organization. Today, we continue to see the value of diversity within an organization.

Systems Theory

Each organization should be considered interdependent and interact with various stakeholders to survive and thrive. **Systems theory** can help public relations

FIGURE 0.1
Systems Theory

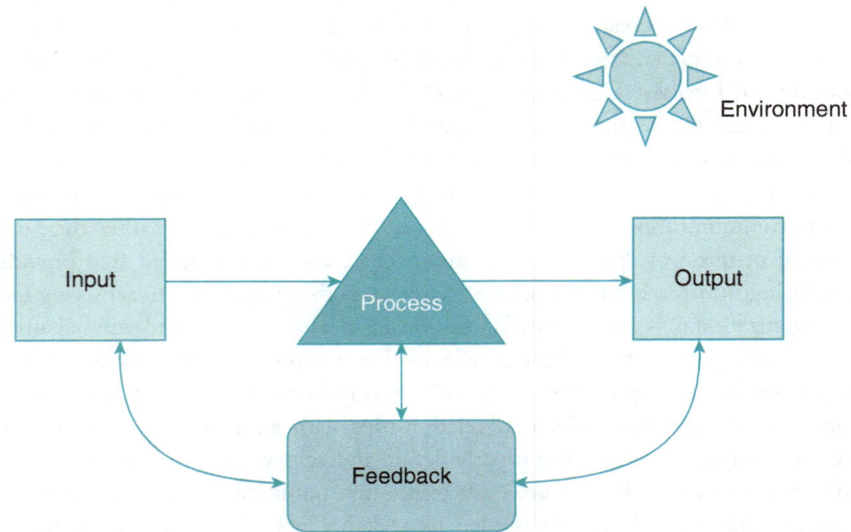

Systems theory positions organizations as part of systems, where one action or process creates feedback and impacts all actors within the environment.

practitioners recognize many of the boundaries found within organizations. This theory understands that organizations are comprised of interrelated parts, adapting and adjusting to changes in the political, economic, and social environments in which they operate.[7] Consider the following example. Envision, for a moment, that you work for a company that makes ice cream. This organization must rely on farmers to provide milk, sugar, and other essential ingredients; customers to purchase their product; the government to set food regulations; the media to help spread their message; and financial institutions to keep them moving forward. As a public relations practitioner, how might you approach any disturbances/evolutions that may occur in the overall business environment? According to Cutlip, Center, and Broom, in an organization such as this, one of the essential roles of public relations is based on a systems theory approach: to help this organization adjust and adapt to changes in its environment.[8]

Diffusion Theory

Diffusion theory is a specific area of communication concerned with the spread of messages that are perceived as new ideas. This theory was developed to explain how, over time, an idea or product gains momentum and spreads through a specific

FIGURE 0.2
Diffusion Theory

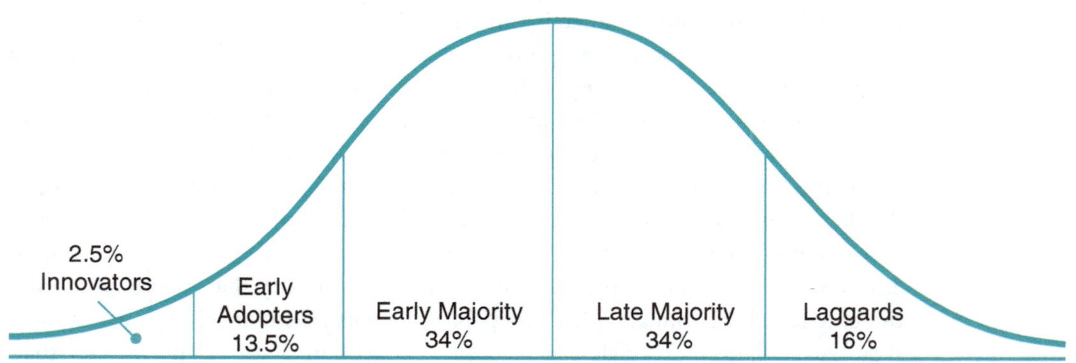

While many companies and organizations focus on the first people to try a new product or technology (innovators and early adopters), the majority of consumers wait and see rather than rush to adopt.

population or social system.[9] Everett Rogers, communication researcher, claimed that people make decisions or accept ideas based on the following principles:

1. "Awareness: Individuals are exposed to an idea.
2. Interest: The idea stimulates the individual.
3. Evaluation: The individual considers the idea as potentially useful.
4. Trial: The individual tests the idea.
5. Adoption: The individual acceptance or adoption of the idea after having successfully moved through the four earlier stages."[10]

Public relations practitioners use this approach when planning campaigns to understand how information about organizations, events, products, or issues will be received by the intended audience. It is also useful when evaluating how to appropriately segment messages and develop outreach approaches for different audience groups, as some individuals seek out new experiences, processes, and products (innovators and early adopters) while others wait until nearly everyone else around them has a new piece of technology before using it (laggards).

Framing Theory

The development of **framing theory** has been attributed to sociologist Erving Goffman and anthropologist Gregory Bateson. Framing involves the process of calling attention to a particular aspect of the reality described.[11] Essentially, Goffman and Bateson are suggesting that what is presented to the audience, often called "the frame," can influence the choices that people make about how to process the information they are receiving. For example, when journalists and editors make decisions about whom to interview, what questions are appropriate to ask, and the article content, they are "framing" the story.[12] In essence, framing is the way that a communication source defines and constructs any piece of communicated information.[13] The most common use of frames for public relations practitioners is in how they define problems, diagnose or identify the root cause of the problem, make decisions on how to proceed, and develop solutions to the problem.[14] The media are often thought to influence the perception of the news because they not only tell the audience what to think about but also how to think about a particular issue simply by the way that the news is written, presented, and disseminated. Because public relations practitioners often act as sources themselves, these individuals can be seen as contributing to framing a story that is presented in the media.[15] Framing and the **agenda setting theory** are often connected.

Agenda Setting and Agenda Building Theories

Maxwell McCombs and Donald Shaw were the first researchers to solidify the idea of **agenda setting**. They originally proposed that the media sets the public agenda by not necessarily telling people what to think but what to think *about*.[16] McCombs and Shaw noted,

> In choosing and displaying news, editors, newsroom staff, and broadcasters play an important part in shaping political reality. Readers learn not only about a given issue, but also how much importance to attach to that issue from the amount of information in a news story and its position.[17]

While this theory was originally intended for the news media, public relations professionals can be perceived as using agenda setting when they create and disseminate messages to various audiences, as well as when they work with media as sources on news stories and articles.

Similarly, **agenda building** is the process by which active publics and organizations focused on a cause to attract the attention of the news media and public officials to add their issue to the public agenda.[18] The **agenda building theory** is considered to be an extension of agenda setting. Examples of agenda building can include the release of a report on the effects of global warming, a speech about the movement Black Lives Matter, or even a Facebook page promoting the worldwide rallies held by the Women's March to advocate for legislation and policies regarding human rights and other issues, including women's rights, immigration reform, health-care reform, reproductive rights, the natural environment, LGBTQ+ rights, racial equality, freedom of religion, and workers' rights.

PRo Tip

AGENDA SETTING

In political campaigns, the media may not be effective in swaying public support toward or against a particular issue or candidate. But by continually raising particular questions and issues, or simply by showing an interest in a particular political candidate or issue, the media can lead the discussion toward or away from issues important to the candidate and even to the public (as identified through polls).[19]

Professor Ron Smith, The State University of New York at Buffalo

The difference between the two theories can be understood in this way: traditional agenda setting explained the news media's influence on audiences by their choice of what stories to consider newsworthy and how much prominence and space to give them, whereas agenda building theory suggests there is an exchange between the media and sources or society broadly to build an agenda.[20]

Situational Crisis Communication Theory

One of the most widely used theories is **situational crisis communication theory**, also known as SCCT. One of the leading researchers in this area, W. Timothy Coombs, notes that SCCT attempts to predict the level of threat to an organization's reputation during a crisis situation. Crisis management is a growing area within public relations and should play a central role in public relations practitioners' planning. As described in this theory, a crisis is defined as "the negative event that leads stakeholders to assess crisis responsibility."[21] Public relations practitioners often use this theory when faced with responding to a crisis. SCCT provides a recommended framework for response strategies when facing a reputational threat by helping practitioners assess the initial crisis responsibility, crisis history, and prior relational reputation.[22]

As with any discipline based on numerous models, theories on how to properly practice public relations will continue to evolve and develop over time. The seven aforementioned theories present a solid foundation to build upon as we begin to introduce different models for public relations planning. As you will see, these models give practitioners a way to organize concepts and ideas by types of public relations practice. Theories, coupled with planning models, help public relations practitioners predict more effectively what will and will not work in the practice of public relations.

FIGURE 0.3
Two-step Flow Model

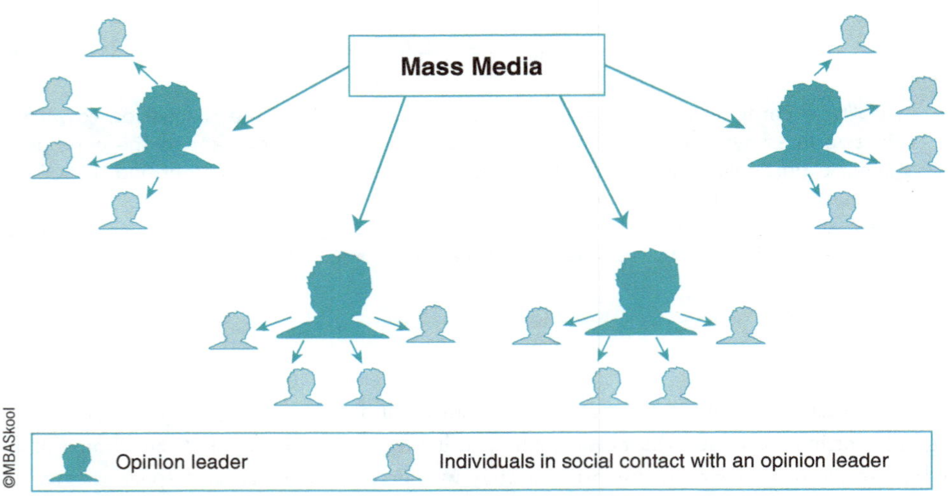

Two-step Flow Model

One of the earliest mass communication models of adoption in the field of public relations is the **two-step flow model**.[23] This model states that an organization initially targets its message to the mass media, which in turn delivers that message to the throngs of viewers, readers, and listeners. Individuals that take the time to seek out and understand information on particular societal topics are considered "opinion leaders." Opinion leaders can have substantial influence over their followers. Research indicates that opinion leaders who share the same social status as their followers are the most effective.[24] Opinion leaders consist of individuals from a large range of backgrounds, including family members,[25] doctors, local politicians, mommy bloggers, parish leaders, or educators. Most of the time, opinion leaders are individuals who are well respected within their circle of influence. In the social media world these leaders are often referred to as "influencers."

MODELS OF PUBLIC RELATIONS PRACTICE

Organizations can practice public relations from a variety of different perspectives, whether it is to get information out into public view; to serve as an objective, journalistic voice within and for an organization; to advocate on behalf of an organization in public view; or to provide perspective and insights to balance the relationship

PRo Tip

THEORIES IN PRACTICE—MODELING MEDIA RELATIONS

Public relations scholars Lynn Zoch and Juan-Carlos Molleda created a theoretical model for media relations by combining framing theory and agenda building with the concept of information subsidies. In this case an *information subsidy* represents the value of content within a particular pitch made by a public relations professional to a journalist. It could include access to a difficult-to-reach source, a head start on information not yet available to the public, or details about a particular situation not shared with other media outlets.

To create the theoretical model, Zoch and Molleda explain that practitioners create information subsidies for journalists that frame issues based on the way the organization would prefer to see an issue addressed publicly. Journalists can accept or reject the frame presented as part of their research and preparation in writing a story. In this way, practitioners contribute to agenda building by supporting journalistic interest and coverage of desired issues by mainstream media.

Source: Lynn M. Zoch and Juan-Carlos Molleda, "Building a Theoretical Model of Media Relations Using Framing, Information Subsidies and Agenda Building," in *Public Relations Theory II*, ed. Carl H. Botan and Vincent Hazleton (Mahwah, NJ: Lawrence Erlbaum, 2006), 279-309.

between an organization and its publics. These viewpoints are captured in Grunig and Hunt's four models of public relations: press agentry, public information, two-way asymmetrical, and two-way symmetrical.[26]

Press Agentry

In the **press agentry model**, or publicity model, public information flows in one direction—from the organization to its audiences and publics. Grunig and Hunt noted that persuasion is often used to achieve organizational goals. This model is one of the oldest forms of public relations and is often synonymous with promotions and publicity. Public relations practitioners using this model are generally looking for "ink": media coverage. Essentially, these practitioners are hoping to get their organization mentioned in the media for purposes of promotion. This model can include propaganda tactics and publicity stunts such as giveaways, large events, or celebrity sponsorships.

Public Information

The purpose of the **public information model** is to provide relevant and useful information directly to the public rather than for promotional purposes or targeted publicity. This model, positioning public relations practitioners as journalists-in-residence, employs one-way communication and is widely leveraged within the areas of government relations, educational institutions, nonprofit corporations, and some corporations.[27] While this approach is neutral in its overall outreach, it is considered "craft" rather than "professional" public relations due to its nonstrategic nature. For example, many government officials leading communication efforts go by job titles such as *public information officer*, with their mandate to inform the public—using both traditional earned media and digital channels—about what is going on in their specific department or agency.

Two-way Asymmetrical

By implementing scientific persuasion methodologies, the goal of the **two-way asymmetrical model** of public relations planning is to convince others to accept an organization's message. Public relations practitioners capitalize on the use of surveys, interviews, and focus groups to measure relationships in an effort for the organization to design public relations programs that will gain the support of key, targeted publics. Information does flow between the organization and its publics; however, the organization is more interested in having their publics adjust to the organization rather than the opposite. Political campaigns as well as traditional public health initiatives are examples of the two-way asymmetrical model.

Two-way Symmetrical

The **two-way symmetrical model** presents a balanced, strategic, and informed approach to public relations. Organizations and their publics adjust to each other and attempt to achieve mutual understanding using two-way communication, not persuasion. When public relations practitioners employ the two-way symmetrical model they not only provide information to their intended publics but also listen and receive information. Some believe that the development and adoption of social media as a communication platform provides an effective and efficient avenue for conducting two-way symmetrical communication.[28]

Public relations is a strategic process established to influence public opinion, through sound ethical and accurate implementation, based on mutually satisfactory two-way communication. In practice, public relations departments use a mixture of these models depending on the goal, message, or public at hand. Some of the more historically well-known models are also extremely valuable as tools in strategic planning.

PUBLIC RELATIONS PLANNING MODELS

Several useful planning models identify central ideas within public relations and inform development of campaign objectives, strategies, and tactics. Each of these models is presented below, including the R.O.P.E., R.A.C.E., and R.O.S.I.E. planning models.[29] Let us take a closer look.

R-A-C-E, R-O-P-E, or R-O-S-I-E

We've already seen that planning and processes are an integral part of the successful execution of a public relations campaign. John Marston developed the four-step management process for public relations in his 1963 book, *The Nature of Public Relations*, which he called the R-A-C-E model.[30] To this day many public relations practitioners implement and follow it regularly:

Research: Practitioners must first conduct research to understand the problem or situation.

Action: Practitioners decide what actions will be taken to address the problem or situation.

Communication: Practitioners determine which channels will be used to communicate the plan of action to the public.

Evaluation: Practitioners assess whether or not the defined goals were achieved.

Shelia Clough-Crifasi expanded on the R.A.C.E. model in the year 2000 to encompass a more managerial approach when she developed the R.O.S.I.E. model: R—Research, O—Objectives, S—Strategies and planning, I—Implementation, and E—Evaluation.[31] Other iterations of the R.A.C.E. and R.O.S.I.E. model exist in public relations planning as well, including the P-A-C-E (planning, action, communication, evaluation) model, the A-C-E (assessment, communication, evaluation) model, and the S-T-A-R-E (scan, track, analyze, respond, evaluate) model.[32] Regardless of which model is subscribed to, planning is essential if practitioners want to achieve positive outcomes that enhance an organization's relationships with its public. Each of these models outlines the importance of several key factors: the role of research and planning to understand the situation at hand; the identification of clear, measurable objectives; the planning and execution of the campaign itself; and the evaluation of the campaign's success based on its achievement of those objectives.

ROSTIR: Research, Objectives, Strategies, Tactics, Implementation, and Reporting

This book is organized around a new evolution of this approach, the ROSTIR model, which emphasizes the steps in this process necessary for successful campaigns in today's rapidly changing public relations landscape. ROSTIR stands for Research (including developmental research, diagnosis, and goal setting), Objectives, Strategies, Tactics, Implementation, and Reporting/Evaluation. As we'll explore in the chapters to come, this model clearly reflects the campaign planning needs of practitioners and can be understood in conjunction with the other models.

PRo Tip

STRATEGIC MESSAGING

When creating strategic messaging, Jamie Turner from the *60 Second Marketer* advises practitioners should do the following:

- Prioritize and crystallize information
- Ensure consistency, continuity, and accuracy
- Measure and track success

Source: Jaimie Turner, "Three Tips to Overcome Email Fatigue in the New Year," *60 Second Marketer*, January 20, 2015, https://60secondmarketer.com/blog/2015/01/20/three-tips-overcome-email-fatigue-new-year/.

Each of these models enriches our understanding of how public relations is practiced, but they can only take public relations planning so far. Every approach to campaign planning should be thought of as either circular or ongoing and including research and evaluation as a central component during every stage of the planning process. As a strategic management function, public relations adds value to organizations by continually assessing the organizational environment and adjusting communication strategies and tactics accordingly. Campaigns may end, but the planning process never does: the end of one campaign becomes the beginning of the next. That being said, any good model also relies on the development of solid strategic communication targets with appropriately defined goals, objectives, and purpose.

Communication Goals

Strategic communication can be either informational or persuasive in nature; however, its overarching purpose is to build an understanding and garner support for ideas, causes, services, and products. Given that public relations is a deliberate process, every instance of communication must contain a goal, objective, and purpose. There are four standard communication goals that are regularly referred to in the industry: to inform the recipient, persuade the recipient, motivate the recipient, and build a mutual understanding between the recipient and the originator of the message.[33] Patrick Jackson, former editor of *pr reporter*, believes that when creating a piece of communication, "the communicator should ask whether the proposed message is appropriate, meaningful, memorable, understandable, and believable to the prospective recipient."[34]

Just as the development of appropriate content is important, public relations practitioners must also pay special attention to the objectives of the messages being communicated. In addition to contributing to multiple public relations theories, James E. Grunig has also introduced five objectives for a communicator in order to provide a clear set of potential outcomes for strategic campaigns.[35]

1. **Message exposure**: Audiences are exposed to messages in various forms. From newsletters to brochures, blogs, and social media channels, public relations practitioners often provide materials to the mass media to disseminate their messages.
2. **Accurate dissemination of the message**: Information can be filtered by editors, journalists, and bloggers, but the overarching message stays intact as it is transmitted through various channels.
3. **Acceptance of the message**: The audience retains the message and can accept it as valid based on their perceptions and views.
4. **Attitude change**: The audience members will make a mental or verbal commitment to change their behavior as a result of the message.
5. **Change in behavior**: The audience genuinely changes their behavior. This could be to purchase the product and use it or vote for a different candidate in an election.

PULLING IT ALL TOGETHER

Theories and models related to practical public relations execution continue to evolve and contribute to the predicted successes in practice. Theories and models provide practitioners with guidance on how to organize concepts as warranted by the differing types of public relations practice. By moving the mindset of public relations beyond the early models of planning toward a more clearly defined set of measurable variables, researchers such as Grunig, Cutlip, Scott, and Allen introduced to the field a far more sophisticated way to evaluate public relations.

THINK CRITICALLY

1. Evaluate each theory presented in the chapter, and discuss the one(s) you believe are used most often in public relations planning.
2. Search the Internet to find examples of organizations using theory as the foundation for their public relations campaigns.
3. Compare and contrast the public relations planning models, then discuss which planning model you perceive to be most effective and why.
4. According to AdAge, Netflix's *Gilmore Girls* revival ranked as the No. 3 most-watched original series on the platform. The four-part series "averaged 5 million viewers among 18- to 49-year-olds and pulled a 3.59 rating in the demo in the three days after it dropped on Netflix."[36] Using what you have learned in this chapter, explain what theories and public relations models were implemented that help explain the success of the revival. Critique whether or not Netflix successfully applied James E. Grunig's five objectives for communicators.

KEY TERMS

Agenda building theory 6
Agenda setting theory 6
Communication theory 1
Excellence theory 3
Framing theory 5
Press agentry model 9
Public relations 2
Public information model 9
Situational crisis communication theory (SCCT) 7
Systems theory 3
Theory 2
Two-step flow model 8
Two-way asymmetrical model 10
Two-way symmetrical model 10

CONCEPT CASE: COMMUNITY FLOW YOGA*

This textbook features a reoccurring Concept Case that takes readers through exercises based on a fictitious client, Community Flow Yoga. This growing company is an aspiring national chain, but also emphasizes local ownership for individual studios and seeks to connect with local communities as part of its business model and corporate purpose. As you progress through the textbook, you will consider and apply the learnings of each topic to the operational activities of Community Flow Yoga.

- Choose two theories in this chapter and explain how Community Flow Yoga might use them when planning a marketing or community engagement campaign.
- How can strategic thinking be incorporated into the models presented in this chapter, and how could it fit with planning an integrated campaign for Community Flow Yoga?
- Research other fitness companies that share some of the same traits or values as Community Flow Yoga. What types of strategies, tactics, and messages are they using to communicate with their audiences?

**Community Flow Yoga is an imaginary organization created to be an example of the types of challenges a real company might face in planning and executing integrated public relations campaigns.*

Introduction to Integrated Campaigns

©iStockPhotos/Leonardo Patrizi

THINK AHEAD

1.1 Identify the need for new models of public relations planning.

1.2 Describe the six steps of the ROSTIR public relations planning model.

1.3 Articulate the significance of planning models.

1.4 Summarize the diversity-first approach and understand how to utilize the Diversity & Inclusion Wheel when developing integrated campaigns.

There are moments in the life cycle of an organization when public relations (PR) efforts may signal the difference between the success and failure of a brand. Our approach to planning begins with the premise that, while there are many valid choices that PR practitioners can make over the course of a campaign, not all are created equal. How can we craft objectives and select strategies and tactics that serve as the foundation for successful, ethical campaigns and respected organizations? Our industry has long suffered mixed perceptions regarding the role of PR professionals. We have been called "PR flacks" and "spin doctors," and have battled mightily in defense of our expertise, budgets, and professional worth. By using a research-first approach and addressing challenges, failures, corrections, and revisions incorporating real-world, integrated campaign situations, students will be provided the necessary tools to make more thoughtful and informed choices as practitioners.

A NEED FOR NEW PUBLIC RELATIONS PLANNING MODELS

A recent study[1] by Marlene Neill and Erin Schauster highlighted that traditional competencies required to be successful within PR, including writing and presentation skills, remain a foundation within the profession; however, additional proficiencies are now necessary. Newly created roles in today's workforce including **content amplification** of earned media, **native advertising**, **online community management**, **programmatic buying**, **social listening**, and **social media analytics** are contributing to the rapidly expanding vocabulary for those teaching and learning about the profession of PR. Content amplification allows practitioners to use paid tactics to increase the reach of messages to publics across multiple channels, including websites, and social media sites. At present, a gap exists in PR education as a result of the evolution that our field has experienced over the past ten years. Two factors of particular importance are the impact of **social media**[2] on the profession and the need to incorporate **diversity and inclusion** within the PR curriculum.[3] The second edition of this book identifies three new models supporting successful integrated campaign planning and execution and also highlights methods that today's practitioners use to plan, execute, and measure their PR campaigns.

Emerging Models

The process of conducting effective PR is grounded in sound methodologies for solving problems and robust planning. The role that research plays to fully understand a situation and set communication goals; the identification of clear, measurable objectives; the execution of the campaign itself; and the evaluation and reporting of the campaign's success are all critical elements to consider as a practitioner. Within this text, we will explore a new evolution of this process using the ROSTIR (Research/Diagnosis, Objectives, Strategy, Tactics, Implementation, and Reporting/Evaluation) model. This emerging model emphasizes those steps critical to the development of successful campaigns in today's rapidly changing PR landscape, including the incorporation of **PESO's** (paid, earned, shared, and owned media) wide variety of related tactical elements. In fact, these two models reflect work practiced on a daily basis in PR agencies around the globe. As a result of the integration of many PR, **marketing**, and **advertising** functions within organizations, new models need to be adopted that prepare the next generation of professionals.[4] The third and final model we will explore is the Diversity & Inclusion Wheel, which incorporates diversity at the very start of any integrated campaign—the research phase—and follows through to reporting and evaluation.

PRo Tip

AMPLIFYING CONTENT

Developing integrated campaigns blends complementarity communication channels and tactics, which is why content amplification is used so frequently. This method allows practitioners to use paid tactics to increase the reach of messages to publics across multiple channels, including websites and social media sites.

FIGURE 1.1

The ROSTIR Model

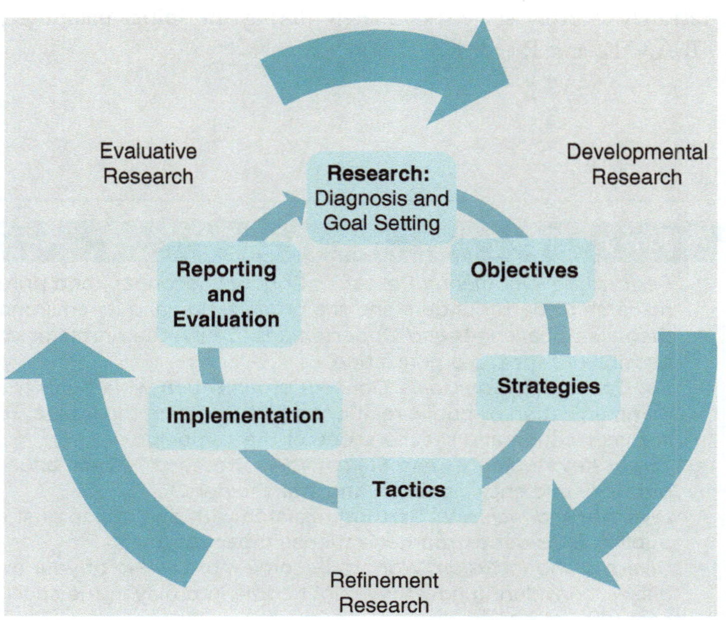

Research is critical at every stage of campaign development and execution. Insights from before (developmental research), during (refinement research), and after (evaluative research) implementation should inform public relations outreach and future campaigns.

THE SIX STEPS OF ROSTIR

ROSTIR stands for Research/Diagnosis, Objectives, Strategies, Tactics, Implementation, and Reporting/Evaluation. As we explore in subsequent chapters, this model appropriately reflects the needs of today's practitioners. While the traditional models of PR including R.A.C.E. (Research, Action, Communication, Evaluation) and R.O.P.E. (Research, Objectives, Programming, Evaluation) certainly apply, the industry has experienced a clear shift toward approaches that not only position an organization as a strategic leader in its respective industry but also as a genuine, authentic, and progressive organization desiring to connect with its audience.

THE VALUE OF PUBLIC RELATIONS PLANNING MODELS

The value of any model is in its ability to help enrich our understanding of how an industry or function is practiced. In the world of PR, traditional models can only take the task of planning so far. Plans should be reviewed and revised on a regular basis, leveraging research at every stage, not merely during the initial planning phase as depicted in R.A.C.E. and R.O.P.E.

TABLE 1.1

ROSTIR PR Planning Guide

Stage	Actions
Research and Diagnosis	• *Perform Developmental Research*: Conduct secondary and primary research to better understand the organization and its environment. • *Diagnose Challenges and Opportunities*: Define the problems or possibilities for the organization. • *Set Communication Goals*: Connect organization-wide goals to communication or public relations goals to define the impact role for communication and set the scope of the campaign. • *Target Key Audiences and Stakeholders*: Research, select, and prioritize audiences, publics, and stakeholders. • *Diversity and Inclusion*: Perform research with publics, not just on publics; consider extraorganizational impact of goals. • *Diversity and Inclusion*: Work to become more aware of your own biases, considering how they might come into play in the specific campaign at hand. • *Diversity and Inclusion*: When soliciting participants for original research, ensure members are from heterogenous groups.

Objectives	• *Set S.M.A.R.T. Communication Objectives*
	  ○ *Specific*: Focus on the situational communication problem or opportunity at hand for a particular public.
	  ○ *Measurable*: Define success through output, outtake, and (preferably) outcome metrics.
	  ○ *Attainable*: Make objectives realistically achievable within budgetary, time, and competitive constraints.
	  ○ *Relevant*: Support and prioritize an organization's mission and goals.
	  ○ *Time-Bound*: Create a clear timetable for execution and measurement.
	• *Diversity and Inclusion*: Consider why some audiences are targeted and not others, as well as how achieving objectives might impact diverse publics and stakeholders.

Strategies	• *Leverage Organizational Strengths*: Strategies should reflect the unique internal and external organizational environment to place the campaign in the best possible light. • *Complementary Channel Selection*: Support objectives through complementary channel approaches reflecting different audiences, implementation stages, or message components. • *Diversity and Inclusion*: Develop messages and select channels with publics, not just for publics.

Tactics	• *Craft Effective Messaging*: Create memorable campaign-wide and audience-specific messages supported by research.
	• *Define a Campaign's PESO Approaches*: The tactical mix should reflect audience(s)/publics, timeline, budget, messaging, and team expertise.
	  ○ Paid Media
	  ○ Earned Media
	  ○ Shared Media
	  ○ Owned Media
	  ○ Converged Media
	• *Diversity and Inclusion*: Review the diversity wheel and look for opportunities to include more representative examples, stories, images, and experiences in campaigns.

Implementation	• *Project Management*: Define the budget, timelines, and workflow processes needed to execute the campaign.
	• *Implementing the Plan*: Demonstrate persistence, perseverance, and flexibility in communicating with stakeholders.
	• *Continuous Improvement*
	  ○ *Self-awareness and Self-evaluation*: Create space for reflection and to regularly adjust personal processes in outreach efforts.
	  ○ *Refinement Research*: Track metrics and responses to outreach and messages to see which strategies and tactics are most effective.
	  ○ *Embrace Change*: Rather than executing a plan exactly as written, practitioners should regularly examine the lessons learned throughout a campaign and adjust accordingly.

	• *Diversity and Inclusion*: Monitor for unintended consequences; willingness to revise, update, and adjust tactics and messages as conversations and publics emerge and change.
Reporting and Evaluation	• *Evaluative Research*: Review objective-centered metrics and examine unexpected results—both qualitatively and quantitatively—to create a holistic perspective on your campaign. • *Turning Evaluation into Improvement*: To inform future campaigns, define lessons learned for the PR team as well as for the organization itself. • *Reporting Results*: Generate easy-to-understand, scannable, and customized reporting documents for key stakeholders and organizational leaders. • *Diversity and Inclusion*: Evaluate for social and community impacts. Segment reporting (how did the campaign impact a variety of audiences differently). If needed, communicate outcomes to diverse audiences inside and outside the organization.

PR should be considered a strategic management function, adding value to organizations through the continual assessment of the organizational environment and then adjusting communication strategies and tactics accordingly. It is important to note that many of the best **public relations campaigns** are rarely ever finished. Real-world campaigns are judged on impact, actions that consumers take, and awareness with regard to a brand, product, event, or even an individual. When planning and executing a PR plan, organizational leaders are interested to see that their audience is connecting, purchasing, attending, sharing, and engaging with them. Campaigns are not only about creating a perfect plan, rather, they are also about connecting the targeted audience(s) with the correct message(s) at a specific time in order to drive action/change. In truth, **C-suite** (Chief Executive Officer, Chief Marketing Officer, Chief Operating Officer, etc.) leaders are generally less interested in the approach or tactics (media relations, marketing, or social media) used in developing a successful plan and more interested in the results. This is why it is critically important to understand the appropriate tools to implement at the right time. At the end of the day, good PR models incorporate the development of solid **strategic communication** targets with aptly defined goals and objectives, tied to a clear organizational purpose.

The process of appropriately planning a campaign requires a practitioner to anticipate challenges, ensure that audiences are clearly defined, identify objectives, and prioritize resources efficiently in order to work best with each **stakeholder**. The practice of PR should take on an integrated approach. When we commit to our audience, mission, and goals, we ensure that the best resources are being allocated to our campaign efforts. Let's face it, not every challenge or opportunity will be solved in the same way. Tactics may change over time, but the underlying rules of effective communication will remain the same.

FIGURE 1.2
The PESO Model

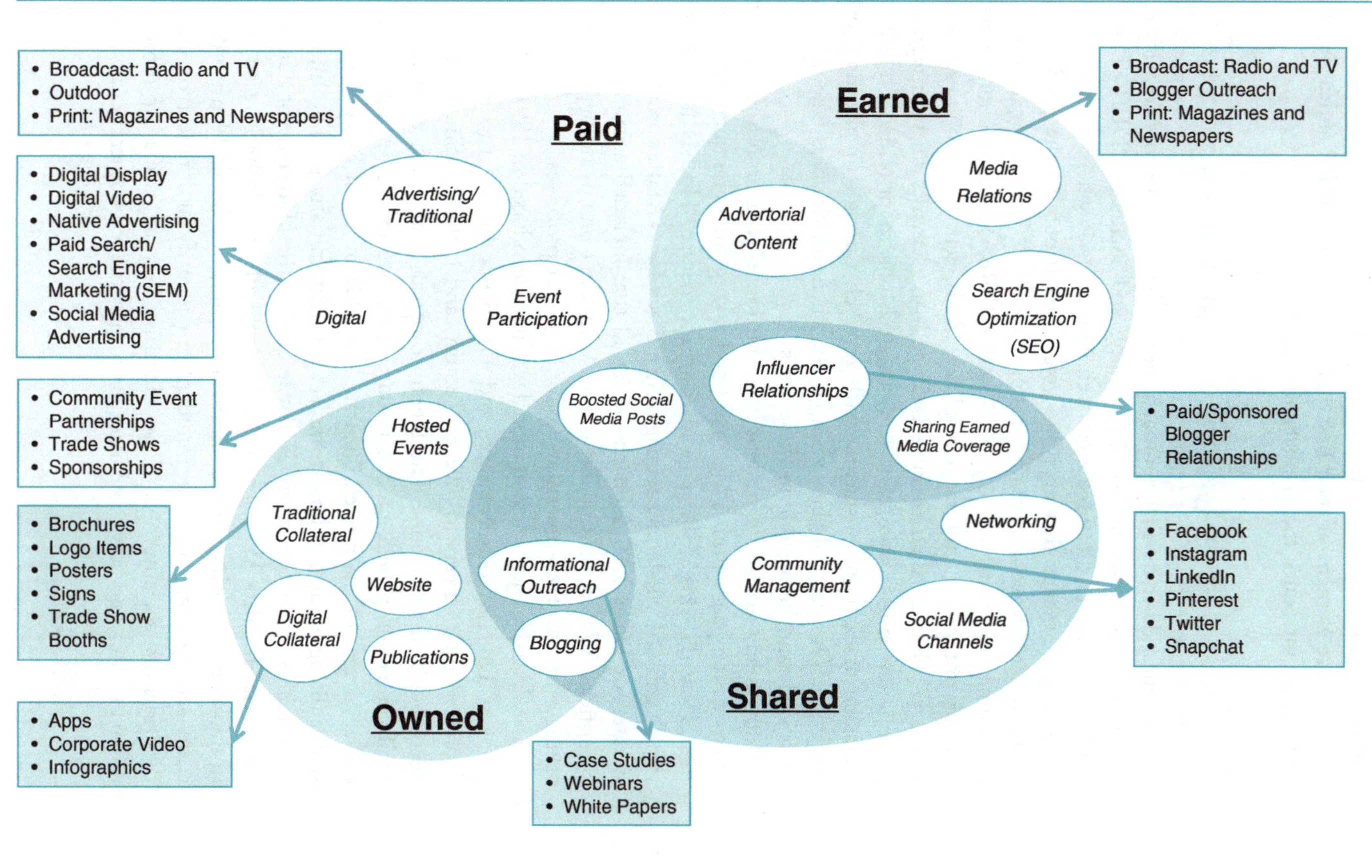

What's more, as organizations attempt to engage with diverse stakeholders through purposeful campaigns, it is their responsibility to make **diversity**, **equity**, and **inclusion (DEI)** a core element of their brand and its subsequent PR endeavors. In this second edition, we introduce the diversity-first approach.

THE DIVERSITY-FIRST APPROACH

Employing a diversity-first approach means that we have to start with understanding the differences between diversity, equity, and inclusion (DEI). The University of Michigan sums up the three areas well: "Diversity is where everyone is invited to the party. Equity means that everyone gets to contribute to the playlist. And inclusion means that everyone has the opportunity to dance."[5] To be truly inclusive, according to the Public Relations Society of America (PRSA), organizations must "champion diversity of thought, cultures, disciplines, ideals, gender, disabilities, sexual orientation and age."[6] Rather than making DEI add-on elements of an integrated campaign, practitioners must make conscientious decisions to prioritize diversity, equity, and inclusion at each step—starting with research through to planning, execution, and reporting. This can only be accomplished when practitioners take the time to develop their skills and knowledge in these areas.

How many times as a student have you found your professor showing yet another offensive campaign from a big brand and asking the same questions: "Who approved this? How did this make it to mainstream media?" H&Ms Monkey of the Jungle, Pepsi's gaff of Kylie Jenner reimagining a Black Lives Matter protest, Gucci's blackface sweater, or Dolce and Gabbana's racist ad that included a woman eating pizza with chopsticks. We are continually asking: Why can't brands do better? We have to stop asking ourselves these questions and change our processes.

The diversity and inclusion model was first introduced in 1991[7] and created by DEI pioneers Dr. Lee Gardenswartz and Dr. Anita Rowe,[8] two researchers who have dedicated their careers to diversity, equity, and inclusion. Since then, the model has been modified repeatedly. The literature reveals that much of what we know about DEI centers on people, human resources, and workplace settings. In fact, one of the earlier images of the model, illustrated in 2008 by Lynn Perry Wooten, was used to start a dialogue surrounding workplace diversity initiatives.[9] The Intergroup Relations Researchers at the Spectrum Center housed at the University of Michigan developed the Social Identity Wheel and the Personal Identity Wheel based of early research in this area. According to the Spectrum Center, "the Social Identity Wheel worksheet is an activity that encourages students to identify and reflect on the various ways they identify socially, how those identities become visible or more keenly felt at different times, and how those identities impact the ways others perceive or treat them."[10]

While the Personal Identity Wheel encourages students to reflect on how they identify outside of social identifiers.[11] Both help people consider their individual identities and how privilege operates within society to normalize some identities over others. As PR practitioners, we can learn much from previous research in this area and apply it to our tasks as professionals and brand advocates.

The model illustrated in this book is yet another modified version of Gardenswartz and Rowe's original model. Building upon previous research, scholars have adapted these tools and developed a version for PR students and practitioners, calling it the Diversity & Inclusion Wheel for PR practitioners.[12] As you will see, this is an amalgamation of similar identity tools that can be found widely in journals and online.[13,14]

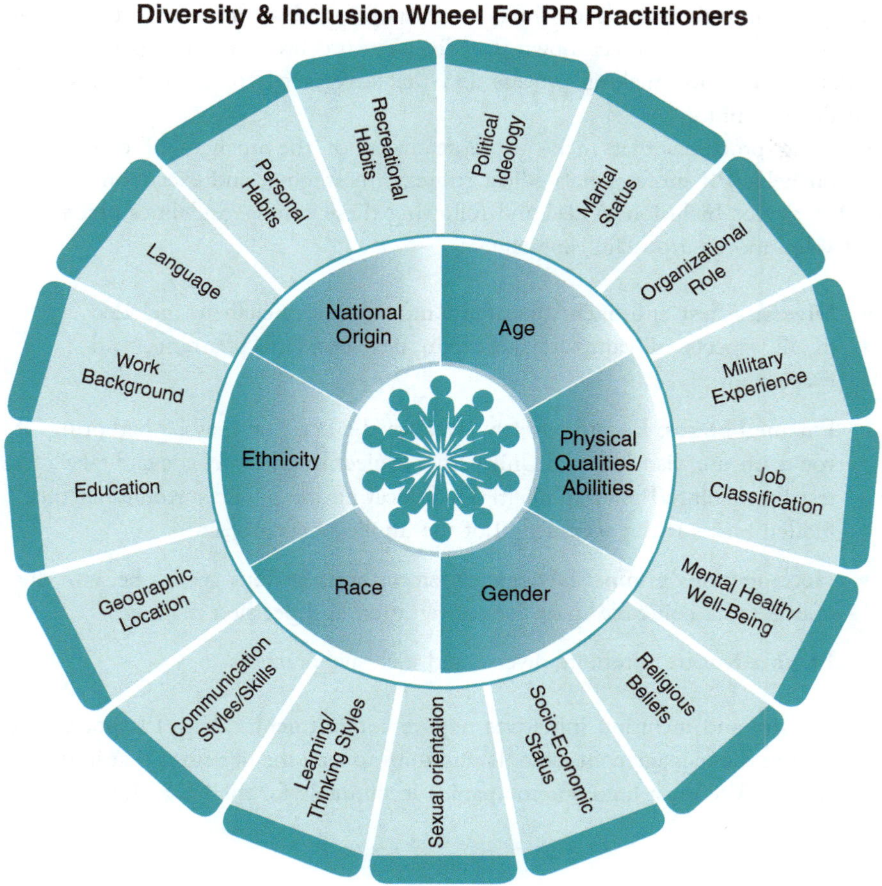

The center of the wheel has six core spokes that organizations should consider when first beginning to develop a campaign. Did your initial research include people from heterogeneous or varied groups and identities? Is your planning team made up of people with diverse thinking styles, life experiences, management skills, or team members with different roles in the company? Does your campaign or plan represent people of various genders, ages, physical qualities or abilities, different ethnicities, or places of origin? If not, deepen and expand your initial research and the overall campaign you are about to develop. The outer layer of the wheel, beginning at the top and moving clockwise around the wheel, includes 17 diverse and inclusive areas such as marital status, religious beliefs, mental health/well-being, language, communication styles, thinking styles, education, or language. The idea is not to incorporate every spoke or external layer represented in the Diversity & Inclusion Wheel, but to consider deeply whether the same people are continually represented and create a campaign that includes two or three inner spokes and an array of external layers presented here. Research has shown that diverse teams bring multiple perspectives to the strategic decision-making process and that diverse outcomes more fully reflect client demographics.

Creating processes that make us more aware of the nuances of diversity and inclusion helps PR professionals adjust strategy, messaging, and execution. By using the Diversity & Inclusion Wheel and following these simple guidelines practitioners can develop more purposeful campaigns:[15]

- **Diversity-first approach**: Be intentional with every element included in all aspects of campaign research, development, planning, and execution.
- **Personal biases**: Become overtly aware of the bias you may be harboring. If you're unsure, visit Harvard University's Project Implicit website and take a free test http://bit.ly/ProjectImplicitHU. Educating the public surrounding their hidden biases is the overall goal of the implicit bias project.[16]
- **Heterogenous groups**: Deliberately create heterogenous groups because they offer a more equitable space for conversation and decision making.
- **Be an advocate**: Promote diverse and inclusive practices.

True diversity and inclusion initiatives require commitment. Many PR practitioners have a seat at the management table. It's up to us to lead the decisions that impact our organizations. We must hold our companies accountable for their DEI initiatives—or lack thereof.

CONCLUSION

When considered together, the ROSTIR and PESO models fortified with the Diversity & Inclusion Wheel create a comprehensive framework for PR practitioners to plan effectively and use all of the resources at their disposal to create inclusive, award-winning campaigns. ROSTIR helps practitioners to execute each critical step within the campaign planning and implementation process. PESO reminds us of the wide variety and complementary value in a diverse array of channels and tactics for outreach. The Diversity & Inclusion Wheel ensures a variety of perspectives are taken into consideration when developing integrated campaigns. The remainder of this book will provide an in-depth review of these frameworks and the tools for practitioners to implement them with organizations large and small.

THINK CRITICALLY

1. Can you identify which communication and media trends are transforming the PR industry? In which ways are they most impactful? What is the importance of developing a clear set of outcomes for strategic campaigns?
2. In what ways has PESO influenced the way in which PR strategies and tactics are formed? How does ROSTIR build an organization's strategic plan implementation? Give specific examples.
3. Identify a recent campaign from one of your favorite brands. Using the Diversity & Inclusion Wheel ascertain whether or not the campaign represents a broad spectrum of people, opinions, voices, images, languages, and views.
4. After reading the case study "Ambev Wants You to Dirnk Repsnosilby" consider the following stance. The nonprofit organization Alcohol Justice (https://alcoholjustice.org/) maintains that there are inherent problems with the notion of *drink responsibly* coming from alcohol companies. They have asserted that awareness campaigns, such as the one highlighted in this chapter, are distractions and lack evidence-based true reform. They are quoted as saying "There is no evidence to show that 'drink responsibly' messages are an effective strategy for reducing alcohol consumption or related harm. Much like Big Tobacco's anti-smoking campaigns, alcohol industry facades like 'drink responsibly' are counterproductive and could backfire, increasing intent to use the product instead of decreasing alcohol-related harm."[17] Do you agree with this statement? Support your response by first conducting a search on the Internet for data that support both the pros and cons of this issue. As a future PR practitioner, imagine your creative agency was hired to develop alcohol conscious campaigns on behalf of a beverage company. What do you do?

KEY TERMS

Advertising 16
Content amplification 16
C-suite 20
Diffusion Theory 32
Diversity 22
Diversity and inclusion 16
Equity 22
Inclusion (DEI) 22
Marketing 16
Native advertising 16
Online community management 2
PESO 16
Programmatic buying 16
Public relations campaign 20
Social listening 16
Social media 16
Social media analytics 16
Stakeholder 20
Strategic communication 20

CONCEPT CASE: INTRODUCING COMMUNITY FLOW YOGA

The fitness studio industry has grown by leaps and bounds over the past decade, with dozens of new concepts opening nationwide. Cycling, boxing, aerobics, barre classes, and interval training have turned into a multi-billion dollar business. Yoga, by contrast, has been left largely to mom and pop local studios, with the exception of the US-wide CorePower Yoga chain. Community Flow Yoga is a new startup chain, designed to offer a high standard of quality and consistency (like CorePower), but also give back to the communities where it does business like a local studio.

As discussed in this chapter, effective integrated PR and marketing campaigns take considerable planning. You have just been hired as the company's new Vice President for Public Relations. Executives are looking to you for direction and leadership of the communication department and programs, including media relations, social media, community relations, brand management, studio/employee communication, and member/customer engagement.

Founded by a collective of long-time yoga instructors and studio owners in several cities, the chain aspires to bring a local, humane approach to the chain concept. Ownership is private, but communal. The chain's leaders are focused on making tangibly beneficial contributions to each of the communities where they operate, such as free classes for local elementary and middle school students, reduced rates for college students and seniors, and an environment that promotes conscious community-building among members. Each studio puts 5 percent of membership dues into a fund for community development and charitable projects, the focus of which is decided with the help of local studio members. It's approach puts corporate values—such as inclusion, community, acceptance, equality, and harmony—at the center of its brand and customer experience. These values have driven community giving projects, which have included supporting localized refugee resettlement, low-income housing assistance, mental health programs, and rehabilitation/anti-recidivism programs.

The company operates (like CorePower Yoga) on a primarily monthly subscription model, with rates based on the cost of living in each metro area. Additionally, members can take classes at any studio in the network. Today, the company has fifty studios in twenty cities across the US, but they have several important goals: To grow the brand (by converting existing studios and owners) to ten new cities in twenty-four months, to improve brand perception in the twenty cities where it does business, and to gain national and international brand awareness to lay the groundwork for further expansion. These values, while a differentiator in a crowded fitness marketplace, may be at odds with a low-margin business model and with prevailing political views in some areas where the company may want to expand.

A few initial thoughts to consider:

- What would you see as the main strengths of the brand in the marketplace?
- What would you see as significant weaknesses?
- Who are the key stakeholders and publics for this company?
- Where can communication play the most important role in helping this organization to achieve its goals?
- Consider how the ROSTIR planning model informs the creation of a strategic PR campaign.
- Highlight how the Diversity & Inclusion Wheel can be applied strategically for Community Flow Yoga. Identify the areas of the wheel that can be used in their PR planning and execution.

CASE STUDY: AMBEV WANTS YOU TO "DIRNK REPSNOSILBY"

Contributors: Sophie Estep, Laura Nolan, Jessica Zuk
Ambev with SunsetDDB
Campaign Focus: Consumer Engagement, Consumer Awareness

Initiated in the spring of 2019, Ambev, the largest brewing company in Brazil and a branch of Anheuser-Busch InBev, deployed a strategic campaign to help consumers "Dirnk Repsnosilby." Ambev partnered with one of the leading marketing firms in Brazil, SunsetDDB, to develop a clever and well-thought-out integrated campaign. The agency redesigned labels on specific brands of beer sold in Brazil, then distributed the new bottles to consumers to bring attention to the impact of alcohol and inebriation.

Research/Diagnosis

Ambev (NYSE: AMBV), the Latin American branch of Anheuser-Busch InBev, developed an ingenious campaign by shuffling the letters on eight of its most well-known beer labels—Stella Artois, Budweiser, Corona, Brahma, Skol, Colorado, Original, and Antartica—to emphasize the perils of drinking and driving while emphasizing the safe consumption of alcohol. The campaign, titled "Dirnk Repsnosilby," caused a global reaction from audiences worldwide.

The campaign, derived through Ambev and SunsetDDB, crafted a message through strategic alterations on their beverage labels. Ambev is active in nineteen countries, manages thirty-two breweries in Brazil, and distributes 30 brands. The company currently employs 35,000 people in Brazil. The campaign, created by SunsetDDB, a marketing and advertising firm in São Paulo, Brazil, wanted to bring awareness of altered perceptions, but also fulfill with Ambev's goals of educating consumers on the benefits of developing smart drinking habits.

Brazil has an entrenched history of drinking and driving, making this campaign particularly relevant.[18] The international journal, *Sleep Medicine and Disorders*, published a report dealing with drinking implications specific to Brazil. The findings included a trauma center showing 28.9 percent of patients had alcohol in their systems with similar results in a neighboring city, at 27.2 percent.[19] Of course, impaired driving is not limited to Brazil: According to the World Health Organization, 500,000 people are injured and 17,000 die from alcohol-related vehicle accidents in the US each year.[20] The costs associated with such accidents exceed the billion-dollar threshold on an annual basis. Between 25 and 50 percent of all car accidents worldwide are associated with at least one driver being inebriated and above the legal limits set forth by that country.[21] Brazil is considered one of the largest consumer markets of alcohol in the world, and it continues to grow. The consumption of alcoholic beer is expecting to surpass 13.48 billion liters annually by 2021.[22] In 2010, the annual revenue related to alcohol products revealed 56 billion reals, compared to 128 billion reals eight years later in 2018.[23]

In 2010 Ambev, in concert with public health officials, launched what they called Global Smart Drinking Goals. These were programs and initiatives centered on changing social norms, consumer behaviors, and their own business practices to help reduce the harmful use of alcohol globally.[24] By 2014 the company had exceeded all six initiatives which included partnerships, public education initiatives, retailer training, and other activities that reinforce responsible drinking.[25] Realizing the importance of addressing drinking implications worldwide, Ambev determined taking these goals to the next level would assist with the company's goals and objectives.

Objectives

The "Dirnk Repsnosilby" campaign objectives falls under Ambev's overall Global Smart Drinking Goals, which is a set of programs and initiatives that focus on shifting public perception, social norms, and consumer behaviors regarding safe drinking practices. The desired impact of this campaign was reducing the harmful use of alcohol globally. The four specific S.M.AR.T. objectives that Ambev implemented included these:[26]

- **Objective 1:** Reduce the harmful use of alcohol by at least 10 percent in six cities by the end of 2020. Implement the best practices globally by the end of 2025.
- **Objective 2:** Invest $1 billion USD across our markets in dedicated social marketing campaigns and related programs by the end of 2025.
- **Objective 3:** Ensure No- or Lower-Alcohol beer products represent at least 20 percent of AB InBev's global beer volume by the end of 2025.
- **Objective 4:** Place a Guidance Label on all beer products in all markets by the end of 2020. Increase alcohol health literacy by the end of 2025.

The "Dirnk Repsnosilby" campaign itself aligns most closely with the first objective of reducing the harmful use of alcohol by at least 10 percent in six cities, including São Paulo, Brazil, where Ambev is headquartered. Beyond targeting drinking and driving, the campaign connects to the objective of investing money into social marketing campaigns, as this is an effective and educational advertisement that brings awareness to the dangers of harmful drinking habits, such as drinking and driving.

Strategies

Ambev's objectives were substantiated by specific strategies created for the organization's customers and Brazilian society. To tackle the objectives outlined in their Global Smart Drinking Goals, Ambev designed a subliminal graphic design campaign to encourage consumers to think about their safe consumption. The idea started with the company purposely misspelling popular adult beverage names by shuffling the letters on their most popular labels. Modifications were made to physical product containers, social media posts, and advertisements all indicative of the disorienting effect of alcohol on the mind. SunsetDDB deliberately designed the campaign components in this manner to spark consumer awareness on the thought that sometimes things appear clear after alcohol consumption, but in reality, you are impaired.

SunsetDDB and Ambev wanted to use communication channels that were familiar to their consumers. The first release of these modified designs occurred during a Brazilian national televised event.[27] Then, social media and traditional print were utilized to target consumers accustomed to seeing these brands online and in print. This campaign employed a secret release, and eventually carried weight from earned media, influencer engagement, and consumer engagement. Strategically, the primary component of the campaign—switching labels with misspelled versions—propelled them into the next phase of the campaign allowing them to encourage safe and thoughtful drinking.

Tactics

The "Dirnk Repsnosilby" campaign used memorable and sticky tactics to deploy their messaging. Ambev decided to change the labels of their eight most popular beers in Brazil: Stella Artois, Budweiser, Corona, Brahma, Skol, Colorado, Original, and Antarctica.

These beers chosen for this campaign have well-known labels that utilize special typefaces,

The images here illustrate the new misspelled labels presented on various brands of their most consumed beer.

imagery, and coloring. Shuffling a few letters of the beverage names was subtle enough that a consumer would have to be paying attention to notice the change. "Budweiser" became "Bwedusier" and "Corona" turned into "Cronoa." Without notifying the public about the switch, the first twenty-four hours spurred an avalanche of organic reactions from consumers of the switched labels and advertisements. This campaign used all elements from the PESO model (paid, earned, shared, owned).

Paid

Paid ads were purchased on the Globo television network during one of their largest events of the year, Campeonato Brasileiro, the national football championship, adding to the legitimacy of the campaign.[28] Because 18 million people were watching or attending this game, this was an effective paid ad that hit the target audience more than social media ever could. In addition, featured billboards, print, and social media ads were purchased.

Earned

The agency relied on consumer and influencer sharing to spread the message of the campaign. Earned media loved to carry this story. Upward of forty Brazilian media outlets reported on the confusion, and later the message that came from the campaign. Because this issue is impactful to a large portion of Brazil's news-consuming audience, the story was repopulated to share with more viewers.

Shared

Social media sites were used to perpetuate the dissemination of the campaign's subtly altered images and brands. Because of the large followings of these brands, this campaign could be seen and shared easily. Brahma, the popular Brazilian beer first changed for this campaign, has over 4 million page likes on its Cerveja Brahma Oficial Facebook page.[29] The subtle messaging that was shared through these social networks drove significant engagement.

Influencers were a core component utilized by SunsetDDB. They shared specific content while posing with misspelled bottles and pointing out the misspellings, without indicating any idea of the underlying meaning. The influencers connected to this campaign, who were geographically and culturally relevant to Brazil, had a potential reach of 22 million people in total. Some of the partnerships included accounts like ale_oliveiraoficial, who has 1 million followers, and naiaraazevedo, who has over 3 million followers. These partnerships were a great way to further the message and combines paid and shared media for a wide-reaching message.[30]

Owned

Within owned media, traditional collateral materials are found. This includes logos, brochures, and signage among other items. Ambev took a risk in altering its labels and logos. The powerful ownership of these iconic images added to the mystique that arose from the small changes. For instance, the Budweiser: King of Beers logo has been the same since 1999, utilizing a proprietary typeface and icons specific to the beer. Many viewers of this campaign were left wondering how a brand could have misspelled their own famous label in such a public way.

Implementation

Secrecy was a central component of the success of this campaign. The campaign launched on Sunday, April 28, 2019, during the opening matches of the national Brazilian football championship, or the Campeonato Brasileiro. An impressive 18 million people were watching this championship on Globo, Brazil's most popular TV network, when the first advertisements aired. With no further explanation, the traditional logo of Brahma, one of Brazil's most popular beers, was changed to read "Bhamra." This was strategically planned so it would surprise those who were watching or attending the game, and lead to speculation on social media about the misspelled labels. Simultaneously, other Ambev brands like Budweiser, Skol, Antarctica, and Stella Artois changed their social media profile pictures and covers on Facebook, Instagram, and Google to instead show labels with changed letters, which grabbed the attention of those who followed the beers on social media, or were told about it through word of mouth.

These changes were quickly noticed by the brands' followers, which proved to be extremely effective in gaining attention on social media. Hundreds of thousands of people tweeted about the confusion. One fan, @DaniloMaciel said "I think the graphic designer intern drank too much, probably the marketing guy too to pass up that wrong name."[31] To which Ambev replied, "Without blaming the interns. This idea is an action by Cervejaria Ambev to remind everyone that, when we drink, things seem to be in order, but they are not. So don't forget: if you drink, don't drive. #Everythinginorder."[32]

The misdesigned labels were then released everywhere in Ambev's home district of Brazil. The company worked with bars and restaurants to serve beer bottles with altered labels, which matched all the new social media avatars for the different brands. Influencers further spread the message by posting with the altered products, but did not reveal the secret.

Because the change was made so quickly and without warning, the majority of viewers eagerly awaited a response from the company to explain what had happened to their labels. This, of course, set Ambev and SunsetDDB up perfectly to share their warning message to a captive audience who already had piqued interest in the company. A buzz grew through social media and, by the next day, the reasoning behind the switches was revealed through popular social media channels, as well as print advertisements and out-of-home advertising like billboards. The company responded to tweets pointing out the "mistakes," thanking those engaged for their sharp vision and urging them to think twice about their own impairment after drinking. The campaign explained that "*soemtimes* you *drnik* and *evethyring appaers* to be ok. But it's not. If you drink, don't drive."

The labels reflected the idea that sometimes people drink and feel as if everything is in order (the labels "looked" correct in color and likeness), but it isn't. As one of the world's largest brewers, Ambev felt a responsibility to change their labels to start a conversation around safe driving habits, and, hopefully, to change people's behaviors to reduce the number of drunk drivers. In the company press release, the CEO of Anheuser-Busch InBev, Carlos Brito said, "As the leading global brewer, we believe we have a unique role to play in championing a culture of smart drinking globally. For more than thirty years, we have invested in initiatives to promote responsible drinking and discourage harmful drinking. Now, we are taking our efforts to the next level, moving beyond awareness raising to driving real impact for the communities in which we live and work."[34]

People shared their delight on social media, stating with posts such as "[I]t wasn't a mistake, it was so clever," and that it was an "amazing idea to switch the letters." This short turnaround of confusion to enlightenment allowed the public to become intrigued and invested and revealed the hard-hitting awareness message in a timely fashion, as to not lose the interest and buzz that had been built around the labels.[35]

These ads illustrate the focus of the campaign: to visually represent how easy perceptions can be altered after drinking.[33]

Reporting/Evaluation

The campaign drove impressive results. Within its first twenty-four hours, more than 200,000 people noticed the "errors" on the beer labels and responded via social media. The number of interactions quickly increased after the campaign message was revealed through print ads, magazines, and direct social media responses, leading to 619,000 interactions within the first forty-eight hours of the campaign. The engaged audience was more susceptible to the lesson-based campaign messages because they had engaged in the first part of the campaign with the scrambled words on the beverage labels.

In just twenty-four hours, Google searches regarding the names of the eight beers increased by 1,550 percent, driving more engagement to the campaign.[36] Partnerships also arose from this campaign. Cabify, a Spanish network transportation network similar to Uber, took this as an opportunity to partner with Ambev to promote safe drinking habits.[37] They offered 30 percent off of a customer's next two rideshare trips by using the code "Cafiby." This misspelling of the company's name was a spin on the campaign itself, engaging more of the Brazilian population in the campaign's message.

Earned media also added to the campaign's stickiness. The campaign resulted in coverage from 40 different news channels and sites that are popular in Brazil, sharing the message and thoughtful reflection that came from the confusion.[38] Finally, overall engagement of the campaign enhanced regular brand awareness by 15.6 percent.[39] In total, the campaign garnered more than 157 million impressions on social media. These are quite successful metrics, considering the location-specific efforts of the campaign and the brief length of time it ran.

Theories

Diffusion Theory: This theory is typically concerned with the spread of messages that are perceived as new ideas. By secretly launching the campaign, Ambev and SunsetDDB created buzz among consumers arousing their curiosity and creating a natural bridge for fans to engage and respond on various social media channels. Additionally, by unveiling the campaign during a national football game, Ambev's reach and visibility skyrocketed.

Agenda Setting Theory: Agenda setting theory states that the media does not tell people how to think, but it does tell people what to think about.[40] The "Dirnk Repsnosilby" campaign could be considered a public awareness campaign. Ambev attempted to raise the public's level of understanding about the importance and implications of drinking responsibly.

Diversity- and Inclusion-First Approach

Evaluate for social and community impacts: Through the company's Global Smart Drinking Goals they attempted to educate the public by reinforcing the importance of drinking responsibly. This campaign was a direct result of their initiative. While the Global Smart Drinking Goals represent a positive first step toward recognition and management of the potential harms and dangers of alcohol abuse, they did not seem to be deeply integrated into the measurement and evaluation framework of this campaign. For example, Ambev could also have investigated whether there were any short- or long-term campaign-related impacts on behaviors such as drunk driving or binge drinking (two of the factors explicitly mentioned in the Global Smart Drinking Goals) in Brazil.[41] A broader conceptualization of the campaign impact and evaluation may help PR professionals help companies such as Ambev to live up to the mission and values they espouse.

Strategic Communication Campaign Fundamentals

2

Anadolu Agency/Anadolu Agency/Getty Images

The *We the People* campaign aimed to restore hope, imagination, curiosity, and creativity into the conversations happening across the US. This piece of art titled "Greater than Fear" was created by Adhami and Shepard Fairey in response to the Trump administration's Muslim ban.

THINK AHEAD

2.1 Understand why public relations practitioners plan and make connections between campaign development and organizational goals.

2.2 Explain the importance of each step in the planning process beginning with research and ending with reporting.

2.3 Recognize how the elements of an integrated and strategic plan come together by examining tangible results.

In 2017, Aaron Huey, National Geographic photographer and Stanford Media Designer, launched a Kickstarter campaign with one goal in mind—to counter "hate, fear, and open racism that were normalized during the 2016 presidential campaign."[1] Amplifier Art, built upon free and open source images, describes itself as an organization that turns artists into activists and observers into participants. By galvanizing like-minded people this organization promotes messages of hope. It has sponsored visually stunning integrated campaigns to raise awareness of a wide variety of issues, such a voting rights, climate change, and criminal justice reform. The goal of the organization according to Huey, "is to reclaim and rebuild an American identity rooted in equality, dignity, diversity, truth, and beauty. At Amplifier, we believe that each piece of art we create and distribute with our partners can be a compass that leads us away from the chaos and negativity of this polarizing time."[2]

Since its inception, the organization has grown tremendously as it has developed campaigns with stakeholders front and center. In just a few short years and with a dedicated group of 18 artists, the organization has impacted more than 20,000 educators nationwide. Even receiving support from the Bill & Melinda Gates Foundation Discovery Center.[3] Its first campaign titled *We the People* disseminated 46,535 posters, 9,788 free graphic downloads, distributed 79,260 stickers, and amassed 201,233 shares and impressions via

Hear Our Voice by Brooke Fischer is one of many pieces of art found on the Amplifier website.

social media channels.[4] Since then they have launched the following socially driven campaigns, *Women's March on Washington*, *Power to the Polls*, *March for Our Lives*, *#MyClimateHero*, *Voting Rights*, *Unbroken by Bars*, *The Truth Is Prisons Are...*, *Honor the Treaties*, *Close Rikers*, and a special call for art during the COVID-19 worldwide pandemic.[5] The organization has accrued support from people across the **social sphere**, the broad network of interactive digital and social media channels that collectively create a new form of public sphere. Between downloads, photographs, tweets, Instagram posts, Facebook follows, check-ins, and likes, blog articles, and news coverage, the organization is thriving. Its success and its tools are multimedia, multimodal: This is integrated communication today.

Public relations campaigns come in an almost infinite variety of forms and combinations. They utilize channels from social media and digital advertising to media relations and public events. They combine words, images, audio, and video in a multitude of audience-centered formats to convey their messages. They incorporate cutting-edge research to develop strategies and tactics, continuously improve content, and evaluate impact. They continue to strive for more inclusive language and imagery reflective of the diverse organizations they represent and the societies where they exist. Yet, in all of their complexity, campaigns begin with a simple purpose: To help solve a problem.

As PR practitioners, we are professional communicators developing and orchestrating these campaigns. Management relies upon this role to be better than most at communicating an organization's messaging. All too often, PR practitioners are pigeonholed into being labeled media liaisons or relationship managers; however, this role is more than that; PR practitioners are strategic marketing counselors. In order to successfully execute strategic integrated campaigns, we must be able to see the big picture and the minute details. It is impossible for organizations to disconnect from the world around them and to operate in a vacuum.

WHY WE PLAN

The foundation of a well-developed PR plan is an effective approach devised from a robust communication blueprint. Using a strategic approach has everything to do with identifying key stakeholder outcomes, targeting the right audience, formulating the most impactful objectives and message, and incorporating the most effective tactics to accomplish the necessary goals. A plan is an avenue that is used to propose and obtain approvals, as well as a mechanism for monitoring and evaluating a product that distinguishes true PR professionals.[6]

The goal of strategic PR is to contribute to the overarching mission of an organization by supporting its defined goals. In order for the strategies to be successful, it is imperative that PR practitioners obtain accurate information about the challenges at hand, the publics with which they communicate, the effectiveness of each communication initiative, and the relational impacts that each program has with critical stakeholders.

PRo Tip

THE CASE FOR LISTENING FIRST

To ensure effective communication, PR depends upon the need to listen. Stakeholders including employees, clients, and diverse audiences help inform integrated campaigns. According to researcher Katie Place, "When listening occurs, clients and agency consider themselves as partners in achieving shared goals."[7]

Source: Katie Place, "Listening as the Driver of Public Relations Practice and Communications Strategy Within a Global Public Relations Agency," *Public Relations Journal* 12, no. 3 (May 2019): 1–18, accessed May 2019, https://prjournal.instituteforpr.org/wp-content/uploads/katieplace_listening.pdf.

The strongest and most strategic campaigns are informed by what customers, prospects, and stakeholders are sharing and posting in the public and social spheres, so listen to what they are saying or, for that matter, not saying. Listening is one of the most important but underused tools of the PR practitioner.[8] Shayna Englin, founder and CEO of 42 Comms and graduate instructor in strategic communication at Georgetown University and George Washington University, notes that **strategic communication** "means communicating the best message, through the right channels, measured against well-considered organizational and communications-specific goals."[9] Understanding the specific executable tasks and their impacts can ensure that programs are delivered more effectively and highlights the value that the PR function brings to the organization.

One approach to planning is a process called **management by objectives**, commonly referred to as **MBO**. Organizations have missions and goals, which can be broken down into measurable objectives. Responsibility for execution and completion of goals is held by different parts of the organization. PR professionals often use communication objectives to provide focus and define direction when formulating a strategy targeting or supporting specific organizational objectives.[10] Norman Nager and T. Harrell Allen outline several steps of MBO that assist practitioners in building a plan that includes examining client and employer objectives; audience analysis; media channels; primary and secondary sources; communication strategies; message sentiment; and visually appealing artifacts such as photos, infographics, artwork, or videos.[11] These steps can be used to form a checklist to spur PR practitioners in formulating a comprehensive plan and a sound foundation for strategic development.

As presented in the introduction, a simplified approach to planning is typically composed of four steps. First, practitioners use **research** to define the problem or situation; then they develop objectives and strategies that address the situation; once complete, they implement the strategies; and finally measure the results of the PR efforts. John Marston's **R.A.C.E.**[12] model (Research, Action planning,

Communication, Evaluation) or Jerry Hendrix's **R.O.P.E.**[13] model (Research, Objectives, Programming, Evaluation) are commonly used to describe the process.

Both planning models begin with research and end with evaluation. The four steps encompass the following:

1. Conduct research to analyze the situation facing the organization and to accurately define the problem or opportunity in such a way that the PR efforts can successfully address the cause of the issue and not just its symptoms.
2. Develop a strategic action plan that addresses the issue that was assessed in the first step. This includes having an overall goal, measurable objectives, clearly identified publics, targeted strategies, and effective tactics.
3. Execute the plan with communication tools and tasks that contribute to reaching the overarching objectives.
4. Measure whether the campaign was successful in meeting the goals using a variety of evaluation tools.

All planning models have varying strengths and weaknesses. In this book, we expand our focus on the planning stage using the ROSTIR model to emphasize the importance of understanding and diagnosing the problem, challenge, or opportunity at hand; setting communication goals and objectives; and building strategies and tactics from them.

ELEMENTS OF A STRATEGIC PLAN

It may seem proper to begin the process of planning with tactics including brochures, press releases, an event, or even a blog post; however, an appropriate plan should precede the selection of tactics. By first conducting research, practitioners are able to define the overall goals, objectives, and strategies of the plan, otherwise efforts may be wasted from the outset. Some practitioners create a brief outline, while others develop an expansive document that includes a substantial amount of detail. Another model for the planning process, the ROSTIR strategic planning model, includes six key elements, all of which will be expanded upon in upcoming chapters. The following is a brief summary of each element:

- Research: diagnosis/goal setting
- Objectives
- Strategies
- Tactics
- Implementation
- Reporting/evaluation

iStock.com/South_agency

Secondary and primary research, diagnosing the organizational problem or opportunity, and setting communication-specific goals are critical first steps to a successful campaign.

Research, Diagnosis, and Goal Setting

The term **diagnose** means to ascertain the cause or nature of something, usually an issue or problem that must be solved.[14] In this initial stage of planning, practitioners ask themselves the following question: Why is a PR plan necessary? There are many situations that prompt the need for strategic PR planning. Some include the following:

- overcoming a problem or negative situation;
- conducting a specific, one-time project supporting the launch of a new product or service;
- reinforcing an ongoing effort to preserve a reputation or public support;
- expanding your organization's outreach to a new audience;
- creating and reinforcing a brand and professional corporate image;
- mitigating the impact of negative publicity and/or corporate crisis; or
- establishing expertise among your peers, the press, or your potential clients or customers.

Once the decision to create the plan has been made, regardless of the rationale, the foundation for the overarching strategy has to be defined. Research accompanies this stage of development. Research is the methodical collection and explanation of information used to increase understanding of needs, audiences, channels, and communication baselines.[15] Strategic planning cannot work without intimate knowledge of the intended audience. Research is key to understanding the target audience and the needs of the plan. This initial developmental research provides practitioners with the insights to diagnose challenges and opportunities, before prioritizing and reframing them as communication goals.

Diversity First

Incorporating the diversity-first approach should begin in this initial stage. We often see campaigns fail when **diversity** and **inclusion** (D&I) are not part of a campaign's initial research and planning. It has never been clearer that homogenous groups lack diversity of thought, opinions, and ideas. Implementing a true D&I first approach is more than ensuring messages or images represent a variety of backgrounds. It's about the people developing the campaign—ensuring they too are diverse—in more than merely race. Nysha King, a communications council member for Forbes, says that brands should strive for "promotional activities that reflect the society that they are a part of, and avoid offensive references to race, gender, sexual orientation or religion—thereby, increasing the chances that audiences respond to the call to action."[17]

Forward-thinking brands are paving the way. For example, Tylenol's four-year **hashtag** driven campaign "#HowWeFamily" is a celebration of diverse families[18] while brands like Shutterfly and Snapfish regularly include images portraying an array of couple/family images illustrating variety of life celebrations through inclusive photos. Microsoft's "We All Win" 2019 Super Bowl commercial highlighted the Xbox Adaptive Controller for people with disabilities. The campaign centered on hassle-free gaming equipment which has an accessible, user-friendly controller.[19]

PRo Tip

DIVERSITY AND INCLUSION FIRST

"PR and marketing departments have the power to shape new approaches, while at the same time, demonstrate that their organizations are employers of choice and industry innovators." Nysha King, Forbes[16]

Source: Nysha King, "Making the Case for Diversity in Marketing and PR," Forbes (blog), entry posted February 15, 2019, https://www.forbes.com/sites/forbescommunicationscouncil/2019/02/15/making-the-case-for-diversity-in-marketing-and-pr/#4007d073424d.

More than an item to check off a list, diversity and inclusion should be embedded in the campaign development process. Just as PR practitioners develop thorough objectives, they should also embed sound D&I principles into their campaigns. And that starts by having a diversity of individuals and experiences as part of an integrated PR team.

Objectives

After research is conducted, a clear diagnosis is realized, and broad communication goals are set, the next step of the process is to establish appropriate **objectives** for the plan. Objectives must be measurable. At the end of the day, the C-suite executives place emphasis on the bottom line. Executive management is looking to see data, analysis, measurement, and how each relate back to PR efforts. Statistics and data are often necessary to show that efforts put forth by a PR department are contributing to the overarching goals of the company. Outcomes can evaluate whether or not a change in behavior or relationships is influenced by the PR strategy. Examples of high-quality outcomes might include an increase in the sale of a product or an uptick in donations due to an executed PR campaign. As organizational resources are precious and companies are becoming increasingly frugal, executives are often unwilling to spend money unless an outcome contributes to a business objective.[20]

Objectives should connect four key elements: the target audience or public, the specific outcome, the measurement or magnitude of the change required to reach this outcome, and the target date.[21] Campaign objectives should contain an impact factor, such as a knowledge outcome, a change of opinion, or a change of behavior.[22] Strategies and tactics should be designed to support the achievement of the objective.

- **Example**: Focused on bottom line metrics, objectives are outcomes that can be quantified. Armed with $2.75 million in grant funding, the Texas Council on Family Violence launched two public awareness campaigns, "There is Help, There is Hope" and "Family and Friends." The goals for both campaigns were measurable.[23]
    - **Objective**: Achieve 20 percent increase in Texas-based calls to the national family violence hotline during paid media flights.
    - **Strategy**: Connect with families directly by creating an informational brochure to increase awareness for the program.
    - **Tactic**: Distribute 1 million educational campaign brochures over the duration of the campaign.

It can be difficult to measure how well a particular informational objective has been achieved. Objectives should have clear metrics that can be tracked and quantified. The PR practitioner, along with management, must set the objectives together. As noted earlier, objectives must be realistic, achievable, and measurable in order to illustrate success. To simply state "increase awareness by 25 percent" is not enough. A solid baseline is needed to indicate whether or not the target audience increased awareness by 25 percent. Therefore, developmental research must provide an initial baseline (e.g., initial awareness may be at 40 percent among the public in question, therefore 65 percent would be the target). Measurement before, during, and after the campaign is critical to understand whether the objective has been achieved.

Strategies

Strategies are the choices made to select specific channels and approaches, focusing efforts toward achieving the objectives. For each objective, there may be a single overall strategy, or there may be multiple strategies depending on the PR plan. Some strategies may also support multiple objectives. In many campaigns, this means building a combination of paid, earned, shared, owned, and converged channels that are most appropriate for the campaign's purpose and its publics.

Tactics

Tactics are the tangible aspects of the strategy. There are various methods to reach a target audience, such as face-to-face interactions and media outreach through paid, earned, shared, and owned channels. Face-to-face tactics might include special events such as annual meetings, open houses, grand openings, recognition events, group meetings, town halls, round tables, and meetups. Owned media tactics are comprised of any material that is managed and owned by the company, such as a company blog, annual report, blogs, case studies, books, infographics, mobile apps, logos, letters, brochures, websites, podcasts, webinars, videos, photographs, and newsletters. Earned media is one of the most powerful vehicles for getting messages out to the masses. Earned media refers to publicity gained through promotional efforts rather than publicity gained through paid messaging like in advertising. When a practitioner's pitch to a journalist or blogger results in some type of media placement, this is considered earned media. Social and digital media channels with opportunities for interactivity constitute the space for shared media. Mediated and nonmediated approaches should work together to create effective campaigns.

Let us examine the combination of a strategy and tactic collectively at work. Consumers often prefer products that are all natural, healthier options to those that may be less environmentally friendly or less wholesome. Coffee creamer is probably not the first product that jumps to mind when considering natural, healthy, and organic options. As a way to differentiate themselves from the competition, Nestlé Coffee-mate set out to change opinions with its line of all-natural coffee creamers, Natural Bliss. Its strategy was developed to turn heads and garner attention. Nestlé Coffee-mate surprised consumers with an all-natural coffee experience where they least expected it—at their local coffee shop. Nestlé Coffee-mate staffed a New York City

PRo Tip

KEEP TACTICS TOP OF MIND

Review tactics regularly. While an organization's mission and goals should be relatively stable over time, and many components of a PR plan can be considered fixed elements, tactics require constant review. Unexpected external developments, a change in the business atmosphere, emerging media channels, or the actions of competitors can require a fresh perspective and second look.

coffee shop, temporarily renaming the establishment "Natural Bliss Café." Actors who looked the part of baristas, wearing little more than body paint, served coffee with Natural Bliss creamer. This strategy was successful in large part because the target audience, millennials, were not only shocked but also had the opportunity to sample free coffee and Natural Bliss.

The strategy can be considered as the idea (a direct consumer experience of the product in a surprising setting), and the tactic is the method through which that idea is carried out (the uniquely revealing pop-up coffee shop, actors, and free products to sample). In the above example, the intent behind the strategy was to introduce the shock factor to the targeted audience, and the tactic was the unexpected pop-up coffee

Nestlé emphasized the *natural* in its Natural Bliss Café coffee shop takeover.

shop managed by scantily clad, painted baristas. This strategy also relies in part on shared social media and traditional earned media to spread the story, ensuring coverage and awareness beyond those who entered the shop itself. In this way, smart strategies and tactics can impact multiple audiences through multiple channels.

Implementation

Determining the right timing to implement a campaign and identifying who is responsible for executing the campaign is the next step in the planning process. Factors such as the complexity, duration, steps, and intricacy of the campaign play a key role during the **implementation** phase, the point in the campaign process where the campaign plan is put into operation. A calendar or timeline should be developed to help guide practitioners through the implementation process. Some campaigns may only last a month while others may be staggered over several months or longer. Appropriate timing of the campaign, scheduling of the correct sequence of tactics, and building a calendar can help contribute to the development of a seamless implementation schedule and workflow.[24]

Reporting/Evaluation

The process of reporting and **evaluation** relates the results of the campaign directly back to the stated objectives. Evaluation includes the analysis of completed or ongoing activities that determine or support a PR campaign. PR practitioners must put measures in place to track the results of each PR campaign, then contextualize and communicate those results to key stakeholders. Reporting and evaluation should not only take place at the end of a campaign. In fact, quite the opposite is true. Savvy practitioners continually evaluate the metrics throughout the process. In doing so, a practitioner will know whether or not the stated objectives, strategies, and tactics are resonating with the intended audiences. It is appropriate to measure objectives at multiple points during the implementation phase through the conclusion of the PR campaign. If strategies and tactics are not working as expected, this process provides the opportunity to revise them before the end of the campaign. Experienced practitioners know that flexibility is a key part of successful campaigns.

As previously noted, objectives must be measurable; therefore, it is vital to understand the appropriate metrics that will be used in order to properly evaluate if the objectives have been achieved. Reporting should reiterate the specific objectives and how each was measured. Informational objectives might include metrics such as surveys of awareness among key publics, media content analysis, number of fliers distributed, or number of hits to a website. Motivational objectives, on the other hand, are more easily evaluated using metrics evaluating the number of attendees at a specific event, direct increase in sales, or surveys that benchmark consumer's beliefs before and after using a product.

Budget

When evaluating the previous steps, it is important to not forget about the all-important **budget** that has been reserved for the campaign. At the initiation of any project, the PR manager should sit with both the internal and external teams to establish the program costs and expectations. Budgets are generally divided into two basic categories: staff time and out-of-pocket expenses (also known as OOP expenses).

Staff expenses include the time required by the practitioners to create and execute the plan. This varies widely, but can often account for 70 percent or more of the overall budget.[25] Media kits, collateral material, website development, video production, transportation, staging, and even media costs such as radio advertising or paid social media are some examples of OOP expenditures.

PUTTING IT ALL TOGETHER

This chapter began by highlighting one of the most unique grassroots social movements of the past decade—the launch of Amplifier Art. At the time its origin, founder Aaron Huey launched a **crowdfunding** campaign hoping to raise a mere \$60,000 by attracting 10,000 backers. Crowdfunding is the practice of funding a project or venture by raising small donations from a large number of people, typically through digital channels. By the end of the campaign the organization accrued 22,840 supporters and raised \$1,365,105.00.[26]

Of all of the organization's social media platforms, it's no surprise that Instagram boasts the most with 54,000 followers and an average of 400 comments per post. According to analysis from Similar Web 100 percent of the organization's traffic is organic.[27] Nearly unheard of in today's paid media market. This indicates a strong brand affinity and a keen understanding of the organization's audience.

100.00% Organic

Top 5 Organic keywords

0% Paid

Top 5 Paid keywords

Further examination indicates that traffic to the organization's website is led by Facebook with 31.27 percent followed by Pinterest then Instagram and finally Reddit.

In this example, Huey solicited support from everyday citizens using powerful imagery along with a strong foundation built upon community allies such as the Women's March and an understanding of the overarching issue, seizing the opportunity, setting realistic goals and objectives, and forming strategies that aligned with tactics that were easily implemented.

Facebook 31.27%

Pinterest 26.72%

Instagram 22.91%

Reddit 19.11%

For PR practitioners, this campaign represents a clear example and opportunity for identifying the objectives, strategies, and tactics behind the campaign. Taking a closer look, in the simplest form, the *objective* of this campaign was to raise awareness surrounding the polarization of America the Trump campaign initiated; the *strategy* was to formulate a far-reaching, widespread, earned and owned media outreach approach; and the *tactic* was to allow for the downloading of free art images to be used in classrooms, at marches, and within the community at large.

CONCLUSION

Planning is critical to effective campaigns. There are many approaches to strategic planning, but the most useful follow the practices of MBO: setting clearly defined targets and building out a plan of action to implement them. This allows for work to be broken down into digestible pieces and to empower every individual involved with the responsibility for their piece of the larger plan. The ROSTIR model is one approach particularly well suited to PR campaign planning in that it emphasizes the research necessary throughout the process, as well as a clear separation of the objectives, strategies, and tactics that provide a playbook for implementation, while the Diversity & Inclusion Wheel helps practitioners center on all areas of DEI to create meaningful, genuine, and impactful campaigns that represent today's America.

THINK CRITICALLY

1. What are the differences between goals and objectives?
2. What qualities go into well-written objectives?
3. How do strategies and tactics relate? Identify the best way to distinguish the two by giving examples.
4. Why are measurable objectives important during the evaluation phase? What are some advantages and disadvantages to incorporating measurable objectives into a strategic campaign?
5. Consider how Aaron Huey's crowdfunding campaign helped to support a campaign

whose overarching message was hope. Do you think it was a well-designed campaign? Support your response with evidence found in the chapter and secondary research you find online while examining Amplifier Art. Does the art found on the Amplifier webpage embody any spokes from the Diversity & Inclusion Wheel? If so, which ones? And how are the areas represented?

KEY TERMS

Budget 44
Crowdfunding 44
Diagnose 38
Diversity 39
Evaluation 43
Hashtag 39
Implementation 42
Inclusion 39
Management by objectives (MBO) 36
Objectives 40
R.A.C.E. 36
Research 36
R.O.P.E. 37
Social sphere 35
Strategic communication 36
Strategies 41
Tactics 41

CONCEPT CASE: MISSION-DRIVEN PLANNING FOR COMMUNITY FLOW YOGA

The mission statement for Community Flow Yoga is as follows: *Community Flow Yoga believes that the lessons learned in a conscious yoga practice can be spread to enrich our communities and our world. We believe in inclusion, community, acceptance, equality, and harmony at the center of our teaching philosophy and in the way we run our business. Helping others, both in our teaching and through community outreach, is central to who we are. As a decentralized company, we understand that power should be shared among our studio leaders, instructors, members, and communities. As a privately held company, we have the autonomy and the freedom to live these values in the pursuit of long-term stability and sustainable growth.*

Given this mission your task is to think about elements from each stage in the ROSTIR model that reflects this mission.

- What research would need to be done to learn more about this organization and its publics?
- What communication goals could reflect these organizational aspirations?
- What measureable objectives could serve as specific, useful points of achievement and direction?
- What messages would best reflect the organization's needs?
- What communication strategies, tactics, and communication channels would be most effective for this organization?
- How could diversity and inclusion be conveyed in the organization's outreach?
- What ongoing and evaluative research should the organization perform on its communications, its publics, its industry, its competitors, and its communities?

CASE STUDY: [UNLABELED]™

Coca-Cola with Anomaly LA
Campaign Focus: Diversity, Inclusion, and Equity

What happens when one of the world's largest and most recognizable brands tosses away its iconic logo and replaces its labeling with a simple silver can and a solid red stipe? Well, it turns out, quite a bit.

The Coca-Cola Company, partnering with the agency Anomaly LA, developed one of its most integrated, diverse, and multitiered PR campaigns ever: [unlabeled]™. In a world driven by labels, the company decided to strip its own label of all words to start a much-needed conversation surrounding the ill-effects of labeling others.

Research/Diagnosis

Diet Coke, produced and distributed by the Coca-Cola Company, has been a supporter of LGBTQ+ rights for years. The company prides itself on fostering an atmosphere of diversity, inclusion, and equity. In fact, every year since 2006, Coca-Cola has received a perfect score of 100 on the Human Rights Campaign's (HRC) Corporate Equality Index.[28] The HRC, a nonprofit organization representing over 3 million members, is considered the largest national lesbian, gay, bisexual, transgender, and queer civil rights organization nationwide.[29] The Corporate Equality Index is their benchmarking tool that tracks policies and procedures pertinent to LGBTQ+ employees.[30] What's more, a campaign such as this draws upon research indicating that younger generations, including millennials and Generation Z, are loyal to brands that support causes that are important to them. The Brands Taking Stands 2019 study, *Cause Is Working, Your Marketing Isn't* from DoSomething Strategic, reported that "66 percent of young consumers say that a brand's association with a social cause or platform positively impacts their overall impression of the brand and 58 percent say this association will impact their likelihood of purchasing that brand."[31]

Developing the [unlabeled]™ campaign was a natural part of the company's core values as well as the next in a series of initiatives deducted to its diversity and inclusion efforts. In 2015 the company sold logo-free cans in the Middle East near Ramadan to combat prejudice,[32] and created limited edition cans for Australia in 2017 supporting marriage equality.[33] Additionally, during the 2018 Superbowl, its ad touched upon the importance of gender fluidity.[34]

As part of the research efforts before the launch of the larger campaign, the PR and marketing practitioners at the Coca-Cola Company worked with their community partners including American Association of People with Disabilities, the American Indian College Fund, Ascend, Essence Communications, Human Rights Campaign, National Urban League, Hispanic Federation, Essence Communications, and GLAAD to garner insights and feedback surrounding the campaign.[35] According to Kerri Kopp, group director, Diet Coke, "Social media chatter around stereotypes and discrimination has increased almost five-fold over the last three years."[36] The premise behind the [unlabeled]™ campaign was simple: While not all labels are negative, most create an experience of feeling inadequate or "less than" as perceived within the boundaries of societal norms. The Diet Coke [unlabeled]™ website reads "some labels are earned. fought for. demanded. proudly owned. but then there are labels that are imposed upon us. weapons aimed to limit. box us in. make us feel lesser than. but imagine a world where we aren't limited by the way others label us."[37] By removing the label from their can, the hope was that the move would spark a deeper conversation surrounding labels in this country. The initial campaign featured various people sharing their experiences of being labeled. The labels addressed in the campaign range from mental illness to physical abilities to sexual orientation. You can watch their stories on YouTube here: https://www.youtube.com/user/dietcoke/videos. After watching some of the videos and looking at Diet Coke's social media pages on Instagram and Facebook, refer to the Diversity & Inclusion Wheel to see which areas of D&I were prioritized in this campaign.

Objectives

Grounded in the Coca-Cola Company's core values of equity, this campaign furthered its support of diversity and inclusion initiatives. In a word, the campaign challenges stereotypes and hopes to empower individuality. The campaign's overall purpose was to start a national conversation surrounding the importance of removing barriers so that we can begin to value one another for who we are. The company pledged to use their resources, global reach, and relationships to create an open space for everyone to simply be themselves.[38] One could assert that core elements of brand awareness were a critical component of this campaign. Cans of any Coca-Cola product are quintessential examples of brand awareness. The classic red, the stripe down the side—recognizable in any medium. It would not be unrealistic to conclude that in this case the company wanted to be associated with equality, diversity, and inclusion at every level.

Strategies

Using their own iconic cans as the centerpiece of this campaign, the Coca-Cola Company stripped themselves first of their own label to encourage others to discard theirs. This was a bold move for the brand. Packaging is the identity of a product. They took a risk in "unlabeling" themselves.

Tactics

Using a multipronged approach, the Coca-Cola Company employed tactics across paid, earned, shared, and owned channels through the development of a microsite dedicated to the [unlabeled]™ campaign, videos, social media posts, and sponsored events during the summer of 2019.

Paid

At a Pride event in Los Angeles, the company distributed stickers with words including "Independent" and "Misrepresented" to drive home the labeling points. In addition, they purchased ads on social media channels that reinforced this messaging.

Earned

Coverage of the campaign was picked up by traditional media coverage and by outlets including Forbes, Essence, Adweek, Ad Age, and PR Daily among others.[39]

Shared

The campaign relied heavily upon social media. To launch the campaign, the company developed a series of three separate ads that highlighted the rules for "unlabeling" others.

Additionally, to gain additional reach, those featured in the campaign used their personal social media accounts to share the message. Ketzi, Ayani, Justina, Keri, and Brendan are a few of the people that utilized their sphere of influence to share the significance of the campaign.

Owned

A microsite, [unlabeled]™, was created as the online space for the campaign. In addition to explaining the premise behind the campaign, the site featured the 16 people included in the initiative. If a visitor to the page clicked on an image, they could watch a video about the person and the labels they have had to overcome.

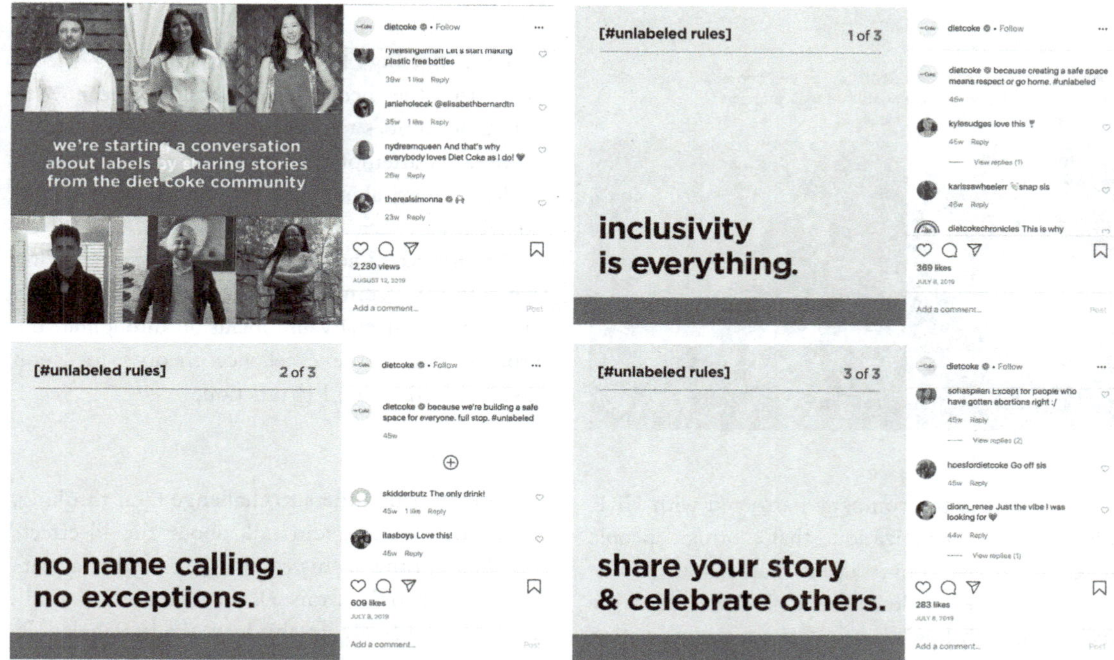

In this image posted to the Diet Coke Instagram account the company launched a series of their [unlabeled]™ videos.

The Diet Coke [unlabeled] cans debuted at NYC Pride on June 30, 2019.

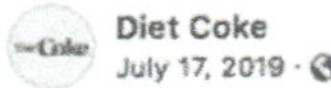

we're removing our labels, to start a conversation about yours. see how we're celebrating individuals and their stories at dietcoke.com/unlabeled. #unlabeled

In addition, the company partnered with Civic Dinners, an organization that "brings people together to have conversations that matter."[40] Visitors to the site can download a PDF that walks the reader through how to host a dinner conversation surrounding "labels and how they help us and how they hinder us in society."[41]

Implementation

The campaign employed a soft launch strategy in select cities during the summer of 2019, including events such as Pride parades. According to media coverage, [unlabeled]™ is a multiyear campaign that will continue to be refined and eventually rolled out nationally.[42] Coca-Cola designated Instagram and Facebook "safe spaces" where consumers could share their own stories and read comments from others.[43]

Reporting/Evaluation

As part of the one-month concentrated efforts of the campaign, it can be concluded that the campaign was successful, based on social media comments, likes, shares, and video views. This initial phase of this multiyear campaign explored the nuances of labels and what they mean to different people.[44]

Theories

Agenda Setting Theory: Agenda setting theory states that the media does not tell people how to think, but it does tell people what to think about.[45] Coca-Cola attempted to raise the public's level of understanding about the importance of diversity, equality, and inclusion.

Excellence Theory: In addition to reflecting symmetrical communication, the campaign's emphasis on diversity and inclusion throughout the process reflects the excellence theory's focus on diversity within the PR function.

Model

By empowering others to challenge their thinking, open their minds, and talk about the ill-effects of labeling others, this campaign provided a platform for people from all backgrounds to talk candidly and freely. In this way, the [unlabeled]™ campaign exemplifies a **two-way symmetrical communication model**, with the organization and the campaign shaped by engaged participants and putting value in societal and community outcomes.

Diversity- and Inclusion-First Approach

This campaign is the embodiment of diversity, inclusion, and equity and could be used as a benchmark for other organizations incorporating such initiatives. Within each step of the ROSTIR model, Coca-Cola incorporated meaningful D&I efforts. During the research and diagnosis phase, the company worked with GLADD, AAPD, the National Urban League, and the Hispanic Federation to ensure the elements within the campaign were aligned. The strategy and tactics employed were well thought out and included nearly every element from the Diversity & Inclusion Wheel.

Understanding PESO

"Did you see a cocktail napkin with our entire marketing campaign on it?"

©iStockPhotos/andrewgenn

THINK AHEAD

3.1 Understand the PESO model and the differences between paid, earned, shared/social, and owned media.

3.2 Recognize when companies should use paid, earned, shared/social, and owned media.

3.3 Identify how each area works together to form strategic, holistic campaigns.

WHAT IS PESO?

As you will discover, the **PESO model** is an approach that connects paid, earned, shared, and owned media to deliver integrated marketing communication programs that extend reach and establish brands as leaders within their industry.[1] The PESO model takes these four media types—paid, earned, shared, and owned—and merges them together. Understanding when to use each element and how they complement each other is paramount. Tailoring and customizing PESO campaigns to the audience and company goals is essential to successfully executing a public relations campaign today.

FIGURE 3.1

The PESO Model

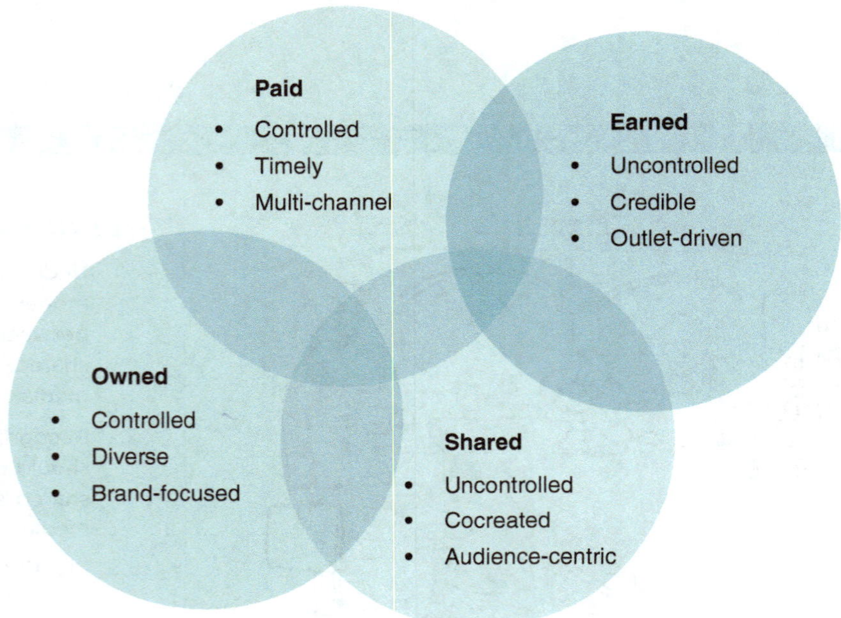

Paid, earned, shared, and owned channels allow practitioners to choose from a variety of approaches: controlled or uncontrolled, narrow or diverse media or audiences, as well as favoring a singular organizational voice or many voices (cocreated).

The four areas of the model can be understood as paid, earned, shared, and owned media. Areas of overlap—where a channel includes multiple parts of the model—can be referred to as "**converged media**." Practitioners can understand the campaign process as a painter: selecting the right colors from a palette, sometimes mixing multiple colors together to get the best possible shade. While no individual could be an expert in all four areas, public relations today requires that professionals have a familiarity with each of the four major types of media to understand when and how they can connect with specific organizational audiences and strengthen campaigns.

Paid Media

Paid media (PM) is often thought of as "traditional" advertising through online channels, display ads, pay per click search ads, commercials, print ads, and sponsorships.[2] The rise in popularity of advertising on sites like Facebook, Twitter, YouTube, and LinkedIn has driven renewed interest in this area. Companies use PM to gain a presence on channels where consumers and buyers are spending their time.[3]

PRo Tip

WANT TO MAXIMIZE SHARED MEDIA? START SHARING

You'll need to follow these simple tips:

- Instagram: Post new content one or two times per day using a multitude of hashtags to capture a larger audience. Tools like hashtagify.me help organizations find the right hashtags, amplify their message, and even identify possible influencers.
- TikTok: It has 800 million active users and the highest follower engagement rates across 100,000 user profiles according to Influencer Marketing Hub. That means those creating videos must post a constant stream of content. Many top users share at least five videos per week to keep fans engaged. More if you want to grow a following.
- Twitter: The day you publish content, tweet the link four times, three hours apart. Day two: tweet the link twice. Day three: once. Social dashboards like Hootsuite or Cyfe can assist in scheduling when to tweet.
- Pinterest: Conservative pinners will pin five times per day. Companies that have the audience and threshold will pin up to 30 times per day. Know your audience and know company resources. But, if there is only one person managing social media, pinning 30 times per day may not be advantageous.
- Facebook: Post content at least once a day and be sure to include an image or video. Consider sponsored content as part of a larger, overarching PM campaign.
- Snapchat: Post anywhere from one to five times daily to build a loyal audience. Use Storyheap to help measure and analyze a campaign's performance.
- LinkedIn: Post once a day to the company account, the company page, and your personal account. Encourage employees to share company posts.
- YouTube: Establishing a subscriber base is most important with YouTube. Post compelling videos at least once a week, and use targeted keywords through Google AdWords to reach your target audience.

Cross-promote your content across all social channels for the most effective coverage because converging media is critical to amplifying brand messages.

Sources: Nathan Ellering, "How Often to Post on Social Media According to 14 Studies," *CoSchedule Blog*, December 12, 2017, https://coschedule.com/blog/how-often-to-post-on-social-media/.

Tom Roy, "Social Media Frequency 2016: How Often Should You Post," LinkedIn, April 18, 2016, http://www.linkedin.com/pulse/social-media-frequency-2016-how-often-should-you-post-tom-roy.

Irfan Ahmad, "How Often and When to Post on Social Media [Infographic]," *Social Media Today*, November 10, 2017, https://www.socialmediatoday.com/news/how-often-and-when-to-post-on-social-media-infographic/510206/.

Earned Media

Earned media (EM) is commonly referred to as either publicity or media relations. Examples include having a newspaper or trade publication write about you, your company, or its offerings.[4] EM is often associated with public relations professionals and the industry as a whole. This could be because it is one of the tangible tactics unique to public relations initiatives.

Shared Media

Shared media (SM) is also known as social media and is the result of a brand and followers, customers, or fans interacting and mutually creating content. Customers many times feel empowered to publish and create content on the brand's behalf inspiring buzz and word of mouth.[5] SM uses **influencer** relations. Influencers can be bloggers, journalists, celebrities, or people who are held in high regard within varied social circles, marketplaces, or industries. Influencers know their audiences. They have a keen awareness of what their audience likes and have built a following by consistently posting high-quality content that resonates with their audience who, in turn, may become loyal advocates.[6] In order for SM principles to be effective, brands must relinquish control and grant a level of editorial and creative freedom to their influencers. In this way, they feel empowered to produce authentic content, benefiting both the brand and their fans.[7]

Owned Media

Content and assets that the brand controls, like websites, blogs, newsletters, brochures, and social media accounts, are all considered **owned media** (OM).[8] Brands are increasingly behaving like publishers by employing editorial staff that manage content creation streams.[9] Content is written with the idea that it will engage its customers and help foster relationships throughout the customer lifecycle.

Recent research has demonstrated that shared and owned channels have grown significantly in importance over the past several years.[10] As advertising and public relations departments and agencies have collaborated and, at times, challenged each other for organizational support and budgetary dollars, the convergence of channels makes these distinctions among media types increasingly blurry. While public relations, social media, and advertising practitioners may be far from fully integrated, collaboration is necessary and beneficial.[11]

WHEN SHOULD EACH OF THE PESO CHANNELS BE USED?

By using the PESO model, organizations are employing the all-channel, all-inclusive approach to strategic planning. In the PESO model, each channel delivers unique

PRo Tip

UNIFIED EMPLOYEE ENGAGEMENT

When creating content for the company's social channels, encourage employees to retweet, share, and pin the content to their personal social networking sites. PR leaders can choose from a variety of digital tools that help facilitate employee engagement, making it easier for employees to review, modify, and share organizational content through their personal social media channels. These include Bambu, Dynamic Signal, Hootsuite Amplify, and many others.[14]

value. For example, PM are the channels public relations practitioners use in which money is paid to place the message and control its distribution; EM assists practitioners with creating the opportunity to have the company story told by credible, objective, third-party influencers such as journalists, bloggers, trade analysts, and industry leaders;[12] SM allows a company's community of users to pass along messages through various social networking sites while at the same time commenting on the messages; and OM are the editorial messages written, published, and controlled by a company-owned blog, website, or other channel.[13]

Campaigns in Action

The following examples highlight each function of the model being used in individual campaigns. The final campaign uses all four areas of the PESO model.

Paid Media

American sporting brand Under Armour has created multiple campaigns emphasizing and showcasing women. They worked with advertising agency Droga5 to create the "I will what I want" campaign, focused on empowering women and creating a space for the Under Armour Women's brand to grow. The campaign encouraged women to go after what they want and not be held back, wait for affirmation, acceptance, or permission from others.[15] Leanne Fremar, senior VP and creative director for women's business, said that the insight behind "I Will What I Want" was not "you go, girl." The goal was to celebrate women "who had the physical and mental strength to tune out the external pressures and turn inward and chart their own course."[16]

The campaign features the stories of Misty Copeland, ballerina for the American Ballet Theatre; Lindsey Vonn, US Down Hills Skier; Gisele Bundchen, model; Brianna Cope, pro surfer; and Kelley O'Hara, US Women's National Team (Soccer).

© Under Armour

Renowned ballet dancer Misty Copeland lent the strength and power of her personal brand to Under Armour's "I Will What I Want" campaign.
#IWILLWHATIWANT

The campaign was an overwhelming success. The videos have been viewed more than 2.8 million times on YouTube, there was a 293 percent lift in brand conversation, and, most importantly, traffic to underarmour.com increased by 42 percent.[17] The campaign proved that women's sports marketing is no longer an afterthought. Sales in Under Armour's North American women's apparel division are on pace to reach $1.8 billion by 2019.[18] The PM campaign won the Cyber Category Grand Prix award at the Cannes Lions Festival. According to the Cannes judging panel, the video was an obvious choice for the top prize as it used technology to deliver an empowering message, "this is the entry that demonstrates how a well-crafted digital experience creates an uplifting impact to bring a brand closer to people, from the point of engagement to the point of transaction."[19]

For International Women's Day in 2020, Under Armour teamed up with three-time NBA Champion Stephen Curry and actor Storm Reid (*Euphoria*, *Twelve Years a Slave*, *A Wrinkle in Time*). The partnership resulted in a newly designed basketball shoe (Curry 7 Bamazing Colorway), a collaborative effort showcasing Reid's Bamazing initiative to empower young women. Under Armour will also support additional scholarships for women through Curry's Eat. Learn. Play. Foundation.[20]

Storm Reid and Stephen Curry both added their design influence to Under Armour's Curry 7 Bamazing colorway basketball shoe in celebration of International Women's Day 2020.

Earned Media

IBM has been a technology leader since its founding in 1911, but maintaining a perception as a leading-edge, innovative company can be challenging for a twenty-year-old brand, let alone one with more than a century of history. As part of this effort to position the organization as future focused, IBM created the "5 in 5" campaign to share annual tech predictions.[21] This long-running campaign received multiple accolades in 2019 (its twelfth year), including a Digital PR Social Media Award from Ragan's PR Daily (Media Relations Campaign category)[22] and a PRSA Bronze Anvil (Media Relations—Business-to-Business [B2B] category).[23] The campaign, titled "From Seed to Shelf: How IBM Innovations Will Transform Every Stage of the Food Supply Chain," examined the positive and expanding role of technology in food production and distribution. The integrated campaign (including a variety of digital content such as a website, videos, social media, and five livestreamed "subject matter expert" talks) generated significant high-level media coverage, including coverage from *Forbes*,[24] *Fast Company*,[25] and BBC News.[26]

An imaged captured from the homepage video on IBM's "5 in 5" campaign website, featuring Top Chef season 17 winner Melissa King discussing the future of technology in the food supply chain.

As a B2B campaign, IBM's "5 in 5" targets high-prestige EM coverage as a desired outcome—in contrast to consumer campaigns that may position EM as a means to additional social media conversations with marketing ends. In this way, the campaign highlights the value of EM as part of an integrated campaign structure. It demonstrates how content generated by organizations (such as the dedicated website and expert videos) and shared through social media can help position an organization for media relations coverage.

Shared Media

When brands use SM initiatives they usually revolve around content such as word of mouth, referrals, community-driven content, and cocreation. This is an area of the PESO model where content marketing and social media marketing work together. Reese's has been a sponsorship partner of the National Collegiate Athletic Association (NCAA) for more than a decade. According to the public relations team, the brand celebrated the passion and roller coaster of emotions that the NCAA tournament evokes in college basketball fans through a variety of creative advertising, social media content, and in-store promotions.[27] Content strategy was clearly a strength for Reese's as they curated incredible pieces with beautiful visuals that celebrated both March Madness and the Reese's brand. Moreover, the copywriting for these posts was engaging and sharable.[28]

In their joint press release, Walt Disney Parks and Resorts and the Make-A-Wish foundation announced that in honor of the 100,000th Disney wish granted globally, and in celebration of Disneyland Resort's 60th Anniversary, fans were invited to share images of Mickey Mouse ears, or any creative ears at all, to help grant wishes. By using the Share Your Ears photo frame on Facebook and sharing photos with the hashtag #ShareYourEars on Twitter and Instagram, community users unlocked a $5 donation from Walt Disney Parks and Resorts, up to $1 million.[29] The campaign used the social media entries on their websites to drive audience engagement and boost campaign awareness. The #ShareYourEars campaign became a trending topic on Facebook, and Disney Parks doubled their original pledge, donating $2 million to the Make-A-Wish Foundation.[30]

The emotional roller coaster has come to a glorious end. #MarchMood #NCAAChampionship #MarchMadness

8:37 PM - 4 Apr 2016

12 Retweets 33 Likes

1 12 33

© The Hershey Company

A sweet partnership between the NCAA and Reese's has embraced energetic content to capture the spirit of March Madness.

Owned Media

OM expresses brand portability by extending a company's presence both within and beyond its website through social media sites and unique communities. Proponents of capitalizing on OM strategy believe that content should live on organization-controlled channels that then lend pieces to outlying owned social networks, such as Twitter, Facebook, Instagram, Snapchat, or other social channels.[31] Owned content is more than just a website; it includes blogs, white papers, ebooks, webinars, podcasts, video campaigns, catalogs, and email marketing, as well as hosted events and other in-person opportunities. While social channels are also part of SM, the content posted to those channels is owned by the company. Content can flow across channels and can be used in multiple ways to reach audiences and publics. Crossover between and among each area of the PESO model is common.

As COVID-19 swept across the US in early 2020, organizations of all types and sizes adjusted their products, services, and messages to reflect the unprecedented events. Amid the cancellations, thousands of couples were forced to cancel or postpone weddings. Signet Jewelers, parent company of Jared, sought a way to give these couples a way to connect and share their special day, even if it was not the way they originally intended. The company created a new online platform (Jared.com/VirtualWedding) and provided 1,000 free ceremonies, giving couples the opportunity to select a variety of elements and build guest lists, create invitations, and craft a theme.[32] This OM-centered campaign also included a paid TV ad from agency Publicis and used #LoveCantWait on multiple social media channels.

© Disney

User-generated content helped Disney and #shareyourears raise millions of dollars for the Make-A-Wish Foundation.

Jared's Virtual Wedding website used owned-media to help couples share their special day during COVID-19.

CONTINUOUS INTEGRATION

All four media types—paid, earned, shared, owned—contribute to establishing a brand's reputation. They should continually overlap through a series of strategic and diverse approaches. Brands should share their content on all of their social media pages as well as owned channels in order to deliver their messages to as many users as possible in an effort to engage in meaningful conversations with them.

CONCLUSION

All organizations use a mix of outreach approaches and channels to share information with their stakeholders. The PESO model helps practitioners to consider channel selection holistically and strategically: by regularly asking ourselves what the best mix of channels might be for a specific campaign, project, or program, we give organizations the greatest chance of success in execution. If we consider this in the early stages of planning, we're better able to craft content that can be repurposed across channels, to consider the needs of organizational stakeholders and publics, and to use integrated campaigns to build relationships, not just achieve short-term objectives.

PRo Tip

INCORPORATING CONVERGED MEDIA

Combining paid, earned, shared, and owned media is known as converged media. According to Rebecca Lieb and Jeremiah Owyang from Altimeter,

converged media utilizes two or more channels of paid, earned, shared, and owned media. It is characterized by a consistent storyline, look, and feel. All channels work in concert, enabling brands to reach customers exactly where, how, and when they want, regardless of channel, medium, or device, online or offline. With the customer journey between devices, channels, and media becoming increasingly complex, and new forms of technology only making it more so, this strategy of paid/owned/earned/shared confluence makes marketers impervious to the disruption caused by emerging technologies.[33]

Source: Rebecca Lieb and Jeremiah Owyang, "The Converged Media Imperative," Report, Altimeter Group, July 19, 2012, https://www.slideshare.net/Altimeter/the-converged-media-imperative.

THINK CRITICALLY

1. What is PESO, and how is it applied to public relations?
2. How does the PESO model differ from R.O.P.E. and R.A.C.E.?
3. Conduct a search of a small business using social media. Analyze its paid, earned, shared, and owned channels. What role does the PESO model play in the success or failure for the organization?
4. It has been said that today's public relations practitioner must embrace the PESO model in order for a strategic campaign to be effective. Do you agree or disagree?

KEY TERMS

Converged media 52
Earned media 54
Influencer 54
Owned media 54
Paid media 52
PESO model 51
Shared media 54

CONCEPT CASE: APPLYING PESO TO COMMUNITY FLOW YOGA

Community Flow Yoga is looking to tackle two short-term communication challenges:

1. Improving communication with existing members and supporters
   a. Strengthening relationships with the organization
   b. Balancing communication from the national brand and local studios
   c. Building a feeling of individual ownership and contribution to the larger brand
2. Increasing brand awareness at the national level
   a. Developing relationships with influencers (traditional and digital media)
   b. Prioritizing specific target audiences and publics
   c. Improving name recognition
   d. Raising its favorability relative to other fitness and yoga brands

From a public relations perspective, consider which channels would be the best fit from among the paid, earned, shared, owned, and converged media universe to convey each of the crucial messages and approaches described above. How might they work together to achieve some of these goals? Which channels would be best to convey certain messages? What would be less effective or efficient for specific messages and audiences?

CASE STUDY: THE TAMPON BOOK

The Female Company
Campaign Focus: Advocacy, Activism, Social Impact

Many of today's for-profit organizations are increasingly committing to give back, to connect with the community, to make real change happen, and to be more authentic with consumers. For many businesses, a community focus such as this is just a small part of a larger approach. This is precisely the case with the Female Company, with an eye on the community residing at the center of its mission and values. Accordingly, this case study highlights what can happen when two women set out to end the luxury tax on feminine hygiene products. The impact of which can be seen in both their home country of Germany, and well beyond their borders.

Research/Diagnosis

Ann-Sophie Claus and Sinja Stadelmaier, founders of the Female Company, an organization that produces and sells pesticide-free and fair labor organic tampons and pledges the proceeds to support economically disadvantaged women,[34] took on antiquated German legislation. With one simple question, "What do caviar, truffles, and oil paintings have in common? They are all taxed at lower rates than tampons." The founders, along with their creative agency Scholz & Friends, developed a calculated and inventive way to circumvent the 19 percent luxury tax imposed on feminine hygiene products.

Within Germany, tampons are considered a luxury item and therefore taxed at top value-added rate allowable by law, wherein items such as caviar, art, or books are taxed at a mere 7 percent. Armed with research from all around the globe, Claus and Stadelmaier found that the tampon tax issue was also a concern beyond just their home country, even provoking international protests.[35,36] Canada, Kenya, and Australia along with individual US states including New York and Minnesota had already eliminated a tax on feminine hygiene products.[37] At the time, the original tampon tax was voted into law in 1963 with a majority vote of 499 men to 36 women in Germany's parliament.[38]

This integrated campaign centered on a book that concealed tampons between its pages because books are taxed at a much lower rate of 7 percent. Carved out within the pages was a secret compartment that held fifteen organic tampons. According to the company press release, the book was so much more than a nifty carrying case for tampons: "The Tampon Book is a fun read. The forty-six pages offer surprising and often humorous stories around menstruation from biblical times until today. The aim of the authors is to show how interesting and culturally relevant menstruation actually is. A topic that is still not spoken about openly."[39]

Objectives

Through the entire month of April 2019, the program aimed to meet the following objectives:

- Change Legislation: Petition German parliament to abolish the 19 percent tampon tax altogether
- Gender Equality: In many countries, there is a shame associated with menstruation, making education about/access to feminine products difficult. Through this campaign, Claus and Stadelmaier worked to create an open environment where women everywhere can ask questions, speak freely, and understand further the biological aspects of their being.

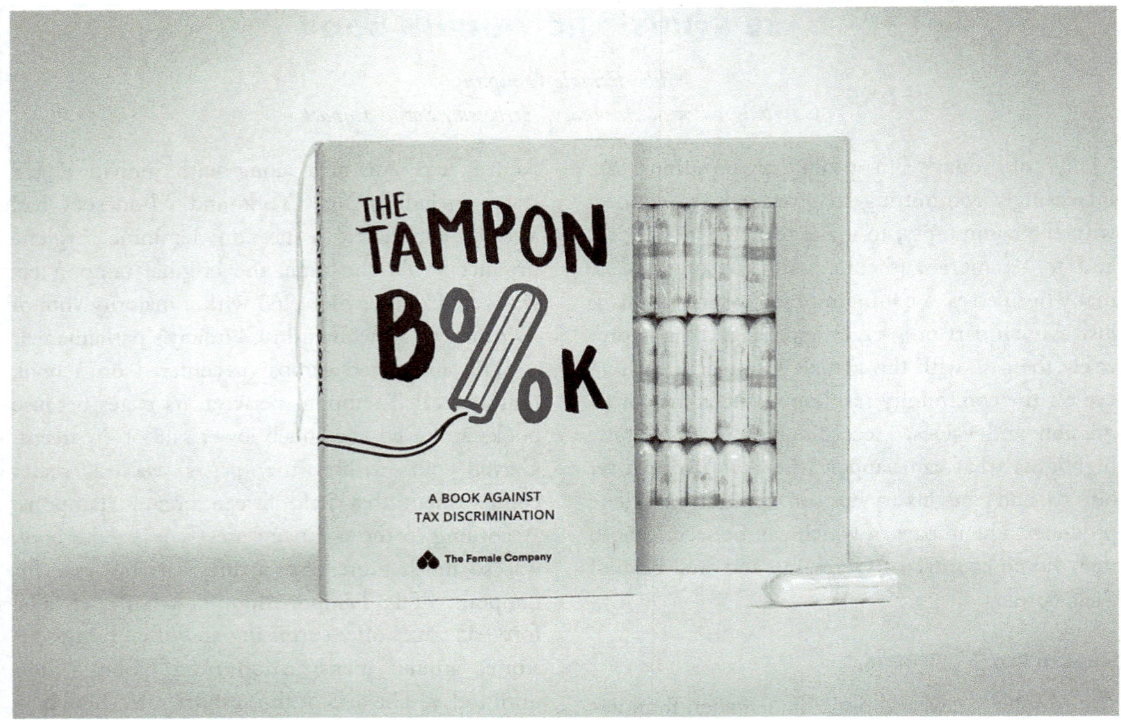

The Female Company

The Tampon Book displaying the hidden tampon compartment.[40]

Strategies

The strategy hinged on the ability to convince the German parliament that the law was antiquated. Based on their research and overarching objectives, the Female Company devised a strategy to circumvent the 19 percent luxury tax—create a book that concealed the tampons and educated readers about menstruation while selling the tampons at a reduced rate. Through this effort, coverage and discussion of this novel, newsworthy, and attention-grabbing approach through earned, shared, and owned media would support both direct legislative advocacy as well as broader societal awareness and support.

Tactics

A series of integrated strategies using multiple aspects of the PESO model were planned and included the following:

- The Tampon Book
- Traditional media relations including a well-crafted press release
- Website
- Company Facebook page
- Change.org petition
- Endorsements by female political leaders and influencers

Paid and Owned

Used as an inventive political statement, the most important component of the campaign centered on the actual tampon book. Consumers could purchase the book via the company's website: https://www.thefemalecompany.com/tampon-book-en/. In addition, the company started a change.org petition where they collected over 190,000 signatures.

change.org Start a petition My petitions Browse Membership Log in

The period is not a luxury - lower the pad tax!

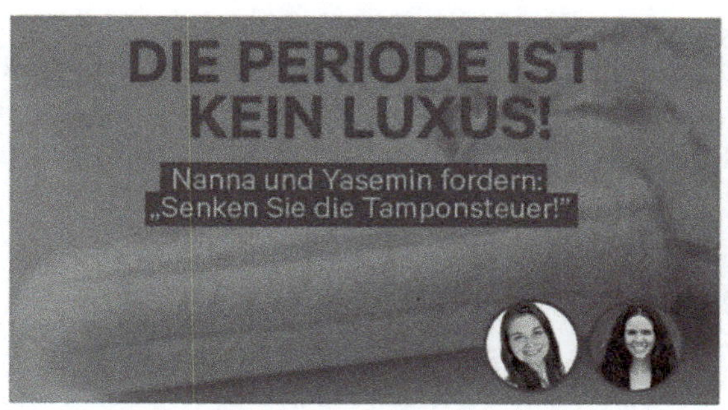

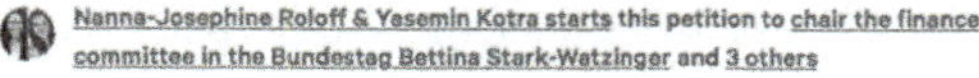

Earned and Shared

A carefully written and artfully crafted press release was sent to the media. The release announced the sale of the Tampon Book and outlined the unfair and gender-biased tax on feminine products.[41] Mainstream media, including *Berliner Zeitung*, *RTL*, *Glamour*, and the country's nightly news forums, covered the topic thoroughly. With news media sharing the report, German influencers quickly joined in and began sharing the story on a variety of social media channels. This, in turn, sparked interest from leading female politicians, including Dr. Franziska Brantner and Nicola Beer. The company Facebook page was used as a vehicle to promote the book and the agenda. At one point Facebook banned the content for being too political.[42]

Implementation

This is an example of a short-run campaign that had a significant public impact. As quickly as the Tampon Book was released, the book sold out. In fact, the initial 10,000 copies sold on the first day with a second print selling out within a week.[43] Demand for the book could not be satisfied.

Reporting/Evaluation

When coverage from Germany's largest television networks began to put pressure on the German Federal Minister of Finance, Olaf Scholz, the public conversation became more directly political and parliament started to pay attention.[44] Eventually, Germany voted to eliminate the 19 percent luxury tax on feminine hygiene products. The campaign was a success on many levels.

The Clio Awards, which recognize innovation and creative excellence, awarded the Tampon Book five gold awards and three silver awards.[45] The campaign also took home the PR Grand Prix at the Cannes Lions. Jury president Michelle Hutton (Edelman's managing director of global clients) said, "the tampon book is a great example of modern communications. The campaign combined creativity with the craft of public relations and when these two go hand in hand this is the type of magic that is produced."[46]

Theories

Framing Theory: Framing theory emphasizes that individuals construct their worldview through a variety of interwoven and interconnected symbols. The campaign served to provide a new public context for understanding this crucial public issue. The tampon book served as a symbol aligning the Female Company's agenda with the public's interest.

Agenda Building Theory: The Female Company honed in on an issue which they took a strong public stance. Through their action and public relations efforts, they leveraged the idea of agenda building, catching the attention of the media, the public, and German legislators who, in the end, voted to reduce the tax on tampons.[47]

Diversity- and Inclusion-First Approach

Fighting for gender equality was among the top priorities when considering various aspects within the Diversity & Inclusion Wheel. With creativity and determination Ann-Sophie Claus and Sinja Stadelmaier fought and won to change an unfair and biased law that had been enforced for more than half a century.

Research, Part 1

DIAGNOSIS AND DEVELOPMENTAL RESEARCH

iStock.com/kate_sept2004

THINK AHEAD

4.1 Describe the importance of research in understanding an organization and its environment.

4.2 Connect research to building knowledge around organizational challenges and opportunities.

4.3 Define different types and stages of research (primary/secondary, quantitative/qualitative, formal/informal, developmental/refinement/evaluation).

4.4 Consider the use of different research tools (interviews, content analysis, experiments, and so on) to help answer different research questions.

The creation of any successful public relations (PR) campaign begins with recognition of a specific situation: the challenges or opportunities the organization faces. This chapter and the following chapter provide an outline to investigate and clarify your approach before planning a campaign. Research allows practitioners to diagnose an organization's aspirations and needs—the challenges and opportunities within its environment—then craft communication goals to address them. Research involves a **methodology** (a framework for systematically processing understanding information) for analyzing **data** (such as survey results, a sample of written content, or the conversations of a focus group).[1] Research should be seen as important to inform individual campaigns as well as ongoing strategic decisions for the organization.

PR professionals can use secondary and primary research techniques as well as qualitative and quantitative methods to develop a clearer understanding of a situation. In *Advertising and Public Relations Research*, authors Jugenheimer, Kelley, Hudson, and Bradley argue that proper research positions organizations to save money, gain on competitors, adapt to change, and improve internal operations.[2] By helping organizations to better understand diverse publics, stakeholders, and communities, PR research can also create more inclusive campaigns and contribute to improving the community awareness of leaders and managers.[3] Research enables PR campaigns to provide strategic insight and support to the organizations that they serve.

Yet, many practitioners make assumptions and begin tactical work without initially understanding the **audiences**, **stakeholders**, **publics**, challenges, competitors, and risks in the environment. Even seasoned PR professionals are guilty of this mistake from time to time. It is always more efficient in the long run to invest time and effort at the onset of campaign development, to properly inform the goals, objectives, strategies, and tactics that will follow.

DEVELOPMENTAL RESEARCH: DIAGNOSING THE PROBLEM AND/OR OPPORTUNITY

Research comes into play throughout a PR program or campaign cycle. Eminent PR researcher Dr. Don W. Stacks explains research as "a continuous process that continually assesses an organization's position among its publics on a variety of outcome measures."[4] He groups these into three categories: developmental, refinement, and evaluation.[5] **Developmental research** helps practitioners to understand the environment and current situation. **Refinement research**, undertaken while the campaign is underway, assists in the regular adjustment and optimization of messages, as well as the clarification of audience needs and perspectives. Finally, **evaluative research** looks back on a campaign to understand areas of success, methods for improvement, and lessons learned. As noted, developmental research is a critical and often overlooked stage of the PR planning process, which allows practitioners to understand the organization and the communication environment, define publics, clarify problems or opportunities, and set baselines from which to measure improvement.

As the link between the organization and its societal and industry environment, PR practitioners may be asked to create a PR campaign with limited or incomplete knowledge of the situation at hand. Even organizational leaders who value the work of PR teams may unwittingly withhold information or have an unclear vantage point to

iStock.com/sanjeri

Research can deepen the understanding of external and internal organizational stakeholders and publics, informing campaign goals, objectives, strategies, tactics, and messaging. These publics may include local families, businesses, employees, or other members of your community.

fully understand and diagnose potential communication challenges. It is often valuable for PR teams to lead an internal discussion that can help create distance from the most pressing issues at hand and considers the larger perspective of the company as situated in its industry at a specific point in time.

- In your industry, how is today different from yesterday?
- How will tomorrow be different from today?
- What are competitors doing differently?
- How is the industry changing?

Asking some of these broad questions provides an organization with competitive, as well as historical context. This this type of conversation can also help prioritize and create a framework for initiating a situational investigation to develop detailed strategic insights about the role of PR and the best approaches to position an organization for long-term success. This inspection is considered a form of primary research (discussed in more detail later in the chapter) that informs subsequent investigative work and can provide an initial hypothesis regarding the challenge or opportunity at hand. It also begins the process of understanding the organization's goals and aspirations as defined by leadership.

Researching Your Brand

Research can deepen the understanding of external and internal organizational publics, informing campaign goals, objectives, strategies, tactics, and messaging. These publics may include local families, businesses, employees, or other members of your community. As professional communicators, this starts with a deep understanding of an individual organizational brand. In *Public Relations Writing and Media Techniques*, Dennis Wilcox and Bryan Reber outline a number of approaches to consider when conducting research on a brand:[6]

Review the organizational mission statement: The majority of organizations have a mission statement that defines their purpose for doing business.

- Evaluate its clarity, simplicity, and trajectory as a statement of purpose.
- Review the organizational website and other owned media, social media channels, and additional external facing materials such as collateral to determine whether actions and messages support the mission statement.
- Look at discrepancies as areas where improved communication can positively impact the organization:
  - For example, a manufacturing organization details in its mission statement that "the customer always comes first" but rarely references its customers in any public-facing language or materials.
  - **Desired outcome**: The PR team diagnoses the disconnect and recommends, as its goal, closing this identified gap by revising specific materials and updating content standards, trade media outreach topics, and internal-facing language to support the shift in focus.

Look for the "uniqueness": Every business or nonprofit should have a clear understanding of what differentiates them from their competitors, but many have difficulty articulating the specifics.

- PR professionals can evaluate a company relative to its competitors to establish, from their strategic vantage point, what the public-facing content says about each organization. This content may or may not align with leaders' perceptions.
- By examining the gaps between internal and external messaging, as well as identifying any unused communication "real estate" in the industry of interest, strategies and tactics can be further refined to help a company stand out relative to its competitors.
  - For example, three local theater companies are competing for the attention and financial resources of the same audiences, supporters, and

reporters; often repeating the same messages with similar "calls to action."

  - **Desired outcome**: A PR practitioner identifies and advises one of the nonprofits to differentiate itself in the region by targeting a specific audience within the broader spectrum (perhaps students and recent graduates). By developing and promoting unique incentives, opportunities, and rewards specific to this audience, the theater creates messaging that resonates with its targeted demographic, driving media interest providing a differentiator among its competitors.

Talk to individuals on the front lines: Speaking with customer service representatives, salespeople, fundraisers, and others who have regular interaction with an organization's most critical external publics can provide an excellent perspective on how the organization is perceived.[7] Several research techniques can gather and synthesize the insights from these critical internal stakeholders.

- **Informal interviews and conversations** with key informants can point toward potential areas of strength and weakness—both can be valuable for additional in-depth or formal research.
- **Focus groups** provide a structure for efficiently gathering the insights from many individuals with a shared perspective (hence the term *focus*), which can be useful for understanding a group's perspective, as well as—by carefully watching the interactions among the individuals as part of the discussion—additional pain points, fears, challenges, and, through what is not discussed, taboos.
- **Desired Outcome**: Surveys of relevant teams or departments within the organization allow practitioners to formalize and support the findings from earlier qualitative or informal research. Additionally, they can provide a relatively efficient and wholly anonymous way to gather information—particularly for teams or organizations that are rarely in the same geographic location. Digital tools such as Survey Monkey make these simple for respondents.

By considering some these aspects of brands and their communities or publics, practitioners can begin to understand the importance organizational brands play.

RESEARCHING AND MEASURING THE PROBLEM/OPPORTUNITY

After completing the initial audience identification analysis, PR professionals then rely on a variety of research techniques to develop the objectives and strategies that will contribute to the development of a campaign. In *Using Research in Public Relations*, Glen M. Broom and David M. Dozier describe a *communication problem* as the gap between what a group of people perceive and what is actually desired.[8] This approach recommends drafting a problem statement as the first step of the research process, summarizing the issue at hand.

All formal research (qualitative and quantitative as well as secondary and primary) begins with a clear statement of the research problem at hand. The problem statement should be concise and strive to meet the following criteria: written in the present tense, specific, measurable, and blame free.[9] Examples of statements adhering to this methodology include the following:

- Company X's product market share has declined by 20 percent over the past two years, resulting in lost revenue and overproduction.
- A nonprofit organization is hiring for various positions but has struggled to attract qualified applicants over the past two months.
- The State Department of Transportation has seen a 7 percent increase in traffic deaths over the past three years (the period over which it has also been running a similar public safety outreach campaign).

Although these challenges are not entirely within the realm of communication, as strategic leaders, PR practitioners can and should serve a role in prioritizing the areas where improved communication can have the greatest impact.

Problem statements lead to a variety of potential questions, which can be answered with both formal and informal techniques. Using **formal research** techniques can help define an organization's challenges, identify audiences, select strategies, refine tactics, and evaluate success. That said, practitioners should not overlook the value of **informal research**, particularly in the early stages of the diagnosis process. Informal research can help form a general understanding of an organization and its environment, including work to read and understand organizational documents and language (as well as competitors'); building relationships and asking for the perspective of management; and gathering external viewpoints from external experts, media, and other audiences and publics. This research does not need to be done using a scientific process to be valuable, but it can still be thoughtful and thorough. The main distinction from more formal approaches is that such methods are not **generalizable** to larger groups.[10] Informal research can be extremely valuable, but it represents educated guesses in relation to formal systematic research.

iStock.com/kate_sept2004

Data can come from many different sources, including secondary research, interviews, and content analysis.

Research on the same set of data can be performed in formal and informal ways. For example, a PR practitioner may be interested in the coverage of a specific issue or organization by a certain media outlet. An informal approach could involve reading a small sample of articles to understand recent coverage in terms of structure, tone, or content, producing qualitative findings. This could end up as a report or client presentation informing future strategies, tactics, and messaging. Alternatively, a formal approach could use a quantitative method such as content analysis. This might involve selecting a time window (past five years), collecting all articles or a large, representative sample, and analyzing each using a systematic process with a group of trained researchers. Analyzing all or a representative proportion of the sample would reinforce generalizability—the idea that findings would be reflected in a wider sample than the one chosen—as well as the validity of the results themselves. Note that the two approaches do ask and answer different questions: rather than being right or wrong, better or worse, they may both be valuable in discerning a complete picture of the situation. **For more on matching the research question with specific research methods, see the Appendix, p. 241**.

RESEARCH TERMINOLOGY AND TECHNIQUES

As mentioned at the beginning of this chapter, research involves the analysis of data. Such data include both numeric and qualitative (written words, interview transcripts, images, and so on) and can come from a wide variety of sources, from national databases to experiments to individual observations.

Data

PR practitioners should be aware of all of the communication data they collect or have access to about their organizations, including media coverage (qualitative and quantitative), social media analytics (quantitative), and customer service information (often qualitative and quantitative).

Types of Research

Both qualitative and quantitative research methods can be applied in valuable ways to answer PR-related questions. While quantitative approaches dominate the business world, practitioners often underestimate the importance and the degree to which they already use **qualitative research methods** to analyze difficult-to-quantify concepts like tone and brand voice in writing, media coverage, and social media content. **Quantitative research methods** reflect a scientific method approach to research: reducing phenomena to their component parts, measuring them, and using the results to make predictions about future events. It narrows the field of vision, which can be useful for efficiency and planning purposes, if the right factors are part of the focus. By contrast, qualitative research often starts with a wider lens, taking into account holistic situations.

Selecting the correct balance of methods should be based on the questions at hand as well as the available resources and expertise for analysis. For example, a content analysis project using quantitative methods could preselect the most important words and count them to see how often they occurred. This would be useful if the research question centered on *whether* certain subjects were brought up by the authors. A qualitative analysis of the same data would most likely begin with a complete reading. This would be the better approach if the main question at hand was *how* the subjects were discussed. If the data sample is only three articles, a qualitative approach may be more effective. But if the sample is 3,000 articles, a quantitative approach might be necessary for efficiency. Additional approaches that would increase the quality of the research are clearly devising and articulating how the sample articles were selected, having multiple researchers read the articles to compare their notes and discuss/address inconsistencies, and using both qualitative and quantitative methods to triangulate results. Additionally, such research projects can have several substages, moving back and forth between different methods and research questions as initial results emerge. Often initial qualitative questions prompt quantitative investigations. The best researchers follow the questions through multiple stages of analysis to create a complete picture of the situation at hand.

Just as every campaign is unique, each formal research approach must be carefully sourced, designed, and calibrated to ensure that it is gathering the desired information.

PR practitioners should have the skills to select and develop these tools as well as (in many cases) to implement them and interpret the results. Practitioners perform secondary research constantly, such as reading existing articles, reports, and studies. They also regularly take on primary research tasks such as media coverage analysis. While some primary methods, such as large-scale surveys or big data analysis, may be beyond the capabilities of the average practitioner, we each have a responsibility to understand the tools available and be able to recommend the best research methods for a given situation—even if they require external assistance. Both primary and secondary research can be appropriate and valuable tools in diagnosing organizational challenges and orienting practitioners toward strategic solutions; however, the relative value depends on many variables including the specific situation at hand, the budget, timelines/deadlines, and the level of research experience that the team possesses.

Validity

The term ***validity*** refers to whether research is measuring what it is intended to measure, whether that is at the level of a specific concept, the desired subjects/data set, or the most applicable methodological choice.[11] For example, when attempting to evaluate the quality of a relationship between an organization and a public, practitioners should begin by examining existing research on the key components that make up a relationship (such as commitment, control mutuality, trust, and satisfaction) as well as the questions that have been tested to reflect each component making up the measurement.[12] In this way, practitioners begin with proven tools for their analysis. Validity is also important when considering a data set. Are you interviewing or surveying the right individuals to answer your questions? Are you analyzing media content relevant to future campaign outreach? And, finally, validity also follows from methodological choices. A small but in-depth set of qualitative interviews would certainly be a valid way to understand *why* or *how* a certain audience interacts with a product, but it would not be a valid method for understanding the socioeconomic circumstances of a wide range of potential customers, as the sample would not be representative. In quantitative research, supporting validity is demonstrated through statistical measures, while in qualitative or case study–based research, the concept of **triangulation**—using multiple sources of data and or multiple methods of analysis to increase the reliability and credibility of findings—is a key indicator.[13] Qualitative research demonstrates quality through rigor in data collection and analysis, detailed descriptions of findings, and collaboration with other researchers.[14]

CONDUCTING RESEARCH

All PR research should strive to involve a rich variety of voices, perspectives, viewpoints, experiences, and communities in research and decision-making processes.

Diversity supports inclusive organizational decisions and actions, inclusive messages, and inclusive environments inside and outside of organizations.

Diversity in Data and Sources

Practitioners can advocate for inclusion of such diversity from the beginning of the research process, including along a variety of intersections (age, culture, ethnicity/race, faith/religion, gender, nationality, sexual orientation, weight, and more).[15] This should involve finding diverse participants for surveys and interviews, seeking out community groups that may not have interacted with the organization in the past, or engaging with traditional and social media leaders that fully reflect the diversity of an organization's publics. Such an approach helps organizations to avoid what PR scholar Dr. Donnalyn Pompper refers to as "selective listening": Using research and listening tools to only hear what the organizations want or expect to hear.[16] It is often more time consuming to build these new relationships than to use what has been done in the past, but organizations, publics, and communities all benefit when PR does its job to nurture diversity among these groups.

Secondary Research

Secondary research can be defined as the selective sampling of the research of others. While it provides less specific, tailored insights for individual campaigns or publics, carefully defined secondary research has the added benefits of providing outside credibility for the goal, objective, strategy, or tactic that it directs or supports. Reputable sources for secondary research include the following.

Case Studies

PR practitioners can find publicly available case studies through Public Relations Society of America (PRSA) that reference similar challenges and potential strategies and tactics. Award-winning campaigns, such as the PRSA Silver Anvil entrants, provide a best-practices approach that can serve as a checklist and idea generator for future campaigns.

Government Data

There is a wealth of information that has been compiled and made public by the US federal government (as well as many other governments around the world). From the Census Bureau's detailed and localized demographic content, to regular reports put out by the Bureau of Labor Statistics, PR professionals have many resources to draw from when looking to investigate basic information before formalizing a campaign. Government reports tend to be free of political or industry bias and carry significant credibility with journalists and consumer audiences. Common challenges of working with government-generated data include sorting through a vast number of volumes and correctly interpreting their meaning.

Scholarly Research

Many PR practitioners are not aware of the research created and updated by academics. Several PR organizations and publications are working to fill this gap, including the University of Florida–based Institute for Public Relations (www.instituteforpr.org) and the open-access *Public Relations Journal*. Both focus their efforts on making applied research accessible to PR practitioners.

Think Tank/Nonprofit Reports

Nearly every industry has multiple organizations that provide relevant, data-rich content on specific topics. They can be university-affiliated academic centers, independently funded nonprofits, or grant-driven research organizations. Oftentimes, these reports are a source for news coverage at the time of release but can also provide strong insights for strategic communicators looking to better understand a specific issue or industry. With this in mind, while many organizations are ideologically neutral, these types of reports may be cause driven or carry an inherent bias and should not be taken as the sole source of authority on specific content.

Trade Association Research

For industry-specific data, research generated from a trade association may provide a valuable starting point for practitioners to pursue. Are you wondering how many manufacturing jobs there are in the US today? It's more than 12 million, according to the National Association of Manufacturers (NAM).[17] Are you interested in the impact of health-care industry consolidation? The American Medical Association (AMA) is, too.[18] Trade associations compile and share significant amounts of useful data with the public at large. However, strategic communicators should be wary, as these associations

Think tanks can provide a valuable source of data and information, but practitioners should check for an organization's political bias when using this research.

are generally advocacy-based organizations. This means that the data that they make available are often built to support a specific organizational or industry purpose, as opposed to government data or scholarly research. Of course, the vast majority of trade associations act and communicate ethically in the content that they share. PR practitioners simply need to be aware that there may be a perspective in these numbers and findings for which they need to account.

It is important to remember that all available information can be used to support a specific element of a project or campaign, or it may be general demographic or geographic data that can generate useful assumptions about the audience at hand. With that being said, the data alone are not inherently useful. The real value of data analysis is to create the appropriate context so that it can be properly understood by a larger audience.

Primary Research

Primary research is loosely defined as devising and executing original research. This could include a systematic round of informal interviews with internal and external stakeholders; creating and executing a survey of a relevant constituency to gauge interest in a new product; or performing textual media analysis on geographically specific coverage for a specific topic over a particular time frame. By researching these topics directly, a project can yield highly specific insights into the challenges that organizations may face or work to overcome.

However, as with any research methodology, primary research does require investment, whether financial in nature, resource based, or simply a timing commitment. Many informal approaches (including information gathering via conversations with internal stakeholders) are common, efficient, and inexpensive. Often, outside research firms are brought in to conduct large-scale, quantitative research. The following list includes a variety of commonly used PR research approaches.

Polling and Surveys: Opinion and Awareness

Surveys are one of the most widely used tools of PR researchers. Organizational leaders and PR practitioners regularly lack detailed insights into their key strategic publics. Practitioners can better understand an audience or public's perspective by asking them questions directly. Both internal groups (employees, volunteers, board members, or shareholders) and external groups (current customers, potential customers, community members, or social media followers) can offer valuable and often unexpected insights. Surveys, when planned well, make participation relatively quick and easy, can maintain anonymity for participants, can be analyzed in a variety of ways (including across demographic groups), and can be given in multiple forms. **See the Appendix, p. 239 for more information on constructing and conducting effective surveys**.

While a larger, scientifically validated poll or survey intended to reach a significant population (such as opinion polling on a statewide ballot initiative) is both time consuming and expensive, the following strategies outline a number of techniques and processes that can easily fit within the budget of many organizations. Additional challenges include incomplete answers or inattentive respondents, gathering information from incorrect respondents (those outside the prescribed sample), or, particularly if the survey is too long or poorly constructed, the potential for confusion and fatigue.

Survey Details and Terminology

Survey Questions: Depending on the information desired, potential questions can range from a series of open-ended qualitative prompts to **Likert-type scales** (a series of statement followed by an odd-numbered range of answers such as "Strongly Agree" to "Strongly Disagree"). For example, a multiple-choice approach would help a practitioner determine which parts of a nonprofit's mission statement were most valuable to donors. A Likert-type scale would allow a practitioner to measure the opinions of external or internal publics regarding trust or other relationship factors. An open-ended approach (either done with a questionnaire or through in-person interviews) could provide a holistic perspective on consumer complaints or challenges to catch organizational blind spots.

- Types of Survey Data Collection
    - Digital survey: Qualtrics, SurveyMonkey
    - Mail surveys: Practitioner or direct mail vendor
    - Intercept interviews: Hired or trained on-site interviewers
    - Telephone survey: Professional call center
- Sampling versus Census Data
    - Sampling: Selecting some members of a group to represent the whole
    - Representative sample: A sample that represents the makeup of the group as a whole in regard to relevant factors such as age, socioeconomic status, race, gender, or sexual orientation
    - Purposive sample: A nonrepresentative sample, where the researcher selects individuals to participate because they have certain, specific characteristics or shared experiences
    - Census: Gathering information from every member of a specific audience or public

See the Appendix, p. 238 for more details on developing survey questions.

Content Analysis

PR practitioners often need to make sense of vast numbers of words and images. They could come in the form of media coverage, social media conversations, books and reports, advertisements, or speeches. Practitioners often want to understand what is being said about an organization: is it positive or negative? What issues are being discussed? What words and phrases are used to describe an organization? In these cases, the content itself becomes the data for **content analysis**. The methodology can take several forms, from a qualitative approach to read, understand, and interpret, to a heavily quantitative approach measuring the frequency or words or phrases, the use of specific images, the tone, or the structure.[19] With the widespread availability of both traditional and social media–based research tools, an organization should have a clear and detailed picture of relevant data prior to initiating any campaign.

Most forms of content analysis use a process called **coding**, where researchers select the relevant units of analysis—such as specific words or symbols, themes, and stories; organizational identification or messaging; or tones and perspectives—and collect that information while reviewing each article. Ideally, a team of researchers develops the criteria for what constitutes each unit and category (commonly called a **codebook**) and divides the data for analysis so that multiple individuals examine each individual piece. Often, the process also includes the gathering of metadata: data about the data itself. This would include identifying information such as the media outlet, date, author, and media type for collected coverage. For social media, it may include the platform, author, format, and length.

iStock.com/Katleho Seisa

The coding process involves multiple individuals tracking a variety of themes including tone, key messages, or client/organization inclusion.

PRo Tip

MEDIA COVERAGE ANALYSIS

Media coverage is one type of data often examined by practitioners through the lens of content analysis. Practitioners define a data set, select categories, themes, or variables to track, and develop a methodology for analysis. The data set should include relevant publications and a time frame for analysis. Next, keywords or authors (among other categories) can be used to narrow the set. The best practice is to include all articles based on these search categories. Once the data set is finalized, practitioners can examine variables such as prominence, tone, sources, key messages, and competitors when analyzing media coverage. These individual features are known as "codes." The full data set should be analyzed to report on the codes, which should be clearly defined so that a reader could identify whether the feature was present or not.

Content analysis can be qualitative or quantitative. Qualitative approaches would include in-depth reading and analysis to interpret key themes and messages from the articles.

By contrast, quantitative analysis would entail counting the specific words, themes, or codes relevant to the research needs at hand.

For example, imagine a local financial institution interested in raising its profile among community members. This organization can begin by conducting qualitative research on community events and media outlets for a specific geographic area (most likely based on a media market breakdown) and using financially relevant terminology as part of their search (such as "personal finance," "mortgages," "auto loans," and "savings rates" in conjunction with location-specific terms). The results of this exercise provide a number of media outlets that cover those key terms that can then serve as a starting point for conducting a deeper level of media research. **See the Appendix, p. 246 for more details on content analysis.**

In her book *Measure What Matters*, K. D. Paine approaches content analysis by separating automated or computerized and manual forms. While automated analyses have evolved over time and provide unparalleled speed and efficiency, they also have significant drawbacks in their inability to distinguish quality, tone, messaging, subtext, and perspective. Conversely, manual content analysis traditionally takes far more time to complete, depending on the approach, but can yield much more detailed, tailored insights.[20] In many cases, the most effective and efficient approach tends to be a combination of both automated and manual approaches. By implementing an iterative approach to conducting an automated analysis, additional clarity can be realized that often helps define the most critical points, questions, or insights.

Competitor Analysis

There are numerous approaches that a practitioner can use to uncover valuable insights about an organization's market competitors or peers. By examining the tools, tactics, strategies, and results of competitors, PR teams gain perspective on historical successes and failures, approaches that may be less common, and what brand space or positioning may be advantageous in a particular market.

Output-based. What are your competitors saying? By researching the media output of select competitors (press releases, company website news, social media channels, and so on), PR practitioners can begin to understand the objectives and messaging existing within the market. These insights can lead to differentiation from competitors (such as choosing distinctive tactics or easily distinguishable key messages) or even lead an organization to focus on an entirely different (potentially untapped) audience. It may also encourage organizations to join and become a part of specific conversations, by incorporating or diverting resources toward specific channels, in order to balance a competitive environment.

Competitive media coverage analysis. What is the media saying about your competitors? From a competitive perspective, the same media analysis lens employed above can be aimed at key competitors in a specific market. Although the range or depth of analysis is often reduced based on the availability of resources, selecting multiple, specific variables for analysis can create an enlightening portrait of the larger competitive landscape and highlight areas for improvement or unidentified competitive advantages.

Experimental Research

While we don't often think about PR professionals conducting social scientific experiments, there are several areas where they can be practical. **Experimental research** techniques test whether one factor (the independent variable) causes a change in a second variable (the dependent variable).[21] Experiments are controlled, meaning that different subjects or participants will go through distinct experiences in order to understand whether the variables in question have an impact on their awareness, beliefs, or behaviors. For example, PR practitioners could use the marketing/advertising technique of message testing prior to implementation of specific campaigns. A robust experimental design could use multiple groups, composed of either randomly selected or representatively selected individuals, who view different messages and are asked relevant organizational questions before and after the presentation of these messages. Experiments should only change one variable at a time. Therefore, such an experiment could be constructed with similarly composed groups, the same initial information and initial questions (pretest), then a separate campaign message and relevant questions to gain insights into any changes in awareness, belief, or potential behavior (posttest) depending on the nature of the campaign. In this way, an organization can relatively easily gather feedback as to how potential messages may affect audiences.

There are some potential challenges to conducting effective experiments. The most common is establishing causation: Did the single change made to the situation truly cause any differences between the groups? Or were any changes based on the groups themselves or

©Starbucks

Competitive research should examine multiple facets of an organization's communication channels, including earned media, owned media, and a variety of social (or shared) media. Brands such as Starbucks demonstrate how they perceive themselves and their audiences as they communicate across multiple channels.

other external variables? For this reason, it is always valuable to carefully consider what else could have caused changes. If possible, additional experiments can be set up to examine additional variables. To anticipate such challenges, experiments must consciously eliminate potential third variables.[22] In the aforementioned experiment, participants were drawn from a similarly random or representative pool, provided with the same introductory information, and the same posttest (albeit based on different content).

Interviews

Interviews can be used to produce large amounts of extremely useful qualitative data. They are particularly well suited to helping practitioners uncover complicated situations and to better understand how publics or audiences perceive a particular event, challenge, or opportunity. In contrast to an informal conversation, research interviews start with the researcher defining the goals and purpose; finding the best willing candidates; carefully drafting questions; and investing the time to schedule, complete, and analyze each interview.[23] They can range from in-depth informant interviews—planned, long-form sessions where the interviewee is a clear representative of a specific group—to intercept interviews, where the researcher tracks down individuals on the street for quick engagement.

While interviews are more open ended than surveys, experiments, or content analysis, they still have a variety of best practices to ensure validity in execution and analysis. Research interviews are generally conducted one on one or in pairs (either two interviewers or two interviewees). Any larger and the interview begins to lose both intimacy and depth of conversation. Questions should be ordered to ensure that interviewees are comfortable, that the most important information is covered, and that there is time for flexibility and follow-up when interesting or unexpected answers arise. When research teams conduct multiple interviews with multiple interviewers, regular collaboration and discussion before and after each interview are crucial to ensure that similar processes are in place and common challenges are addressed with similar revisions. Interviews should be audio recorded, allowing researchers to review the content, create transcripts, and verify quotes. Transcripts and audio can be analyzed using a process not unlike content analysis, looking for commonalities and differences among the responses to similar questions from the participants. Analysis of interviews done by a team should include multiple individuals listening and providing perspective on each interview, which can help to speed the development and accuracy of themes and topics for further investigation.

Focus Groups

The term *focus* implies similarity and narrowing: The purpose of a focus group is to bring together individuals with similar perspectives to hear their conversations and interactions around a specific topic. Focus groups have the benefit of being more efficient than traditional interviews, in that they can gather the sentiments of more participants quickly. They are excellent venues for soliciting opinion on a concrete product, new design or brand, or a specific message. Additionally, focus groups allow researchers a unique perspective into how groups navigate the social challenges of talking about certain issues—in this way, they can be informative when observing discussion of delicate or taboo topics.

PRo Tip

INTERVIEWING TIPS

- It is helpful for the researcher to take notes and record the interview audio for future reference.
- The order of questions factors into any interview's success.
  - Warm-up questions: Interviews often begin with closed-ended, easy-to-answer background questions. This establishes rapport and makes the interviewee feel comfortable before asking more difficult questions.
  - Open-ended questions: The most important interview questions should be both open-ended and unbiased in their framing. In response, the interviewer should appear interested but not overly encouraging in their facial expressions and body language.
  - Probing questions: More details can be obtained related to key open-ended questions using more specific probes to gather more detail on particular aspects of the question or the response. This allows for a more conversational, back-and-forth flow to the interview.
- Be flexible: The prearranged order of questions should be thought-out and logical but should always be flexible to reflect the natural flow of the conversation, the interests and perspective of the interviewee, as well as the time available.

Source: Sarah J. Tracy, *Qualitative Research Methods* (Malden, MA: Wiley Blackwell, 2013), 138–52.

PRo Tip

SWOT[24]

A business management tool that is widely used in PR campaign development consists of a strengths, weaknesses, opportunities, and threats analysis, or **SWOT**. This type of analysis can highlight many important elements of an organization's internal and external environment and is often developed through brainstorming exercises at different levels of an organization. According to Broom and Sha, this approach is important in identifying both internal strengths (to take advantage of opportunities) and minimizing weaknesses (to combat challenges).[25]

- Strengths: Organizational attributes helpful to achieving the goal
- Weaknesses: Organization attributes harmful to achieving the goal
- Opportunities: External conditions helpful to achieving the goal
- Threats: External conditions harmful to achieving the goal

Often, SWOT analyses are done by bringing together multiple organizational leaders or teams to provide a variety of perspectives. For example, front-line staff might see different external challenges than management based on their daily customer interaction. Both of these perspectives are critical for a complete picture of an organization's strategic environment. This could be done in a series of small group meetings, potentially carried out by department, and including both individual brainstorming of ideas for each of the four boxes as well as group discussion. Practitioners would benefit from comparing the results across departments to more deeply understand the similarities and differences in perception across the organization. Compiling results in this manner produces an informed SWOT analysis to drive strategic discussions and planning.

Sources: *APR Study Guide* (University Accreditation Board, 2017), 76. Glen Broom and Bey-Ling Sha, *Cutlip & Center's Effective Public Relations*, 11th ed. (Boston, MA: Pearson, 2013), 244–45.

Even with these benefits, focus groups must be managed and constructed carefully. It is easy for one or several individuals to dominate and drive conversation, essentially shutting out the rest of the group. A strong moderator can help to refocus discussion on the content at hand and ensure everyone has the opportunity to participate. **See the Appendix, p. 244 for additional moderator tips**.

CONCLUSION

Research plays a critical role in understanding an organization and its environment. Before any campaign begins, practitioners should engage in developmental research, driven by the questions at hand. Crafting research questions, selecting methods, and executing research are all critical skills for success in crafting effective PR campaigns. While not every organization may have the expertise and resources to implement statewide public opinion surveys or conduct big data analysis, every practitioner can develop research skills to better analyze content, gather information from a variety of key individuals, and measure what is genuinely important for the success of the organization.

THINK CRITICALLY

1. What is the goal of developmental research? How is it different from other types of research?
2. How can practitioners demonstrate validity in their research to others inside their organization?
3. Why should practitioners conduct research inside their organization as well as outside?
4. What are key benefits of qualitative research? Quantitative research?
5. When would you use secondary research versus primary research techniques?
6. What should drive the choice of a specific research method or approach over another?

KEY TERMS

Audience 68
Codebook 80
Coding 80
Content analysis 80
Data 67
Generalizable 72
Likert-type scale 79
Methodology 67
Publics 68
Research, Developmental 68
Research, Evaluative 68
Research, Experimental 82
Research, Formal 72
Research, Informal 72
Research, Primary 78
Research, Qualitative 74
Research, Quantitative 74
Research, Refinement 68
Research, Secondary 76
Stakeholders 68
SWOT analysis 85
Triangulation 75
Validity 75

CONCEPT CASE: RESEARCHING COMPETITORS, COMMUNITIES, AND CUSTOMER EXPERIENCE AT COMMUNITY FLOW YOGA

As a new staff member at Community Flow Yoga, you'll want to begin the process of understanding the industry and the company in greater detail. First, it will be important to consider the existing fitness and yoga companies who may be vying for the same customers: Who are the major players? What are their strengths? Where are they geographically? Next, consider the communities where the company does business [feel free to pick your metro area and two others to focus on]: What community concerns and aspirations align with Community Flow Yoga's values? What barriers might there be to establishing a thriving studio? What particularly successful partnerships or involvement could the studio develop there? Finally, consider the experience of studio members and customers: What do they see, hear, touch, and smell as they enter the studio? What does a class feel like physically and emotionally? What incentives are there to return? How do instructors and studio staff build community among members?

As a vice president, you should aspire to gain your own personal understanding of the questions mentioned above. You should also seek to generate both qualitative and quantitative data to inform your findings. Select one qualitative and one quantitative research approach and explain how they can each help to answer multiple questions listed above.

CASE STUDY: A NEW DAWN BREAKS FOR BARBIE

Based on PRSA Silver Anvil Winner
Mattel with Ketchum
Campaign Focus: Consumer Products

For the last six decades, Barbie has been built upon the mission of breaking "boundaries and sparking imagination."[26] Ruth Handler, founder of Barbie and a businesswoman, mom, and a pioneer of her time, created Barbie to inspire imagination, discovery, and expression through play.[27] Yet, over time, the doll has become associated with outdated, rigid, and limited understandings of femininity—the brand today is more closely associated with restricting positive perceptions of body image for girls than for expanding their imaginative and professional horizons. How could a company that was built on the idea of empowering young girls to think beyond being a homemaker have become one that is universally known as the anthesis of female empowerment? This case study looks at Barbie's attempt to change its presentation of the ideal female body image radically through Project Dawn, the creation of tall, petite, and curvy Barbie dolls, which were launched on January 28, 2016.[28] Mattel, the American multinational toy company that produces Barbie,[29] seeks to redefine its image about American beauty.

A collection of Barbie dolls from Project Dawn, a new line of Barbie dolls that include several body shapes, sizes, and skin tones.[30]

Research/Diagnosis

The media plays a critical role in the way women view themselves.[31] Because of unrealistic body standards, many women strive to be "attractive, youthful, and thin."[32] Undeniably, this definition of beauty, in which skinniness is standard, is depicted on a daily basis through traditional and online forms of media. Much of the backlash surrounding Barbie concerns the degree to which Barbie helps feed into these misnomers surrounding female beauty. The traditional doll's design makes her proportional to a woman who is 5′9″ tall with a 39″ bust and an 18″ waist. Based on these measurements, she would most likely meet the medical criteria for anorexia.[33] Barbie critics "complained that the doll's body was so thin that she lacked the body fat to menstruate."[34]

Barbie has suffered from the ongoing debate surrounding what women should do, be, look like, and represent.[35] Her physicality, however, has been a continuous issue from the beginning. Barbie's form has been altered many times over her sixty-year-long history, but her consistent blonde hair and white skin spread the idea to young girls that eventually resulted in one hair color and ethnicity.[36] *Tiny Shoulders: Rethinking Barbie*, a documentary created by Andrea Nevins,[37] follows Kim Culmone (Barbie's head of design) as she and her team embark upon an initiative that attempts to push existing beauty values toward an appreciation of body acceptance.

Mattel's goal was to create a new line of dolls with "diverse body types, along with the new skin tones and hair textures introduced last year,"[38] to reflect more individual and diverse people and experiences.

Despite legitimate criticism of the Barbie's shape and features, many elements of the doll have always reflected progressive values. Barbie's mission has always been to inspire "the limitless potential in every girl."[39] As of 1960, fewer than 40 percent of American women worked outside the home,[40] but Barbie has been pursuing a career as a business executive from the start.[41] From a Major League Baseball player, an astronaut, an army ranger, to the president, or even a NASCAR driver, the brand has allowed little girls to imagine themselves in any role. Committing to its mission, Barbie demonstrates that its societal shift is powered by the idea of keen, contemporary, and diverse women inspiring children through play to see themselves within the new line of dolls.[42] Nevins's *Tiny Shoulders* captures a "behind-the-scenes debate at Mattel, among feminists and Barbie fans, about what the doll should symbolize versus what realities she should reflect."[43]

"Project Dawn," led by Culmone, represents Barbie's mission to create a new line of dolls. At the time of this campaign, Barbie's sales dropped 3 percent in 2012, 6 percent in 2013, and 16 percent the following year, globally.[44] This 92-minute documentary uses Barbie as "a metaphor for a culture that is still infinitely more preoccupied with what a woman looks like than what she says."[45] The documentary showcases the behind the scenes of an iconic brand, taking an honest look at themselves and creating a new line of dolls that emphasizes stronger diversity and inclusivity among Barbie fans, an issue that has been in debate throughout the doll's life.

Time Magazine displaying a new cover for Barbie with the headline: "Now can we stop talking about my body? What Barbie's new shape says about American beauty."[46]

Objectives

Over the course of a year, the team at brand Barbie hoped to achieve the following:

- Increase Sales: Create a new and different line of Barbie dolls to increase sales.
- Create Positive Conversation: Andrea Nevins created *Tiny Shoulders* to change the negative conversation about Barbie's ethnicity and body shape.
- Create Social Change: Inspire and empower young women and children to develop higher self-esteem by redefining what American beauty means.

Strategies

The strategy used within this project centered on reimagining, or rethinking, Barbie's brand values. "Project Dawn" focuses on inclusivity and empowerment by portraying an active, fun, positive, and valuable influence. Through this effort, Mattel addresses Barbie's negative image along with what the brand hopes to achieve by reinventing Barbie and creating a new line of dolls that features different ethnicities and body shapes. Mattel used an attention-grabbing approach through earned, shared, paid, and owned media to demonstrate the brand's turnaround as well as creating social change and empowerment.

Tactics

This integrated campaign used the following:

- *Tiny Shoulders: Rethinking Barbie* documentary featured on Hulu
- Extensive media relations campaign including press releases and honed pitches to media outlets
- A Barbie Wellness website page
- Documentary distribution rights handed over to Entertainment One (eOne), a Canadian entertainment company of development, production, marketing, and distribution[47]
- World premiere during the Tribeca Film Festival, which highlights a diverse collection of independent films at Spring Studios in New York City[48]
- Events around the world including an exhibition in France showcasing the evolution of Barbie

Paid and Owned

The documentary, *Tiny Shoulders: Rethinking Barbie*, featured on Hulu was a central component to their tactics. The brand has launched a website page dubbed "Barbie Wellness," which emphasizes the benefits of self-care through play.[49] In 2018, Entertainment One, also referred to as eOne, has handled international distribution for the documentary since 2018.[50] The documentary can be found on Hulu (www.hulu.com).

Earned and Shared

Barbie has received over 6 billion media impressions since her reinvention.[51] Major news outlets, such as *The New York Times, Time Magazine, CNN, The Atlantic*, and *The Wall Street Journal*, have heavily covered the topic. In addition, Mattel produced numerous press releases and specific pitches to reporters highlighting its diversity and inclusivity goals. The most recent press release, titled "Barbie™ Celebrates 60 Years as a Model of Empowerment for Girls," talks about the Dream Gap, an initiative that gives children the encouragement and resources they need to "continue believe in themselves."[52] As a result of this media coverage, "#rethinkingbarbie" went viral on Twitter. Mattel consistently posts and shares information with their followers on Twitter, Instagram, Facebook, and Pinterest. Consumers rely on other consumers when making purchasing decision, that's why using social media is a core component of their strategy.[53]

Implementation

In the documentary, we see that over many months of research and planning, Mattel created a new line of dolls that became the next evolution of the brand. Going back to its roots, it now sells dolls that are more ethnically diverse and include a variety of body sizes and shapes.

Reporting/Evaluation

Following the press coverage earned from the news forums mentioned earlier, Barbie's new collection, which includes an unparalleled variety of skin tones,

A new line of Barbie Dolls, Barbie Wellness, highlights self-care and physical well-being.[57]

The Fashionista line includes a doll with alopecia, vitiligo, prosthetic limbs, long-haired Ken, and one in a wheelchair.

hair textures, and body types, generated 5 billion clicks and impressions globally.[54] Positive sentiment remained in the high nineties throughout the launch of the new line. The Barbie brand has over 99 percent brand awareness worldwide.[55] *TIME* magazine devoted a cover story dedicated to Barbie's new collection, with the headline "*Now can we stop talking about my body? What Barbie's new shape says about American beauty*," and listed it as one of the "Top 25 Inventions of 2016."[56]

Building on the success of Project Dawn, Mattel introduced a collection of self-care dolls called Barbie Wellness in 2020. This line of dolls highlights daily routines that encourage emotional well-being through meditation, self-care, and physical activity—"because Barbie knows to be one's best to give yourself the best care."[58] In addition, Mattel also released a line of "Shero" Barbies featuring Adwoa Aboah; Bindi Irwin, Yara Shahidi; Naomi Osaka; and film director Ava DuVernay in Barbie figures.[59]

In addition, the company unveiled dolls with vitiligo, a condition in which a person's skin loses pigment in patches across their body, alopecia, a hair loss condition, as well as dolls with prosthetic limbs and in wheelchairs.[60] When the company made the announcement on Twitter, Mattel said "What makes us different makes us beautiful."[61] The company said their latest line depicts "a multi-dimensional view of beauty that represent global diversity and inclusivity."[62]

Theories

Agenda Setting Theory: Project Dawn emphasized the powerful influence of the media by introducing and highlighting the new definition of American beauty. Through this campaign, Mattel addressed "what the public thinks is important."[63]

Diversity- and Inclusion-First Approach

Ethnicity, race, and physical qualities/abilities were some of the most important issues addressed during the creation of this documentary and reinventing Barbie overall within the Diversity & Inclusion Wheel. Mattel fought to change the societal attitudes toward these aspects and succeeded.

Research, Part 2

GOALS

iStock.com/PeopleImages

THINK AHEAD

5.1 Understand the difference between organization-wide goals and communication or PR goals.

5.2 Connect developmental research findings to the goal-setting process.

5.3 Examine the different types of goals applicable to diverse organizations and situations.

5.4 Anticipate the potential challenges of setting public relations goals within an organization.

Creating effective and actionable communication and public relations goals balances the need for practitioners to understand the organization with the imperative to carve out the appropriate role for communication. Does your community know what your organization is? Do your customers have an outdated image of what your products can accomplish? A nonprofit organization expanding its services must let the community know. Stockholders may need their profit expectations reset in light of new competition. A company's employees may not be taking advantage of all of the benefits offered to them. Whatever the situation, once you understand the challenge at hand, the next step is aligning communication goals with the organization's goals to best position public relations programs to make an impact.

To begin the process, it is important to understand the distinction between **organization-wide goals** and communication or **public relations goals**. Broom and Sha explain that "an organization's vision, its mission, and its operational goals serve as the framework for public relations goals, which in turn address the problems and opportunities facing the organization."[1] In this way, practitioners must start with a thorough understanding of the organizational goals, followed by a research-based application of knowledge about the internal and external environments. From there, they can generate more specific campaign-related communication goals.

According to Stacks, a communication goal is the overarching, long-term achievement a particular communication campaign or program attempts to accomplish.[2] Goals should be informed by research on the organization and its environment. Finally, goals are crafted to start the process of defining or narrowing audiences/publics for communication, to focus the campaign's efforts, and to apply the tools of public relations in useful, appropriate ways. Goals act as a compass for a public relations campaign, pointing practitioners toward the objectives, strategies, and tactics that best fit the organization's needs. They also help to prioritize efforts. It can be easy for public relations campaigns to attempt too much: to take on so many strategies and tactics that resources are stretched thin and completing objectives becomes difficult. Effective communication goals allow practitioners to judge potential objectives, strategies, and tactics by the degree to which they will contribute. Such a rationale for activities makes the processes of budgeting and coordinating with management significantly easier. Clearly aligned goals demonstrate a thoughtful practice and process for communication: they put public relations in the driver's seat.

Another way to begin to conceive of goals, building on Wilson and Ogden's writing about an organization's situation and environment, is as "a positive restatement of the core problem."[3] From this perspective, part of the process of researching and developing communication goals—in conjunction with organizational goals—is to understand and reframe problems as opportunities. Practitioners can consider the problem (such as growing competition, loss of government funding, or a restrictive regulatory action) and reconceptualize it as an opportunity:

- Problem: Competition; Goal: Differentiate a brand in a crowded marketplace
- Problem: Funding; Goal: Expand fundraising efforts
- Problem: Regulatory action; Goal: Increase public awareness of the positive of a particular industry, product, or process or (if it's not a particularly media-friendly or consumer-friendly issue); Goal: Inform key decision makers about the positive impact of a particular industry, product, or process

UNDERSTANDING YOUR ORGANIZATION AND ITS GOALS

When defining opportunities for any public relations campaign, it is important to focus initially on two key factors: understanding both the organization as a whole and the business model that it is built upon. All organizations, including for-profits and nonprofits, have structures that support their work. Considerations such as size, shape, vision, and history are all key elements to take into account when working to understand the company. How does it generate revenue? What are its expenses? Who are the major stakeholders it serves?

The larger the organization, the more variety it often has in its operations. Large organizations tend to be more complex due to their wider variety of product and service offerings; additional geographic, demographic, and industry-based audiences; and the volume of internal stakeholders. Such additional organizational details complicate the goal-setting process for PR practitioners but also multiply the opportunities for success. There are more stakeholders and constituencies to manage, generating more challenges, but also greater resources to address them.

Organizational structure also plays a role in the goal-setting process. Some organizations are top heavy, with more highly skilled employees. A law firm, for example, may have twenty attorneys, ten paralegals, and a support staff, while a manufacturing company is more likely to have a small executive team with a much larger number of skilled workers. The structure of a business can influence different dynamics and present various internal and external communication challenges. These situational factors may point toward very different challenges and goals for each organization. The law firm may struggle to retain top talent, while the manufacturing company may need to balance the internal and external issues of unionization, outsourcing, and cost controls.

Keep in mind that improved communication is never a silver bullet or an end in itself. Communication is a means to an end, and identifying the best possible "end" or "ends" is the clearest path to a measurably successful campaign. Strategic public relations professionals constantly relate their actions at the planning and implementation stages to organizational goals. Creating effective communication goals helps to point a campaign in the right direction to support broader organizational goals.

The Evolving Role of the Corporation in Society: Community-Centered Goals

The goals of all types of organizations tend to put themselves at the center of issues, problems, products, or services. Yet, the purpose of corporate goals may have more flexibility than ever before to consider external, societal, environmental, and community factors. The 2019 Business Roundtable "Statement on the Purpose of a Corporation" marked a watershed moment in that a large, powerful group of corporate leaders explicitly stated that profit was no longer the primary purpose of businesses. In

PRo Tip

ISSUE PRIORITIZATION

When setting goals, how do practitioners know which issues, challenges, or opportunities to tackle first? Otto Lerbinger[4] presents three criteria to help narrow a long list of potential organizational issues down to those most important for setting communication goals:

1. **Imminence of action**: How quickly will the environment change? Concentrate on issues or opportunities that will arise more quickly.
2. **Impact on the organization**: How much will the issue or opportunity affect the organization? Prioritize those that have the largest potential impact.
3. **Actionability**: How much impact will public relations and communication have? Focus on issues and opportunities where communication can make a significant positive impact.

Source: Otto Lerbinger, *Corporate Public Affairs: Interacting With Interest Groups, Media, and Government* (Mawah, NJ: Lawrence Erlbaum, 2006).

this way, the statement made clear that financial gains for stockholders were not necessarily more important than supporting the broader needs and values of the organization's stakeholders.[5] Therefore, public relations practitioners have additional support in valuing a corporation's customers, employees, suppliers, and communities, creating opportunities for community-centered goals.

THE GOAL-SETTING PROCESS

When developing a campaign's goals, research should inform the focus, priorities, and audience selection. The most important points to establish are (1) the impact role for communication and (2) the scope of the campaign, including initial decisions about the target audience(s) and publics, as well as the program's size, budget, and duration.

Seeking the Impact Role for Communication

Public relations evaluation leader Katie Paine urges practitioners to "measure what matters": to set goals and track efforts in areas where communication can make a clear, definable impact for organizations. Public relations goals should be clearly relevant to the organization as a whole but also focus on areas where communication itself can make a difference. In practicing the insights highlighted by Paine, it is critical to set goals (and subsequently define objectives and measurement techniques) that accurately reflect the work done by communication programs.[6] It is somewhat easy to define, for example, increasing product sales as the top organizational goal and divert budget to a marketing program dedicated to supporting this task. However, when the goal is not achieved, communication may easily be viewed as the reason for failure; even when there are many additional factors in play (economic environment, sales team, competition, product quality, and so on). It points practitioners toward two key questions before setting public relations goals: What can we control? Where can we have the greatest impact?

To improve goals, one approach would be to begin by taking a holistic look at multiple parts of an executable and measurable process. For example, consider the general consumer purchasing cycle to identify the communication's impact role: If the sales team is struggling to get in the door of retail stores because the potential customer bases have not yet heard of the product or organization that offers the product, awareness may be the most important component to consider as impactful for communication when considering the components of a campaign. Conversely, if potential customers are already aware of a specific product, but may have misconceptions about its use or potential, measuring specific content and defining an improved brand position in the marketplace may be a more valuable strategy.

PRo Tip

THE POWER OF "YES AND ... "

Inherently, the process of planning a PR campaign will unearth many challenges that cannot be addressed through communication alone. In this way, it is critical to set goals based on those perceived areas wherein improved communication will have the greatest impact:

- Question: Can improved internal communication raise awareness for new employee incentives?
- Answer: Yes, with the cooperation of internal stakeholders.
- Question: Can improved media relations exposure increase sales?
- Answer: Yes, if the sales team is working in tandem with media outreach to capture, share, and integrate positive coverage into the sales process.
- Question: Can improved marketing communication increase awareness of a new product or service?
- Answer: Yes, with the appropriate budget and audience targeting.

Whether tackling these challenges from an internal viewpoint or as an outside agency professional, understand the limits of what public relations can do on its own.

The "Yes and..." or "qualified yes" approach allows public relations experts to underline the potential impact of a campaign while providing context for limitations based on process, budget, approvals, and timeline. "Yes and..." encourages practitioners to present themselves as problem solvers, rather than obstacles, and to frame campaigns realistically, rather than simply agreeing to the terms proposed.

Source: Regina M. Luttrell and Luke W. Capizzo, *The PR Agency Handbook* (Thousand Oaks, CA: SAGE Publications, 2018).

Defining the Scope

Realistic goals must be set with an awareness of the available resources, preferred timeline, necessary expertise, and desired impact of the campaign. Combined, these comprise a campaign's **scope**. Public relations practitioners cannot accomplish everything. First, communication itself has its limits. Second, the resources available for a particular campaign bind the available toolbox of strategies and tactics for outreach. Program goals should be crafted with this concept of the appropriate scope of outreach. Four key areas for addressing this issue of scope are the budget, timeline, the desired change, and the expertise of the team. Considering these factors holistically informs realistic goal setting.

The budget provides one way to examine how much of an impact a potential campaign can achieve. From this perspective, practitioners can make judgments of priority and scope based on what resources are available to them. Campaigns may be planned with a predefined budget, where practitioners are given freedom to spend a set amount strategically. In other scenarios, the public relations team may need to make the case for their budget for a particular campaign or communicate to leadership that an initial budget is not sufficient to accomplish the desired goals. Budget may also impact factors such as the choice of media and outreach techniques (earned vs. paid media within the PESO model, for example), which can bring additional constraints (such as the potentially slower pace and lack of timing control of earned media).

At each step of diagnosing challenges, defining audiences, and planning a campaign, PR practitioners must make strategic decisions about the best uses for the organization's time, human resources, materials, media budget, equipment and facilities, and administrative items.[7] Before defining objectives, it is essential to conduct budgetary planning and the associated fiscal processes and research. Based on Broom and Sha's three guidelines of budgetary planning, the following are useful considerations:[8]

1. Identify all costs to the organization and resources allocated to the campaign.
2. Define the cost necessary to achieve specific results.
3. A budget is an estimate—manage and track it at each step in the process.

iStock.com/Eblis

Publics and stakeholders (internal and external) should be top-of-mind for practitioners from the first stages of research and planning a campaign.

Selecting Audiences for Outreach

Identification of key audiences and publics should be among the first steps that a PR practitioner considers when diagnosing an organizational problem or opportunity. A more detailed and informed stakeholder research initiative can help form decisions about campaign prioritization and how best to connect with the identified public or audience.

Approaches for audience outreach should be based on the importance of the specific audience, organizational priorities, and the potential impact of communication. Beginning with the initial research (primary or secondary), the challenge that many PR practitioners face is evaluating each audience based on the probability of achieving the campaign objective using strategic communication. Some audience groups will inherently have a greater potential to take action: to buy a product, attend an event, or donate to a nonprofit organization. With that being said, these groups may not always be the highest priority audience at a given moment. Strategic communicators should look at the specific goal of interest (what type of product? when is the event? how is the fundraising drive being positioned?), in conjunction with initial audience-focused research, to begin to define the best targets.

For example, an organization's goal may be to increase sales of a product. If this particular product has significant market penetration among one group, but limited penetration among another, the second group could represent an opportunity for growth. Initial research can help to identify the specific demographic, ideological, or interest-based difference between various audience groups, and the results can create a strong rationale for a more tailored campaign. It may also indicate that certain media channels are less valuable because their distribution may be considerably broader and less defined. Striking the right balance is key.

Defining the Desired Change

While goals do not need the specificity of objectives as to narrowness and focus, they still must clearly identify the desired overall change. Is the highest priority financial (such as increasing revenue, market share, or fundraising)? Reputational (such as crisis communication)? Relational (such as improving trust with employees, stockholders, or lawmakers)? Communication can drive change in multiple areas, and setting goals is where the focus and direction are set. The magnitude and measurement of this change should be developed and included as part of the objectives.

Prioritizing Budgets and Resources

While budgets should inform public relations goals, such goals also point toward the most effective use of budgets. An important point to consider is that organizations and campaigns always have limited budgets and resources. Certainly, not all costs can be estimated at the goal-setting stage, but knowing general budgetary limitations for the organization or campaign, understanding the priority of the project, and considering anchor strategies or tactics (and their costs) can contribute to smart planning. For example, a campaign with a very short timeline, a narrow audience, and a clear direction (such as driving attendance) might require a significant investment in paid advertising to meet organizational goals. Media relations may not be able to reach publics quickly enough, organic social media may not be a feasible approach if the publics are not already connected with the organization, and owned media may not be impactful enough if publics do not already visit the organization's website. If the budget is not available for the paid outreach needed to reach the desired publics, different goals may have to be set or additional resources redirected.

WRITING GOALS

Crafting communication goals continues the process of understanding the similarities and distinctions between organizational goals and communication goals. It also reflects the necessary balance between a long-term and short-term focus. Finally, goals must reflect a visionary perspective, distinguishing them from concrete, measurable, time-bound objectives.

Types of Goals

Different organizations with different purposes can have very different organization-wide goals, which in turn create a variety of distinct communication goals. At a certain level, every organization has a "business model" and an activity focus: a major source of revenue for its operations as well as a functional purpose. In the case of a for-profit business, these are generally the same. The products or services are the company's purpose. In the case of nonprofits and public sector organizations, their purpose can either be the same as their source of revenue (such as a hospital) or radically different (such as a homeless shelter). Practitioners must understand both components of the organizations they work with in order to develop beneficial communication goals.

Despite these differences, all organizations have stakeholders on whom their success depends. Most communication goals, in one way or another, explicitly work to inform, persuade, or build relationships with these stakeholders. Campaign goals help to bridge the gap between what the organization should accomplish and the individuals or groups that enable such achievements or stand in their way.

Context: Mission Versus Situation

In the creation of communication goals, public relations practitioners must balance an organization's long-term mission and direction with the immediate challenges and opportunities of its current environment. While both organizational and communication goals should be connected to an organization's mission,[9] they also must reflect the circumstances at hand. At times, unusual opportunities or challenges may arise and become more pressing. Public relations planning should be continually responsive to changes inside and outside of the organization.[10] This begins with setting goals that are in line with current circumstances as well as the organization's history, mission, and overall strategic direction.

When setting communication goals, practitioners should ask themselves the following questions:

- In what ways does this goal reflect the organization's long-term mission and vision?
- In what ways does this goal reflect the organization's short- to medium-term circumstances and opportunities?
- Do circumstances justify a temporary reprioritization of communication activities?
- What opportunities might be missed (or challenges prevented) by not prioritizing this goal? Are they more or less important than other opportunities or challenges?

TABLE 5.1

Examples of Typical Organizational Goals and Relevant Communication Goals

	Organizational Goal	Potential Communication Goals
Business Sector	Maintain profitability Gradually improve stock rating Achieve a positive trust ranking Minimize governmental regulatory interference	Maintain external awareness/exposure Improve trust perception among key publics Change opinion of regulators/stakeholders toward reducing interference
Public Sector	Increase use of funded social programs Increase efficiency Decrease fraudulent use of social programs Improve citizen access to and use of information Increase government funding	Raise awareness of funded social programs Lower perceived barriers to access funded social programs Improve citizen access to and use of information Advocate for increased funding
Nonprofit Sector	Expand research efforts Expand program reach Secure private financial support of programs	Raise awareness of organizational success and growth Improve perceived reputation and trust among key publics Increase private financial support of programs

Source: Adapted from Laurie J. Wilson, and Joseph D. Ogden. *Strategic Communications Planning: For Effective Public Relations and Marketing* (Dubuque, IA: Kendall Hunt Publishing Company, 2008).

Visionary Goals, Concrete Objectives

As mentioned at the beginning of the chapter, goals should be—as Wilson and Ogden explain in *Strategic Communications Planning*—"broader and more generic than the objectives that follow."[11] To use a travel metaphor, goals provide direction, while objectives describe the destination.[12] Goals need not be specifically measurable but should be attained when several underlying (and measurable) objectives are completed. Hallahan distinguishes goals that "center on organizational activities" from behavior-based objectives, which focus on knowledge, attitude, and awareness.[13] Therefore, communication goals should be the visionary statements that connect the organizational mission with the impact focus for communication. Goals may include how an organization is uniquely distinguished in the minds of its key publics. For example, to become the recognized leader in our industry that provides patients and physicians with convenient, complementary, and cost-effective medicine. Objectives represent the concrete steps to achieve this.

GOAL-SETTING CHALLENGES

Working With Organizational Decision Makers

Within an organization, the functional area of public relations cannot exist in a vacuum, as the success of campaigns depends on many internal stakeholders in various departments. As part of early-stage campaign planning, being able to properly understand the individual challenges faced by key internal decision makers in relation to the current challenge, including integrating their insights into the campaign, is vitally important. Not only does a collaborative approach lead to the development of a more comprehensive plan, but a more inclusive process promotes an increased sense of buy-in from the stakeholders involved. Such insights can be gained through formal research but also through informal conversations and relationship building with individuals from across the organization. Simply getting to know a variety of individuals at different departments and different levels can make a world of difference in providing a more informed perspective when setting communication goals.

©iStockPhotos/vgajic

The PR team may receive pushback when presenting campaign goals. It is important to make a strong case for why they represent the best approach for the organization.

Prompting More Research

Research is an ongoing process. It's difficult to craft goals that do not prompt additional questions, which can be addressed by various types of research. At the beginning of the planning process, practitioners cannot know all of the questions they'll need answered. Initial developmental research may not address an important issue that arises while drafting goals. For example, initial research and direction from leadership may point out that a new product has not been adopted as often as has been expected, based on similar launches in the past using similar tactics and resources. Additional research into the situational differences from past campaigns (such as changes in the product, changes in the environment/economy, or changes in communication) may uncover a more specific area to focus the goal and future planning efforts. With a second look, it may be a question of *who* rather than *why* that must be investigated.

Often this creates an **iterative planning** cycle: drafting goals leads to additional research, which leads to revision of the goals, which prompts additional researchable questions. Actionable and impactful goals are not easily clarified and defined. They should take multiple drafts and be informed by several stages of research. Again, this research can help to understand the true problem or opportunity the organization faces; where its competitors match up; and what broader environmental, economic, or social factors may come into play.

This iterative process of research and goal setting as part of diagnosis should not be intimidating. "Stages" of research may be as simple as a quick investigation or competitor products or a review of secondary research on a particular audience demographic. More fully and accurately developed goals will yield more focused, effective, and achievable objectives. A clearer understanding of stakeholders, audiences, and publics will drive more appropriate strategies and tactics, as well as more resonant messages.

CONCLUSION

Diagnosing the problem or opportunity is an essential role public relations practitioners must play within a larger organization. Often, PR is relied upon to be the "interpreter" for management. In the long run, helping the organization see strategic challenges, and how communication can address them, strengthens the position of the public relations team. The better the public relations team's reputation is among organizational leaders, the more likely that necessary resources and information will support future campaigns. Smart goal setting that positions communication goals within organization-wide goals provides a strong foundation to achieve and measure success.

THINK CRITICALLY

1. What are three important factors to remember for writing effective, useful campaign goals?
2. Why is it important to connect campaign goals with developmental research?
3. How can goals prompt additional research?
4. What are three issues that can arise in the goal-setting process? How would you overcome each of them?
5. How should public relations practitioners balance the organization's mission (long-term) with the current (short-term) environment, situation, or immediate communication needs?

KEY TERMS

Communication/public relations goals 94
Iterative planning 104
Organizational/ organization-wide goals 94
Scope 98
Situational theory of publics 107

CONCEPT CASE: FLOW YOGA SETS COMMUNICATION GOALS

Finding the Impact Role for Communication
Setting effective communication goals for Community Flow Yoga requires uncovering the impact role for communication and public relations outreach. The CEO has laid out two aspirational goals: Growing the company to new regions, and becoming the industry leader in community engagement and giving. What potential communication goals could support these organization-wide goals? Using the following considerations, draft three to four potential communication goals for Community Flow Yoga.

Consideration #1:

Remember that all goals should be:

- Broad rather than specific
- General rather than measurable
- Aspirational rather than attainable
- Open-ended rather than time-bound

Consideration #2:

In what areas could Community Flow Yoga be "the best" or "the most" or "the leader" from a communication or perception perspective? These are the best places to start when carving out the impact role for communication in writing goals.

Consideration #3:

How do the communication goals fit together? Ideally, these goals should address the areas where communication can make the biggest impact toward an organization's goals, while complementing each other. Drafting more communication goals than necessary, then prioritizing them by (1) how closely they support the organizational goal and (2) how big of an impact integrated public relations can have toward them is an excellent place to start.

CASE STUDY: BURGER KING—BE YOUR WAY

Campaign Focus: Community Relations

In 2014 when Burger King unveiled its new "Be Your Way" tagline, the company leveraged a fully integrated campaign and the prevailing social issues of the day to reposition its brand.[14] As the company moved away from the forty-year-old "Have It Your Way" tagline to its updated language, it sought to connect with younger audiences and align with changing societal values. The Proud Whopper was born.

At the time, momentum to legalize same-sex marriage nationwide had been building and Burger King decided to use its product packaging to take a public stand on this issue. The company supported these efforts with paid, earned, and shared media outreach, as well as fundraising support for LGBTQ+ youth, creating a fully integrated campaign.[15] Taking place during Pride Week in San Francisco, California, the Proud Whopper and the "Be Your Way" campaign was Burger King's way to show support for same-sex couples.[16] Through this campaign, Burger King strengthened its progressive identity as a brand, while connecting on a personal and supportive level with those who identified as or supported same-sex couples. Beyond the immediate local audience and owned-media approaches, Burger King used social media (shared) and media relations (earned) efforts to connect with others across the country and around the world.

PESO Model

Owned

Multiple tactics were used as part of the "Be Your Way" campaign. The first was the use of owned media in The Proud Whopper design. A standard Whopper hamburger was wrapped in colorful paper reflecting the rainbow symbol of gay pride. As customers unwrapped their meal, the powerful campaign message was delivered: "we are all the same inside." This item was only sold at Burger King locations in the San Francisco area during Pride Week, but this seemingly geographically narrow audience included tens of thousands of visitors from across the country as well as the significant local and national media presence for Pride events.[17] In another owned media tactic, Burger King also used its signature paper crowns to encourage others to show support, handing out more than 100,000 rainbow paper crowns for the crowd at pride parades in New York and San Francisco, where the brand was a major sponsor.[18]

© Burger King

The Proud Whopper.

Shared

To leverage the campaign online, Burger King released a video that featured the reactions of consumers when the Proud Whopper was unveiled. Shared across all company social media platforms, the video generated conversation both with those participating in the San Francisco Pride Week events as well as those tuning in from farther away. Burger King capitalized on social media to spread the news about its Pride Week endeavors and to continue to support the cause of equality even online. Social media gave audiences an outlet to share the campaign, comment on the Proud Whopper and paper crown designs, and showcase the campaign with those not in the San Francisco area. By interacting with consumers on their pages, Burger King encouraged stakeholders to create conversation about the campaign, generating social media conversation and engagement during and after the ten days that the Proud Whopper was available. Expanding the reach of the campaign outside of the city limits of San Francisco was crucial in both promoting the Burger King brand and the cause being supported. Across all social media platforms, the video that Burger King released of the reactions to the Proud Whopper garnered more than 7 million views in its first year, with 5.3 million of those views being on YouTube alone.[19]

Earned

The "Be Your Way" campaign, along with the Proud Whopper that played a large role in the campaign, had a vast reach and produced commendable results despite its very focused target group in the San Francisco area. Major media helped to spread the story nationally and internationally, with coverage from dozens of significant outlets including the *L.A. Times*,[20] MSNBC,[21] *Time*,[22] *USA Today*,[23] and *The Washington Post*.[24]

Paid

The advertisement reached more than 20 percent of the United States' population, and all of the profits made from sales of the Proud Whopper benefited the Burger King McLamore Foundation, an organization that provides scholarships to LGBTQ+ identifying high school teenagers.[25]

Burger King executives made internal changes to improve the company's policies toward LGBTQ+ employees and, importantly, to credit the campaign as a significant part of driving US sales and revenue higher after several years of brand stagnation.[26] The Proud Whopper campaign demonstrates the power of integrated approaches to strengthen and unify brands to connect with consumers and make an impact on the business as a whole.

Be Your Way Continues

Six years after the initial campaign, Burger King continues to support LGBTQ+ initiatives. In 2019, the company transformed two very burnt Whoppers into diamonds for couple Alvar and Dima's wedding.[27] The carbonized ash from the whoppers were used to create diamonds for the couple's wedding rings. The two men flew to Germany to say their nuptials as same-sex marriage is still illegal in their country. Burger King was there to not only capture every moment, but also sponsored the largest Pride celebration in Germany—Cologne's Christopher Street Day festivities.[28]

Watch the video: http://bit.ly/WhopperDiamonds

Theories

Situational Theory of Publics: Through recognizing the challenge and opportunity of the same-sex marriage debate, acknowledging the effect that this issue had on people's lives, and creating a campaign to address and intervene in the situation, Burger King's "Be Your Way" campaign exemplified the **situational theory of publics**, as defined by Patricia Swann.[29] By centering the campaign in San Francisco during Pride events, Burger King targeted a specific audience they knew would be highly involved and invested in the issues at hand.[30] These three components of the campaign process demonstrated Burger King's ability to use its platform to take a stance on issues that greatly affect the lives of their stakeholders.

Agenda Building Theory: During this campaign, Burger King zeroed in on an issue on which it could take a stand and used its platform as a global organization to draw attention to the issue through action and public relations tactics. This demonstrates the agenda building theory, as the organization was able to catch the attention of the media and of the publics and work toward getting same sex-marriage accepted and legalized.[31]

Diversity- and Inclusion-First Approach

Continued and sustained efforts by Burger King illustrate the company's commitment to diversity, inclusion, and equality. The Proud Whopper, Be Your Way, and Whopper Diamond campaigns are examples of corporate initiatives that reflect the values of the company as well as its publics and communities.

The company website reads "At Burger King Corporation, we recognize that each individual's unique characteristics have an important impact on all aspects of our business. Individual expression is the cornerstone of diversity and helps BKC lives its values of being Bold, Empowered, Accountable, and Fun."[32] Take a moment to find the company's full diversity and inclusion policy on its website. Then connect its company policy with the Diversity & Inclusion Wheel and the campaigns they develop. Are they aligned? What are your initial thoughts around their D&I initiatives. Find the policy here: https://company.bk.com/diversity.

Objectives

6

iStock.com/marchmeena29

THINK AHEAD

6.1 Understand why objectives are crucial to the creation of successful campaigns.

6.2 Define S.M.A.R.T. objectives for public relations campaigns that contribute to organizational and communication goals.

6.3 Understand how to share and communicate objectives to build internal support and enthusiasm.

WHAT MAKES HIGH-VALUE OBJECTIVES?

The process of setting appropriate objectives in the planning of public relations (PR) campaigns is critically important to a campaign's success: Objectives provide PR practitioners the opportunity to define a positive outcome. Without clear, measurable, and agreed-upon targets, the road to building momentum toward your campaign's success—both inside and outside of your team or department—is far more difficult. Objectives force clarity for yourself and others, answering the question, "What, specifically, do you want to accomplish?"

PR departments never work in a vacuum but constantly interact with other organizational functions and leaders. By defining objectives, practitioners support clear conversations with internal stakeholders regarding their definition of success. It is easier for leadership to provide constructive feedback for a campaign plan if the proposed results are clearly defined. Who wouldn't agree that *raising awareness of our new product* would be beneficial? But that feedback is not strategically helpful in understanding the expected *scope* of change and the resources necessary to achieve it. Alternatively, an objective of *raising awareness of our new product from 15 to 30 percent of current customers over the next four months* is much more clear-cut. It answers *what* as well as *who, when*, and *how much*.

Objectives are also about setting expectations. Particularly for leaders who may be unfamiliar with how PR can influence opinions and behaviors, writing a clear, measurable definition of success can align expectations with reality. While there is often give and take during the process of setting objectives, the PR function should take the lead, demonstrating a depth of understanding related to the associated challenges and how to best communicate them.

So, just how reasonable is it to expect a *30 percent* increase in product awareness when we take the budget into consideration? Do the projected goals allow for the team to ask for more resources (if appropriate)? If the anticipated timeframe must be expedited, it might also require a larger investment or a change in strategy to ensure success. Alternatively, if the budget has little flexibility, the objectives may need to be modified. When these types of discussions happen in the early stages of campaign planning, they make the situation much easier to negotiate. It is only after a campaign has failed to meet expectations that PR teams lose both budgetary support and decision-making clout for future programs.

Clarifying and specifying objectives is not possible without a well-defined audience or public. You may find it difficult to measure the objective of *raising awareness by 30 percent*; however, it may be easier to measure *raising awareness of current customers by 30 percent*. Without a defined audience, there can be no actual target. Objectives only exist relative to the audience or public for whom they are created and intended.

MANAGEMENT BY OBJECTIVES

Business scholar Peter Drucker's concept of "management by objectives," from *The Practice of Management*, outlines the structural and organizational benefits of setting clearly defined, narrow, and actionable objectives.[1] Drucker's approach allows leaders to empower employees throughout the organization by giving them clearly defined targets for success. As you may imagine, the first step toward success relies on the executive leadership setting high-level, overarching goals for the organization. These may include entering new markets, launching new products, expanding geography or infrastructure, growing market share, or increasing revenue or profit. Executives must work with their management teams to develop actionable, measurable objectives for each department that will contribute toward achieving the larger organizational goal.

Managers should collaborate with organizational leaders in the development of objectives for their teams to implement.[2] Drucker indicates that this process centralizes empowerment and accountability for large organizations.

Business performance therefore requires that each job be directed toward the objectives of the whole business, and each manager's job be focused on the success of the whole through his or her specific objectives. Managers must know and understand what the business goals demand of their team, and their superiors must know what contributions to demand and expect of their direct reports—and must judge them accordingly. If these requirements are not met, managers are misdirected. Their efforts are wasted. Instead of teamwork, there is friction, frustration, and conflict.[3]

This description has been widely accepted as an ideal management approach for both for-profit and nonprofit organizations. Guided by clearly measurable, actionable, time-bound objectives that are coordinated with other departments, PR practitioners are in a unique position to develop a clear understanding of what must be accomplished and how individual and departmental successes contribute to strengthening the entire organization.

The Public Relations Society of America (PRSA) strongly supports this narrow definition of objectives as the central step in communicating the business value of the PR outreach: "Public relations programs cannot be successful without proactive, strategic planning that includes measurable objectives, grounded in research and evaluated for return on investment."[4] They are the tool through which practitioners show their strategic acumen and set the standards for their own success and value to the organization.

It should be noted that the process of setting formal objectives is not universally subscribed to within the practice of PR. Some agencies make the reasonable case that, since awareness and opinion change are difficult to predict, these items should be tracked and measured but not used as the definition for success. Oftentimes, practitioners tend to overlook this step or set objectives that cannot be measured for the simple reason that defining success also requires defining failure. By defining failure, it makes it a potential reality. Overcoming a fear or hesitancy of setting objectives is an important step to take toward creating campaigns that clearly connect with larger organizational and communication goals. By defining objectives, an element of transparency and accountability is clear for those within the communication department and throughout the organization.

Types of Objectives

Objectives can be defined in a variety of ways, falling into three distinct categories based on the nature of the specific information being measured: **outputs**, **outtakes**, and **outcomes**.[5] Most campaign plans include a mix of the three in order to track efforts at several levels. Output objectives are limited in their direct connection to organizational goals. These may include metric-based targets such as the number of press releases distributed, the number of media placements secured, or the number of messages posted on a particular media channel. While output objectives are valuable to track for departmental purposes, they only provide process-related insights, rather than measuring the impact of campaigns.[6]

Outtake objectives measure whether targets "received, paid attention to, understood, and/or retained" organizational messages.[7] This information may be obtained using quantitative methods (e.g., formal surveys), qualitative methods (e.g., focus groups), or other approaches, including digital tracking of social media platforms, e-blasts, websites, or other content. These objectives provide insights with substantially more value than output objectives but are also only measuring the transactional side of outreach, rather than the impact on key audiences or the progress toward organizational goals.

Finally, outcome objectives tend to hold the most value and connection to organizational goals, measuring change in opinion and behavior. Examples of outcome objectives might include increasing event attendance, shifting public opinion on a ballot initiative, or convincing an activist group to end a boycott against your organization. Clearly, one challenge of defining outcome objectives is that communication is rarely the only factor involved. The closer an objective moves toward an organizational goal, as outcomes do, the more cooperation will be required between departments to achieve success. When possible, practitioners should aim to develop outcome and outtake objectives first to measure their own success. This is not to say that they should not track outputs rather, that outputs alone do not equate to impact or progress toward organizational and communication goals.

Writing S.M.A.R.T. Objectives

One framework for addressing the challenges of writing objectives is outlined using the "S.M.A.R.T." framework: Ensuring they are specific, measurable, attainable, relevant, and time-bound. By using this structured approach, practitioners can develop objectives that are both actionable and valuable to organizations. The S.M.A.R.T. framework serves as a reminder that crafting objectives effectively helps to set a campaign and its expectations on the right path.[8]

Another important consideration that requires attention while developing objectives is the intended audience itself. In this way, each specific audience should be segmented and have its own distinct objectives.[9] By taking this approach, each objective and associated measurement is connected to a specific result that clearly demonstrates success or failure within a target population. These objectives should also serve as part of a larger communication and organizational goal. For example, an industry trade association might focus on raising awareness among its members and supporters for a new piece of legislation, connecting to a larger organizational goal of mobilizing either support or opposition. This objective focuses on one narrow aspect of the larger goal. Being able to define a timeline and specifying a measurable degree of change would complete the criteria.

NurPhoto/NurPhoto/Getty Images

Objectives may relate to achieving political or public policy outcomes, such as teachers unions lobbying for additional school funding.

PRo Tip

A FORMULA FOR S.M.A.R.T. OBJECTIVES

Action + Context + Audience + Volume + Duration

Example: Increase the awareness of Bill 123's potential negative industry impact among ABC Association members and key supporters (predetermined contact list) from 25 to 50 percent over the next three months.

Specific

As we have seen, objectives must be specific to the campaign, to a defined audience, and to the individual piece of the larger goal they reflect. *Improving awareness* is too broad. Improving awareness of a specific brand, product, event, or initiative is better. Improving awareness of a specific brand, product, event, or initiative for an important, definable audience is best.

PRo Tip

COMMON ERRORS—MEASURING WITHOUT A BASELINE

One common misstep that PR practitioners make is to measure an objective without having an appropriately defined baseline from which improvement can be tracked. When writing a measurable objective, it's critical to have a clear starting point. Often, this can come from data gathered during the developmental research or *diagnosis* phase of campaign planning, but the need for a baseline may also come to light as the objective is developed. Without a baseline, there is no way to demonstrate growth or success (or to see where changes need to be made). An appropriate baseline could be defined by the click rates for prior e-newsletters, RSVPs to last year's annual event, or precampaign public opinion surveys to quantify attitudes or awareness for the issue at hand.

Measurable

Once objectives are specified to the audience and an associated challenge or opportunity, their projected impact or outcome can be defined. A variety of measurement tools and tactics exist, ranging from the number of clicks on an e-newsletter link (an outtake objective) to changing the opinion or behavior of an audience (an outcome objective).

Depending on the broader goals of an organization, a number of methods exist to support the measurement of a desired objective. Measurement should connect intimately with larger, overarching goals. For example, advocacy campaigns for local ballot initiatives generally use public opinion polling of likely voters throughout an election season (as budgets allow) since their goal is, by definition, to drive a change in opinion. Efforts supporting this type of initiative would most likely include qualitative research to inform and assess message creation, as well as elements of quantitative research to define and measure progress toward an objective (awareness, attitude, intention to vote, and so on).

Attainable

S.M.A.R.T. objectives must be realistic. Communication alone cannot transform organizations or publics overnight. Individuals will rarely change their mind after reading a single e-newsletter, viewing a promoted post, or reading one newspaper article. A functional objective hinges on the ability to appropriately set a measurable goal that is reasonably attainable with the resources and time involved. It is impossible to know what is attainable without first measuring and researching the situation.[10] This legwork establishes a baseline and provides both quantitative and qualitative insights that inform the degree of change that can be achieved.

Practitioners should also keep in mind that awareness and a change in opinion must occur before behavioral change.[11] Behavioral change, whether it is discouraging smoking or encouraging the purchase of a new consumer product, takes significant time and budget. The more specific the behavioral focus, the more effective the message can be.[12] Successful campaigns are more likely to occur when the attempted change is low cost and high reward and when budgets include sufficient resources to execute based on the size of the audience or public, the magnitude of the change, and the necessary timeline.[13]

Additionally, organizational leaders may not necessarily want to hear that the proposed objectives are unreasonable within the constraints mentioned above. Communicators must work to ensure the best-possible strategic, integrated approaches and to clarify a clear rationale for their choices in order to best position their recommended objectives and strategies for approval and success. The more that practitioners can have honest conversations with organizational leaders about attainability at the objective-setting stage, the more realistic everyone's expectations will be when reporting and evaluation occur.

Relevant

Practitioners should avoid tracking only *output* objectives that measure the number of tweets or Facebook posts, the number of press releases distributed, or the number of reporters contacted. The most useful outtake and outcome objectives measure the impact of a campaign's efforts, and generally fall into three categories: awareness, opinion change, and behavioral change. An awareness objective could involve increasing familiarity for a specific organization, event, product, or service. Opinion change might involve issue advocacy work on one end of the spectrum or sales-focused competitive product outreach on the other. Behavioral change may include efforts related to recruiting (both for employees and organizational membership), purchasing a product, **lead generation**, or **lead capture**.

While these outcome objectives tend to highlight the best-case scenario, it is not always possible to measure this way based on available expertise, resources, and timelines. Objectives that may be based wholly on output or organizational results are considered outtake objectives and include **competitive objectives**. Objectives of this nature allow organizations to measure the quality of a PR effort in a way that can clearly connect to communication priorities, including **share of voice** or quality of media coverage determined through content analysis. Organizations can benchmark themselves against key competitors and also measure progress. While competitive objectives do not necessarily carry the same connection to organizational goals as outcome objectives, they can still add significant insights to campaign measurement.

The more relevant an objective's measurable component is to a broader organizational goal, the more valuable it becomes. This connectivity is a key component of demonstrating the success of PR campaigns.

Time-Bound

One of the hallmarks of a good campaign objective is the inclusion of a defined timeline for its overall execution. Identifying an appropriate duration is determined by a variety of factors, including the overall campaign timeline, the scope of change desired, how the objective integrates into larger goals, and the volume of work needed by the communication team to complete the strategies and tactics involved. A larger team or a larger budget may allow for an expedited projected timeline.

Organizations should also plan to have multiple objectives running simultaneously, all following separate, overlapping timelines. Short-term objectives generally focus on knowledge and awareness, while long-term objectives can more successfully drive attitude and behavior change, as knowledge-based change necessarily comes before behavioral change.[14] Setting objectives within a time-bound campaign helps to connect projects with higher-level organizational goals. Multiple layers of objectives pointing toward tangible results demonstrate a valuable strategic understanding of the PR discipline's most valuable contribution: how PR can improve organizations' relationships with their publics over time.

Considerations for Inclusive Objectives

As discussed, PR teams and organizations benefit when individuals with a diversity of perspectives and experiences take part in decision making. That said, objectives can be made more thoughtful and inclusive through a broader understanding of the following questions practitioners should ask themselves when crafting objectives:

- **Why are some groups targeted and not others?** Practitioners can question how audiences, publics, and stakeholders have been selected for communication and engagement. This may bring to light questions of equity that otherwise would not have surfaced.
- **How might attaining these objectives affect diverse stakeholders?** Objectives are chosen for the impact they generate for the organization, but that may not fully take into account the completion of objectives for internal and external stakeholders.
- **What might some unintended consequences be of achieving these objectives?** Practitioners would benefit from considering the potential for unexpected outcomes, particularly for (1) publics underrepresented in the organization and (2) for internal and external stakeholders with fewer resources to adjust to changing circumstances.

Additional Objective Frameworks

Leading PR scholars note that various recipes exist for formulating successful objectives. Practitioners should use the framework that resonates best with them, allowing them to envision the results of their campaign.

Broom and Sha indicate that there are four elements that ultimately contribute to campaign or program objectives: a target public, outcome, measurement, and target date.[15] Identification of a target public should reflect a key constituency for the organization. The outcome should reflect a meaningful change and must be measurable using organizational resources prior to, as well as after, the communication activity. Of equal importance is the clear communication of the timelines in which the result will be achieved. If each of these elements is accounted for in the planning stage, the resulting objective will be clearly defined. As the milestone date arrives, organizational leaders should be able to clearly see whether it has been achieved or not.

Similarly, PRSA defines four components of successful objectives in the *APR Study Guide*: (1) the result or outcome, (2) the public or publics addressed, (3) the "expected level of accomplishment," and (4) the time frame.[16] While using slightly different language, it outlines the same focused four-component approach.

A complement to this formula for appropriately developing objectives, Stacks and Michaelson have defined three types of useful outcome objectives to consider: *informational objectives* measure awareness and knowledge, *motivational objectives* track information received and understood to measure opinion change, and *behavioral objectives* chart whether the audience takes an intended action.[17] If a particular message does not reach its intended audience, their opinions will remain unchanged. An opinion must change before a behavior. In this way, the three types of outcome objectives work together to drive long-term impact.

PRo Tip

CONSTRUCTING YOUR OBJECTIVES

Example objectives from the PRSA's *APR Study Guide*:

- To increase ridership of public transportation in the Los Angeles metropolitan area [behavioral outcome] by 8 percent [level] among workers earning less than $25,000 per year [public] within the first six months [time frame] following launch of the communication program.
- For at least 10 percent [level] of a randomly selected sample of public transportation riders in the Los Angeles metropolitan area [public] to identify as their reason for using public transportation one of the communication tactics employed in your PR campaign [behavioral outcome] by the end of the second year of that campaign [time frame].
- To have confirmed reports that 50 percent [level] of the natives of one Asian, one African, and one South American developing country [public(s)] are applying multiyield agricultural practices [behavioral outcome] by 2020 [time frame].

Source: *APR Study Guide* (Universal Accreditation Board, 2017), 60.

Perhaps even more important than the framework used to develop objectives is following a consistent and comprehensive approach. Each approach can act as a checklist to ensure that objectives are created with the necessary components to position a campaign for success. Practitioners can experiment to identify the approach that works most effectively for them, their organization, and the campaign at hand.

CONNECTING OBJECTIVES TO KEY INTERNAL AUDIENCES

Whether working at an agency or as a consultant, practitioners should keep in mind the internal or executive audience(s) for their objectives. During the *diagnosis* phase, formal and informal research provides insight into what leadership sees as the goal of a project as well as its communication objectives. The role of a practitioner is to gather a variety of perspectives on the challenge or opportunity, as well as to craft potential objectives. With that in mind, these may not always be the best communication objectives for that particular moment. Approved objectives also often reflect—for better or worse—the organization's internal politics, personalities, and priorities. Successful practitioners not only write objectives that are S.M.A.R.T. and focus their team's efforts on campaign elements likely to have the biggest impact but also act as counselors to provide a strategic perspective with support for their positions. Communicators who have mastered the internal "client" pitch tend to get more buy-in from their organization's dominant coalition and more opportunities to put their ideas into action.[18]

iStock.com/SDI Productions

Objectives will not be successful if public relations team members are unable to convince organizational leaders that they are relevant and valuable to achieve.

Do Your Objectives Make Organizational Decision Makers Excited?

Keep in mind that the content and the objectives matter when presented to an audience comprised of internal leaders. The diagnosis phase should point not only toward organizational need and priority but also to enthusiasm. As communication teams never work in isolation, successful objectives take into account internal attitude to ensure that energies are channeled in the most useful direction.

This process does involve a degree of politicking. Practitioners must anticipate and respond to internal coalitions, key decision makers, and organizational history. Two organizations with similar goals will inherently have different objectives based on their resources and assets, as well as their structure and leadership. Goals are aspirational, but objectives must clearly reflect organizational and environmental realities. If the leadership does not agree with a campaign's direction, it will not succeed.

Proving Relevance: Will Completing Your Objectives Drive Positive Change?

If the primary goal of a campaign is to increase the number of dues-paying members for your organization, your PR objectives should be judged by how closely they support that goal. For example, assuming final responsibility for membership growth falls within a separate member relations department, here are multiple potential communication objectives:

- Potential objective #1: Raise awareness of the organization among potential members in the community (defined demographically and geographically) from 15 to 20 percent over six months.
- Potential objective #2: Target the attendance of 100 potential members at organizational events as the guests of current members in the next six months.
- Potential objective #3: Identify and capture contact information for 100 potential members over the next three months.

While each of these approaches point to particular elements in the puzzle of raising membership, the second and third objectives more clearly address the problem at hand. The third objective may be the easiest to execute as only the communication department is involved. All three approaches could be implemented, but the second and third should be prioritized based on their closer relationship with the organizational priority. The final decision on which objectives to focus on may be based on the available resources as well as organizational and departmental circumstances for execution.

iStock.com/SDI Productions

Event attendance may be a useful objective, but it may only be the first step toward attracting new customers. Ensure campaign objectives reflect the multiple stages often needed to influence the opinions and behaviors of publics.

Another item to keep in mind is that the scope of the communication department's work or an agency's agreement changes from organization to organization over time. Ideally, clear demonstration of successful and impactful communication objectives help expand the influence of top communicators and the resources and responsibilities of communication departments.[19] Overreliance on another department can doom objectives to fail if the communication team does not receive necessary information, resources, or support. The expectations for such support should be made exceedingly clear to all campaign team members when developing objectives.

Are You Connecting Short- and Long-Term Objectives?

Objectives may come in multiple simultaneous, overlapping, or separate stages, reflecting short- and long-term steps toward achieving organizational goals. For example, an internal campaign-specific objective may be to increase employees' awareness of a new health-care benefits package from 0 (prior to launch) to 80 percent over a three-month period. The organization may have a larger, overarching goal of improving employee satisfaction and retention, which the new benefits program supports. For the PR function, the long-term objective may be to increase employee awareness of all company benefits or (along with the human resources department) to increase employee retention by 15 percent over the course of the year. In this case, the short-term campaign objective clearly connects to the long-term organizational objective.

If the short-term objective moves out of alignment with the organizational objective or goal, practitioners should consider making an adjustment. As an example, if the top priority of the human resources function shifts to a lack of qualified job applicants in a growing division, rather than a retention problem, communications professionals should adjust or reprioritize their objectives as needed to reflect a new audience, a new message or focus, a new technique for measurement, and a new timeline. Promoting new employee benefits may still be the campaign's purpose and central message, but the most important audience could be outside the organization. This would necessitate different channels, and the measurement may be related to capturing information about incoming applicants to the organization, including whether their application had originated from the specific outreach campaign. In this way, objectives and measurement approaches should be flexible and responsive to the shifting needs of the organization as a whole.

PRo Tip

HOW *NOT* TO WRITE OBJECTIVES

- **Does the measurement matter?** Output-based rather than outcome-based objectives may mean that practitioners can easily check objectives off a list, but that they lack organizational impact. Counting Facebook "likes" and media clips or calculating ad value equivalency does not assess whether a campaign has achieved the intended result for an organization. Using awareness, attitude change, behavioral change, or content analysis metrics, for example, can more accurately measure success.
- **Is the objective primarily communication driven?** Objectives not tied directly to PR efforts can present practitioner challenges because they are too dependent on others within organizations to complete or do not end up being a result of communication strategies and tactics.
- **How much impact will achieving the goal have?** Objectives not closely related to organizational goals will lack impact and, eventually, reduce overall organizational support for PR efforts. Organizational goals should drive communication goals, and each goal should be represented by objectives.
- **Is it organizationally feasible?** Sometimes, there is just not enough organizational enthusiasm, time, or resources to complete the desired objective. Practitioners must be aware of such limitations when calibrating the amount of change in each objective.

For more details and to see common errors in writing objectives before and after reviewing them with the questions listed above, see the Appendix, p. 249.

CONCLUSION

There are many benefits to PR that cannot be easily measured. Community goodwill, volunteer or donor enthusiasm, and brand equity or trust do not translate smoothly to numerical data, graphs, and charts but may be clear outcomes for successful campaigns. In some cases, these can be measured using proxies (positive vs. negative media coverage or social media discussions, for example). With that being said, PR will always be undermeasured. It is impossible to record each of its effects (positive and negative) on perception and behavior simultaneously. Practitioners must take on the responsibilities of understanding what is measurable with the resources at hand and develop objectives aligned with the goals that are most important to the organization. With a bit of creativity, it is possible to measure many significant components of campaigns.

By writing objectives with existing organizational structures and focuses in mind, as well as having a clear understanding of the value of each priority, practitioners can make a meaningful and sustainable impact. Organizations tend to end up stale and static. Change may be met with resistance even in situations where it is deeply needed. The PR function within an organization can act as a "cooperative antagonist," supporting policies that encourage long-term, mutually beneficial relationships with external *and* internal publics rather than short-term advantage over them.[20] Practitioners should be able to understand and explain the organization-wide implications of their ideas and objectives. Communication cannot win every internal battle, and this will sometimes result in less-than-ideal objectives. However, over the long term, practitioners that prioritize strategy; understand their industry and competitive environment; and those that research, quantify, and justify their recommendations will make their departments and their organizations measurably better.

What word hasn't been mentioned in this chapter? You might notice we haven't often used *how*. Objectives should be written in a way that is neutral in how they are accomplished: the strategies and tactics we choose to implement.[21] In particular, thinking strategically and planning consistently successful campaigns means that we are not working backward from tactics but understanding what will be value-added to our organization and public. Objectives grow from necessity and from prioritizing organizational opportunities and challenges. Strategies, covered in the next chapter, connect those objectives with the tactics, the toolbox of PR practice.

THINK CRITICALLY

1. What is Management by Objectives, and how is the concept applied in PR?
2. Why is it important that objectives are measurable?
3. What are some examples of potential objectives that are measurable but not relevant to organizational or communication goals?
4. What would you do if an objective you presented was met with a negative response from organizational leaders, such as "we don't have six months to wait for that change to happen"?

KEY TERMS

CONCEPT CASE: SETTING MEASURABLE OBJECTIVES FOR COMMUNITY FLOW YOGA

The collective leaders of Community Flow Yoga have targeted ten new cities to expand their operations over the next two years, including their first locations outside the US: Atlanta, Georgia; Austin, Texas; Baltimore, Maryland; Boston, Massachusetts; Copenhagen, Denmark; London, United Kingdom; Oakland, California; San Diego, California; Toronto, Canada; and Vancouver, Canada.

In order to expand successfully, they need to raise awareness and generate a positive impression of their brand with multiple audiences and stakeholders in each city, including potential instructors, potential members, community leaders, local political leaders, and local nonprofit partners.

Given this prompt, how might you craft S.M.A.R.T. objectives to reflect the necessary steps to build relationships and make inroads in these new communities? Begin to brainstorm options from the following prompts:

- Different objectives for different audiences:
  - Consumer
  - Industry
  - Community
- Awareness, opinion, and behavior change objectives
- Differences in geography, country, language, and media market

CASE STUDY: SHINING A NEW LIGHT ON THE HEFORSHE MOVEMENT AND GENDER EQUALITY

Based on PRSA Silver Anvil Winner
United Nations with FleishmanHillard
Campaign Focus: Activism

Gender equality is not only a women's issue; it is a human rights issue. The United Nations HeForShe movement is "an invitation for men and people of all genders to stand in solidarity with women to create a bold, visible and united force for gender equality."[22] Gender equality is an issue we face regularly and is now more timely than ever. One in three women face physical or sexual abuse worldwide, and many choose to remain silent because of shame, fear, or embarrassment.[23] Unfortunately, the fact that men and boys are also victims of physical and sexual violence goes unacknowledged. Men are statistically less likely to report an assault.[24] Accomplishing gender equality involves an inclusive approach that highlights the essential role of men and boys as "partners for women's rights, and as having needs of their own in the formulation of that balance."[25] So, how can men contribute to improving gender equality? How can they help prevent violence against women? This case study looks at how the HeForShe movement rekindles momentum around gender equality to inspire change.

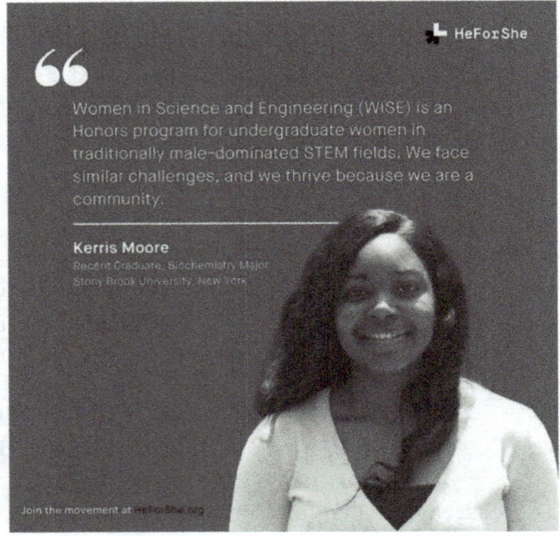

HeForShe mentee Kerris Moore, a biochemistry graduate from Stony Brook University in New York.[26]

Research/Diagnosis

The HeForShe movement's primary goal was to create a plan that encourages men to advocate for gender equality in a sensitive #MeToo era.[27] Through insights and survey research, the United Nations found a variety of obstacles for women in the workplace, along with fear of mentoring and socializing, due to sexual harassment. Such obstacles are not only unfair and intolerable for any person but also may additionally act as barriers for career success and financial independence. Indeed, "our societies remain marked by critical gender issues, and latest figures estimate that 35 percent of women experience some form of violence in their lifetime—an unchanged statistic."[28] As such, the United Nations set to develop a worldwide campaign to encourage men to advocate for women instead of isolating them.[29]

Launched in 2014, Emma Watson, UN Women Goodwill Ambassador, actress, and activist, presented a speech at the UN General Assembly persuading men to help promote gender equality:

> *I am reaching out to you because I need your help. We want to end gender inequality—and to do that we need everyone to be involved.*

Men—I would like to take this opportunity to extend your formal invitation. Gender equality is your issue too. This is the first campaign of its kind at the UN: we want to try and galvanize as many men and boys as possible to be advocates for gender equality. And we don't just want to talk about it, but make sure it is tangible.[30]

Achieving gender equality can only occur through addressing the authoritative imbalances that men have over women that limit people's chances to live to the fullest. Watson emphasizes the crucial need for men to join the feminist pursuit of social righteousness; "it's a matter of human rights, not of enlightened self-interest."[31]

Upon its launch, the HeForShe movement aimed to prompt 1 billion men and boys, globally, to act in preventing discrimination and violence against women. Secretary-General Thorbjorn Jagland, a Norwegian politician, pledged his support for the movement: "When you work in human rights, you see that the strongest, safest and most prosperous societies are those in which women are empowered, and the genders are more equal."[32] That said, the UN aimed to raise awareness about the consequences of excluding women and emphasize the contributions they offer society. This idea led to the core perception that "half of the world's power is lost when women are excluded," which led the UN to look for ways to make this reality more tangible.[33]

Objectives

The UN Women's HeForShe campaign had to be global, cost nothing for supporters to participate, and compete for media attention with other worthy and related causes.[34] To that end, over six months, the United Nations Women HeForShe movement hoped to achieve the following objectives:

Rob Kim/Getty Images Entertainment/Getty Images

Emma Watson speaking about HeForShe at the UN General Assembly.

- Generate widespread, positive social media engagement
- Increase site traffic to their website and social channels
- Rekindle global dialogue and media coverage around HeForShe
- Reignite momentum in the HeForShe movement around the world five years after the campaign's initial launch

Strategies

The strategy used within this project focused on creating an entirely new message that intended to redefine where the world's power comes from: "Men and women are more powerful together."[35] Through this effort, the UN Women's HeForShe campaign developed the "More Powerful Together" message, and invited Mark Consuelos, a star of the television show *Riverdale*, to speak at the campaign launch.[36] Moreover, the UN asked iconic buildings around the world to power down half of their exterior lights on September 24, 2014, to set a visual statement, demonstrating the type of power lost when women are excluded from society. This campaign, which intended to drive consumer-focused media attention, was focused on raising awareness and sparking interest in the HeForShe week of the annual UN General Assembly in New York.[37]

Following the "More Powerful Together" campaign the UN planned the "HeForShe 10x10x10 IMPACT Summit," which is an annual, invite-only event also during the UN General Assembly. Discussions of the state of gender equality during this summit led to the development of the annual "Emerging Solutions for Gender Equality Report." This report includes thirty-four solutions on how to achieve gender quality, including women's economic empowerment, putting a stop to gender-based violence, closing the gender pay gap, and accomplishing parity.[38]

Tactics

To bring their strategy to life, this campaign used the following tactics:

- Encouraged some of the most iconic buildings and landmarks in different countries to turn down half their lights on the night of September 24, to send a powerful message to the world that the world is more potent with women
- Secured Consuelos as a celebrity spokesperson and supported the announcement through a media alert that was sent out on September 21. Consuelos also presented a speech and attended media interviews and photo opportunities during the Empire State Building lighting ceremony
- Recruited hundreds of social media influencers to share campaign content, and created sample social signage and graphics
- Used a layered approach to traditional media for the "More Powerful Together" message, and the "IMPACT Summit" by reaching out to local and national broadcasts to share information about the campaign
- Leveraged the global head for HeForShe, Elizabeth Nyamayaro, as a spokesperson
- Reached out to media after the "More Powerful Together" announcement and the "IMPACT Summit" to package and distribute assets secured from the buildings to hundreds of media outlets
- Created a dedicated website for people to commit, take action, and donate

Social media signage example shared with social influencers.[39]

Paid and Owned

The UN Women's HeforShe campaign created a website that provides people the opportunity to commit to gender equality for free by signing up on the website. As of 2020, HeForShe has reported over 3 million commitments.[40] The UN Women's HeForShe website does not only allow people to commit but also take action by offering individual and organizational action kits through materials, such as flyers, for events and social media. People are also able to donate to raise critical funds for UN Women to fight violence against women and girls.[41]

Earned and Shared

The HeForShe campaign took major steps to achieve earned and shared media. UN Women managed to convince the owners and managers of twenty-five buildings in eight different countries to turn down half their lights to bring to light the consequences of excluding women from societies. These buildings were often built and run by men. Also, as previously mentioned, not only did the UN secure Emma Watson as the face of this campaign but also convinced Consuelos to speak at the Empire State Building lighting ceremony, and supported the launch by including his name in media outreach. The UN also encouraged social influencers, at no cost, to promote, share, and create content heavily emphasized on persuading men and boys to pledge support for gender equality.[42]

"More Powerful Together" outreach focused on media outreach to local and national broadcasts to share information on the campaign, which resulted in earned media on *Live with Kelly and Ryan* and multiple other forums across the country. Upon the launch day, September 24, the campaign shared videos, images, quotes, b-roll, and more of the lighting ceremony, which earned more media mentions online and on broadcast news forums. As for the "IMPACT Summit," media in New York or those attending the UN General Assembly were invited to cover the event by setting up interviews and offering live stream links. Furthermore, the campaign shared a commentary postlaunch for those who were unable to attend.[43]

Implementation

Over six months of research and planning, the UN Women HeForShe campaign launched two main activations; the "More Powerful Together" messaging and the "HeForShe 10x10x10 IMPACT Summit" to encourage gender equality.

Reporting/Evaluation

The campaign created a meaningful representation of the need for change and positioned HeForShe as a leading, globally unifying movement for gender equality. The campaign garnered 424 million impressions through earned media in 200 articles and 159 outlets in 13 countries and languages and has achieved a 100 percent positive and neutral sentiment across social media platforms.[44] The integrated campaign generated 145.7 million social media impressions, and the #HeForShe hashtag went viral on Twitter within the first three days of the campaign's launch with 1.1 million Tweets from 1.2 billion unique users.[45] UN Women's HeForShe website received a 500 percent increase in site traffic compared to the week before the launch. Emma Watson's speech has been viewed 1,927,122 times.[46] Finally, HeForShe has earned strong political commitments, including the US government offices conveying solidarity by powering down half their lights on their capitols, and Minnesota declaring September 24 as HeForShe Day.[47] Also, Queen Rania of Jordan gave a speech at the summit, and Burj Khalifa participated during the lighting event in Dubai, both of which raised awareness in the Arab world. Today, the Middle East is one of the leading regions for international media engagement with HeForShe.[48]

As of 2020, there are more than 2 million gender equality web commitments, 1.3 billion relevant social media conversations, and 3.3 million HeForShe commitments. More than one thousand community events have taken place.[49] HeForShe has earned significant commitments in countries including the US, Mexico, India, Rwanda, and the Democratic Republic of Congo.[50] Most recently, it was announced that Mr. Luis Carrilho, United Nations Police Adviser in the Department of Peace Operations, is the newest HeForShe Advocate supporting gender equality.[51]

Theories

Framing Theory: The UN Women HeForShe has reshaped what it means to be a woman in society. That said, they took the perception that men yield power over women in the workforce, and framed it in a way that demonstrates to people the kind of power the world loses when women are excluded.

Diversity- and Inclusion-First Approach

Gender equality was the most crucial aspect of the Diversity & Inclusion Wheel that the campaign has focused on. HeForShe has also highlighted thinking styles, education, and political ideology by reframing what it means to be a woman in the workplace and persuading world leaders to commit to achieving gender equality.

Strategies

7

iStock.com/Drazen_

THINK AHEAD

7.1 Demonstrate proficient use of each area of the PESO model.

7.2 Articulate how elements of the PESO model work together to achieve objectives and create integrated campaigns.

7.3 Recognize the differences in audience segmentation to accomplish campaign strategies.

7.4 Leverage an organization's resources.

7.5 Learn to work within competitive environments.

Strategies demonstrate synthesis in a public relations (PR) campaign. The situation has been defined, audiences have been selected, and the objectives have been developed, but it's the job of the PR team to drive the best possible direction for implementation. This is where strategies come into play. It is the moment when concrete objectives—crafted from research, organizational goals, communication goals, and situational realities—meet the skills, talents, and creativity of PR professionals. Strategies are the approaches through which objectives are accomplished. They act as a compass for practitioners to navigate from written objectives to completed objectives.

Broom and Sha define strategies as "the overall concept, approach, or general plan for the program designed to achieve an objective."[1] In this way, they connect objectives to tactics, or "the events, media, and methods used to implement the strategy."[2] Strategy development involves a deep understanding of audiences and publics, of the competitive environment, and of the **channel** or medium within which the communication will take place.[3]

CHOOSING YOUR CHANNELS: THE PESO MODEL

The PESO (paid, earned, shared, and owned) model provides a helpful checklist to ensure campaigns include strategies in multiple facets of campaign communication.[4] It serves as a framework to help communicators think systematically about the tools at their disposal for a specific campaign. Developed and championed by Gini Dietrich of Chicago-based PR firm Arment Dietrich, PESO builds on the traditional marketing duo of paid media (such as advertising) and earned media (media relations) to include shared media (social media outreach) and owned media (brochures, fliers, digital properties, physical locations, events, and other wholly controlled environments). It also maps what can be referred to as converged media: additional overlaps between the four main types of communication channels, such as social media advertising (paid and shared), social media influencer campaigns (paid, earned, and shared),[5] or event sponsorships (owned and paid).

Keep in mind that these categories work together and are not prioritized over one another. Campaigns do not force us to choose between paid and shared media or earned and owned media, rather they allow us to choose from a menu based on what fits the needs of the organization and the situation. Like a painter, practitioners begin with distinct categories or colors but choose the degree to which we mix them together, place them side by side on the canvas, or leave them out of the picture entirely. These choices should not be made arbitrarily but based on the knowledge of organizational goals and audiences from the diagnosis stage in order to achieve defined campaign objectives.

While not every medium is a fit for every campaign, different channels are often complementary. For example, paid media and social media allow for repetition and timeliness, but earned media's editorial processes create more credibility and trust for the messages being shared. On one hand, paid opportunities offer a clear selection of channels, choice of timing, and message control, while, on the other, earned media comes with the tacit endorsement of the outlet.[6] Luckily it does not need to be a choice. Earned and paid strategies should work together to provide both repetition and credibility. Many campaigns benefit from a mix of channels designed to reach audiences with approaches that support each other to achieve objectives.

The terms *controlled* and *uncontrolled* are applied to make the distinction between earned or shared media and paid or owned media. Broom and Sha define controlled media as "those in which practitioners have the say over what is said, how it is said,

FIGURE 7.1

Practitioners can select from a palette of paid, earned, shared, or owned channels, as well as converged approaches that share characteristics and benefits of multiple media types.

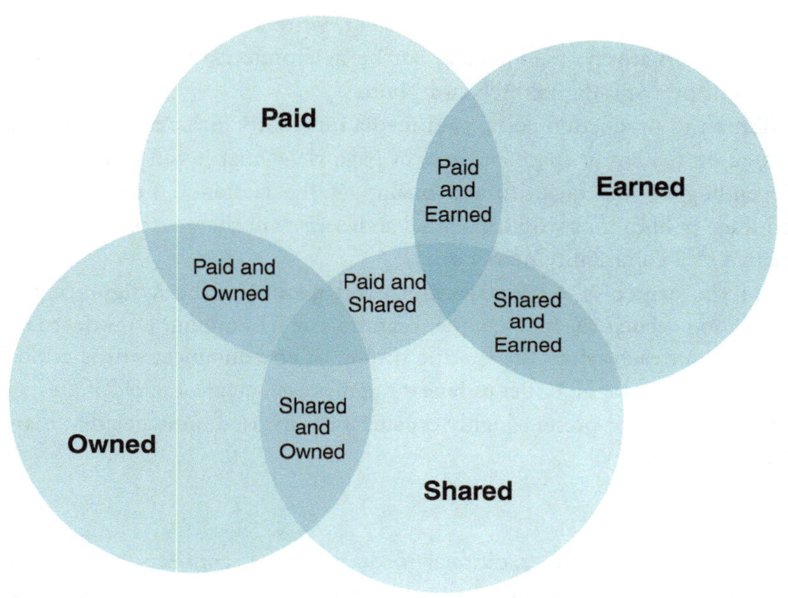

when it is said, and—to some extent—to whom it is said."[7] Conversely, they define uncontrolled media as "those over which practitioners have no direct role in decisions about media content."[8] The PESO model expands on this distinction by breaking down these categories further. In this case, the lines between categories are not absolute: there are degrees of controlled and uncontrolled media within each part of the model.

The Model

Paid

Paid media includes advertising, but it is certainly not limited to this function alone. It includes the ads on television, radio, and in newspapers and magazines, as well as traditional and digital billboards and sponsored posts and tweets.[9] These are

©MTA

While we think of paid media as "controlled" by organizations, publics often remix many facets of brand communication.

opportunities where funding is the most important factor and the major barrier to access. Generally, organizations have near-total control of the content and its timing. Some paid content has extremely high production value, meaning significant resources are spent to create a photo or video, hire talent, write a script, craft a design or logo, and so on. Alternatively, paid media can be as simple as a black-and-white print advertisement or a still digital billboard photo.

In addition to production costs, paid media inherently includes the cost of the buy itself, based on the layout space, airtime, or page views that it will generate. The costs vary depending on the quantity and quality of the audience. For example, highly targeted trade publications with influential audiences will charge a premium per-reader cost relative to a community news outlet.

Due to the degree of content control, paid media can be a significant asset in communication related to, for example, branding or rebranding, a product launch, or event-related outreach when the specific timing of an announcement is critical. This type of media allows for an outlet to repeat the message, create a series of messages that build on each other, or present highly organization-focused messages that may not be considered newsworthy.

Earned

Earned media, the work of traditional media relations, connects organizations and reporters, providing many of the same publicity benefits as paid media, along with the added asset of the tacit endorsement of the reporting organization. Because organizations don't pay for the coverage, it carries an implication that the message has inherent news value beyond the organization promoting itself.[10] Organizations give up control of the story (making earned media *uncontrolled*) in order to reach audiences consuming news content rather than advertising content.

Newsworthy stories—those appealing to or having impact with broad audiences—can generate significant coverage. When envisioned as part of integrated campaigns, such news-friendly announcements, trends, and events can be planned to maximize earned media coverage and reinforce organizational messages. While many assume media relations strategies must appeal to a broad consumer audience, the explosion of media channels from traditional print, radio, television news, industry trade publications, and valuable digital-only channels allows for significant audience variation and nuance.

That said, earned media does not fit every campaign situation. Some organizational stories may be too complicated or narrow for audience-appropriate media outlets. They may be difficult to fit to a particular media outlet's concept of **newsworthiness**. Others might have a specific objective that requires significant repetition or personalized outreach to key audience members. They may require a very narrow time window.

iStock.com/Chaay_Tee

Social media influencers often have very loyal followings and generate specific focused content, such as food, fashion, or parenting bloggers.

Earned media may not be the most effective or efficient approach in such situations, but resources could allow it to be valuable as a secondary or complementary strategy.

Shared

Shared media is most simply defined as social media outreach—channels where the initial message is controlled by an organization but that facilitate direct, uncontrolled conversation with individuals and other organizations without the mediation of reporters and editors.[11] Regularly updated content drives successful shared media outreach, whether campaign-related or not.[12] While the list of social media platforms changes regularly, Facebook, Instagram, LinkedIn, and Twitter account for the majority of social media use by practitioners, and all must be considered by organizations.[13] Each of the four platforms include a varying degree of largely static profile content and opportunities for microblogging: creating short posts that often include images, videos, or links to other content.[14] The expectations for the type of content and timing for each channel can vary significantly.

Organizations participate in conversations on these channels through their own branded handles or through individuals speaking for themselves or on behalf of the company. Social media conversations also reflect the impact of influencers—individuals with high credibility and visibility in specific social media communities or on specific channels that "shape audience attitudes."[15] Brands often work directly with bloggers or influencers (bloggers can also *be* influencers) using a similar framework as they would when researching, pitching, and collaborating with journalists. Social media channels are comprised of self-selected networks, and organizations best serve the interests of all stakeholders by thinking of these channels as places of dialogue and engagement, rather than primarily promotional spaces.[16]

Owned

Despite the importance of earned and shared media, owned media still can, and should, act as the center of an organization's content universe. A broad definition of owned channels could include, for example, an organization's digital footprint (including, but not limited to, their website) as well as physical branded offices and the printed brochures for specific programs and projects. Owned channels provide a place for those outside an organization to gather information about it. They allow the organization to curate this path for the audience member. Wholly owned channels (such as a website) and partially owned channels (such as blogs hosted through third-party sites such as WordPress that could allow user comments) house content that is created and controlled by an organization. Owned channels provide a central point for an organizational brand, along with content that can be shared and distributed directly to audiences or through social channels.[17]

The first, and possibly the most impactful, evolution of the digital restructuring of organizational communication occurred when companies began creating their own websites, greatly expanding the reach and scope of channels where they had complete control over the content and the environment. Not unsurprisingly, many early websites functioned much like what they replaced or were based on: the print brochure. As programming expertise has expanded and the tools for creating more elegant and functional websites have become more affordable and easier to use, owned content has become more democratic. Now, all organizations can establish a respectable digital presence, making it a near requirement for public legitimacy today.[18] Technology has also facilitated the evolution of owned channels, and brands themselves, to become more responsive to their audiences. Brand monitoring, ranging from a wide variety of easily accessible free digital tools to large-scale systematic brand research, provides deep and actionable insights about how communities interact with organizations and their products and services.[19] In this way, well-designed websites and organizational blogs bridge the gap between owned and shared media, becoming interactive spaces used to listen as well as speak.

HOW THE MODEL OVERLAPS

There are areas of overlap between and among the paid, earned, shared, and owned categories. Collectively, we can refer to these as converged media although they are more accurately depicted as individual areas of convergence. Most social media channels offer a variety of paid options, which create a continuum between fully shared content and static display advertisements. For example, "boosted" posts on Facebook still reflect many qualities of shared content, with relatively inexpensive additional reach.[20] Native advertisements or "sponsored posts" on social media streams provide content that fits directly into the natural consumption of a channel but with more distinctive markers of advertisement. Native advertisements avoid ad blockers but must reflect content users want to engage with to be effective.[21] Social media channels can also have opportunities for display advertisements—the digital equivalent of a newspaper advertisement on a page, separate from the news content. All of these examples are both paid and shared media, reflecting options that may be a better fit than purely shared or paid approaches depending on the context of the campaign.

How to Build an Integrated Campaign Strategy Around PESO

Strategies should be conceived to work together using multiple channels as part of the same campaign. In this way, campaigns can target multiple publics and connect with individuals through multiple channels. While it is important to identify commonalities among target audiences to reach them, there will always be significant variation within a group.[22] Employing multiple strategies using multiple channels helps bridge this gap.

The importance of integrating multiple channel approaches is also beneficial from a timing perspective. In the case of a grand opening for a new retail store, there can and should be multiple phases that draw on different parts of the PESO model. Prior to the opening, using paid, shared, and owned media channels may be the most timely and efficient ways to generate interest in the new facility. Earned media could be integrated immediately before, during, and after a grand-opening event. Finally, that coverage could be used and shared with key audiences through earned and owned media channels as part of an ongoing campaign to sustain interest after the grand opening. In this way, multiple channels within the model are most appropriate at different stages in a specific campaign.

Crafting Winning Strategies

Successful strategies combine a specific audience or public and the best channel to connect with them.[23] The following tips from *Strategic Communications Planning for Effective Public Relations and Marketing* by authors Laurie J. Wilson and Joseph D. Ogden help to demonstrate how strategies can work together to support objectives:

- **Deepen audience segmentation**: Objectives define audiences/publics, but strategies should add a more granular level to identify the channels that can, when combined, reach the desired group.
    - **Role**: Director of public relations for a school district.
    - **Goal**: Pass a bond proposal during a local election to provide funds for necessary facilities upgrades across the district.
    - **Sample Objective**: Increase support for the bond proposal by 10 percent among

likely voters in the community over the next three months.

- Strategy #1: Share information with *parents of current students* through presentations at parent-teacher organization meetings at each school.
- **Strategy #2**: Connect with *local seniors* through earned media outreach, starting with the monthly senior-focused community newspaper.
- **Strategy #3**: Identify *community leaders* (political, business, religious, and so on) for personal outreach and potential public support statements.

- **Follow your publics**: Following the **uses and gratifications theory**, selecting the right channel to reach a specific audience begins by understanding what media and messages they already consume.
  - **Role**: Director of corporate communication for a medium-sized manufacturing company.
  - **Goal**: Increase employee use of new company-provided fitness center and equipment.
  - **Sample Objective**: Raise awareness of new fitness center from 40 percent to 80 percent over the next six months.
    - **Strategy #1**: Share consistent (monthly), image-rich updates about the fitness center through *traditional employee communication channels* (e-newsletter, departmental bulletin boards, and so on).
    - **Strategy #2**: Provide content about the fitness center *to managers to share with their employees* during staff meetings.
    - **Strategy #3**: Showcase information about the fitness center on *company social media* (knowing many employees follow these channels).
- **Let the creativity flow**: Fun, engaging, and original content approaches capture each public's attention.
  - **Role**: Vice president of communication for a community bank.
  - **Goal**: Increase the share of home mortgage lending in their hometown.
  - **Sample Objective**: Increase mortgage loan market share (in the town) made to current homebuyers by 5 percent over the next year.
    - **Strategy #1**: Create *a series of humorous, but informative first-time homebuying tips*, package them in creative formats (short videos, blog posts, and so on), and share them through paid or boosted social media channels.
    - **Strategy #2**: Target real estate agents (who can point their clients toward mortgage services) through *high-visibility, memorable event sponsorships* at local professional events.
- **As long as it serves the objective**: Creativity for creativity's sake does not achieve objectives—audience reach and audience relevance should guide what strategies are selected.[24]

Source: Laurie J. Wilson and Joseph D. Ogden, *Strategic Communications Planning for Effective Public Relations and Marketing* (5th ed.) (Dubuque, IA: Kendall-Hunt, 2008), 102.

THE RIGHT APPROACH FOR YOUR AUDIENCE(S)

Audience or publics segmentation is at the heart of successful strategic PR and strategic campaigns. It is a simple idea with extremely complex implications: audience matters.

The message, the medium, the tone, and the timing all hinge on who the intended (and unintended) recipients might be. Audiences should be defined in a campaign's early stages, and analyzing them can point toward the most effective strategies.[25]

The following list of potential factors to segment audiences moves from broad to narrow restrictions. It is just one approach to segmentation, and those interested in learning more about the process should also reference *Cutlip & Center's Effective Public Relations*, where Broom and Sha provide a list of nine approaches.[26] Narrowing down audiences or publics using these or other factors helps point practitioners toward the best strategies, channels, and messages for a given campaign. Looking for areas of overlap, practitioners should research both their intended publics as well as the audiences of a variety of existing channels that may be potential campaign strategies. Significant overlap can indicate a strong fit.

All channels have a defined audience. Media outlets are themselves particularly targeted to specific publics, so practitioners employing media relations strategies should find overlaps between their targets and a given outlet's audience. Individual channels or outlets may define their audience based on geography, demographics, psychographics, interest, or industry.

As technology and opportunity continue to shift, the field of PR will continue to see increased diversity in the number of channels available for distribution. This serves as both an opportunity and a challenge. The increased variety allows for more targeted, unique, and scalable strategies. It also makes it more difficult for organizations to keep pace with public expectations of increasingly instantaneous communication in a variety of formats. What will remain is the value of strategic thinking: audience-focused, objective-driven approaches will continue to pay dividends.

Demographics

Demographic factors include age, education, income, gender, and can, along with geography, narrow down a mass audience to those with the most potential interest or stake in a given product, service, or issue. For example, a campaign to support the passage of a local millage to support a new senior center may differentiate messaging based on demographics between those who would have the opportunity to use the center personally and those who would see the benefits for their parents and their community rather than in their daily lives. Additionally, both demographic and geographic data are often publicly available through the US Census Bureau and other sources, making it accessible.

Geography

All organizations have geographic boundaries (zip codes, school districts, cities, regions, nations, or continents) where their campaigns will take place. All relevant stakeholders exist within an organization's relevant geography, but many targeted publics have their own, more limited geographies. Traditional local media outlets (print, radio, television)

FIGURE 7.2
Top Ten US Media Markets

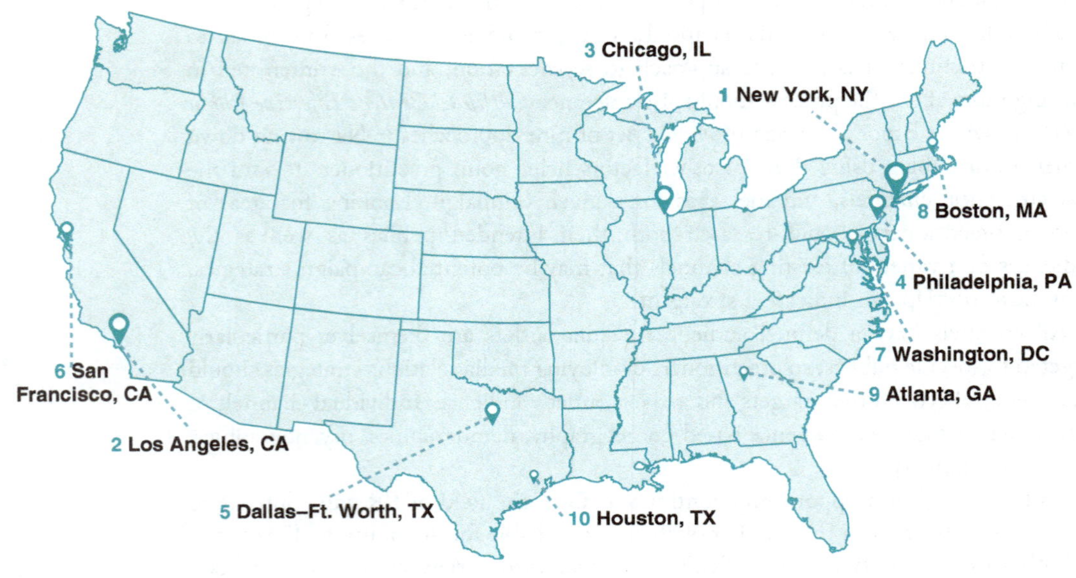

clearly define their geographic boundaries, while national and digital outlets may take additional research to determine their impact in specific regions.

Psychographics

Characteristics related to the values and preferences of specific publics allow for psychographic analysis, another form of segmentation.[27] This approach creates a more holistic picture of audience groups that can be used to align channels with behavior. More focused than demographic or geographic approaches, psychographics analyze group audience members through their responses to a series of statements that can indicate ideological, spiritual, economic, and familial attitudes.[28] Many media outlets perform psychographic research to provide potential advertisers a clearer picture of their audience. PR practitioners can use such information to inform decisions about strategy and tactics (including messaging) related to audience values and perspectives.

Activity/Interest

Publics may share a profession, a passion, or a predicament. They may or may not interact with one another, and they may have an active or passive stance toward the organization or issue at hand.[29] A group of doctors, surfing enthusiasts, or those who have purchased tainted spinach at the grocery store may have nothing else in common aside from the categories above, and they often will not know each other in any meaningful sense but may constitute a critical group for the organization based on the campaign at hand. Similarly, the readers of a specific blog or magazine may have little in common outside of their passion for a specific subject. Often, the most valuable campaign channels are those with a direct interest overlap between the subject matter at hand and a channel or media outlet.

Influence

Not all members of a given public are created equal. Some individuals are decision makers within their organization, and their opinions, attitudes, or behaviors are significantly more important than others. Creative practitioners can create strategies and select channels to target these individuals as a unique audience across multiple organizations within the same campaign.

Channel Consumption

Often, practitioners can make assumptions about specific audiences based on the media they choose to consume. For example, those reading a specific industry's trade publication

PRo Tip

DIFFERENCES IN CHANNEL CONSUMPTION

- Television
  - Passive viewership but evolving with on-demand and streaming options
  - Local news continues to be a significant draw
- Newspapers and magazines
  - Mix of digital and traditional readership
  - Deepest reporting resources lead to widely shared content
- Radio
  - Mix of digital and traditional listenership
  - Drive time is prime time
- Mobile Devices
  - Regularly used simultaneously with other channels
  - Accessible size and layout are critical for content
- Laptop & Desktop Computers
  - Often used at work or while working—use peaks midday[30]
  - Many online purchases are still made from computers, despite the rapid growth of mobile devices[31]

clearly have a stake in that industry. The majority of those reading a community weekly newspaper generally live in the community itself. In this way, channel consumption connects demographic, psychographic, and activity/interest to media outlets. To take the process one step further, targeting specific newspaper sections, local television shows, or specific bloggers marks an even narrower audience definition based on the readership/viewership/listenership of that specific show.

Generally, such decisions are not *either/or*: multiple audiences for a campaign, as well as wide variation among members of specific publics, make it so that multiple channels should be used. That said, these questions support prioritization of strategies and channels and help decide what is necessary, what would be nice to include, and what does not need to be done. Practitioners can use audience research and understanding combined with a deep knowledge of the potential strategies and channels at hand to make a thorough case to organizational leaders in support of the recommended approach.

Intersectionality: Moving Beyond Segmentation to See Intersecting Identities

PR campaigns address varied audiences. To connect with these groups, it's as easy as slicing them into their relevant demographic parts, researching what each group needs and reads, and then crafting and distributing messages accordingly, right? *In practice, it's rarely that simple*. Publics overlap, and tactics and messages are visible far beyond their intended audiences.[32] In fact, an overly simplistic approach can easily alienate publics and reinforce stereotypes. How can practitioners with finite time and resources address all of these challenges? One place to begin is by considering publics not just as separate audience segments based on demographic factors (such as race and gender) but as groups of individuals each carrying their own layered identities. To address this need, scholars Natalie Tindall (PhD, APR) and Jennifer Vardeman (PhD) have introduced the theory of **intersectionality** to PR research and practice.

An intersectional perspective helps practitioners see that every individual's experiences are different, and we all share a multitude of interdependent identities that become more or less relevant or *salient* depending on the situation. Age, gender, race, and socioeconomic status (as examples) each tell part of a story about an individual or members of a community. These identities mean that organizational messages can be interpreted or experienced in very different ways by each individual. Even with the best of intentions, PR can contribute to *othering*: reinforcing existing stereotypes and privilege structures by separating certain individuals from those with more power in a group or broader society. Here are several practical recommendations, based on the work of leading PR scholars, to help practitioners create more inclusive and community-centered campaigns:

Attempt to be aware of and remove your personal biases. We all carry subconscious biases. Rather than only seeing a campaign's goals from the organization's perspective, practitioners must place themselves squarely in the shoes of their publics.[33]

This starts the processes of understanding and connecting with publics on their own terms. Targeted heath campaigns, for example, often begin with assumptions that "groups don't know what's good for them" rather than using research to understand the priorities, perspectives, and experiences of publics.[34]

Bring publics into the planning process early. Research at several stages of a campaign can integrate ideas from and with (not just about) publics. From a developmental research perspective, consider asking how a public's goals are relevant to the issue at hand, rather than only focusing on organizational goals. This can help shape mutually beneficial campaigns, rather than only including publics for message testing in the later stages.

Consider identities together rather than separately. Rather than isolating different publics or audiences by single demographic factors, consider how identities fit together and how they are influenced by the environments and experiences of individuals.[35]

Broaden your conception of diversity. Many organizations and communication campaigns focus on racial or gender diversity, but there are many different types of diversity that should be considered, often dependent on the issue at hand. Considering sexual orientation, gender identification, religious beliefs, educational background, health status, occupation/employment status, parental status, and many other factors can contribute to a more complete understanding of publics.

As practitioners, we should continue to challenge ourselves to avoid stereotypes and *essentialization*—singling out representative or core characteristics of groups of individuals—and instead aim to understand our publics' intersections of identities and experiences.[36] The end result should not be campaigns that avoid segmenting publics and messages entirely but rather campaigns that prioritize understanding and communicating with whole people rather than just one part of them at a time.

LEVERAGING YOUR ORGANIZATION'S STRENGTHS AND RESOURCES

In developing strategies, there is always value in identifying and leveraging the resources your organization has at its disposal to better connect with audiences and tell its story. Ragas and Culp refer to these broadly as "intangible assets," including an organization's vision and strategy, skilled management and employees, reputation, and brand value, as well as leadership in research and development.[37] From a rich history of community engagement to a new leader with a strong reputation, many organizations have people, products, policies, or successes that help them stand out from the crowd. These components of newsworthiness transcend specific or tactical opportunities and should be considered at the strategy development stage of the campaign planning process. Using PESO, practitioners can identify multiple tactics that could emanate from each asset.

Subject Matter Expertise

Issue-specific credibility, either from the organization's reputation or an individual spokesperson's reputation, can become a central element of many campaigns. For example, in a political environment where complex financial and investment regulations shift quickly, an organizational leader with a knack for explaining changes in easy-to-understand terms would add significant value to earned and shared media outreach. Armed with the right messaging, these opportunities could easily support related campaign objectives.

Imagery/Visuals

Knowing a particular campaign will generate or include strong, camera-ready visuals means strategies should maximize their use. A project with excellent photographic opportunities should absolutely be pitched to earned media (such as television and newspapers) that can take advantage, as well as shared through social media channels, such as Instagram, where they will have the most impact. Planning on-location events that make for easy media access (location, day, and time) allows journalists to capture these images, which makes content more newsworthy. Strategies could also ensure that post-event content, such as e-blasts or media relations outreach, take advantage of valuable visual elements.

ROBYN BECK/AFP/Getty Images

Major trade shows like the Consumer Electronics Show (CES) provide opportunities for communicators to make significant progress toward objectives with a variety of paid, earned, shared, and owned media strategies.

Dynamic Presenters/Personalities

Having a company spokesperson with a flair for public speaking and the experience to provide quotable, media-friendly content creates a strong opportunity for multiple earned, paid, and owned media opportunities (all of which can later be shared through additional social channels). It also could open the door for more in-person or digitally mediated events and programs. Positioning an organizational leader as a speaker at local, regional, or national conferences and events can provide a compelling and highly credible platform for sharing content in the service of organizational objectives.

Data

New studies, data, and statistics can provide fuel for multiple strategic directions, including earned media outreach based on newsworthy findings or using internal design capability to create compelling and shareable infographics. Depending on budget, departmental skill sets, and the relationship to the objectives at hand, practitioners can take full advantage of the growing media appetite for accessible data.

Organizational Vision or Narrative

A powerful story could encourage practitioners to choose channels and strategic approaches that allow for the best use of such content. Depending on the resources

©Andrew Toth/Getty Images for AWXII

Increased access to big data is fueling the growing field of data journalism, such as the work of Nate Silver and FiveThirtyEight.com, and creating new opportunities for PR practitioners to utilize data in their campaigns.

available, that could include creating a dedicated microsite to create a complete, owned version of the narrative (as a center for content that could be shared to multiple channels) or a proactive earned media campaign focused on outlets and reporters with the interest and bandwidth to value the story. If the story is more concise or delicate, it may be a better fit for paid media channels where the organization's message can be placed front and center.

History/Institutional Authority

An organization with deep community roots can leverage its historical impact as a campaign asset. For example, strategies can integrate current and historical content (such as classic black-and-white photographs, which can be used in all PESO media channels) as well as added clout and credibility for earned media. Both local and trade publication reporters see value in historical perspectives, particularly around milestone anniversaries and other timely events.

Of course, not all (or most) of these advantages would apply to individual objectives and individual strategies simultaneously. But organizations often underutilize and undervalue their inherently compelling resources and stories. Content generated across PESO channels should reflect a strategic approach that makes use of these potentially valuable assets.

THE COMPETITIVE LANDSCAPE

Previous chapters discussed several approaches to competitor analysis, including output-based analysis (studying an organization's messages), competitive media analysis (reviewing how media portray an organization to their audiences), and a SWOT analysis (outlining an organization's strengths, weaknesses, opportunities, and threats in a competitive context). These research processes can inform not only audience choices and creation of objectives but also the subsequent strategies and tactics.

Understand Competitors and External Challenges

Organizational competitors may be strong communicators or weak communicators across the board. More likely, they will have some areas of strength and other areas of weakness. For example, a manufacturer may have strong relationships with industry trade media, including earned and paid media, as well as a top-notch website, but lack a vibrant social media presence and relationships with local reporters. When setting a strategy, a competing manufacturer may decide that it is worth the extra effort to tackle the uphill battle of gaining coverage from industry trade publications, or it may decide that the untapped opportunities through social media offer a better use of company time and resources. Either way, the strategic choice should be informed by an understanding of the competitive landscape in the industry.

PRo Tip

POSITIONING CAMPAIGNS FOR MAXIMUM IMPACT

- **Put the audience first**: Smart strategies reflect their intended audience's knowledge, needs, preferences, and experiences.
- **Play to organizational strengths**: Winning strategies put the best messages forward using the most effective channels.
- **Be memorable**: Concise, unique strategies stand out in the memories of those who hear their messages.

Get more detail on winning strategies in the Appendix, p. 252.

Avoid What Everyone Else Is Already Doing

Organizations should seek distinctive strategies and messages to stand apart from competitors. If six companies are selling a similar product to a similar audience at the same conference, chances are that it will be difficult for customers to differentiate them from each other. If all six explain that they provide the highest quality product with the best service, built by the best team, consumers will have good reason for confusion. Particularly in a crowded market, when organizations use the same message or approach, they often cancel each other out. This rule applies as much to nonprofits angling for donors or members as for businesses seeking to grow revenue.

If a company sees that all of its competitors are on Facebook, but only one is on LinkedIn, that may signal an opportunity. Or, if Facebook is clearly the best channel to reach the desired audience, an organization can investigate *how* their competitors are using it: shared, sponsored/boosted, or paid content? How much interactivity are they generating? These and similar questions can point practitioners toward creating a strategy that distinguishes their organizations from the competition.

CONCLUSION

Effective campaign strategies never succeed because of a single channel, tactic, or message, but they can fail because of incorrect strategy. This chapter alone cannot teach budding practitioners to develop strategies, a skill that can only truly be honed through practice, but it can provide a toolkit for thinking strategically about channels, organizations, and audiences. It should remind all PR professionals that effective campaigns are built on research and investigation, rather than on instinct. In this way, communication departments and their leaders can enable and promote smart strategic choices in this crucial period of campaign development.

THINK CRITICALLY

1. Strategy is critical in PR planning. Discuss how effective strategies are developed.
2. What role does PESO play in PR?
3. How does a PR practitioner discover the right approach to strategic planning? What tools are used to effectively promote an organization? How does a practitioner consider multiple identities?
4. What does converged media allow PR practitioners to do?
5. How can the history a company possesses be leveraged in a strategic campaign?

KEY TERMS

Channel 130
Intersectionality 140
Newsworthiness 132
Uses and gratifications theory 136

CONCEPT CASE: CHANNEL SELECTION FOR POTENTIAL MEMBERS OF COMMUNITY FLOW YOGA

Based on its existing membership, Community Flow Yoga defines its core target demographic as individuals between twenty-five and forty-five years old who are physically active and community conscious.

Consideration #1

Consider both geographically targeted and general consumer (i.e., US national and international) media channels that would be appropriate to reach these demographic groups:

- Paid?
- Earned?
- Shared?
- Owned?
- Converged?

Consideration #2

Different channels—different environments to send and receive the messages—might dictate changes or tweaks in the core message being presented. Consider language, images, audio, and video as you answer the following questions.

- How might the messages be optimized for each of these selected channels?
- How might audiences interpret the message differently on different channels?

Consideration #3

As inclusion and diversity are core values for Community Flow Yoga, how might you adjust the selected channels above, or the messages within them, to give particular prominence and care to historically underrepresented groups?

- How might these considerations shift in different geographic locations?
    - Remember that this includes multiple US cities as well as Denmark and England.
- What steps could you take to include diverse publics in the planning of this content?

LONG-LASTING POSITIVE CHANGE: WASHINGTON UNIVERSITY IN ST. LOUIS

Washington University in St. Louis
Based on PRSA Silver Anvil Winner
Campaign Focus: Internal Communication

2014 was a crucial year for Washington University in St. Louis (WashU) as the university felt the eruption of tension between law enforcement and the local community. This long-simmering animosity between Black residents and police officers put the faculty, staff, and students of WashU, an elite, private university, in an unusual position as a neighbor and witness to significant violence and unrest. These events ultimately sparked the university's campaign to create a bridge between the university and the community. Through this plan of action, members from both parties were able to start and/or continue often uncomfortable conversations about diversity and inclusion that had yet to be expressed when being fully backed by a university. Years after the introduction of this campaign, WashU has continued to maintain the initial intent of their campaign successful, through expansion and continually updating the campaign as the underlying issues remain relevant.

On August 9, 2014, a Black teenager was shot and killed in Ferguson, Missouri, in an altercation with police. It was a tragic loss of life, which, under any circumstances, would have brought an outpouring of grief. But, beyond what anyone might have imagined, the event sparked an intense community and national response in which "Ferguson" became synonymous with police brutality, social injustice, economic disparity, and political disenfranchisement. Months of simmering public unrest followed, and the St. Louis region is still healing.[38] For WashU, the shooting and its aftermath cut deep. St. Louis has been home to the university for 165 years. The institution is a regional leader: when St. Louis hurts, Washington University in St. Louis hurts. Many of the faculty, students, and staff members have for decades been actively engaged in serving the extended St. Louis community to address social, economic, and educational disparities. Others, through their leading research, are experts in addressing the difficult issues that triggered public unrest.

At WashU, the shooting became a pivotal moment for the university community. Faculty, staff members, and students had been grappling with the difficult issues of diversity and inclusion. Several incidents on campus exposed serious racial divides. Students, in particular, were questioning the administration's commitment to achieving greater racial, ethnic, and socioeconomic diversity—it was even expressed as a top university priority. "Ferguson" had the potential to drive a wedge more deeply into the university community.

Research/Diagnosis

- ***Campus climate***: Through surveys of the faculty, students, and staff, an assessment was conducted regarding the sentiment about diversity and inclusion and how these issues play out in everyday lives. The results helped to better understand the problem and inform planning and execution.
- ***Others' experience***: Such issues are not uncommon on university campuses throughout the country. Through secondary research of universities' experiences—particularly among top tier peer institutions—WashU learned from others' best practices (and missteps).

- ***Academic experts***: A relevant database was compiled for the university's academic experts on diversity issues in a variety of fields. Representing all schools—including medicine, law, social work, art and architecture, business, and arts and sciences—these experts helped to frame dialogue on campus and brought important perspective to media coverage of "Ferguson" (and adding resonance with internal audiences).
- ***St. Louis Regional Disparities***: A landmark study conducted by WashU researchers and local partners detailed disparities in St. Louis, including Ferguson. *For the Sake of All: A Report on the Health and Well-Being of African Americans in St. Louis and Why It Matters for Everyone* helped to inform a response and has become an important resource for policymakers and community leaders working to strengthen the region post Ferguson.[39]
- **Diversity and Inclusion**: The killing of Michael Brown Jr. exacerbated the divide between law enforcement and the community. Historically, police officers have been known to target people of color and more often, Black people. Hedwig Lee, of Washington University in St. Louis's Department of Sociology, along with two other professors from separate universities conducted a study that measured the risk of being killed by a police officer in the US. The researchers used verified data on police killings from 2013 to 2018 compiled by the website Fatal Encounters, created by Nevada-based journalist D. Brian Burghart. Under their models, they found that roughly 1 in 1,000 Black boys and men will be killed by police in their lifetime. For White boys and men, the rate is 39 out of 100,000.[40]
- WashU increased efforts to cover the vast sections and intersections that define diversity. This is done online and on campus through databases, forums, events, and speakers, to name a few.

Objectives

WashU faced a crisis and had to manage it. But the university had the opportunity to do much more. It could turn this tragedy into a force for positive change. Through "Ferguson," the university was determined to find and amplify WashU's voice: to help this institution "do better and be better."

The university created a bridge between the institution and the community by working together to create a collection of content including images, stories, artifacts, and so on that defines and allows space for the surrounding area's thoughts to be included.

Strategies

In addition to relying on detailed and regularly updated crisis plans, the initiative stayed on track using the following strategies:

- *Checklists, timelines, and tactical roadmap*: Because events unfolded so quickly and the effort easily could have been overtaken by reactive crisis management needs, planning was essential. A detailed step-by-step, scenario-by-scenario roadmap guided the work and focused on core objectives.
- *Messaging*: Volatile, divisive issues had to be managed. Sensitivity and understanding had to be conveyed. Confidence had to be instilled in those worried about safety on and around campus. To strike the right balance, WashU developed a strong message matrix and pulled it through all communications. A call to action ("do better and be better")

framed this experience and set the stage for a long-term effort.

- *Media targets*: The media relations team created a targeted list of traditional and nontraditional media contacts leading/influencing coverage of Ferguson and pitched academic experts as informed local sources.
- *Events, shows/plays, and funding*: For six years, WashU has continued to foster the St. Louis/Ferguson community by supporting faculty and community-based endeavors that used events, arts, and creativity to bring diverse stakeholders together. This includes the Ferguson Academic Seed Foundation, book talk series, plays held by community organizations and speakers.

Tactics and Implementation

Integrated efforts were aimed at (1) engaging the university community in open and meaningful dialogue about race and racism; (2) demonstrating WashU's leadership on important issues; and (3) when necessary, keeping the faculty, staff, and students informed and safe, without feeding into the heated rhetoric fueling public unrest. The primary tactical components included the following:

Earned + Shared

- *WashU Experts*: A diverse group of WashU thought leaders were identified with expertise in a range of related topics and they proactively pitched to local and national media covering Ferguson. From criminal justice, to the history of race relations, the social construct of race, health/educational/economic disparities, the influence of media, and more—the experts contributed important context and helped frame the debate. On the WashU campus and far beyond it, their input opened minds to the complexity of the issues and potential solutions.
- *Executive communication*: Communication from university leadership had to convey empathy, challenge the community to become stronger, and maintain calm even as the region erupted with protests. It was a difficult balancing act, particularly given the range of audiences and history on the issues of race and racism. Parents wanted to know their children were safe; students wanted to know the university cared. Staff members working just blocks away from protest activity needed to be reassured; students and faculty engaged in protests wanted to feel supported. No single message, messenger, or channel would be sufficient.
- *#WashUVoices*: The use of a shared hashtag was encouraged to connect social media efforts and conversations.
- *#InSTLProject* is a hashtag that was created by the university in 2019 for the fifth-year anniversary of Mike Brown's death. In St. Louis is a project of Washington University's Academy for Diversity, Equity, and Inclusion, in partnership with the Office of Public Affairs.[41]

Owned

- *Voices.wustl.edu*: Within days of the shooting, the university launched *WashU Voices*, a digital gathering place to inspire and motivate conversation and engagement. Despite the inherent risks, *WashU Voices* became the place where differences of opinion were not only shared but also celebrated. On the WashU website (https://voices.wustl.edu/) tabs titled "Do Something," "In the News," and "Resources" were established to provide students various outlets of information. A blog "Perspectives"—to which students, faculty, and staff members submitted personal thoughts—opened hearts and minds to others' everyday realities. A social media feed provided a real-time capture of perspectives. For those who wanted to take action, "Do Something" was a clearinghouse for opportunities to engage in activities on campus and throughout the region. "In the News" captured the breadth of the thought leadership on issues underlying the public unrest. When necessary, "Resources" was used to keep the community informed of safety concerns and support services, rather than elevate fear by broadcasting via the crisis communications/emergency channels. Scheduled 7 a.m., noon, and 4 p.m. updates were particularly helpful for parents who were watching events unfold from afar.

©Washington Universityandresr

Day of Discovery and Dialogue on Race and Ethnicity: In early February 2015, a first-ever, daylong series of conversations among students, faculty, and staff members was convened. The structure was intentionally unconventional to empower open and honest dialogue. Through small group gatherings, large forums, a livestream, social media–based conversation, and artistic expression, a comfortable way for members of the community to participate was created—knowing different people would have different needs.

This two-day event has been held annually since its creation, with various themes including the focus on inclusion, finding common ground, staying resilient in challenging times, dialogues across difference and most recently, conversations that inspire action long after the event is over. This event is made more accessible through a livestream and allows further conversations held digitally through #WashUVoices.

STL university leaders, @ChancellorWU on right, work to find common ground for campus diversity. Day of Discovery & Dialogue. #WashUVoices

10:25 AM - 23 Feb 2017

3 Retweets 14 Likes

1 3 14

Twitter via @WUSTLnews

"Documenting Ferguson": The WashU library created the only complete archive of the "Ferguson" experience—on and off campus—to provide historical documentation of events but also, more importantly, as an ongoing resource for those involved in finding solutions and strengthening the university and the region.

- ***American Civil Liberties Union of Missouri Archive Internship***: As part of an ongoing project between the Washington University Libraries' Julian Edison Department of Special Collections and the ACLU of Missouri, student interns are reviewing the ACLU-MO's archived records for themes, important historic turning points, and other notable moments in the organization's nearly-hundred-year history. The project began in 2017 and is expected to continue through 2020.[42]

Reporting

In just a few months, WashU successfully managed a serious crisis, transformed the tone and tenor of conversation on campus, and gained momentum for a long-term effort toward a more inclusive community:

- *Voices.wustl.edu* has proven to be a powerful gathering place. In its first five months, the site had 37,527 unique visitors; 143,000 page views; and 62,000 sessions. Noticeable peaks occurred during milestone events and when the site was featured through other communications.
- ***#WashUVoices*** was widely used over the initial three months with more than 26,000 social media engagements, 2,893 interactions on Twitter, and 60+ images shared on Instagram. Tweets by 380+ users generated an estimated 3.4 million impressions.
- ***WashU Experts*** deeply penetrated media coverage, with 330+ stories appearing with WashU commentary and representing a potential audience of 834.4 million; 74 percent of the coverage ran beyond the St. Louis market.
- ***Executive communication*** became an important rallying point. An end-of-year message from the university chancellor reflecting on "Ferguson" and calling for continued effort is widely recognized as groundbreaking.
- ***Day of Discovery and Dialogue*** drew far greater engagement than expected, with 822 faculty, staff members, and students registering for one or more live sessions; and 2,141 participating remotely via live stream and 9,500 social media feed engagements. The event elicited a favorable response from all constituent groups. In 2020, the weekend of the event garnered a social media reach of 7600.
- The ***Documenting Ferguson archive*** already has been accessed by 14,054 unique visitors from around the world as of the 2015 submission date for the PRSA Silver Anvil Awards.
- The **#BlackLivesMatter** hashtag appeared an average of 58,747 times per day in the roughly three weeks following Brown's death, in 2014. This increased to 172,772 times three months after when the officer involved in Brown's death was not indicted. The hashtag was then used 1.7 million times during the subsequent three weeks.[43]

Theories

WashU's campaign exemplifies three theoretical frameworks: systems theory, two-step flow theory, and framing theory. Systems theory is about the organization's interactions with its environment. In this case, the university saw significant changes happening around it and chose to engage rather than simply react. This awareness and proactive approach resonated with internal and external publics. The two-step flow asserts that information from the media moves in two distinct stages.[44] In this case the opinion leaders are the university as they collect information and media content to add to their resources library on their website, which serves to be passed on to the

Joe Madison
@MadisonSiriusXM

Follow

An American Conversation: On Campus Protest to Progress - Lori White & Adrienne Davis #momentormovement #washuvoices

4:41 AM - 4 Mar 2016

4 Retweets 5 Likes

4 5

Twitter via @MadisonSiriusXM

individuals that view this information. WashU has had and continues to have a large impact on how individuals perceive the aftermath of Ferguson after Brown's killing based on the university's continued efforts to provide current information.

From a framing perspective, the university saw the impact of local and national media attention to Ferguson and carefully worked to present and provide information that pointed toward specific elements' importance, positioning the university as a local leader willing to tackle important shared challenges. Through a variety of spokespersons, WashU continued to add its voice to the conversation within the St. Louis community, emphasizing the importance and relevance of its expertise and involvement. In this way, they pointed publics (including journalists) toward vital, engaging, and reputable information.[45]

Model

WashU engaged deeply with publics at each stage in the process and was open to criticism, reflection, and change as circumstances shifted. The open, back-and-forth approach is particularly valuable when considering internal publics whose buy-in and influence should be part of organizational decision-making processes.[46]

Diversity- and Inclusion-First Approach

Diversity, equity, and inclusion were central to the planning and execution of this campaign. It is clear that the university valued the importance of DEI on their campus. What started out as an initial response to community events has become part of the DNA of their campus.

Tactics

8

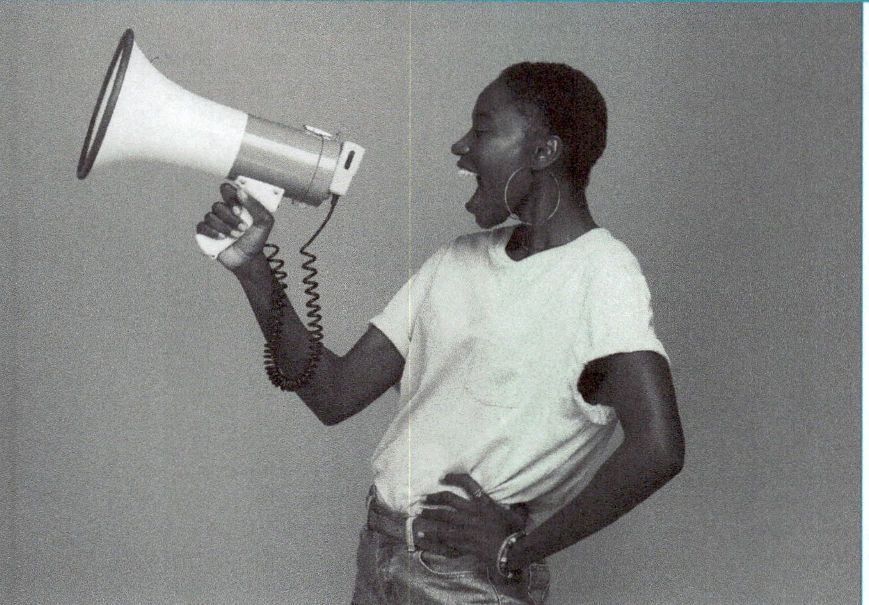

iStock.com/People Images

THINK AHEAD

8.1 Apply the PESO model to selecting public relations tactics.

8.2 Develop inclusive messaging based on objectives and strategies to the best-fit tactics.

After an organization agrees on the strategies to support its objectives, it is up to the public relations team to develop the required tactical approaches for implementing the overall plan. Strategies often broadly define the channel for outreach but not necessarily the specific news media outlets, social media channels, or owned media properties to target or use. Tactics reflect the narrow audiences and focused messages that serve as the building blocks of successful campaigns. Often, practitioners and organizational leaders fall into the trap of moving straight to tactics without first establishing broader objectives and strategies. Without this framework, it is difficult to make the necessary practical and creative decisions that tactics demand or to measure their effectiveness.

Tactics do not exist in isolation. They work together to support objectives and strategies, target audiences, reinforce messages, and tell stories. Regular outreach and conversation using Twitter may be a valuable part of achieving an objective related to stronger customer, donor, or member engagement for an organization, but it cannot succeed by itself. Complimentary tactics may also include earned media outreach, for reach and credibility, and owned media content on the website for deeper information and conversion. Strategies may point toward paid tactics such as building a conference presence for more one-on-one connections, earned tactics like positive media coverage in relevant publications, and owned tactics including an email newsletter. The power of the PESO model comes from the perspective it provides: allowing practitioners to see the wide range of possible tactics to implement.

PRo Tip

CRAFTING EFFECTIVE MESSAGING

Professional communicators craft campaign **messaging** based on incorporating a variety of research findings, audience knowledge, and clear focus on the campaign's most important goal.

1. **Build internal consensus for the overarching campaign message**: Campaigns should have a concise, singular message that carries through all strategies, tactics, and targeted submessages.
2. **Identify segmented publics**: Clarify and prioritize the publics with whom your campaign will communicate.
3. **Develop targeted submessages**: Effective messages should reflect the following criteria:

   Driven by organizational and communication goals: Messages must clearly support and connect to the broader goals of the campaign.

   Reflective of the overarching campaign message: Often submessages are secondary to overarching messages in specific tactics and materials for distinct audiences.

   Supported by audience research: Understanding each audience's interests, habits, channel consumption, and connection to the campaign is critical for crafting messages that resonate.

   Memorable: Messages that stick with audiences are concise, creative, and clearly relevant to their lives.
4. **Pretest overall and submessages**: As communicators, we do our best to put ourselves in the shoes of our publics, but there is no substitute for sharing these messages with publics and gathering feedback for improvement.

TACTICAL APPROACHES

Developing an understanding of multiple paid, earned, shared, and owned media approaches provides practitioners options for selecting the best set of tactics given the situation at hand. The larger your toolbox of tactical skills, the more possibilities you have on the table. That said, there is a difference between understanding the important features and benefits of a given tactic and being able to execute it. Some practitioners specialize in one area where their passion rests, while others have broader knowledge of many different approaches. Practitioners at large organizations tend to be more differentiated and specialized, while smaller organizations need more generalists who can tackle a wider variety of work.[1] All practitioners must identify the right balance between spending their time perfecting their skills for specific tactics and expanding their knowledge. Practitioners should know their comfort level with executing individual tactics and ask for support when needed.

This chapter should not be considered an in-depth overview of all public relations and marketing communication tactics. Instead, its goal is to summarize the key considerations for the core components of the PESO model. Numerous additional resources and references have also been provided in the appendix for those interested in additional details and insights related to specific tactics.

Paid Media

Communication and public relations departments often oversee paid media strategies that work to promote specific, controlled company messages that are delivered to key audiences. Paid approaches come in many shapes and sizes, as well as with wide variation in both initial and ongoing costs. This approach can be particularly useful when a message must target an audience at a specific time, when a message may not be inherently newsworthy (and thus not a good candidate for media relations outreach), or when it must be framed by exact wording or visual tone. Launching a new product, for example, often entails a timing schedule and brand (language, colors, logo, and so on) that advertising can deliver. Many paid outreach approaches require professionals who specialize in such work (advertising, digital marketing, video production, and so on), with organizations generally using agencies or other outside contracts when executing these projects.

Timing

Some paid media opportunities may need months of lead time in order to purchase ad space and produce content. Others, such as paid search advertising, can launch within a matter of days. Each project requires the organization to secure their *space* (such as airtime, digital real estate, or the literal space on a billboard) and to decide what type of message to place within it. The simplest digital display or print advertisements can be created in a matter of hours by expert graphic designers, while large-scale video

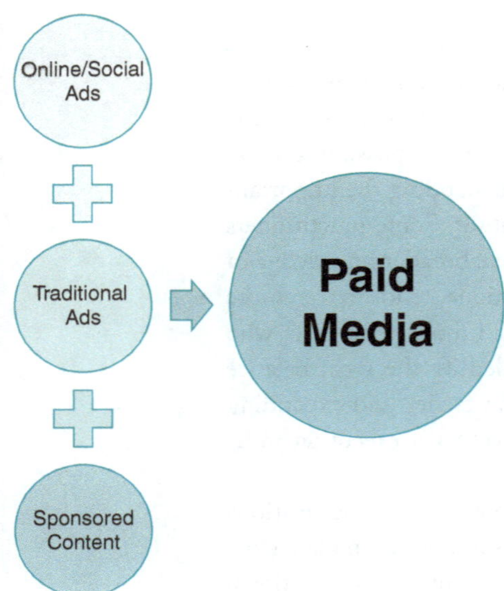

production can easily take months. Advertisers running longer campaigns often schedule using "waves," condensing an ad spend into shorter periods with breaks to increase penetration and retention of information.[2]

Budget

Some paid mediums are more scalable than others. A national television advertisement may cost tens or hundreds of thousands of dollars to produce—not including potentially millions of dollars for national air-time—while a specifically targeted digital display or paid social media campaign could certainly be successful for less than $1,000. The cost of ads in any specific market is dependent on its population size and the viewership/readership/listenership of the individual media channel or location where the ads will be purchased.

Messaging

Paid media often contain the most organization-focused messages. Because there is no outside editorial control, the organization maintains nearly complete decision-making power over the message itself.

Content Creation

Messaging in paid media often leans toward being simple and memorable. Since the audience is not necessarily seeking out these messages, they are designed to grab attention.

Advertising. Advertising in traditional and digital forms remains a key outreach opportunity for organizations and an important revenue generator for media today.[3] The rise of digital advertising has only increased the sophistication and targeting focus available for organizations. As public relations professionals, paid advertising is generally not the center of our work, but it should not go unrecognized as a way to reach specific audiences with specific messages, particularly with time-sensitive or less-newsworthy messages.

In advertising and the subfield of media planning, each potential opportunity should be evaluated based on the target audience demographics and how well they would overlap with the advertising options available to reach them. This includes demographics, habits, and lifestyle.[4] The media options themselves differ according to cost, efficiency, reach, frequency, irritation factor, and complexity. For example, an event awareness campaign must decide whether including more details about the campaign justifies the added cost of a longer or larger advertisement, as well as whether the intended audience would pay attention long enough to digest the additional information.

In evaluating their options, practitioners often start by selecting among broadcast media (such as radio and television), print media (such as newspapers and magazines),

PRo Tip

TYPES OF ADVERTISING

Traditional

- **Event Sponsorship**: Organizations regularly sponsor targeted industry or community events for additional visibility. The flexibility of price and variety of sponsorship opportunities makes this a popular approach.
- **Outdoor**: Billboards can be a price-friendly way to share repeated messages within a specific community or communities.
- **Print**: Newspapers, magazines, and trade publications offer a wide variety of options for selecting specific audiences that fit your campaign.
- **Radio**: Radio—national and local, for-profit, or through NPR—still maintains a strong presence in many Americans' lives, particularly during the *drive time* commuting hours. This continues to make radio a relevant option for reaching metro areas.
- **TV**: Television has higher advertising production costs but offers a wide variety of channel-specific, audience-specific, and time-specific segmentation options.

Digital

- **Digital Display**: Digital banner or billboard advertisements, generally on high-traffic websites and pages in high-visibility locations link back to relevant pages on an organization's website.
- **Digital Video**: Many popular websites, such as YouTube, offer video ads that can be targeted using a variety of content-based or geographic factors.
- **SEM**: Search-engine marketing (SEM) allows organizations to pay search engines directly so that ads pop up when specific terminology is typed in.
- **Social media**: Social media channels offer a variety of advertising options, from the strictly paid (such as sidebar display ads) to more *converged media* such as boosted posts or native advertising and other types of in-feed content.

Practitioners should also keep in mind that traditional media (newspapers, radio, and TV) have as many, if not more opportunities, for advertising as part of their digital properties as in their traditional formats.

For more information on advertising types, please see the Appendix, p. 253.

and digital media (such as online display advertising). Keep in mind that the lines between these media types have continued to blur, as newspapers regularly produce video, digital-only media outlets generate highly credible "print" journalism, and television stations offer advertising on their websites and mobile apps. Despite that, the rules for effective advertising in each of these formats have largely endured.

Advertorial Content. Advertorial content is a growing subset of paid media, where news organizations include advertiser-supplied stories in the same form as their usual articles but mark them as *paid*, *sponsored*, or *advertiser-supplied.* These opportunities exist in print, broadcast, and digital. In most cases, the content is very clearly marked as paid. In others, the labeling is less obvious, and readers unfamiliar with such practices may not be aware that the content has been created without the usual reporting and editing process and that the content should not carry the same tacit endorsement as the media outlet's standard news product. Due to these potential gray areas, practitioners should be cautious when using advertorial tactics. From a credibility perspective, it is always preferable to leverage traditional earned media channels first before turning to paid opportunities. The worst-possible situation would be for an organization to be perceived as attempting to deceive an audience. Some media outlets' lack of clear labeling for advertorial content makes this a concern.

Earned Media

Earned media covers tactics where the public relations practitioner must assist in adding value (in the form of *information subsidies*) to a news- or story-generation process, including media relations, blogger outreach, and organic search strategies.[5] By working with journalists and bloggers, public relations professionals help their organizations participate in public conversations about issues and share content that is of interest to specific audiences. Simply improving search engine optimization (SEO) may also be considered an earned strategy. Because these tactics are **uncontrolled**, they bring significant additional credibility for organizations, but participation may also bring additional risk due to a lack of messaging control.

While different skills and customs are required to negotiate media relations, blogger relations, and SEO, they all require an understanding of multiple layers of communication: the initial audience (journalist, blogger, or algorithm) and the final audience (such as consumers, community members, or potential employees). Successful public relations professionals perfect the processes of working with earned media gatekeepers. This allows them to successfully build relationships to improve their understanding of news generation, better the organization's knowledge of the relevant media environment, and, ultimately, shape the organization's decision making to better reflect the needs of its publics.

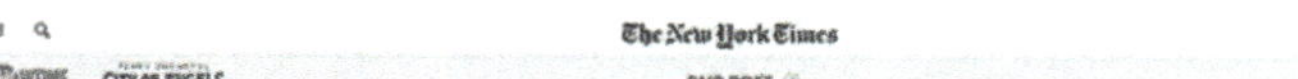

REFORMING THE CITY OF ANGELS

A RESTAURATEUR BATTLED CORRUPTION IN DEPRESSION-ERA LOS ANGELES AND WON. WHO WILL STEP UP NOW?

BEULAH RAYMOND, WHO WAS AT A NEIGHBOR'S HOUSE, feared the worst for her husband. But somehow, he had survived. At the hospital, while surgeons pried metal shards from his muscles, splinted broken bones and stitched his wounds, Raymond was tight-lipped with the detectives. He didn't trust them and was angry at himself for forgetting to check under the car, a routine he'd picked up ever since Beulah spied a prowler in their backyard.

"I know who did this," he told the officers. "I'll take care of the investigation in my own way."

Clifford Clinton, the owner of the popular Clifton's Cafeteria chain, went to Raymond's bedside in the recovery room, where the two were photographed. A self-styled political reformer who conducted his own investigations to uncover government corruption, Clinton was already well respected by the public. He made sure reporters knew that organized crime had tried to assassinate Raymond for getting too close to exposing the truth. The bombing was front-page news the next day — and within months, brought down the political establishment.

A Clifton's Cafeteria postcard circa 1950 features the southbound Harbor Freeway approach to Downtown Los Angeles. Opened in 1931, the Pacific Seas branch was the city's first Clifton's location. PHOTOS BY DON CLINTON.

Even venerable media outlets such as the *New York Times* sell digital space for sponsored content or advertorials, such as this Showtime series, that mimic some of the design characteristics of editorial content.

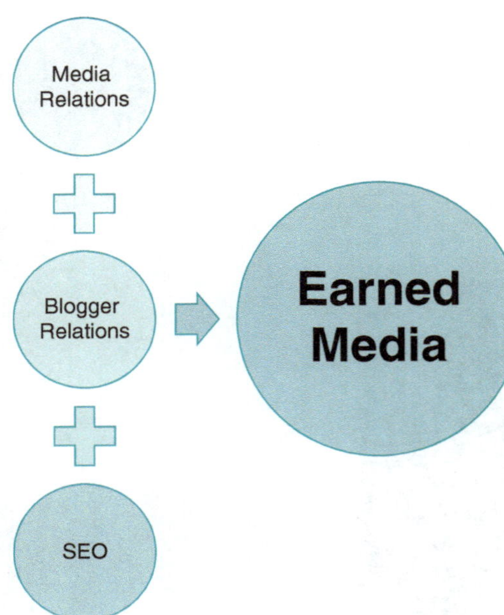

Timing

Earned tactics lack the highly controlled timelines of many paid strategies. Successful proactive media and blogger outreach often requires weeks or months of planning, while search-related web strategies can take months to fully achieve their intent after implementation. Even then, it may be difficult or impossible to guarantee specific timing given the lack of control over, for example, media and journalistic processes or search algorithms.

Budget

By definition, earned media strategies do not require payment for the final product but certainly should include costs for the professional time required for implementation and evaluation.

Messaging

Unlike paid strategies where organizations have full control of the messaging used in each tactic, earned media outreach implies that practitioners only control what their organizations share, not the final product. To meet the needs of news organizations, there is often more variation in what's being shared with individual media outlets. For example, a practitioner can proactively secure an interview on a specific topic with their organization's CEO and an industry trade reporter. They can prepare tailored talking points for the CEO and a fact sheet for the reporter. They can manage a preinterview run-through of the potential questions and answers with the CEO. But the final decisions about the questions and the content used in the article are made solely by the journalist and his or her editors. The CEO may provide eight answers that clearly reflect a specific organizational message and one that does not. The reporter is fully titled to use the ninth response.

Content Creation

As mentioned, the content in an earned media situation is determined by the needs of the reporter, blogger, or the key search terms that an organization is hoping to capitalize on. In earned media, the input content is never the final content. The most successful practitioners should anticipate the needs of those they are creating content for, both inside and outside the organization, and employ such tactics in a way that is mutually beneficial.

iStock.com/seb_ra

Media relations tactics may include those targeted at print, broadcast, or digital media. Today's user consumes media via traditional newspapers, mobile devices, or computers.

PRo Tip

MEDIA RELATIONS TOOLS

- **Bylined articles/op-ed pieces**: Content written by individuals or on behalf of organizations then submitted, reviewed, and (hopefully) published by media outlets; bylined articles are "earned" because they go through an editorial approval process on the publication side
- **Media advisories/media alerts**: Event-specific, bulleted documents that provide the *who*, *what*, *when*, *where*, *why* of media-friendly activities
- **Press conferences**: Inviting multiple journalists to participate in the same conversation and ask questions together; can be held in person or virtually
- **Press releases/news releases**: The ubiquitous, traditional document for releasing a news item in a nonsegmented manner, including key information journalists need to complete a story

For more information on media relations tactics, please see the Appendix, p. 255.

Media Relations. The traditional core of earned media is media relations. The Public Relations Society of America (PRSA) defines this function as "mutually beneficial associations between publicists or public relations professionals and members of media organizations as a condition for reaching audiences with messages of news or features of interest."[6] Media relations comes from the needs of public relations practitioners communicating on behalf of organizations' and journalists' needs to share newsworthy content with audiences. While a journalist's mandate is to provide newsworthy information to a specific public (defined geographically, demographically, or by shared interest), public relations practitioners should be able to see where their organizations would be able to offer value for a journalist's audience. Is a company hiring local workers? Did a nonprofit start a new partnership to connect artists with local elementary students? These items create both compelling company news and valuable information for local consumer reporters. The former would be more valuable for media and may include detailed information about the company's growth trajectory, revenue, and access to executives for additional comments. The latter would be more valuable if accompanied by photos and anecdotal stories about the participating students and artists.

This proactive approach can be called media relations' *publicity* function. **Publicity** is "information provided by an outside source this is used by media because the

PRo Tip

GUIDELINES FOR MAJOR MEDIA EVENTS

In *On Deadline: Managing Media Relations*, authors Carole Howard and Wilma Mathews provide four major reminders for those planning media-focused events.[7]

1. Events should support an organization's brand and be approved by key constituencies within the organization.
2. Invite relevant community leaders: Mayors love to attend new business openings. Even if they are unable to attend, it reminds them of the positive impact on the community.
3. Spokespersons should be chosen carefully. All should be able to speak concisely, stay on message, and be available for reporter questions after their formal remarks.
4. Don't waste time on every detail. Events can become all consuming, and public relations practitioners should maintain their focus on the media-relevant portion while delegating other tasks, such as decorations, food, and other logistics.

Source: Carole Howard and Wilma Mathews, *On Deadline: Managing Media Relations* (Long Grove, IL: Waveland Press, 2013), 129–30.

information has news value."[8] By providing useful information to journalists, media relations professionals create **information subsidies**, reducing the workload of reporters and editors by compiling data, sources, images, and video.[9] At its core, publicity allows organizations to be more visible to their publics. It supports a variety of campaigns, including sales and marketing efforts, community relations, and, when necessary, crisis communication.

Shared Media

Social media outreach has emerged since the mid-2000s as a critical, valuable, and exciting tactic that has become a staple in the public relations toolbox. In many organizations, public relations play a leading role in social media strategy, tactics, and execution. In *The Social Media Bible*, Safko describes the "Social Media Trinity" as blogs, microblogs (such as Twitter), and social networks (such as Facebook and LinkedIn).[10] While not every campaign that integrates social media needs to use all three, the potential impact of each should be considered.

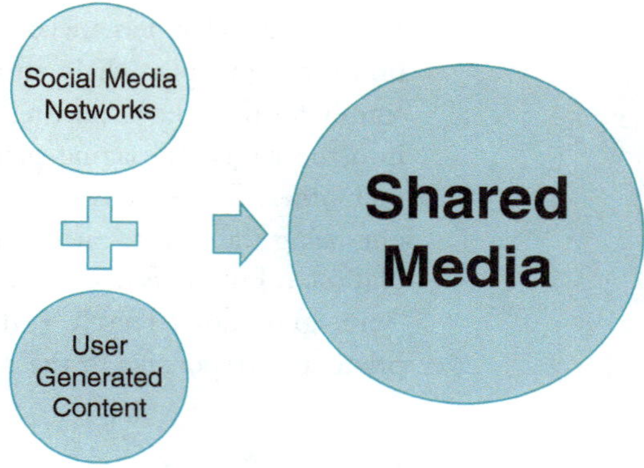

Timing

Social media can be instantaneous, making it both a useful mechanism for immediate response and a significant organizational challenge to monitor. With this in mind, each channel has its own cadence, with Twitter and Snapchat measuring time in seconds, while LinkedIn promotes content over a much longer timeline. The specific timing for any social media campaign can vary widely depending on both the channel and the audience.

Budget

While social media can include a paid component, most platforms allow for organizations to create profiles and participate in conversations for free. The challenge is typically the time required to create content, monitor channels, manage profiles, and respond, sometimes around the clock. As big brands condition consumers to treat social media profiles as customer service channels, organizations must acknowledge the commitment necessary to maintain channels, both during and after campaign-related activity. Additionally, creating a corporate blog can and should require a design and coding investment both for a professional appearance and to ensure that it has the desired functionality and smooth integration with the organization's main site.

Messaging

Social media messages are as diverse as the organizations that create them. Unlike earned media outreach, which generally stays within the messaging boundaries of the targeted media outlet, the direct-to-consumer social media environment provides more freedom to embrace a brand's voice. Its public nature means that messages may need to speak to multiple audiences simultaneously.

Content Creation

Social media channels are constantly hungry for content. Successful practitioners focus, prioritize, and plan their efforts to ensure they are not creating content ad hoc or simply for the sake of posting. As part of a campaign, every piece of content should fit into the larger messaging picture, and efforts on multiple channels should reinforce each other. There are two schools of thought in terms of the **content creation** process, one being the "create once, publish everywhere" (C.O.P.E.) approach, popularized by National Public Radio,[11] and the other, typified in the book *Content Rules* is "reimagine, don't recycle"—stressing the importance of making the message appropriate and responsive to the needs of each channel.[12]

Owned Media

The final and most **controlled** category of content is owned media. This includes traditional marketing collateral including brochures, newsletters, and even embossed organizational logo key chains. Owned media also stretches deep into digital territory to cover organizational websites, corporate videos, many mobile apps, and e-newsletters.

PRo Tip

SOCIAL MEDIA TACTICS

As an example, LinkedIn's function will be used here to demonstrate how one network can fulfill a variety of functions or tactics in the shared media universe.

- **Blogging**: Many professionals and organizations use LinkedIn to share content from their external blogs. The blog functions as a **content hub** while the network acts to spread the content beyond those who would visit the individual blog or organizational website.
- **Community management**: Many organizations host, curate, or participate in a variety

of digital communities, such as employee or alumni LinkedIn groups, which facilitate the sharing of information among those with similar interests.

- **Microblogging**: Individuals and organizations share specific timely, interesting, or valuable information in short posts to their followers, friends, or (on LinkedIn) connections.
- **Networking**: Social media can be used to build relationships at an individual level in ways that can benefit organizations, such as LinkedIn's connections, as well as for organizations to gain followers, opening the door for relationships and continued conversations.

For more information on social media tactics, please see the Appendix, p. 257.

Timing

Full website design and development can take many months depending on the size and functionality. However, day-to-day content updates can be made nearly instantaneously. The creation of other types of collateral materials involves a design phase and a production phase. Often, production and printing (particularly through external vendors) can be the lengthiest part of the process.

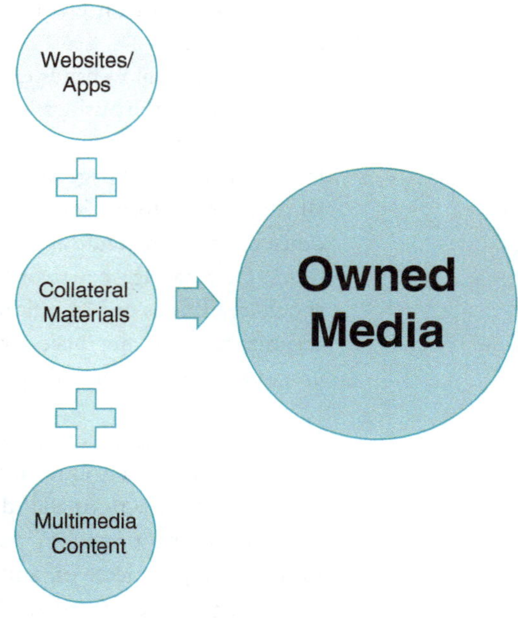

Budget

While the entry-level cost for a website is dropping, most organizations should spend a sizable amount of their budget to create a site that will solve more problems than it causes. Additionally, ongoing website maintenance and updates are critical to include in any budget. Some organizations work with the assumption that a website has a two-year life span and that websites have a two-year development process, moving the website from a project to an ongoing cost of business. Collateral material production costs (and quality) vary widely based on the content.

Messaging

An organization's collateral materials must have clearly defined audiences and messages geared toward those audiences. The danger of these types of materials, as opposed to Twitter, for example, is the tendency to overload them with content and messaging. Messages must be prioritized, organized, and distilled as much as possible. Content must be scannable and navigable so that audiences can quickly find what they need.

Content Creation

For owned media, wherein a significant component of the cost supports production, the act of making a single change can lead to reprinting or redesigning. It is critical to ensure agreement on all content early in the process.

Website Content Management. Organizational websites are nonnegotiable in today's online business world. They are a foundational piece of credibility and are one of the first places any new stakeholder goes to learn about the organization, take actions such as purchasing products, download content, or renew a membership. Campaigns often seek a form of **conversion**, an action such as buying an event ticket or signing up for an email list as an objective, and websites are often where such tactics occur.

Organizational websites exist prior to, during, and after campaigns, and integration should support the business's overarching purpose and message. Campaigns often need a temporary online home as part of this digital presence. This could present itself in the form of a dedicated page or section of the website or a separate microsite that integrates all campaign information and functions, often serving as a place to drive traffic from other digital and traditional channels. Organizational websites also provide opportunities for rotating, newsworthy content as part of their homepage, and campaigns should see this as one significant opportunity to draw in users who are interested in the organization but not necessarily the campaign. Similarly, they can point interested users to dedicated campaign information.

Marketing. PRSA defines marketing as "the management function that identifies human needs and wants, offers products and services to satisfy those demands, and causes transactions that deliver products and services in exchange for something of value to the provider."[13] Many public relation activities are closely connected to marketing objectives and are often underused toward marketing ends. For example, positive earned media coverage should be shared with key organizational publics. This could include integrating the media coverage into paid/**boosted content** shared via social media channels, e-newsletters, or even traditional printed brochures.

Publications. Organizations develop a wide variety of print and digital publications that serve both to distribute content and provide audiences the chance to browse a wider breadth of stories that they may otherwise not be exposed to. The bar for content creation in such outlets is high since the information must be both valuable and interesting to readers. Publications come in several varieties, including recurring *serial publications* like newsletters (print and digital), organizational magazines, and annual reports.[14] Newsletters and magazines, even in print form, are still a popular form of organizational communication and represent an accessible way to share information both within and outside of a campaign structure. While design and production costs vary greatly, particularly when printing and mailing are involved, many organizations still see the value for member/donor outreach, sales and marketing, and event promotion. Many organizations adapt the content produced for such publications for digital purposes. Digital versions of publications, often distributed via email distribution services such as MailChimp, have the advantage of metrics tracking the stories and links that are most popular. Practitioners can use this information to improve story selection, multimedia content, and writing for future issues. The effectiveness of these publications is dependent on having an up-to-date mailing or email distribution list.

Stand-alone (nonrecurring or nonscheduled) publications include e-blasts, reprints, reports, and whitepapers, as well as brochures and flyers. E-blasts are often used to alert specific audiences about more immediately newsworthy content and are timed around the specific event rather than on a weekly, monthly, or quarterly schedule. Reprints are designed versions of media articles that can be repurposed for print or digital use.[15] Copyright law's fair-use provisions provide for some internal and educational use of reprints, but public dissemination generally must be approved and paid for by the media outlet itself. Reports encompass a variety of documents from public-facing research whitepapers (which can be written and disseminated on campaign-specific topics) to customer- or member-focused reports on key organizational issues. Generally, the purpose of such reports is to inform the audience in detail on a specific topic or to provide information tailored for a specific time, event, or campaign. Similarly, fewer organizations have a comprehensive brochure about their work, but many have maintained product- or program-specific brochures. Brochures are made up of folding panels, in contrast to flyers or sales sheets, which often accomplish the same narrowly focused purpose but on a flat piece of paper.[16] One advantage to flyers and sales sheets is that they can be printed easily in-house, although the quality, particularly with color images and photos, often suffers.

An increasingly popular format is that of the infographic, which uses a mix of symbolic imagery and language to represent specific concepts. On one end of the spectrum, infographics can be built as a more detailed version of traditional charts and graphs or process representations. In the extreme, they tend to lean more toward a heavily image-driven approach. The most effective infographics are often the product of collaboration between writers and designers, leading to an output that is both rich in information and easy to understand.

PRo Tip

OWNED MEDIA TACTICS

- **Apps**: Many organizations develop branded mobile applications for consumers, members, event attendees, or other audiences to create a cohesive, branded experience for them.
- **Collateral materials**: Additional materials can be developed for both digital and traditional uses, either as stand-alone pieces or as part of a broader event or campaign. These can range from a variety of branded logo items to trade show booths that represent the business focus. This can expand to a variety of posters and banners ranging from small easel-mounted foam core pieces to specialty printed banners that take up an entire side of a building.
- **Corporate video**: Video allows organizations to tell stories in a gripping and compelling way and is often used on websites and at corporate events, as well as through shared media (social media).
- **E-newsletters**: Digital tools such as Constant Contact and MailChimp have made designing and distributing e-newsletters easier than ever before. These are often image-rich, link-heavy, trackable formats that allow organizations to point readers toward a variety of compelling content and see what they respond to through analytics.
- **Events (hosted)**: By hosting events, organizations can create wholly managed experiences for publics including members, donors, and key stakeholders inside and outside the organization.
- **Infographics**: Infographics use images, icons, and colorful, easy-to-understand graphs and charts to represent data in accessible ways. Their user friendly nature makes them a great fit to share through earned and social media.
- **Publications**: Traditional printed magazines, newsletters, and brochures are becoming more rare due to the low cost of digital editions, but this has created an opportunity. Organizations still willing to invest in the design and printing of high-quality hard-copy materials may be able to stand apart from others in their industries.
- **Website**: The organizational website is the center of communication from an organization to the outside world. All content should emanate from the website and other owned channels, allowing for information, news, and multimedia to be shared (often through social channels) in a way that links publics back to owned media.

For more information on owned media tactics, please see the Appendix, p. 260.

INCLUSIVITY IN MESSAGE DEVELOPMENT

The creation of tactics serves as an important point in the campaign process for a few reasons: (1) reach out to publics and target audiences, (2) seek opportunities for additional diversity and inclusion as part of content creation, and (3) consider the unintended consequences of messages on stakeholders and publics who may not be part of an immediate audience.

Reach Out to Audiences, Publics, and Stakeholders

While traditional message development processes include the step of testing messages with their potential audiences, practitioners can go a step further and bring publics and stakeholders into the process earlier. University of Oregon professor Dean Mundy explains that "stakeholder engagement demands that organizations not only reflect, but also speak to the diverse culture in which they operate."[17] When implementing a diversity-first approach this can become second nature.

Showcase Diversity and Inclusion

At the point of developing tactics, practitioners should ask themselves about ways that they can visibly demonstrate their organizations' commitment to diversity and inclusion. Referencing the diversity wheel can be a very useful tool at this point in the process to examine (1) whether there are additional identities and perspectives that should be considered and (2) whether there are additional identities and experiences that could be represented. In this way, public relations practitioners can be empowered to take a social advocacy role in support of the diverse stakeholders their organizations represent.[18]

Consider Unintended Consequences and Interpretations

Many well-intended messages can be seen out of context as damaging and hurtful. While practitioners can never anticipate every possible outcome, they can help organizations to remember a variety of internal and external stakeholders that make up relevant communities. Multiple constraints to message effectiveness itself can arise, even within culturally similar groups.[19]

CONCLUSION

Campaign tactics should clearly support objectives and strategies. The mix of tactics should be selected and balanced based on the messages to convey and the audiences such efforts intend to reach. While no practitioners will have expertise in all of the paid, earned, shared, owned, and converged tactics described in this chapter, they can be aware of their strengths and shortcomings, budgetary and timeline implications, audience appropriateness, and message fit. Just as several objectives build toward achieving an organizational goal, several tactics can support the execution of a targeted strategy. The limit to what practitioners can achieve and execute is limited only by their creativity and resources.

THINK CRITICALLY

1. What are three characteristics of effective messages?
2. How are the limitations of earned media different from those of paid media?
3. Many organizations tend to see earned media and social media as "free" tactics. How might you address potential costs for outreach using these tactics with departmental or organizational leaders?
4. Owned tactics reach beyond our idea of *media* to include, for example, office spaces and hosted events. How do these tactics share characteristics with websites, blogs, brochures, newsletters, and other owned media tactics?
5. What is the best strategy to develop inclusive messaging? How does the diversity & inclusion wheel empower practitioners?

KEY TERMS

Boosted content 166
Content creation 164
Content hub 164
Controlled media 164
Conversion 166
Information subsidies 163
Messaging 154
Publicity 162
Uncontrolled media 158

CONCEPT CASE: FINDING THE RIGHT TACTICS FOR COMMUNITY FLOW YOGA

The leaders of Community Flow Yoga have approved an objective to raise awareness of the company by 5 percent in Canada over the next year, to coincide with the company's expansion into Toronto and Vancouver (see Chapter 6). As budget for this approach will be low, they've asked you to prioritize three to five specific earned, shared, and owned tactics to help achieve this objective.

- For earned media, what national and major regional earned media opportunities exist that would help achieve this goal?
    - Begin by looking at Canada's major media markets, newspapers, magazines, and TV networks.
    - For the key outlets, who would the best reporters and editors be to pitch?
- For shared media, who might influencers or other partners be to help gain traction within the Canadian market?
- For owned media, what types of content (blog posts, microsites/landing pages, podcasts, videos, etc.) might support outreach and awareness with this market?

Craft brief proposals for the three to five specific tactics that would best fit this objective, keeping in mind the earned/shared/owned strategies selected, and make the case for why these would be effective.

CASE STUDY: PEEPS® COUNTS DOWN TO A SWEET NEW YEAR

Peeps with Coyne PR
Based on PRSA Silver Anvil Winner
Campaign Focus: Product Marketing, Corporate Social Responsibility

Everyone knows about the New Year's Eve Times Square ball drop, but those seeking a sweeter New Year's Eve celebration can head over to Bethlehem, Pennsylvania, the home of PEEPS candy brand. PEEPS, "the colorful marshmallow chicks and bunnies from Just Born Quality Confections,"[20] is known for its Easter gift basket essentials but chose to take over other celebratory holidays. Every year, PEEPS hosts "Peepsfest," an annual two-day New Year's Eve celebration in Bethlehem, where the brand drops a 400-pound, 5-foot-high chick at 5:15 p.m. on December 31 at Bethlehem SteelStacks, a campus devoted to family, arts, culture, and events.[21] This celebration features contests, sculptures, magicians, activities, and more.[22] For the celebration's tenth anniversary in 2018, PEEPS and agency Coyne PR decided to open the factory's doors to consumers while giving back to the Lehigh Valley community, also known as the Allentown-Bethlehem-Easton Metropolitan Area, as part of the brand's "Helping Peeps Sweepstakes."[23] This program included a grand prize trip for up to four people to the PEEPS factory.[24]

Local chapter of the United Way and PEEPS partnership, "Helping Peeps Sweepstakes."[25]

Research/Diagnosis

The primary goals of the "Helping Peeps Sweepstakes" were to improve lives and community conditions by raising funds, investing in programs, and rallying people to action.[26] To do so, the brand studied consumer behavior and identified the target audience as moms between the ages of twenty-five and fifty-four years who are considered "holiday traditionalists and fun enthusiasts who want to make every occasion special for she and her family."[27] Their original research revealed two key outcomes. First, more than half of the respondents said they agree that PEEPS is part of holidays all year long rather than just around Easter. Secondly, Just Born Quality Confections, the owner of PEEPS, determined that there was an increase in the number of PEEPS consumers who wanted a factory tour, which was something that had never been offered to the public before.

In collaboration with the United Way of the Greater Lehigh Valley, PEEPS developed a contest where contestants contributed a minimum of $5 in support of community schools, to be eligible for the grand prize. Much like Roald Dahl's classic book, *Charlie and the Chocolate Factory*, the winner had the opportunity to experience a behind-the-scenes tour at the PEEPS Factory.[28] Matt Pye, the Senior Vice President of Sales and Marketing at Just Born Quality Confections, said,

> *Although we've had many requests and lots of fans show up at our doors over the years, the PEEPS factory has never been open to the public. We couldn't think of a better reason to open our doors for the first time ever than by teaming up with our local United Way to help give back to the*

community that PEEPS calls home. The winner of our PEEPS Helping Peeps Sweepstakes will embark upon a once-in-a-lifetime tour of our factory and witness first-hand how our iconic PEEPS marshmallow is made, all while helping raise funds in support of important community-enhancing programs.[29]

While the launch took place during New Year's, the winner was announced during Easter.

Objectives

Over the course of four weeks, PEEPS aimed to achieve the following objectives:

- Increase awareness for PEEPSFEST overall by 25 percent compared to the previous year.
- Gain media attention for PEEPSFEST with local media and increase coverage by 25 percent compared to the previous year.
- Raise awareness to drive sweepstakes entries along with donations to the United Way of the Greater Leigh Valley.

Strategies

PEEPS and Coyne PR developed strategies that incorporated the brand's well-known Easter essential along with its goal to give back to the community. PEEPS worked with the United Way of the Greater Lehigh Valley to create coverage that "would launch at the culmination of 2018 to drive 'out of season' media coverage."[30] That said, the brand identified media contacts, including *USA Today*, *Forbes*, Travel, and ABC, and maintained regular news coverage through the annual two-day New Year Eve event.[31] Also, PEEPS conducted national and local media outreach a few days before the launch to raise awareness about the drop and its first-ever "Helping Peeps Sweepstakes," hitting multiple markets including Philadelphia and New York City.[32]

Tactics

To accomplish its strategy, PEEPS used multiple tactics:

- Coyne PR took an aggressive approach to target top-tier national media outreach, including targeted pitches, leveraging existing relationships with media professionals, and homing in on a fifty-mile radius hitting major media markets including Philadelphia and New York City.
- Leveraged media relationships and knowledge of each publication's historic New Year's coverage to secure outlets that did not intend on covering New Year's stories.
- Tapped into nostalgic vibes and developed relevancy for PEEPS outside of Easter by bringing a local event to the national forefront with fun facts and impressive visuals.
- Partnered with the United Way of the Greater Lehigh Valley.
- Shared a news release raising awareness about the entire campaign published on Just Born Quality Confections website.

Earned and Shared

Just Born Quality Confection's website created a dedicated page for PEEPS highlighting multiple press releases and media alerts that discuss the brand's partnerships with the United Way of Greater Lehigh Valley, as well as its annual "Peepsfest" event. Its latest press release about the grand prize, titled "PEEPS® Invites Fans Inside the Factory for the First Time," states that the United Way "seeks to improve lives and community conditions by assessing the needs of the community, raising funds, and investing in programs, measuring results, and mobilizing people to action."[33]

PEEPS' "Helping Peeps Sweepstakes" focused heavily on earned and shared media. The brand convinced multiple media outlets, even those that do not cover New Year's events, to cover the grand prize initiative and the drop. News outlets included People.com, *USA Today*, *Forbes*, Yahoo, ABC, Good Morning America, and FOX.[34]

Implementation

Over four weeks, PEEPS and Coyne PR worked together to celebrate the brand's tenth anniversary by not only promoting the annual 400-pound chick drop but also launching the new initiative, "Helping Peeps Sweepstakes," which aimed to assess the needs of the community, raise funds, and improve the community by collaborating with the United Way.

Reporting/Evaluation

PEEPs developed a pop-culture image beyond Easter with the launch of this campaign. More specifically, Coyne PR secured over 800 placements and 1.6 billion media impressions within four weeks, which was a 69 percent increase from the 2016–2017 season. Peepfest was featured in *USA Today*, *Forbes*, Yahoo!, Travel, and ABC with 75 percent of the coverage stemming from media markets beyond a fifty-mile radius of the event.[35] As for the Chick drop, more than 300 broadcast programs featured the event spanning forty states across the country.[36]

Regarding local media coverage, the brand secured more than 116 placements with over 2 million impressions, which is a 41 percent increase from the previous year. More specifically, the event secured twenty-three mentions of Peepsfest on the Lehigh Valley's local cable networks, and thirty-two mentions of the event from the nearest significant media market, Philadelphia, across ABC, NBC, and FOX.[37] Finally, top-tier media placements on People.com, *USA Today*, *US Weekly*, AP, Bustle, and more generated almost 2,000 entries and $25,000 in donations.[38]

Theories

Framing Theory: With framing, the media are used to influence people surrounding what and how to think about an issue. Journalists are often associated with influencing perception through news coverage. In this campaign, PEEPS worked to actively reframe its candy beyond the Easter holiday season.

Agenda Setting Theory: When employing agenda setting, the media sets the public agenda by telling people what to think about. Just Born Quality Confection and Coyne PR focused on media relations to influence the public so they would embrace Peepfest at a time when consumers are traditionally thinking about the ball dropping in Time's Square.

Diversity- & Inclusion-First Approach

PEEPS focused on personal habits of women, specifically mothers, as part of the Diversity & Inclusion Wheel by targeting those who are considered holiday traditionalists and fun enthusiasts.

Implementation

9

iStock.com/RawPixel

THINK AHEAD

9.1 Understand which skills are crucial to the execution of successful public relations campaigns.

9.2 Formulate strategies when the eventuality of change happens within campaign planning.

The execution of a public relations campaign can feel like a tightrope walk. Balancing the demands of organizations or clients with audiences and publics—particularly journalists—is both an exhilarating and humbling experience. Sometimes, everything comes together to achieve objectives and recognition from stakeholders. Often, not everything goes as planned. Veteran PR practitioners have all experienced a moment during a campaign when the pressures of competing deadlines, managing hurried media, and frustrated clients push them to consider an alternate career path. However, these are likely the same moments in which practitioners learn and grow the most, witness the impact of their efforts (good and bad), and prove the value and importance of strategic communication. For Broom and Sha, this stage encompasses "putting the program into operation."[1] Implementation is where the rubber hits the road—where work is sent out into the world.

KEY SKILLS FOR IMPLEMENTING PR CAMPAIGNS

During this phase of a campaign, the distinct lines between project phases are often blurred, as they tend to happen more holistically and simultaneously. Implementation does not mean that we stop researching or planning. Rather, there are a number of new events, audiences, messages, and tasks that will emerge and require additional diligence. It is inevitable that practitioners will continue to learn as projects unfold, and each finding should be considered and implemented when appropriate. This is not to say that the effort spent on initial research, objective building, strategy creation, and tactical definitions is not important. A campaign will not succeed without these components, but changes are required to sustain effectiveness.

Project Management Basics

Successful campaign implementation relies on a mix of preparation, expectation setting, and perseverance. It entails efficient budgeting, effective division of labor among team members, and clear identification and scheduling of tasks. Such tasks are often rooted more in project management than PR. Morris and Pinto's introduction to *The Wiley Guide to Project Organization and Project Management Competencies* highlights that project management must first "deliver projects on time, on budget, and on scope" and then "see the project within its environment" to understand how it supports and interacts with the organization as a whole.[2] Executing this effectively involves a deep understanding of all of the steps in a process, managing timelines, motivating team members, and adjusting to changing circumstances or unforeseen obstacles.[3]

Additionally, there are numerous tasks that must occur prior to beginning work that will set the stage for a successful campaign. These include organizing and managing budgets, assigning tasks, generating timelines, and communicating effectively to all team members and stakeholders.

Budgeting

Budgeting involves estimating planned or projected costs, rather than focusing on a rigid insistence on fixed spending. Therefore, practitioners must research the costs of particular items, work with vendors to quote prices for specific tactics, and communicate with organizational leaders as numbers become solidified and choices are made. The skills of estimation are developed both through experience and effort. The closer a practitioner works with vendors, advertising representatives, and digital advertising channels, the easier it is to estimate costs, ask clarifying questions, and determine which expenditures are necessary for a given situation.

The budgets supporting PR campaigns can generally be broken down into five categories: **personnel**, **materials**, **media costs**, **infrastructure**, and **administration**.[4] Personnel costs cover the professional time spent researching, analyzing, writing, editing, designing, developing, executing, and evaluating campaign work. Items "associated with the tactics" constitute materials, including printing fliers, website hosting costs, video production location fees, and press release wire distribution.[5] Media costs refer to print, broadcast, and digital ad buys or advertorial content. Purchasing a video camera, upgrading editing software, adding a social media monitoring service, or expanding physical space of an organization should be considered infrastructure expenditures, which may be included as part of campaign budgets but are more often spread over multiple projects due to their value beyond a specific campaign. Finally, administrative costs include office activities, travel, and other incidental expenditures for campaign-related work. Such categories are not necessarily the only structure for organizing budgets, but they provide a framework and checklist to ensure that all potential costs are considered during the planning process.

It is also valuable to understand that there are further classifications of each cost associated with a campaign. Some budget items are fixed, known as **hard costs**, while others, **soft costs**, may be more flexible in nature. Hard costs can include vendor payments, event costs, production costs, and infrastructure expansion. Soft costs may include flexible ad buys, in-house production, as well as personnel and other discretionary spending. In many cases, the nature of an individual expenditure allows some degree of flexibility; for example, digital ad buys can be changed on a weekly or daily basis, while print or broadcast advertising is generally locked in. Organizations tend to have fixed personnel costs, while agencies have more flexibility in moving team members from project to project if additional bandwidth is needed. The art of effective budgeting examines the ratio of hard and soft costs to allow some flexibility and reactivity during campaign implementation activity. If certain advertising channels prove to be particularly effective, it is useful to allow for budget flexibility in order to adjust the resources allocated for those tactics. Building in some flexibility allows practitioners to capitalize on opportunities that arise during campaign execution, while feedback provides valuable knowledge and direction.

Of particular importance for agency work, budgets also must reflect the anticipated amount of time that will be spent on the project by agency personnel. Not only should the tasks and tactics be feasible to complete within the timeline, but they must also be possible to complete within the agency's retainer structure. If an agency allocates fifteen hours a month to a specific client, a project requiring an estimated twenty to twenty-five hours of work during a single month would cover the expense of all other efforts and move beyond retainer time (and cost). For some PR firms, this would mean an additional project contract, while others might see the additional time as an important contributor to forming a strong relationship over the long term. Firms have built relationships with both approaches. Many PR agencies bill by the hour or track staff time toward retainer to establish and reinforce project scope. For both in-house and agency staff, tracking time is an extremely valuable tool to understand the duration of specific tasks, creating a clearer picture of personnel time allocation. It also significantly improves the ability of campaign leadership to identify points of efficiency and inefficiency for process improvement at both individual and team levels.

Dividing Tasks Among a Team

Accomplishing PR work efficiently and effectively as a team is often harder than it sounds. Assessing the skills and abilities of team members to identify the project elements best suited to them is critical.[6] With that in mind, implementing process improvements during campaign execution will always be a work in progress. Consider these modifications less like an assembly line and more like the daily modifications required of a high-end restaurant. In a classical French kitchen, each area or station is headed by a *chef*, who oversees the work of his team or *partie*. Meat, fish, sauces, produce, and desserts all entail their own stations and teams, working together to produce a dish. This approach was popularized and perfected by legendary French chef Auguste Escoffier in the late nineteenth and early twentieth centuries. It created a highly organized environment where everyone understood their individual role in a process and, through this efficiency, trimmed the time it took for customers waiting for his dishes at London's Savoy Hotel by up to two-thirds.[7] It is a particularly apt comparison to PR because the work is never a true assembly line: two press releases will never be identical in the same way that two cuts of meat will always need to be seasoned differently based on their size, shape, and fat content. The practitioner will need to use his or her full expertise to make important decisions at each stage in the research, planning, writing, editing, distribution, and evaluation processes.

PR project or campaign teams should also be designed based on the size, scope, and urgency of the task at hand, as well as the skills of those participating. A large team may be broken into media relations, social media, and creative production, with the leaders of each group acting as the station heads in charge of their team's execution. Practitioners should leverage the expertise they have developed in each of these areas. Additionally, like a restaurant kitchen, each step in the campaign has a distinct timeline for planning, development, and production, wherein each group must ensure that their piece of the campaign is timed to meet deadlines and work in tandem with the other pieces. A media announcement, like entrées for a table of diners, must have all components ready to serve at the appropriate time, whether they took three months or fifteen minutes to prepare.

Gantt charts allow practitioners to quickly visualize the multiple timelines that are part of the preparation and implementation process of integrated campaigns.

Creating Timelines and Deadlines

Building functional timelines, or schedules of implementation, begins by working backward. What are the main deliverable due dates? Are these "hard" (immobile) deadlines?[8] If so, it allows practitioners to plan by marking off the time for concept development and approval, content creation and approval, production and approval, as well as final delivery of the items at hand. In the case of a press release, these steps are relatively straightforward, and the timing is more flexible. For example, a project might be set up using the following estimates for writing and distribution:

- Research and information gathering (two hours to one week)
- Initial ideas and approval from staff (two days)
- Drafting (one day)
- Approval and revisions (two days to two weeks)
- Setup and distribution (one to two days)
- Follow-up (one week)

In this case, practitioners would know that the process would need to begin, if possible, one month before the distribution date. However, these timelines might be overly cautious for a small, fast-moving organization or too optimistic for a complex campaign announcement that includes multiple organizations (and thus multiple PR teams and multiple levels of approval). With experience and conscious practice, practitioners can improve their ability to estimate the length of time necessary to complete specific tasks within their own organizations or for individual clients.

Additionally, timelines for creative production can further complicate things, particularly when much of the process takes place outside the control of practitioners. In most cases, PR professionals should schedule recurring meetings with the creative team to discuss timelines and ensure that the larger team understands what the creative team (or outside vendor) expects of them regarding turnaround times. For example, a practitioner might know that the company's executive team takes one to two weeks to approve many of their ideas. This knowledge should be communicated to the creative team to build in this approval time appropriately. The larger the project, the greater the potential exists to run into roadblocks and challenges. Some timeline padding should be built into major creative projects when possible, and PR leaders can take the lead in holding groups involved to agreed-upon internal deadlines.

It is easy to imagine how concurrent timelines supporting various components of a single campaign can easily become confusing and difficult to manage. One tool available for organizing multiple deadlines and projects is called a **Gantt chart**, which provides a clear visual representation of the timeline for multiple campaign components at a glance. Gantt charts are useful to include in full plans because they provide those beyond the PR department a method for understanding the time needed to complete each tactic and task. This can be particularly valuable, as it can be difficult for organizational leaders without a PR background to understand why planning and implementing a campaign may take months of effort.

Setting Clear Expectations and Ensuring Clear Communication

Conveying a clear project vision is the responsibility of the project manager.[9] Those working together on a project should understand how tasks will be divided and what the expectations are related to timelines, quality, and communication. Clarity, in this case, comes in part from defined, measurable objectives connected to the strategies, tactics, and tasks that each team member will perform. This includes processes, results, and direction from appropriate organization and conciseness of communication itself. The more complicated a message becomes, the less clearly it will convey the point. Using a clear information hierarchy and creating scannable, reference-focused language is paramount. Don't expect project directions to be read in full or in order.

Another important facet of team leadership is motivation. Generating enthusiasm for a project is just as important as developing and communicating an effective plan. In doing so effectively, practitioners must sometimes step out of their comfort zones. They should respond to the informational and emotional needs of their team members and provide them with the necessary support to succeed, even if it means a detour from the plan or from their usual day-to-day approach.[10] This can be particularly difficult as PR practitioners are creative and objective driven, potentially making them less tolerant of inflexible rules and management styles.[11] Balancing the needs of deadlines and efficiency with creativity and innovation can only be done with a deep knowledge of each team member and a constant focus on keeping projects interesting and exciting for those involved.

Working With Non-PR People

Oftentimes, those outside of the marketing team become critical pieces in the function of a campaign. They may be sources of information, providers of approvals, or strategic sounding boards. In all cases, PR professionals should take extra care in working with individuals who are outside of their day-to-day function, in part because of the different expectations for timeliness, communication, and approvals. Particularly in working with journalists in need of information or interviews on deadline, practitioners must educate those inside the organization about the need for responsiveness.

Like professionals in any industry, those in integrated marketing communications tend to use industry jargon when communicating. This can ultimately isolate them from others within organizations and undercut their credibility with executive leadership. When working with those outside of the PR field, it is critical to adjust language for easy comprehension. Practitioners should take the opportunity to educate others within their organization regarding the strategies, concepts, and research that go into planning a PR campaign. The more knowledge that others have of strategic, integrated communication processes, the more accurately they will be able to understand recommendations and perspectives from the PR function. Additionally, they will be better equipped to share their own perspectives and insights with the PR team in both constructive and productive ways.

In an agency setting, clients should be regarded as the experts on their industry and their business; keep them included in discussions and decisions about messaging, strategy, and execution in regard to their products, trends, or competitors.[12] The same approach can be taken by in-house practitioners, who can defer to relevant executive team members or other subject matter experts in order to ensure their expertise is used. In both cases, the PR team should maintain ownership of the objectives, strategy, writing, distribution, and measurement.

Working With the Media

Executing media relations not only requires knowledge of the appropriate PR practitioner duties but also the needs of journalists. Ultimately, media outlets have a responsibility to provide a product to their specific audience. PR practitioners must respect this responsibility and act within its limitations. It should govern not only the way information is crafted but also its distribution method and timing.

©iStockPhotos/KreangchaiRungfamai

Working with journalists can be intimidating, but media relations strategies and tactics are still cornerstones of successful integrated campaigns.

When executing media relations, it is critical to remember that journalists, editors, and producers are beholden to daily deadline and editorial pressures. The most valuable pitches are those that are clearly framed for a media outlet's audience and an individual journalist's beat. They should choose topics and use language appropriate and understandable for the outlet's audience. Ease of translation also means that practitioners should always follow *Associated Press Stylebook* guidelines and clearly identify and showcase the facets of newsworthiness that a particular pitch or story requires.

PRo Tip

DEFINING NEWSWORTHINESS

There are six components of newsworthiness by which journalists (and, by extension, PR practitioners) should use to identify the value of their stories and pitches.[13] Of course, no story is considered newsworthy in every category, but news items that rank strongly in multiple categories and are clearly articulated in a pitch will be of greatest interest to journalists.

1. Audience impact: Will the information have significant relevance in the lives of a majority of the media outlet's audience? Is

the story about a widely attended free community festival (highly relevant) or a high-dollar, black-tie fundraiser (less relevant)?

2. Proximity: How much geographical overlap is there between the information conveyed and the audience? Is it happening in the media outlet's coverage area or in a different state?
3. Timeliness: Would the information still be of interest to readers at the time it is published or shared? Did the event happen today or three weeks ago?
4. Prominence: Is the information about a well-known company CEO or an unknown front-line employee? Is the charitable contribution $200 or $200,000? Did the company hire three new employees or 300?
5. Novelty or oddity: Is the information unique and unexpected or something that happens regularly? Is a local business celebrating its 100th anniversary or announcing quarterly sales figures?
6. Conflict, drama, or excitement: Does the information generate interest because of its potentially negative or dramatic consequences? Is the organization responding to a genuine crisis or releasing a minor update to an established product?

Source: Glen M. Broom and Bey-Ling Sha, *Cutlip and Center's Effective Public Relations*, 11th ed. (Boston, MA: Pearson, 2013), 293.

Additionally, practitioners should be aware of editorial processes of specific publications, particularly with respect to deadlines. While there is increasing pressure for many media outlets to provide near-constant updates as news breaks, each media type still possesses a distinct rhythm—whether it's the morning newsgathering, editing at the daily newspaper or local evening TV news, weekly deliverables for regional business weeklies, or the months-long production time for many national magazines.[14] Because of these constraints, the timing of media announcements can be critical to their success. For example, an announcement about an organization that is opening a new location in a new city and hiring several hundred new employees would be largely directed at local media (print, radio, and television) and therefore most effectively released on a weekday morning (not Friday) to maximize quick uptake.[15] If a similar announcement was more important for trade media, it may have a very different timeline for distribution. Content distributed through earned media channels should always be simultaneously posted on logical, easy-to-find owned channels, such as a website's press room, so that other interested journalists can easily access the information.[16]

Self-Awareness and Self-Evaluation

Every practitioner contributes a specific skillset to a project, but practitioners should not be considered experts at every task or tactic. With this in mind, having a clear idea of where your personal strengths and weaknesses are is critical. Howard and Mathews provide particularly pointed and useful questions that communicators should ask themselves:[17]

- **"Am I doing everything I can to stay current on company activities and industry trends?"** Knowing your own organization allows practitioners to see potentially newsworthy stories as they develop. Being on top of industry trends provides significant credibility as well as a wealth of ideas for stories and pitches.
- **"Am I anticipating news and activities in my organization that would cause or generate media interest?"** If not, it might be helpful to follow internal events and news more carefully, build more relationships across departments, and always consider the potential news value for those outside of the organization.
- **"Am I, or is my boss, included in planning meetings and in the decision-making process?"** If the PR function is not included in strategic meetings, it may be worthwhile to ask leadership for the opportunity to participate in, or at least observe, relevant discussions.

Additionally, the following questions relate to individual skill development:

- **"Am I making progressively fewer writing errors and typos?"** If not, consider changing your processes to ensure you have the time and focused energy to proofread your own work. In the meantime, ask a colleague to provide another set of eyes on your writing before sending it to leadership or journalists.
- **"Am I seeing unexpected pushback or disagreement about my best ideas or pitches from coworkers, leadership, clients, or journalists?"** If your sense of what makes an effective pitch or strategy seems not to align with others in your organization, ask for feedback whenever possible. Challenges can arise when junior practitioners are less aware of an organization's history, goals, or internal politics. Having deeper insights into these issues can help improve strategic recommendations. Working with journalists and understanding what is newsworthy often comes from additional reading and research on specific reporters, media outlets, and industries.
- **"Am I spending more time than others writing, making media follow-up calls, or tracking media coverage for similar projects?"** Efficiency, while not as important as overall quality of work, is still an area that can greatly increase a practitioner's ability to make an impact on their organization or client. Speed at particular tasks can increase with time and conscious practice, but the baseline comes from watching the clock to see how long it takes to complete certain tasks and then attempting to gradually improve efficiency over time.

Your own confidence level with a particular task is generally not the best indicator of your skills. The worst writers, the worst public speakers, and the worst designers may be unaware of their inabilities. Conversely, our fear of certain activities often unnecessarily magnifies our lack of confidence. For these reasons, self-awareness (and improvement) comes through working closely with others and regularly asking for feedback. This can function as an informal process, such as asking a senior colleague what else could have been contributed, or a formal one, like scheduling weekly, monthly, or quarterly meetings with staff to provide skills feedback. Often, feedback can be beneficial in both directions: up to superiors and down to staff. For example, structuring meetings so that managers and their direct reports are both comfortable providing constructive criticism to each other allows the working relationship to improve from both sides. Improving both individual skills and group workflow makes the implementation process significantly smoother over time.

Persistence and Perseverance

Successful PR practitioners represent a very diverse cross-section of the workforce, but they have one key trait in common: persistence. When they see an obstacle, they understand that those who break through are the most motivated, hardest working, and most resilient. Young professionals should strive to demonstrate persistence by

iStock.com/fizkes

Follow-up calls support proactive media pitching efforts and serve a critical role in building relationships between practitioners and journalists.

not giving up in difficult circumstances and practice the perseverance and tenacity to work through and overcome obstacles. Of course, this is easier said than done. When discussing the challenges facing new practitioners, "do not expect immediate results."[18]

In media relations, for example, the vast majority of media pitches are not actually used. Failure with one, two, or three reporters does not necessarily mean an idea or a pitch does not have merit.[19] As in Major League Baseball, 30 hits in 100 attempts may be a very good stretch at the plate. For practitioners, this means keeping the energy, enthusiasm, and optimism up, even if seven pitches or follow-up calls in a row don't go your way. Maintaining a balanced, paced approach to the results of this outreach is key to long-term emotional stability and success. No individual pitch, placement, Instagram photo, or advertising tactic should make or break a campaign. Similarly, no individual setback for a practitioner should break his or her spirit. Resilience, or the ability to bounce back from adversity, comes from knowing that you have the right processes, tools, safeguards, and strategies in place, and an understanding that your team has thoroughly researched a problem and identified its cause. It originates from a deep knowledge of the industries, journalists, and organizations that practitioners interact with. All of these small steps build confidence in individual areas, which translates into a broader belief that a campaign can and will succeed with enough effort and resources. Thoroughness, preparedness, and persistence breed excellence and resilience, which is a critical part of perseverance. Long-term campaign success cannot happen without it.

PRo Tip

SCRUM—A STRUCTURE FOR MANAGING CHANGE

PR campaigns take place in dynamic environments. The pace of technological innovation and increasing speed of multidirectional communication mean that today, more than ever before, the world surrounding organizations is in constant change—including while campaigns are taking place.

In response to these challenges, eminent PR scholar Betteke van Ruler has adapted a scrum approach to PR planning and implementation. Originally created for software design and development, the scrum model encourages "permanent monitoring of change":[20]

- **Sprints:** Members execute the plan and maintain focus and direction during short, timed cycles.
- **Team reflections:** Each member is responsible for evaluating their own actions and seeking improvement—concise, regular (often daily or every-other-day) meetings, where team members discuss challenges and issues in their campaign implementation.
- **Interventions:** The team leader has final say in making changes to be implemented during the next sprint cycle.

- **Team responsibility:** Teams are largely autonomous and empowered to achieve their own objectives.

While not all PR practitioners need to become *scrum masters*, they should have regular processes for understanding, reflecting, communicating, and integrating change into the implementation process.

Source: Based on Betteke van Ruler's "Agile Public Relations Planning" article from *Public Relations Review* and her book *Reflective Communication Scrum*.

PREPARING FOR CHANGE

No plan is executed exactly as written. Even the most brilliant campaign plans may not work in the real world. From shoestring small businesses to Public Relations Society of America Silver Anvil winners working with global PR firms, everyone revisits, rethinks, and revises their approach. Circumstances may occur that are beyond the control of the organization or reflect changes in the competitive, regulatory, technical, or local environments. *Plans* are just that: potential approaches that must be flexible and responsive.

Campaigns may also encounter circumstances that could have been anticipated but were not. Actual audience behavior may differ from survey responses. Technological progression occurs in every industry. Practitioners should adjust to the circumstances and recalibrate strategies and tactics. In this way, each new plan and its implementation incorporates the lessons learned from previous campaigns.

When campaigns do not progress completely as planned, flexibility in implementation allows practitioners to make the most of continued learning from the environment. Feedback from audience interaction, in-campaign analytics, and, potentially, structured surveys and outreach can all support the continued focusing (or refocusing) of messages, content, and channels.

One framework for understanding such changes is known as systems theory, which sees organizations as part of a complex, interdependent system within their environment.[21] When one element changes, the organizations within the environment each must respond. Such systems tend to return to a balanced state. This environment includes the company, industry (competitors, vendors, and customers), and communities (local, regional, national, and international), as well as broader political and economic factors. From this perspective, an organization's survival over the long term is tied largely to its ability to adapt to these environmental factors and pressures.

An alternate approach for understanding change has been put forth by Pang, Jin, and Cameron. Their **contingency theory** places an organization's attempts to respond to external change as a balance between "advocacy" (fighting to position the

iStock.com/ibigfish

Crisis may strike an organization when it is least expected, making flexibility and change management a critical part of campaign implementation.

organization in a certain way relative to such forces) and "accommodation" (aligning the organization with the environmental change).[22] This approach asks practitioners to consider constant evaluation of external challenges and opportunities before and during campaigns and to see their work as "dynamic" or constantly evolving.[23] These factors include both internal and external considerations ranging from corporate culture and PR staff experience to customer credibility and the regulatory environment. Changes to any of these factors must be monitored throughout campaigns and, if necessary, reflected by changes in priorities, objectives, strategies, and tactics.

While not all circumstances can be anticipated, there are recurring themes every practitioner can learn from both in their past experience and from the experiences of others. The PR function cannot always predict the results of an upcoming election, but it can prepare and take into account multiple approaches to planning based on hypothetical results. This may be the most important takeaway from contingency theory: it is impossible to predict the future, but our approaches should be flexible enough to succeed when some environmental factors change.

Change and Inclusion

Flexibility can provide significant benefits toward inclusion when practitioners realize their power to adjust and better reflect organizational values. As campaigns progress, organizations receive feedback—from simply paying attention to refinement opportunities through campaign measurement, to making genuine errors in messaging or judgment. Diverse stakeholders and publics will always bring perspectives that practitioners cannot anticipate. Having a mindset of continuous change, of listening to internal and external publics and stakeholders, and of iterating toward a more inclusive approach as campaigns are underway can make any campaign stronger. In any of these cases, practitioners should embrace changes in messaging, visuals, channels, and tone to best learn from the feedback their work is receiving once it has been put out into the world.

CONCLUSION

In the end, balance is critical. Campaigns must employ both strategically planned and reactive approaches. Leaning too much in one direction or the other often has negative consequences. Being overly rigid in execution avoids using the natural and important learning that takes place in the implementation of any plan. Practitioners can make use of the insights that come from the initial stages of implementation. They should budget so that some resources can shift as individual tactics prove more effective than others. The best campaign plans are maps rather than linear directions, showing that there are several paths to successfully meeting objectives. Finally, the best practitioners are adept both at writing and reading their campaign plans for these realities.

THINK CRITICALLY

1. In what ways do PR practitioners act as project managers?
2. Why is it important to be flexible and plan for change?
3. How does inclusion play a vital role in the practice of PR? What value does inclusion bring to a campaign?
4. How might you anticipate some of the challenges of ongoing projects or campaigns with non-PR colleagues?
5. What are three areas of improvement you'd like to focus on based on the implementation recommendations in this chapter?

KEY TERMS

Budget, Administration 177
Budget, Infrastructure 177
Budget, Materials 177
Budget, Media 177
Budget, Personnel 177
Contingency theory 187
Gantt chart 180
Hard costs 177
Soft costs 177

CONCEPT CASE: COMMUNITY FLOW YOGA MEETS UNEXPECTED OPPORTUNITIES AND OBSTACLES

Scenario #1

Due to extremely quick success gaining members in its new London location, the company has decided to add three additional locations in the city over the course of the campaign. In order to keep up with this new goal, what additional engagement would be possible (layered on top of existing paid, earned, shared, and owned tactics) to help take advantage of this opportunity?

- Existing tactics:
  - Boosted social media posts on Twitter and Instagram
  - Media outreach with fitness-focused print and TV journalists in the city
  - A blog post about their (initial) London location

Scenario #2

Community Flow Yoga has always emphasized its community partners, but that does not mean that all partnerships run smoothly. Within weeks after the announcement of a community partnership with an Atlanta-area children's hospital, its CEO is taken into custody for embezzlement. How should Community Flow Yoga adjust to this news and the potential loss of a partner?

- Existing tactics:
  - Boosted social media posts announcing the partnership
  - Media outreach to local journalists covering the nonprofit sector
  - Two events planned to celebrate the partnership (one hosted at each organization's location)

CASE STUDY: INNOVATION GENERATES LEADERS—COMMUNITY-WIDE GIRL SCOUT COOKIE SALES EVENT

Girl Scouts of Greater New York, Kellogg's, and Reilly Connect
Based on PRSA Silver Anvil Winner
Campaign Focus: Consumer Products, Community Outreach

Girl Scouts of Greater New York (GSGNY) is the city's largest girls-only leadership program.[24] With 2.5 million believers in G.I.R.L., Go-getter, Innovator, Risk-taker, and Leader, the organization's mission is to build "girls of courage, confidence, and character, who make the world a better place."[25] In an effort to "practice what they preach," the leadership program created its first-ever homeless shelter–based troop in New York City, called Troop 6000, consisting of approximately twenty-four girls all of whom live in homeless shelters.[26] Troop 6000 and Kellogg's collaborated to create stability for girls whose families may need to move regularly. The campaign, which was the first-ever community-wide cookie sale, connects participants living in shelters across New York City to allow them to be part of the troop, even when they move to different shelters.[27]

Research/Diagnosis

According to the Coalition for the Homeless, a social services organization in New York City, in December 2019 alone, there were more than 62,000 homeless

NBC/NBC Universal/Getty Images

Girl scouts from Troop 6000 raise awareness for their cookie sale with the help of Tonight Show host Jimmy Fallon.

people, including more than 22,000 children and nearly 15,000 families living in New York City's Municipal Shelter System.[29] The shelter system is meant to offer only temporary, emergency housing for families, but it ends up providing housing to individuals for an average of eighteen months. As such, Kellogg's and GSGNY launched Troop 6000 in hopes of raising funds to help facilitate successful transitions from shelters to permanent housing.[30]

With a target of selling 6,000 boxes, Troop 6000 set up a cookie stand at Kellogg's cereal café in Manhattan's Union Square from April 10 to April 14, 2018.[31] The troop and Kellogg's collaborated to create six limited-edition specialty cereals to be sold during the cookie sale week, and 100 percent of the profit going to Troop 6000.[32] This sale served as the central event of the campaign.

Through conducting client interviews, strategy meetings, and planning sessions with GSGNY and Troop 6000 leaders, Reilly Connect, Kellogg's marketing firm, discussed the healthiest approach to promote the event, which is later discussed in strategies, considering the girls' ages and circumstances. Moreover, secondary research illustrated that of the 75,000 residents of Union Square, 140,000 employees, and 60,000 students, millions of tourists needed to be aware of the event.

Objectives

While planning for this campaign took months, execution occurred over five days. Troop 6000 and Kellogg aimed to achieve the following objectives:

- Build awareness of Troop 6000's first-ever cookie program
- Drive event attendance to Kellogg's NYC Café
- Help Troop 6000 hit its cookie sales goal

Strategies

Kellogg's carefully outlined nine proactive earned, shared, and owned strategies to achieve its objectives:

- Focused on national, local, and social media with a predisposed interest in Girl Scouts and homelessness [Earned and Shared]
- Extended national reach beyond New York through the creation of original video content highlighting Troop 6000's story [Owned]
- Mobilized Union Square's businesses and residents through media alerts, café notices, and social media support [Earned and Owned]
- Inspired media and prominent influencers to share information about the event across social channels. Secured on-site media interviews throughout the week with Troop 6000, select Girl Scouts, Girl Scouts leadership, and Kellogg's [Earned and Shared]
- Attracted people in Union Square by having select members of Troop 6000 dressed as cookies to invite them into the café [Owned]
- Promoted the availability of ordering cookies digitally [Owned and Shared]
- Kept the story alive by sharing sales results after the event [Earned and Owned]
- Heavy outreach at the beginning of the sale to create a snowball media effect [Earned]
- Issued multiple press releases and media alerts pre and post event [Earned]

Tactics

To bring its strategy to fruition, Kellogg's executed tactics before, during, and after the Troop 6000 cookie sale event. Through earned media, the brand sent out four media alerts before the event and conducted an aggressive approach to follow up to maximize media outreach. Kellogg's continuously notified surrounding businesses about the event to drive awareness and worked with Kellogg's Union Square event and social team to aggressively reach their followers.[33]

During the cookie sale event, the brand had its scouts available for interviews with top-tier media, such as MSNBC. Digital Marketing firm Reilly Connect also created a B-roll package on site at the event and reached out to local and national media interested in the story but are unable to attend. Finally, after the cookie sale, Kellogg's maintained its aggressive media follow-up to report Troop 6000's sales success.[34]

Owned

GSGNY created an exclusive page dedicated to Troop 6000 featuring news and updates on results, progress, and events since its launch in 2018. These include media alerts and press releases, such as "Troop 6000 Expands to All 5 Boroughs," and "Troop 6000's Inaugural Cookie Sale."[35] In addition, to go beyond national reach in New York, Kellogg's and GSGNY worked together to create original video content emphasizing the importance of Troop 6000 titled "Growing the Girl Scout Sisterhood: Troop 6000."[36]

Earned and Shared

Kellogg's and GSGNY took an aggressive approach using earned and shared media to bring to light its cookie sale event. Both organizations promoted the cookie sale before, during, and after the event on its social media platforms. Additionally, the two organizations focused on local and national media outreach with predisposed interest in such causes. They also encouraged social media influencers to share content on their social accounts on Facebook,

Twitter, Instagram, and Snapchat. In addition, both organizations took extensive measures to keep the social cause alive by maintaining media outreach after the event to raise awareness about the campaign's success and upcoming events.[37]

The launch of Troop 6000 was covered nationally through a cross-section of networks, local broadcasts, national print publications, and online stories. Upon the launch of Troop 6000, Bill de Blasio, the 109th mayor of New York City, announced a $1 million grant from the city to expand Girl Scout Troop 6000.[38] Due to this positive publicity, this campaign heavily targeted Tri-state media, network broadcast media, and journalists who covered stories with a local broadcast affiliate with integration in social media.

Implementation

The community-wide cookie sale event took place between April 10 and April 14, 2018. The immediate goal was to sell 6000 cookie boxes with the help of twenty-four girls within the troop. This event took place in Kellogg's New York City Café in Manhattan's Union Square. The mission of this event was to create awareness and raise donations to help homeless children in New York and beyond.

Reporting/Evaluation

The two organizations have reported successful results from this campaign. Not only did they achieve their goals, they also exceeded their sales objective by 320 percent, selling precisely 32,569 cookie boxes over five days with thousands of people rushing over to the Kellogg's NYC café.[39] Multiple waves of media coverage have carried far beyond New York City and the 2018 cookie sale to create ongoing discussion and support for Troop 6000's success. Over the course of the campaign, this effort generated 419 million earned media impressions including major earned media stories and their amplification through social media.[40]

Additionally, the two organizations garnered social media conversations across Facebook, Snapchat, Twitter, and Instagram from micro- and macro-influencers. These included *Full Frontal* with Samantha Bee, fashion designer Vera Wang, political activist (and first daughter) Chelsea Clinton, and MSNBC reporter Stephanie Ruhle.[41] By 2020, GSGNY expanded its Troop 6000 campaign to all five boroughs of New York. This solidifies and marks their commitment to the G.I.R.L agenda: "to inspire, prepare, and mobilize girls and those who care about them to lead positive change through civil action."[42]

Theories

Uses and Gratifications: By beginning with a genuine community need and a feel-good message, GSGNY and Kellogg's created content that was easily and willingly picked up and shared by individuals, influencers, journalists, and partner organizations. By starting with a deeply moving and positive story that people wanted to read and share, the companies created a campaign that was able to spread nationally without a significant advertising budget.

Diversity- and Inclusion-First Approach

Kellogg's and GSGNY have incorporated multiple aspects of the Diversity & Inclusion Wheel. By creating a campaign that focused on providing a future with education, employment, and shelter, the organizations addressed issues of social equity, access to education, socioeconomic status, and mental health/well-being. What other aspects of the Diversity & Inclusion Wheel can you identify?

Reporting and Evaluation

10

©iStockPhotos/diane39

THINK AHEAD

10.1 Examine the variety of techniques and frameworks available for campaign evaluation.

10.2 Produce reporting strategies that meet organizational and stakeholder needs.

10.3 Understand the special reporting considerations for each of the PESO channels.

The day following a major fundraising event, the CEO of a local nonprofit arrives at the office a bit later than usual. The staff is understandably exhilarated but winded. The director of communication is beginning to sort through the media coverage of the event itself. The CEO asks her, "How do you think the campaign turned out?" Before responding, she pauses. The event nearly met the intended fundraising goals. Its outreach created several new journalist relationships, including one that resulted in an unexpected radio interview the previous afternoon. It certainly energized the organization's volunteer base. Targeted social media ads leveraged the event to broaden the organization's Facebook and Instagram following. A local TV crew covered the event and crafted a highly positive feature story. That said, an influential blogger who was expected to live tweet the event came down with the flu, and one major donor felt the need to share loudly that his contributions the past year had been underappreciated. She replied, almost phrased as a question, "I think it went well," the pitch rising as she spoke.

Evaluating public relations campaigns is rarely clear-cut. Campaign work takes unexpected twists and turns, making the process of evaluation and reporting outcomes challenging; like taking aim at a moving target. Corporate and organizational leaders, understandably, prefer clear, concise, black-and-white reporting; however, the results of integrated campaigns rarely fit into tidy boxes. Successes may be wholly unexpected, while anticipated opportunities may not materialize. The value practitioners provide comes from the rich knowledge gained in the process of executing and tracking paid, earned, shared, and owned outreach to inform future campaigns and organizational actions. By listening to all audiences, practitioners gain an enviable grasp on the perspectives of many critical organizational publics. Understanding how to capture, organize, and synthesize these data allows the public relations function to provide valuable insights for all organizational leaders and departments.

Public relations practitioners have two distinct tasks at the end of a campaign: (1) cataloging, evaluating, and learning from their own successes, challenges, and missteps; and (2) reporting those results to their peers, organizational leaders, and/or clients. Seasoned practitioners understand the importance of both stages of this process and develop a sense for what information is useful to inform future campaigns, as well as what strategic information is valuable for those outside the communication team. Often, mistakes, external pressures, or unanticipated successes lead to the most valuable insights.

Before deciding what evaluative information to share, campaigns must be examined at several distinct levels: foremost, according to their original objectives. Did they succeed in creating the proposed action or change? Were objectives met for the right audiences and within the designated timeframe? Next, they should be analyzed from a more granular perspective focused on lessons learned. Did messages resonate with the community? Were journalists interested in the campaign's biggest news hooks? Did internal audiences participate with enthusiasm or with a shrug? Did relevant content drive interaction on social media channels? Once findings have been collected, they should be analyzed, synthesized, and shared with key stakeholders within the organization. The first section of this chapter addresses the evaluative process itself, while the second portion addresses the work of developing reporting vehicles to fit the needs of an organization and the project at hand.

EVALUATING YOUR CAMPAIGN

As discussed in the research section of the text, campaign evaluation should be tied to valuable, organizationally centered objectives. As Watson and Noble explain in

Evaluating Public Relations, a campaign's "intended communication and behavioral effects serve as the basis from which all other planning decisions can be made."[1] The same sentiment applies to evaluation. Evaluation is an opportunity to look both backward and forward at what areas succeeded and what could be improved for the future. The primary task should be to define and understand the results using qualitative and quantitative methods. This involves examining the execution of objectives as well as their inherent usefulness. For example, if the objective of a campaign was to raise awareness of an event among potential attendees by 20 percent over a three-month timeframe, and it was surpassed but fewer attendees than expected actually showed up, it does not necessarily make the campaign a success. Narrowly, the objective was achieved, but, in this case, it may have been the incorrect item to measure. Sometimes, seemingly valuable objectives appear less central once the campaign is complete. Such feedback and subsequent adjustment leads to continuous refinement of campaign planning and execution that progressively increases impact and relevance to organizational goals over time.

The process of evaluation allows the team to work together to examine and assess the effectiveness of planning, strategies, and implementation processes. Particularly for elements that had unexpected results, this review becomes an invaluable exercise to understand. Was the strategy or message mismatched with the audience? Was the paid media spend more effective than anticipated? Was the paper that the brochure was printed on too low grade for it to have the desired impact? Did event attendance exceed expectations? Were the wrong reporters pitched? Were the right reporters pitched but at the wrong time? Both big-picture decisions and minute details matter.

One approach is to evaluate the campaign in stages. Examining the public relations team's success in the preparation of the campaign, during implementation, and based on its impact.[2] This means examining the quality and thoroughness of preparation and implementation activities, as well as whether their consequences and results were met for each objective. This step-by-step breakdown allows practitioners to understand whether challenges occurred because a particular program did not have time to be executed properly (preparation issue), because an idea did not resonate with reporters to generate coverage (implementation issue), or because, despite a paid media spend, a new website did not receive the anticipated traffic (impact issue).

Public relations campaigns are difficult to evaluate in part because they never operate in isolation.[3] A continually changing environment and a variety of moving parts mean that each component cannot be tested independently to define exactly which features or actions affect the outcome. This is compounded by the inherent uniqueness of campaigns, numerous environmental and situational factors, and lack of **control groups**. In scientific experiments, a control group remains unchanged to demonstrate that the variable or factor being tested creates the expected impact. Real-world campaigns are rarely able to recreate the circumstances of a lab. Multiple factors often work together to influence success in ways that are complex and impossible to separate. The easier areas to evaluate (Facebook "likes," media clips, ad viewership, or website visitors) are, on their own, often the least consequential for campaign success. To this end, Watson and Noble warn against spending too much time and effort evaluating the *process* phase and instead focusing on impact.[4]

Despite these challenges, evaluation research need not require "wide-ranging, expensive and highly technical exercises."[5] Many evaluative tools can be executed simply if they are built into the campaign from the beginning. They may require an investment of time and focus, but many organizations overestimate the resources needed to glean valuable information.

Media Evaluation

A first step in the process of media evaluation includes media monitoring and media analysis. According to Watson and Noble, measuring media coverage should be "systemic, continuous, part of an overall evaluation process, and related to objectives."[6] Today's media monitoring uses a variety of tools, from technology-driven methods such as free Google News Alerts to paid services like Cision. That said, the exercise still relies on many low-tech approaches, such as reading hardcopy newspapers and magazines, watching television interviews, and checking media websites for updates. Not all relevant media coverage appears online in a searchable form, particularly radio

©iStockPhotos/skodonnell

Evaluating media relations is about more than counting the number of media placements earned, it's about measuring their impact toward organizational objectives.

and television content. Digital tools are not perfect, and many practitioners use several simultaneously to attempt to fill such holes. The role of individuals tracking down specific pieces of coverage will never fully be absent from the process.

Once media coverage has been identified, the process of content analysis (as described in Chapter 5) can begin. Some professionals use the mnemonic **I.M.P.A.C.T.** to identify potential criteria for evaluation: *Influence* or tone, *Message* communicated, *Prominence*, *Audience* reached, *Consultant/spokesman* quoted, and *Type* of article.[7] Not all of these criteria are relevant in all media coverage analyses, so practitioners can focus on what is most pertinent to their goals and objectives.

Media evaluation should include both qualitative and quantitative analysis. Some facets are easy to quantify (How many articles were run? How often were key messages included?), while others such as prominence and tone are more subjective. While prominence, for example, can be graded on a 0–10 scale from lowest to highest prominence, such systems implemented by public relations teams have the disadvantage of **observer bias**, where those performing the analysis have a predisposition to favor certain results.[8]

This initial analysis of campaign coverage often leads to broader questions for a wider evaluation of the campaign's results toward objectives. To demonstrate additional nuance, beyond simply reporting the **raw volume** of clips, organizations can share the **relative volume** of coverage.[9] This may be done using time benchmarks (comparing the three months of a campaign to the same three months from the prior year) or competitor benchmarks (comparing three months of an organization's media coverage to the same three months of a competitor's media coverage). Context is added through comparison. Reporting can also be completed using **weighted volume**, based on a scoring system adjusted for the campaign including factors such as organizational prominence, message inclusion, and outlet quality. This approach allows practitioners to quantify the value of media coverage in relation to other coverage and can provide valuable insights related to a campaign's effectiveness, particularly to improve the work

PRo Tip

FOUR QUESTIONS FOR ANALYZING MEDIA COVERAGE

1. How much coverage was received on a specific topic and for what audiences?
2. How often and how prominently were the campaign's messages, spokespersons, and organizations included in this coverage?
3. How did the type of coverage affect audience perception?
4. How positively or negatively were the messages presented or framed in the coverage?

of the public relations team over the long term. That said, such metrics alone rarely connect directly to organizational objectives and therefore should not serve as the only method of evaluation. They are first steps toward following K. D. Paine's advice: a focus on measuring "what matters" rather than on vanity metrics.[10]

Digital Evaluation Metrics and Approaches

The abundance of social media channels and owned media, including websites and blogs, has created a niche evaluation realm in the digital space. A significant amount of data is easily accessible, with major social media channels and Google Analytics providing straightforward quantitative data and, often, a variety of easy-to-share charts and tables. On one hand, the digital world is ready-made for reporting campaign results to a dashboard-driven C-suite. Yet, such metrics often do not tell the whole story. They may not answer questions of awareness, opinion change, or behavior change and do not necessarily address a campaign's objectives. Gaining 200 new Twitter followers may be a valuable step for a campaign but only if they are the right audience members and actively engage with the organization. They may also be of no additional value. It is in the evaluation process where public relations practitioners must dig deeper into both qualitative and quantitative data in order to understand what is important and what is not.

As with media relations, managing digital channels includes both a monitoring/measurement and evaluation component. The four stages of digital audience outreach

A variety of digital tools (such as Hootsuite, shown above) help practitioners track the impact of their campaigns, which often involves analyzing data gathered before, during, and after implementation.

can be assessed as exposure (reach and impressions), engagement ("likes" and shares, as well as the sentiment and tone of interactions), influence (respect and relevance), and action (behavior change, impact, and value).[11] These stages are progressive and build on each other. Depending on their goals and objectives, individual campaigns may value specific stages more than others, but action cannot take place without exposure, engagement, and influence.

The process of selecting the appropriate metrics presents an additional challenge, particularly as *reach* and *impressions* may be calculated very differently based on the channel. These can add to the evaluation only within historical content: did a specific campaign attract more attention on Facebook this year over last year? Often, this is based on more mechanical factors such as the types of posts shared (text, links, images, or video, for example) and their priorities within ever-shifting algorithms. It may be useful for communicators to track and optimize their content and posting approaches, but it is less indicative of true impact, making it less valuable from a reporting perspective. Developing reporting documents in this way, and explaining the choices to organizational leaders, helps to steer them away from vanity metrics and see social media (and public relations more broadly) as integral to success and deeply connected to organization-wide goals and objectives.

TABLE 10.1

Exposure, Engagement, Influence, Action

	Exposure	Engagement	Influence	Action
Paid	• OTS • Click-throughs • Cost per thousand	• Duration • Branded research • Cost per click	• Purchase consideration • Change in opinion or attitude	• Visit website • Attend event • Download coupons
Earned	• Message inclusion • Impressions • Net positive impressions	• Readership • Awareness • URL visits	• Purchase consideration • Change in opinion or attitude	• Visit the store • Vote for/against • Make a donation
Shared	• OTS • Comment sentiment • Number of followers	• Number of links • Number of retweets • Subscribers	• Tell a friend • Ratings • Reviews	• Redeem coupon • Buy the product • Visit the website
Owned	• Unique visitors • Page views • Search rank	• Return visits • Durations • Subscriptions	• Tell a friend • Change in opinion or attitude	• Download white paper • Request more info

Source: Adapted from Richard Bagnall, "Metrics That Matter: Making Sense of Social Media Measurement" (Presented at Public Relations and Corporate Communications Summit, Agra, India, 2014).

Turning Evaluation Into Improvement

Initially, evaluation should take place within the communication department as an opportunity to assess the team's actions. Much of the work performed and lessons learned at this stage may not be entirely useful beyond the department itself. For example, tweaks to pitching and reporter outreach for a media relations campaign, budgetary adjustments to optimize Facebook advertising spends, or deciding to change vendors for the next video production project may/may not be relevant to organizational leadership. Evaluating your campaign means understanding what worked and what could have been more effective. Moving from evaluation to reporting becomes the process of selecting the most important and beneficial information to drive improvement for those outside the department or the agency public relations team.

REPORTING ON YOUR CAMPAIGN

Public relations reporting is the process of organizing and sharing the results of campaign evaluation. It should take into account a broad perspective of a campaign's success or failure, convey lessons learned, and reflect the strategic choices of the campaign's execution. Reporting should clearly explain whether objectives have been achieved. While components should be reported in an integrated fashion, paid, earned, shared, and owned tactics often have distinct considerations for accuracy and clarity.

Ideally, campaign reports are presented in person to key organizational stakeholders. This allows for more detailed explanation and emphasis of major points and the ability to read audience reactions to understand where more explanation may be necessary. Interactivity drives increasingly efficient and effective explanations, as well as a richer discussion regarding how campaign objectives, strategies, and tactics may be improved in the future. Written reporting documents often serve as a more detailed reference and takeaway from such meetings.

The presentation of campaign reports should be selective in content and developed specifically for the audiences at hand. Will leadership be familiar with marketing language? What information does the full group need to know, as opposed to specific departments? While reporting documents are often based on templates, they should allow enough flexibility to highlight different metrics or data based on the campaign and audience. Efforts to get to know executives personally allow for reporting documents to better reflect their priorities, as well as their preferences for receiving information.[12] Such information might drive the decision between bullet points and bar charts or between emailed reports and hard copies presented during a formal meeting.

Objective-Driven Reporting

Objectives can serve as an organizing tool for a campaign's results. While not all evaluation results from objectives, they should always be the center of reporting. As strategies and tactics flow from objectives, results can be framed based on whether the individual objectives were achieved. Eisenmann recommends practitioners "link achievements directly to business goals so that C-suite executives will see what PR results mean to them."[13]

Measurable objectives require a particular level of quantitative analysis, but qualitative approaches may also add significant value and insight. For example, a report describing the achievement of a narrow objective related to lead capture at a conference may describe several strategies and tactics used to build relationships and gather contact information for sales leads, including a trade booth, conference-specific social media outreach, expert presentations, earned trade media coverage, as well as advertisements and sponsorships of conference events. Quantitative analysis may show that two-thirds of the leads captured resulted from the trade booth, but qualitative analysis, which could be based on quick debriefing interviews with the on-site sales team after the conference, may show that the most valuable and promising leads came from the expert presentation. Combined, these two levels of evaluation can provide a much more complete picture of the campaign.

Practitioners should also keep in mind that it is possible for objectives to not add up to a campaign's goal. It is worth stepping back to see whether the objectives, however thoughtfully crafted, S.M.A.R.T., and well executed, may not have adequately captured what the organization needed to achieve its goal. This may be an important point to convey during the reporting stage as well as to inform future campaigns.

Inclusive Reporting and Evaluation

Often, reporting and evaluating processes and priorities reflect existing organizational biases: public relations practitioners seeking to demonstrate the success of their campaigns will be less likely to report initiatives that do not achieve what was intended. The opinions of skeptical or activist publics may be excluded from discussions about impact. Organizational leaders want to know about the impact on the organization, sometimes at the expense of understanding the impact on local communities. In its boundary-spanning role, public relations professionals have the opportunity and obligation to provide evaluation and reporting that presents a representative picture of a campaign's outcomes.

First, evaluation should occur beyond the organization's goals and the campaign's objectives. Practitioners must examine what social and community impacts occurred. This could include (1) tracking unintended consequences (as in the implementation phase); (2) watching for the reactions of stakeholders and publics beyond the campaign's target audiences; and (3) seeking out the broader social implications from campaign messaging and outreach. Each of these may be positive or negative for the organization, as well as positive or negative for the external group(s) involved.

Next, from a reporting perspective, practitioners have an obligation to use smart segmentation to report on a campaign's messages in ways that are transparent and effective for each stakeholder group. This means that campaign reporting should not be too detailed for an audience to take time for or too technical for them to understand. This is always a good practice when communicating to different groups within the organization but takes on a more ethically important role when communicating to groups outside the organization—particularly those who may be marginalized or negatively affected by an organization's actions.

Finally, practitioners should seek out diverse audiences inside and outside the organization for two-way communication. This includes considering who has been impacted (positively and negatively) by the campaign, sharing information with them, and providing conduits for open-ended feedback. Organizations that proactively seek out the perspectives and opinions of such groups will be rewarded with important insights to improve future messaging and campaigns—both for the organization and in terms of broad community impact.

PRo Tip

REPORTING BEST PRACTICES

- Provide an executive summary of key takeaways.
- Be blunt: Did you reach each objective or not?
- Organize by objectives rather than by channels.
- Always report on what worked...and what didn't.
    - Consider what strategies, tactics, and channels made the campaign successful or where they could have been more successful.
    - What internal organizational structures, people, or resources made the campaign successful? Where could priority or emphasis shift next time?
    - In retrospect, were the budget and objectives appropriate?
    - Who from outside your team or department should be thanked or congratulated for their support or efforts toward the campaign?
- Use language accessible to all participants: Be aware of the level of knowledge and expertise of your participants.
    - Choose the report's depth and language accordingly.
    - Explain critical concepts when necessary.
- Include visuals where possible.
    - Graphics can demonstrate success related to output, outtake, and outcome objectives.
    - Visuals should deepen the amount of information included concisely. They should shorten, not lengthen, the overall report.
- Assume the report will not be read in full. Make the contents scannable and reiterate key findings.
- Tie campaign results to broader organizational and competitive goals, objectives, and strategies.
- Move beyond findings: Include recommendations and lessons learned for future campaigns.

- What was learned about the target public?
- How should future objectives be structured differently to better reflect organizational goals?
- What tactics worked particularly well? Why?
    - How can they inform the choice of future tactics?
- What messages were most effective? Why?
    - What made these messages better vehicles for the campaign?
    - How can this improve the crafting of future messages?

Prioritization: What Information Is Most Important for the Reader?

Initially, practitioners must be able to make a judgment call on what information is the most valuable for the intended audience. This begins with an appropriate understanding of the objectives and the core evaluation questions related to the campaign. The highest priority information should describe how and why a campaign has met or not met its objectives. Which strategies and tactics were most instrumental? What external factors contributed to or hindered execution? What unexpected challenges arose? Weaving this information into a coherent, concise narrative creates an executive summary that should be reinforced throughout the report itself.

Beyond the central storyline of the objectives, the next factor to consider should be the takeaways: What information can contribute the most to inform future projects? This may include insights about how key stakeholders react to certain strategies, how competitors take advantage of an organization's lack of resources dedicated to a specific channel, or even information regarding the timing and scheduling of events. Small details can make a difference and often speak to larger issues. Positioning such recommendations early on in reporting allows the audience to glean immediate value from the necessary quantitative and qualitative research that occurs as campaigns are executed.

Additional areas that are valuable in the reporting structure include any challenges, surprises, and/or outright failures. By directly addressing any unexpected events resulting from a campaign, practitioners highlight additional areas of learning and improvement. Each raises the question, why did this catch us by surprise? The process of answering such questions provides a unique opportunity to demonstrate continuous improvement for the public relations team. Sharing such insights with the broader organization can also help other areas anticipate the same challenges and identify the same blind spots related to knowledge of audiences, markets, and the competitive environment.

Format: How Should Your Information Be Best Presented to Your Audience?

Reporting for a specific audience requires appropriate document development to facilitate the delivery of relevant information. Practitioners should ask themselves several questions: What background does the audience have on the campaign and on integrated communication? What organizational conventions exist? How much information are they used to receiving? Understanding their background might, for example, point toward employing more/fewer visuals, a sense of the most valuable overall length and depth, and how communication-centric the content should be.

Expectations play a key role, but practitioners should also consider timing to be an important factor. In some cases, a quick preliminary report may be what leadership requires in order to support key decisions on a pressing strategic challenge. In other instances, they may prefer the accessible depth of a well-constructed, detailed summary with appendices for more information. An extra week or two to complete a full report may matter to the audience, or the circumstance may not necessarily be urgent in nature.

PESO: SPECIAL REPORTING CONSIDERATIONS

Paid Media

An advantage of paid media, particularly within digital opportunities, is the variety and depth of available metrics to track and evaluate success. The danger for practitioners comes when there is an overwhelming volume of data. Determining the value and relevance of tracking and reporting tools, and the subsequent approach, is often half the battle. Working with vendors, whether they are advertising agencies, media outlets, or event planners, should mean having access to the metrics they compile on your campaigns—and they should do their best to present that information in a useful format for your reporting efforts.

Reporting for paid media should have an explicit focus on the budget. Was the spend sufficient? Did the content run for the most effective length of time? Was it allocated to the most effective mix channels in the right proportions? Did the dollar spend have the desired audience impact? As there is more control with the placement and messages for paid media, these factors can be more heavily scrutinized. Recommendations based on how to better scale and optimize the spend for future campaigns are always valuable.

Additionally, as there tends to be more data to share, organization and presentation becomes more critical. Tables, charts, and graphs should be scannable, contextualized, and only contain as much information as needed. Practitioners should only include relevant data, and its purpose within the overall report must be clear.[14]

Earned Media

Evaluation and reporting of media relations should reflect the motivation or purpose for the campaign itself. As described in the evaluation section, it is important to showcase the impact of media relations, not just the coverage itself. Media relations evaluation should also include qualitative and quantitative components (for example, the value of building a new relationship with a key media contact, as well as the share-of-voice percentage in key publications). It should also, whenever possible, reinforce the impact of media coverage on audiences, including actions such as sending traffic back to organizational websites (look for spikes in visitors on days with significant media coverage) or awareness changes (measured in a pretest/posttest survey of publics). Research tools such as content analysis can play a significant role in demonstrating value, as well as understanding potential areas for improvement in future campaigns.

Organizational leaders also should be reminded of the value of earned media coverage toward credibility. When distinguishing between paid and earned coverage, for example, it is valuable to bring up the increased credibility that publics see when organizational messages are conveyed through a trusted, appropriate media outlet, rather than coming directly from the organization.

Shared Media

As described earlier in this chapter, social media reporting provides a wide range of easily accessible data for reporting. The downside to this data-rich environment is that practitioners must wade through many irrelevant metrics to find those that connect with campaign objectives and organizational goals. Is raising awareness

Education Images/Universal Images Group/Getty Images

Practitioners should work with vendors and media outlets to capture data about the impact and influence of paid media outreach.

important? Impressions, page visits, or the right clicks or downloads may be valuable. Surveying retention of the message, event, brand, or product at hand would be best. Building relationships? Engagement through social channels can demonstrate useful activity, and analysis of tone or message content can unpack its types and qualities. Don't simply measure the size of a community; determine the number of active members who meet a campaign's target audience. See if the number of active members is larger than in your competitors' communities. Aiming for online sales or fundraising goals? Connect social media outreach (along with owned media channels) to Google Analytics to track buyers or donors to determine what directed them to your site. Knowledge from any of these areas can help move beyond speaking only to existing digital communities and counting Facebook "likes."

Social media can also be analyzed qualitatively as well. When reviewing engagement, for example, it's important to select key conversation themes and examples to share. Such insights can often help explain or expand on quantitative findings. A brand's tone, voice, and character cannot be fully captured in quantitative data, and reporting on the reactions and interactions among digital communities based on these factors yields valuable information for how organizations are perceived.

Owned Media

Like social media, organizational websites, email newsletters, and other digital owned media provide a variety of metrics through the use of Google Analytics, MailChimp distribution data, and other various reporting tools. They can connect particular drivers (such as an email newsletter) to users who take action on the website by filling out a form, purchasing a product, or making a donation. The more insights the public relations team has about the types of audience members most likely to take action, the better. Additionally, these tools can help identify issues and challenges that may arise during campaign implementation. Are digital forms too complicated for the average user? Many will begin but not complete the form. Is the form too hard to find on the page? Many will go to the page and not click on the form. From a reporting perspective, these findings allow a practitioner to explain the minutia of a campaign when needed but also defend the decisions made throughout. Not all measurement details are relevant to an executive or client audience, but those relating to specific objectives can easily become valuable insights organization wide.

Other types of owned media, from a refurbished office space to event-based outreach, can be more difficult to measure in detail, but these challenges can be overcome with a bit of planning. For example, putting processes in place to ask (both digitally and in person) how new customers who found out about your business can identify how different channels, such as the website, are informing users. Digital tracking can also support traditional owned media efforts. A print magazine can still reference a distinct website landing page, allowing organizations to see which of their tactics sent more visitors. Tracking event attendance is relatively straightforward, but developing a brief qualitative survey can help to provide even more useful insights about publics, successes, and improvements for future outreach.

Integrated Reporting

While various channels require distinct reporting tools and approaches, strategic communication campaigns often are best served by integrated reporting. It is "highly desirable" to combine media coverage from different channels into the same evaluation and reporting documents and formats.[15] Not only does this represent the convergence of media outlets but also reinforces for leadership and clients that the content of the coverage is ultimately as important as the source. As objectives should ideally reflect behavioral and opinion-based change rather than process, reporting can be organized around strategies and tactics contributing to specific objectives. One objective may necessitate paid, shared, and owned approaches, while a second may have focused on earned and shared strategies and tactics. Organizing and connecting the reporting around objectives rather than specific channels reinforces strategic integration. It frames public relations as a solution focused rather than as fragmented and isolated. It positions organizational goals above the vanity metrics of Twitter followers and website hits. Fully integrated reporting best supports the counselor role of public relations as a conduit, a bridge, and a sounding board between and among organizations and their publics.

Integrated reporting may necessitate additional context to ensure clarity for readers. Practitioners should interpret results and connect strategies to impact in order to ensure which findings resonate. What campaign elements were successful across channels? How and why did particular tactics work well together (or not work well together)? What do integrated findings say about specific audiences? Integration should seem natural and obvious to executives or clients, but that often only happens when it is presented in a way that highlights the connections behind such choices.

CONCLUSION

Evaluation and reporting are critical steps to understanding what happened during any campaign, but they also serve as excellent examples of the larger strategic role public relations plays in helping organizations succeed. They demonstrate outreach into the environment and generate direct feedback as to what approach, messages, strategies, and tactics succeed or fail. Evaluative research provides rich insights about stakeholders and publics that are often insightful for organizational leaders beyond the realm of communication. Reporting processes give practitioners the opportunity to make the case that their work matters relative to organizational goals. Together, this understanding of a campaign's impact and the ability to effectively and efficiently share the insights gleaned during and after execution allow public relations practitioners to show their full value.

THINK CRITICALLY

1. Why is it important to evaluate objectives in terms of both achievement and relevance to the campaign?
2. What information is critical for the communication team, and what should be reported to leadership?
3. How might the specific internal audience impact the reporting choices for campaign results?
4. How does evaluation contribute to improving future campaigns?

KEY TERMS

Control groups 197
I.M.P.A.C.T. (mnemonic) 199
Observer bias 199
Raw volume 199
Relative volume 199
Weighted volume 199

CONCEPT CASE: REPORTING RESULTS—COMMUNITY FLOW YOGA'S ANNUAL MEETING

You've been asked to prepare a five-minute presentation for the annual company leadership meeting for Community Flow Yoga. It is a short window to convince these leaders' stakeholders that integrated public relations has made an impact over the course of the past year. Your campaign is still in progress (final results are not in), but you'll need to begin organizing, creating, and formatting your presentation. The immediate audience will not be familiar with public relations and marketing language and terminology, and many have not been involved in the creation of the campaign's goals and objectives.

- What reporting approaches can help you make the case for communication's impact role over the past year?
- What elements could you use to set the scene and provide background information?
- How might your formative and developmental research play a role?
- How might you demonstrate the success of media relations efforts?
- What would be the most useful social media metrics to include?
- What role has owned media, including the website, played in the year's successes?

CASE STUDY: HP'S CONTINUED COMMITMENT TO GLOBAL WELLNESS

Based on PRSA Silver Anvil Winner
Campaign Focus: Employee Communication/Global Employee Communication

Health and well-being are linked to employee engagement, productivity, talent retention, and creativity and innovation. In 2011, HP stepped up its investment in wellness programs, striving to support employees at all levels of health and fitness. HP launched its first-ever Global Wellness Challenge (GWC) to promote employee wellness and help drive wellness engagement. Five years later, HP's annual GWC is still going strong. The company even turns its campus into a mini Olympics stadium.[16]

Research/Diagnosis

For the GWC, HP partnered with an external vendor (RSW, a communications agency) to create a health and wellness platform in order to study the progress of employees.[17] According to research conducted by HP, two-thirds of Americans are overweight and 80 percent of employees work in inactive jobs.[18] Moreover, more than three-quarters of employees feel that their job is stressful, costing businesses $300 billion a year in the US. This stress is only compounded by unhealthy behaviors and chronic conditions such as smoking, diabetes, and alcohol abuse.[19]

The main objective of this health initiative was to focus on a different issue each year. For example, in 2015, the GWC concentrated on contributing to weight loss.[20] That said, fitness trackers were given to employees in nine different countries for them to be able to track their progress online over the course of six weeks. Employees were encouraged to "walk around the world" in an environmentally friendly competition.[21]

In 2017, the HP GWC focused on "The Power of Prevention." In thirty-four countries, outreach raised awareness of skin, breast, colorectal, cervical, prostate, lung, liver, and stomach cancers.[22] The Power of Prevention theme's core message was, "do one thing to fight cancer." HP's online community allowed employees to share stories, developing a unified HP employee community.[23] Two years later, the company conducted a global walkathon, where employees participated to walk in and around the campus for 5–10 km.[24] In another new component, "Run" is a campaign where family members of HP employees can participate in the GWC to encourage family-wide health.[25]

India posed some specific challenges for HP employees, which led to development of a special component of the walkathon. According to Indian employee engagement firm, the Fuller Life, "urban professionals are now combating first-world problems such as lifestyle, illnesses, mental health issues, stress, and that elusive work-life balance."[26] As such, HP has created a second, more focused campaign in India that complements the broader GWC.

Objectives

The team took a multifaceted approach to reach this diverse global employee base and drive registration and participation. More specifically, HP wanted to bring together all of the stakeholders of corporate India's wellness.[27] In addition, 2019's GWC focused on increasing the participation percentage in India to 60–80 percent over the course of two months.[28] Finally, HP wanted to "focus on addressing the fact that talking about some of these issues can be uncomfortable or embarrassing."[29] Of course, these align with the GWC's first-ever objectives: program satisfaction, continued behavioral change, and employee team building.

Strategies

Like the first GWC, HP focused on four key audiences:

- HP Human Resources Community: Ensure Human Resources representatives were aware of the program and could support it locally as needed, as well as serve as role models for participation.
- HP Communications Community: Ensure HP leaders at all levels corporate-wide (and the communicators who support them) were prepared to help promote the event.
- HP "Wellness Ambassadors": Ensure that more than 100 volunteer Global Wellness Ambassadors around the world were informed and equipped to support the event locally.
- HP employees worldwide: Recognizing that employees are people first, HP sought to appeal to their interests in earning incentives, winning prizes, and socializing with their peers in addition to improving their health—regardless of their current state of fitness or physical activity.

In 2019, however, HP added a fifth target audience in India: the family members of employees. The campaign culminates in a "Run" wherein the family members, such as spouses and kids of the employees, can also participate. Participation in the "Run" depends on the number of steps achieved by the employees to make sure they have enough stamina.[30]

Tactics

Owned and Shared

- High-impact initial email to drive participation, with follow-ups: With "push" email recognized as the most efficient way to reach HP's large global population and raise initial awareness, the team wanted this email to stand out and be clearly recognizable as a branded HP communication. Follow-up emails during the registration period gave smaller-population HP countries a chance to shine by showing high participation rates during registration.
- Materials for HP leaders and HR team members: Communication toolkits were posted and publicized for leaders and their communicators to use in team meetings and in their business unit communication channels, such as newsletters and web-pages.
- Materials for local use, translated if necessary.
- Web resources, including ways to share employee-generated content and a social networking platform.
- A GWC welcome kit was mailed to participants at home to encourage participation and add a fun element to recording personal progress with pedometers and a personal logbook.
- Weekly participant emails, with encouragement and reminders.
- Curated content from a variety of relevant sources, including intranet articles and flash videos.
- GWC-themed invitations to participate in local wellness events such as walking tours or exercise sessions were sent to all employees and families.

To bring its strategy to fruition, HP took a comprehensive approach with human-centered benefits. The company has been offering extensive health and wellness benefits and well-being packages to employees. These were posted and publicized for leaders and their communicators to share and promote in team meetings as well as in their business unit communication channels, such as newsletters and webpages. Moreover, HP provided access for its employees to a wide range of resources that include retirement planning, student loan programs, special activities challenges designed for families, and much more.[31]

Every year, HP gives out fitness trackers to its employees to help them keep track of the number of steps they take over the course of the challenge. The more steps they take, the more the challenge's virtual journey translates into a literal, physically rewarding journey for employees and participants around the world. These journeys include the Seven Wonders of the World, the 2019 theme, traveling between iconic buildings within a single country.

In addition to physical health, GWC has added mental well-being to its programming. To achieve its objective of normalizing conversations about mental health, Samantha DuBridge, vice president and global benefits employee at HP, and her team reached out to mental health professionals and pieced together a clinical group to develop an integrated approach to mental health care. This is to raise awareness and make it easier for employees to open up about behavioral health issues.[32] As such, DuBridge provided middle managers with tips and tricks on how to talk about mental health with their teams in a practical yet comfortable way. In addition, HP took significant efforts to educate employees on its employee assistance program to encourage open and honest communication about mental health and focus on delivering accessible and trustworthy mental health services to employees' family members. To drive participation, HP developed a mailing initiative dubbed "Adulting 101," where it promoted HP's employee assistance, program, and benefits such as discounts on movie tickets, food, health care at school, and telemedicine services.

Implementation

Creative execution delivered a consistent look and feel online, at events, and in visual communications to sharpen the focus on wellness as a whole and give a recognizable feel to the GWC campaign. The following guidelines were used:

- Featured realistic-looking people in marketing materials rather than models. They also included actual employees when possible.
- Deliberately shared stories through employees at all levels of the organization rather than traditional CEO/senior executive endorsement, including testimonial videos and ongoing content.
- Communicated about incentives to build excitement and anticipation. For example, Adulting 101 helped build enthusiasm along the way.
- Support localized communication as much as possible.

Reporting/Evaluation

The GWC managed to obtain the participation of 50,000 employees in nearly ninety countries. While there are no specific metrics for the "Run" campaign as part of GWC, a significant benefit was the ability to bring employees together around the world. Indeed, one employee said, "I'm here in the US, and the rest of my family is in India, and we had an opportunity to do something together virtually. So, people were getting their kids involved in exercise and were able to spend more time with their families."[33]

Theories

By providing a consistent flow of materials explaining the benefits of the wellness program, particularly the variety of relatable success stories and group nature, the campaign reflects the work of social cognitive theory (SCT).[34] SCT emphasizes the role of several key factors in changing behaviors and is particularly well tested in health and wellness contexts: the importance of modeling behaviors and giving individuals a sense of agency or *self-efficacy* to believe that they can succeed in making the desired change.[35]

Model

As a persuasion-based campaign, this approach successfully engaged more than 50,000 employees to participate in HP's program through a carefully planned and coordinated communication program.[36] Its objective was specific behavioral change rather than being flexible and audience conscious in its implementation.

Diversity- and Inclusion-First Approach

Beyond focusing on the physical qualities and abilities that are part of the Diversity & Inclusion Wheel, HP also considered thinking styles and learning styles by helping people change their perception that talking about mental health issues is unacceptable. Moreover, the company has touched on personal habits, mental health and well-being, and recreational habits by emphasizing the importance of being healthy: In this case, a holistic approach to health made the campaign more reflective of the values of diversity and inclusion.

Formulating an Integrated Campaign

11

iStock.com/LoveTheWind

This final chapter includes some foundational guides and templates including the ROSTIR PR Planning Guide, the PRSA Independent Practitioners Alliance (IPA) proposal template, an example client report, an audience persona guide, and a crisis communication plan.

This chapter is adapted from Regina M. Luttrell and Luke W., Capizzo. *Public Relations Campaigns: An Integrated Approach* (Thousand Oaks, CA: SAGE Publications, 2018). 227–250.

ROSTIR STRATEGIC PLANNING GUIDE

This text was built around the ROSTIR Strategic Planning Guide. This chapter offers a template that serves as an outline for an integrated campaign and demonstrates what can be accomplished when researching and, ultimately, when executing a complete campaign

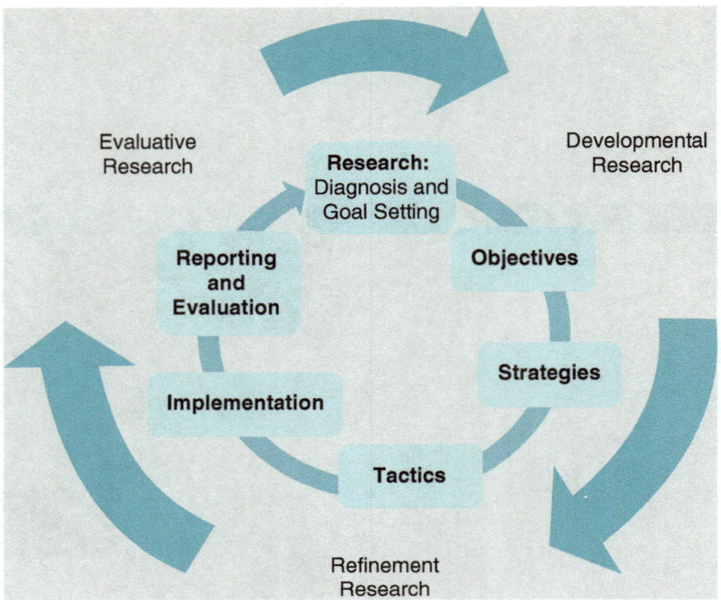

The ROSTIR Strategic Planning Guide helps direct PR professionals through the process of developing a purposeful campaign. R-research (diagnosis and goal setting), O-objectives, S-strategies, T-tactics, I-implementation, and R-reporting and evaluation.

for a client or organization. A number of essential components should be included when preparing a campaign using the ROSTIR strategic planning guide.

Strategic PR Plan
Company Name
Date
Contact Information
Project Lead
Phone Number
Email

TABLE OF CONTENTS
Executive Summary

1. Research—Program Diagnosis and Analysis
    a. Strengths, Weaknesses, Opportunities, and Threats (SWOT) Analysis
2. Objectives and Key Performance Indicators
3. Strategies

4. Tactics
    a. Performance and Monitoring
    b. PESO (paid, earned, shared, and owned media)
5. Implementation and Execution
6. Reporting and Evaluation
7. Conclusion

Executive Summary

The executive summary is a high-level synopsis of the campaign's diagnosis and the solutions offered. This section covers several key points of interest to the client.

Research: Program Diagnosis and Analysis

Research is at the core of all PR activities. Proper research leads to diagnosing the problem and identifying solutions for clients.[1] Depending on the client's needs, various research methods can be used. Research methods can be broadly categorized into two groups:[2]

- *Secondary:* This method involves gathering information from published or professional sources such as peer-reviewed journals, case studies, published reports, white papers, books, professional journals, and archives as well as digital and online sources; internal or proprietary organizational sources; and existing earned media coverage.
- *Primary:* This is research conducted firsthand. Research options include analysis of existing content (qualitative or quantitative), surveys and questionnaires, one-to-one interviews, telephone interviews, focus groups, copy and product testing, psychographic studies, and analysis of digital or social media analytics.
- *Diversity-First Approach:* Applying the diversity-first approach to campaign planning, executing, and reporting starts with research. Use the Diversity & Inclusion Wheel to create diverse campaigns by considering diverse perspectives as to what stakeholders to include, which opinions to prioritize and to reduce potential blind spots in planning. As PR practitioners it is our responsibility to make diversity and inclusion top of mind when developing strategies for our clients.

Within this section, include a summary of the target audience(s). The research helps to identify key publics and stakeholders. The degree of influence, prestige, power, needs, or level of involvement with the client helps identify potential publics.[3] This section should address the following:

- An explanation of those affected by the PR campaign. This section includes data on the demographics, psychographics, audience personas, and overarching characteristics of key stakeholders.
- How the Diversity & Inclusion Wheel was used to develop audience personas and identify key demographics
- Opinion leaders, credible sources, and influencers
- Media to be targeted through PESO
- Benchmarks or metrics that can be used to track progress and success during and after the campaign

SWOT Analysis

A SWOT analysis is a qualitative method that brings together a variety of secondary research about an organization and its competitors/industry peers, combined with primary research to add the input and perspective of organizational leaders. SWOT, which stands for strengths, weaknesses, opportunities, and threats, is an analytical framework that allows organizations to better understand their position in the marketplace.[4] A SWOT analysis enables organizations to pinpoint both internal and external influences that help organizations develop a full picture of all factors necessary for planning.

Goals

It's helpful to connect research and insights on the industry and situation to the broader organizational mission. These areas of connectivity can help point practitioners toward the aspirational goals to set as part of their campaigns.

Objectives and Key Performance Indicators

Once developmental and audience research has been conducted, the central problem/opportunity identified, and goals set, it is time to define the objectives and outline other key performance indicators (KPIs). The objectives should include the end result of the PR activity. Each objective must be SMART:[5]

- **Specific**: Is the objective clearly defined and appropriately focused?
- **Measurable**: Can each objective be measured before, during, and after outreach has occurred to evaluate change?
- **Achievable**: Considering other factors (e.g., budget and time constraints), is each objective achievable?

- **Realistic**: Are you being realistic, given the resources available and constraints?
- **Time bound**: What timing is necessary to achieve the set objectives and by what date do you want to achieve them?

As you develop objectives think: Action + Context + Audience + Volume + Duration

- Increase **awareness** of (*product, event, issue*) among (*public*) by (*degree of change*) over (*period of time*).
- Increase positive **opinion** of (*organization, issue, individual, product*) among (*public*) by (*degree of change*) over (*period of time*).
- Increase **behavior** (*donations made, web pages visited, products sold*) among (*public*) by (*degree of change*) over (*period of time*).

Depending on the desired outcome of the overall campaign there is a hierarchy that can be used.

- *Awareness* (*cognitive*)
    - Focus on information
    - Attention
    - Comprehension
- *Opinion* (*attitudinal*)
    - Focus on feeling about information
    - Interest
    - Attitude
- *Behavior* (*conative*)
    - Focus on response to information
    - Taking action
    - Behavioral change

A KPI, known as a key performance indicator, is a measurable value that demonstrates how effectively a company is achieving key business objectives.[6] Organizations use KPIs to evaluate their success at reaching targets.

Develop KPIs that are easy to measure, quick to report on, and can be checked regularly. Gijs Nelissen offers the following common KPIs that companies use to measure the success of their PR initiatives:[7]

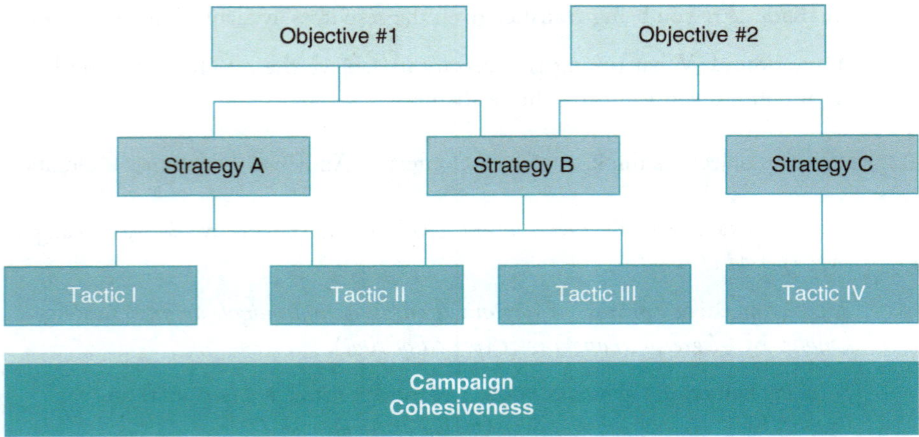

- New social media followers
- New referral links
- Increased organic website traffic
- New leads or sign-ups

Strategies

Strategies define several channels or other communication opportunities that, when combined, help a campaign achieve its objectives. This section includes a broad statement describing how an objective will be achieved. Strategies provide guidelines and key messages while also offering a rationale for the execution. Strategies and tactics are often interdependent. A *strategy* is the approach, while *tactics* are the tangible aspects of the campaign: A strategy may include using consumer media outreach in a specific geographic market, while accompanying tactics could describe the specific PESO channels, media outlets, or other actions to be taken as part of the implementation of that strategy. There may be multiple strategies in a campaign designed for various targeted audiences.

Tactics

Tactics are the activities implemented to carry out each campaign strategy. Practitioners use a number of integrated communication tools to execute a campaign; however, the challenge is identifying the appropriate tactics for each situation and each audience or public. Depending on the campaign, the right tactic may be proactive media relations,

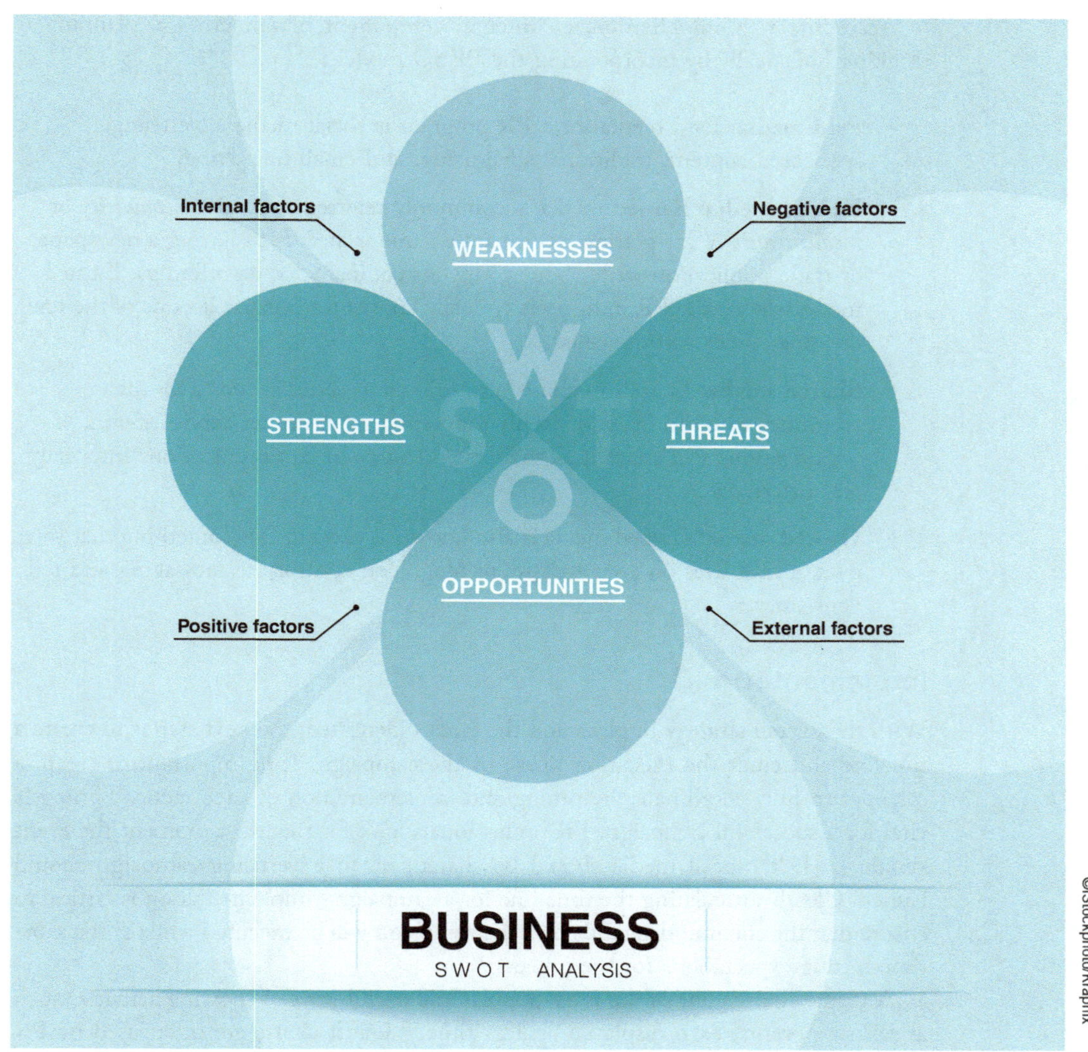

A SWOT analysis that provides business perspectives, lends objectivity, and helps establish organizational goals.

internal communication, lobbying, political advocacy, events, blogger relations, influencer relations, presentations, social media outreach, newsletters (print or digital), case studies, competitions, podcasts, stunts, advertising, and conference presentations in various combinations. Each tactic should help answer the following: What is the next step our organization will need to take to achieve the strategy?[8]

According to Gini Dietrich, an integral component of modern PR planning is thinking holistically by incorporating the PESO model:[9]

- **Paid media**: Paid media for a PR program is social media advertising, sponsored content, traditional advertising, and email marketing.
- **Earned media**: Earned media is commonly referred to as either *publicity* or *media relations.* It's getting a company's name in print. It's having a newspaper or trade publication write about you, your company, or its offerings. Earned media is what the PR industry is typically known for because it's one of the few tangible tactics accomplished.
- **Shared media**: Shared media is also known as *social media.* This area continues to build beyond simply marketing or customer service. Soon, organizations will share it as their main source of communications internally and externally.
- **Owned media**: Owned media is also known as *content.* It is something that you own, and it lives on your website or blog. You control the messaging and tell your story.

Implementation

With the overall strategy in place and the tactics identified, the next step is to create a timeline and enter the execution phase of the campaign. It is important to create a calendar to fully coordinate the timing and implementation of each tactic. Timing is vital for a successful campaign. PR professionals look for the exact moment the event should be held, social media should be shared, or an advertising campaign should launch. Clearly articulating the time line for a campaign's implementation is critical to ensure that the client understands how the campaign will be executed while at the same time setting expectations for the process.

A Gantt chart is one of the most popular and useful ways of showing activities such as tasks or events, each displayed against time.[10] Gantt charts are often used by PR professionals to stay on track and communicate deadlines to project teams within the agency and with a client. Typically, the left side of the chart lists the activities to be conducted and the top is a suitable time scale. Each activity is represented by a bar; the position and length of the bar reflects the start date, duration, and end date of the activity. Gantt charts allow you to see

- the various activities and
- when every activity begins and when it ends.

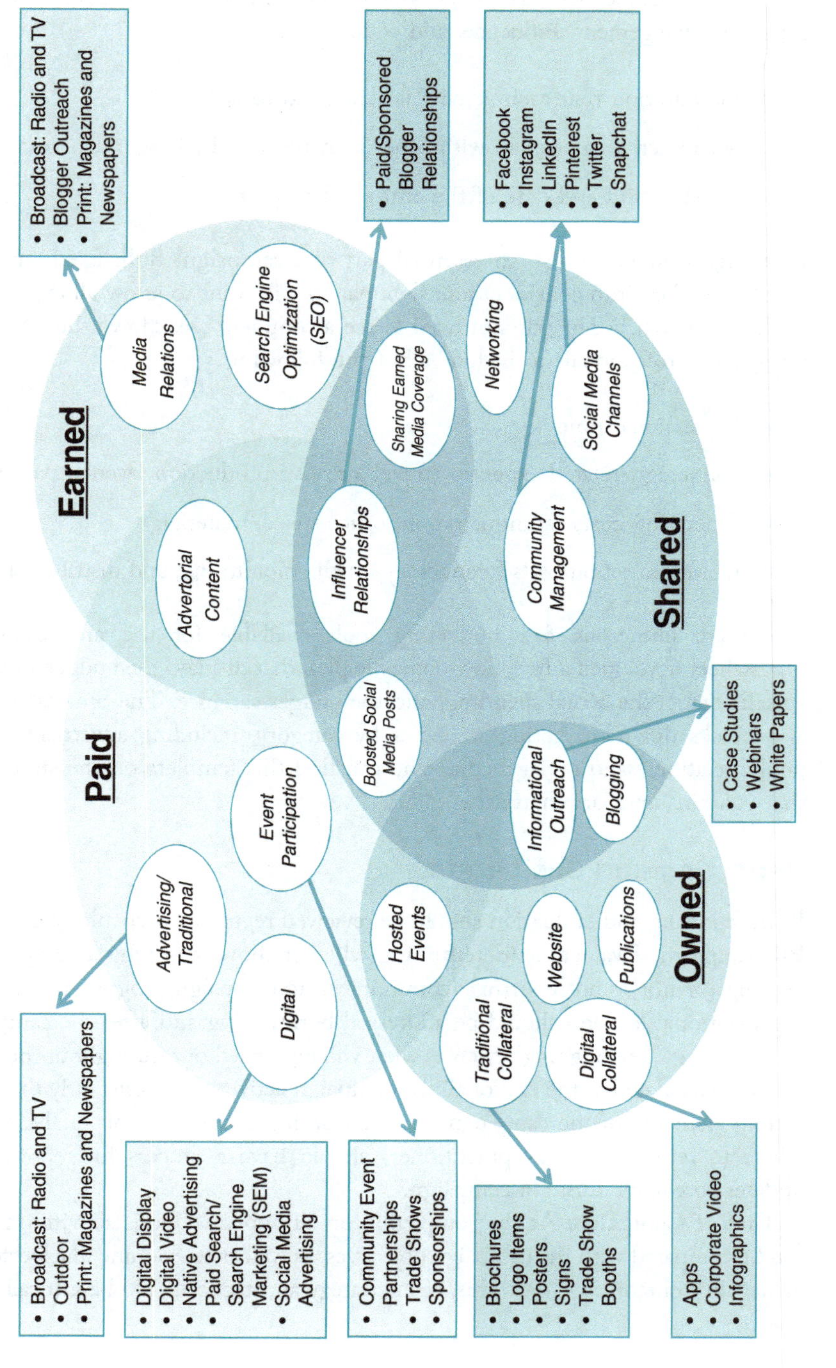

Earned
Paid
Shared
Owned
Media Relations
Search Engine Optimization (SEO)
Advertorial Content
Influencer Relationships
Sharing Earned Media Coverage
Networking
Social Media Channels
Community Management
Boosted Social Media Posts
Informational Outreach
Blogging
Advertising/ Traditional
Event Participation
Digital
Hosted Events
Website
Publications
Traditional Collateral
Digital Collateral
• Broadcast: Radio and TV
• Blogger Outreach
• Print: Magazines and Newspapers
• Paid/Sponsored Blogger Relationships
• Facebook
• Instagram
• LinkedIn
• Pinterest
• Twitter
• Snapchat
• Case Studies
• Webinars
• White Papers
• Broadcast: Radio and TV
• Outdoor
• Print: Magazines and Newspapers
• Digital Display
• Digital Video
• Native Advertising
• Paid Search/ Search Engine Marketing (SEM)
• Social Media Advertising
• Community Event Partnerships
• Trade Shows
• Sponsorships
• Brochures
• Logo Items
• Posters
• Signs
• Trade Show Booths
• Apps
• Corporate Video
• Infographics

The International Association for Measurement and Evaluation of Communication (AMEC) developed standards by which social media is measured. These include exposure, engagement, influence, and action:

- the duration that each activity is scheduled to last;
- where activities overlap with other activities and by how much; and
- the start and end date of the entire PR project.

Including a budget is also an essential part of a campaign. Both fixed and soft costs should be taken into consideration. Companies will want to know all expenses related to the campaign.[11] They do not need to see a complete breakdown, but it's important for agency professionals to include all of the following:

- Professional time
- Campaign-related expenses (travel, creative production, events, paid media)
- Operating costs (administration, office space, materials)
- Communication costs (technology, media monitoring, and distribution services)

There are numerous free budgeting tools available for use and customization. Smartsheet developed a free, downloadable plan that displays the budget allocated for a specific tactic, the actual spending, and the budget variance. The Smartsheet template also breaks down marketing strategies by category, including advertising, branding, public relations, and social media. You can find this template on the student website that contains ancillary materials.

Reporting and Evaluation

Both reporting and evaluation should be reviewed regularly, particularly in a long-term PR campaign. Evaluation (determining whether, how, and why a campaign is succeeding [or not]) and reporting (communicating campaign progress to clients and/or organizational leaders) should be addressed both during and after the campaign:[12]

Ongoing: The ongoing review is what will be carried out throughout the campaign. It is not calculated at the end of all the campaign activity, but constantly throughout. If certain elements of the campaign are not working effectively, this analysis highlights where to refocus. Agency practitioners should have a process for reporting regular updates to clients during a campaign.

End of Campaign: At the completion on all public relations activities, final results can be compared with the campaign objectives, as well as to examine unexpected positive or negative outcomes. To do this, each strategy and tactic should be critically analyzed.

Conclusion

The conclusion ties together the overall PR campaign and discusses future PR plans. Recommendations for future planning and lessons learned are also included.

PRSA IPA PROPOSAL TEMPLATE

To secure new business, practitioners sometimes have to pull together a proposal. This PR prospective client proposal template was developed by and reprinted with permission from PRSA's IPA network. The IPA is made up of more than 200 small business owners and freelance PR and communication practitioners. They offer a number of free resources, including this proposal template, on their website (https://www.prsa.org/independent-practitioners-section/):

PR Proposal
Company Name
Date (+any expiration date)
Name(s): Contact Information
COMPANY NAME HERE
About (YOUR COMPANY)

1. One paragraph about your agency positioning and staff
2. One paragraph about what sets you apart/why you are a good fit for this prospect
    - Promote your key strengths and the experiences that support alignment between you and the prospect/industry.
    - If you are a virtual agency, promote the benefits of doing business with a senior PR professional with low overhead.
3. Link to your website and bio and/or team bios. (Name of Prospect) Situation Analysis
    - Start with demonstrating industry knowledge and any trends/opportunities important to your prospect.
    - Move on to a brief statement of your understanding of the prospect and their products/services.
    - Next, tie these insights to market data and perceived strengths/weaknesses/opportunities/threats to summarize/preview potential communication actions (goals and strategies).

- Make the case for why you/your agency is best prepared to offer assistance.
- Bookend your industry knowledge with a discussion about their messaging and positioning; describe steps for message refinement and the goals of your overall PR program in addressing the current situation.
- Close with a description of what your proposal includes.

For example: This proposal presents a full range of PR strategies and tactics that can be tailored to interact and build upon each other to overcome challenges and best meet the prospect's PR goals. From an initial discussion, the prospect's PR goal, with appropriate supportive objectives, appears to include the following:

1. Build on the existing awareness of the Company's products to improve competitive standing in the marketplace.
    - Objective: Increase share-of-voice within industry trade publications from XX percent to XX percent over the next XX months.
    - Objective: Increase positive word of mouth on social media by XX percent in the next XX months.
    - Objective: Develop and nurture brand advocates and enthusiasts through social media, increasing the volume of content shared by followers to XX over the next XX months.

To accomplish these goals and objectives, we would prioritize the following PR strategies we suggest employing the PESO Model developed by Gini Dietrich:[13]

2. Paid Media
    - Paid media for a PR program is social media advertising, sponsored content, and email marketing.
3. Media Relations
    - Earned media is commonly referred to as either publicity or media relations. It is getting a company's name in print. It is having a newspaper or trade publication write about you, your company, or its offerings. Earned media is what the PR industry is typically known for because it is one of the most tangible tactics.
    - Leverage visibility via a well-balanced media relations program that includes blogs, community offers, and national news articles.

- Issue a national press release and customize outreach to community reporters at newspapers in each of the designated market areas (DMAs) where the company has stores.
- Plan and execute a thought leadership program for the chief executive officer (CEO) through writing/publishing editorial pieces and appearing on various traditional news channels, including television and radio.

4. Shared Media
   - Shared media is also known as social media. This area continues to build beyond simply marketing or customer service. Soon, organizations will share it as their main source of communications internally and externally.
   - Leverage visual storytelling through a series of posts across company social media channels, including Facebook, Twitter, Instagram, and Pinterest, triggering strong engagement and emotional responses.
   - Sponsor Facebook posts with key demographics (age, gender) and keywords related directly to prospective and competitor customers.
5. Owned Media
   - Owned media is also known as content. It is something that you own, and it lives on your website or blog. You control the messaging and tell the story in the way that you want it told.
   - Creating blog posts for your website, white papers, podcasts, apps, email, and marketing communication collateral are all examples of owned media.

***This template assumes that a verbal discussion with the prospective client has taken place, key questions have been asked, and an understanding of their needs is clear. In this section, summarize what you heard to build PR recommendations on stated needs (e.g., branding, messaging, media relations, search engine optimization, etc.).

PR Program Elements

This section should include the key program recommendations for this specific prospect. Examples include the following:

1. A consistent and well-executed analyst relations program
   - Your explanation on why this program is vital to your prospect.
   - Key relationships you already have established in the prospect market area listed by analyst firm, name, and practice area.

2. An aggressive media relations effort
    - Share what this will consist of, how it will support other areas in the program, and specifics on why it's important.
    - Outline your approach and planned focus (business-to-business, business-to-consumer, a combination, etc.) and high-level reasoning behind the recommendations you're making.
    - List established relationships with media by media title only, but cite the coverage area of editors to tie in to the industry/product. It is okay to list as many as fifty in a three-column format, but it is not necessary to have that many. You can list a "Top 10" or "CEO List" recommendation.
3. Social media effort (shared and paid/boosted outreach)
    - Explain the interplay of different social media channels.
    - Underscore the need for a mix of shared, curated, and original content as well as shared and paid/boosted tactics.
4. Key Messages: Distributed (*Sample*)
    - Product reviews and awards
    - Customer testimonials and case studies
    - Developer relations
    - Product launch
    - Tradeshows and user groups
    - CEO thought leadership program
    - Media success measurement

PR Program Pricing

Here, you articulate how much your services will cost and how you will format the invoice. Are you billing by estimating how much time will be spent each month based on known projects (such as an upcoming trade show) or by charging for a monthly fee plus overhead? Will the relationship be a time-bound project or an ongoing retainer?

This is what prospects look for first, so make sure it's clear and straightforward. Potential clients truly value transparency—they are asked to be more transparent, and they appreciate that greatly in their vendors and contractors. Making your costs clear and concise will entice them to read more details before making a decision.

Your Unabashed Pitch on "Why You"

Here's where you restate and add to why you're a great fit, why your business approach is best for them, and how much you look forward to working with them to develop their program.

- Provide them with insight into your management processes (when and how often will you meet how often will you report and on what, when you will send an invoice, what the terms are, what backup you provide, etc.).
- Tell them why you do business this way and how it benefits them.
- Don't forget to thank them for the opportunity and invite them to contact you with questions and/or for a personal meeting.

We'll be happy to answer any questions you may have about this proposal and would welcome an opportunity to meet in person.

Kind regards,

YOUR CONTACT INFORMATION REPEATED HERE

CLIENT REPORTS

Reporting back to the client is paramount. They want to understand how a campaign is going. Weekly or monthly reporting allows the agency and the client to evaluate and communicate progress and challenges. Each reporting document should clearly articulate what has been accomplished (past), what is happening currently (present), and what is in process or coming soon (future). Metrics help to

- track and highlight overall campaign performance monthly,
- evaluate successes, and
- understand what tweaks may be necessary.

Team Gantt, a project management software company, developed a free downloadable template project status report that is easy to customize. Some elements appear within these pages and the template can be found on the student ancillary website.

Agency Logo

Dear Client,

Include an introductory message. Be sure to point out key conversation points, metrics of interest, and even issues that may need addressing.

If you have a call scheduled to review this report, place the date, time, and meeting details here as well.

Thank you,

Your Name
Summary
What happened last week

- Tasks
- Deliverables
- Meetings
- Communications
- Decisions

What's happening this week

- Tasks
- Deliverables
- Meetings
- Communications
- Decisions

In progress

- Upcoming projects and tasks (see list above)
- Content, insights, or approvals needed from the client
- Potential obstacles or challenges to be addressed

Overall project time line completion status: XX% complete (or Stage X of X)
Phase, milestone, or task: XX% complete
Phase, milestone, or task: XX% complete
Total reach grew X% month over month
Overall website visits up X% from [previous month]

**This section could be organized effectively in several different ways, including by campaign objective, by project or initiative, or by previously agreed-upon metrics. Ideally, it should reference larger goals and objectives, contain quantitative and qualitative insights, and demonstrate progress while not ignoring challenges.

Overall budget spent: XX% spent; XX% remaining

**Note: You are tracking hours or dollars here.

Some agencies will report specific time- or dollar-based metrics. Others track specific tasks as well as hours, allowing them to report to a client that, for example,

30% of their efforts for a given month were spent on media relations, 20% on events, 20% on social media, 20% on creative project oversight, and 10% on reporting and account management. Agencies must balance a client's need to know how their dollars are being spent with providing unnecessary or overly granular information.

Upcoming tasks and milestones:

Task/Milestone	Target Date	Detail

Action items:

Action Item	Owner	Due Date	Notes

Project issues, risks, and mitigation plans:

Project Issue	Risk	Mitigation	Notes

DEVELOPING AN AUDIENCE PERSONA

Creating audience personas, sometimes called a buyer persona, is a useful approach to help those developing strategies, tactics, and messages better put a human face on their stakeholders or publics. Audience personas are fictional representations that summarize the traits of a target audience.[14] Personas do not depict any one customer, rather they are an amalgamation of overarching traits made up by various demographics within a brand's target audience. Personas help practitioners refine messaging, create targeted messaging, understand an audience's wants, needs, and habits, and strategically connect with customers. Used thoughtfully, they can aid efforts for diversity and inclusion and help communication teams envision intersectionality. When creating your audience persona be sure to include the following:[15]

- **Name**—Write a name that identifies who your persona is; for example, Foodie Fran, Millennial Mom, or something as simple as first and last name, Ehsan Amari.
- **Photo**—Photos humanize the persona so that the team can connect with a picture of the key audience person.
- **Quote**—Include one sentence that sums up the audience persona in this section.
- **Backstory/Bio**—All personas include a section on who they are, what they like, what their hobbies and interests are. Use company data to help build the biography and backstory for the persona.
- **Personality Traits**—Include a list of behavioral traits, preferences, and habits along with psychographic attitudes. Analytics from the company blog, website, or social media platforms can help identify these traits.
- **Demographics**—Include personal statistics such as income level, gender, educational level, location, ethnicity, race, religion, and family size. Use the Diversity & Inclusion Wheel to help build this section.
- **Goals and Motivations**—Identify what motivates this person. Make a list of both personal and professional objectives identified during the research phase. An easy way to gather this information is to use the data gleaned from social listening tools.
- **Frustrations and Barriers**—Articulate what prohibits your target audience from achieving their goals both professionally and personally. These are key drivers of behavior.
- **Brands**—Include a list of brands they purchase from and stay loyal to.
- **Preferred Channels**—Include a list of where they find news and consume information. The channels change depending on the target audience. Examples include social media, the Internet, or apps.

To design an audience persona you can find an abundance of free templates. Some can be found at Hootsuite, Xtensio, or through platforms such as Piktochart or Canva.

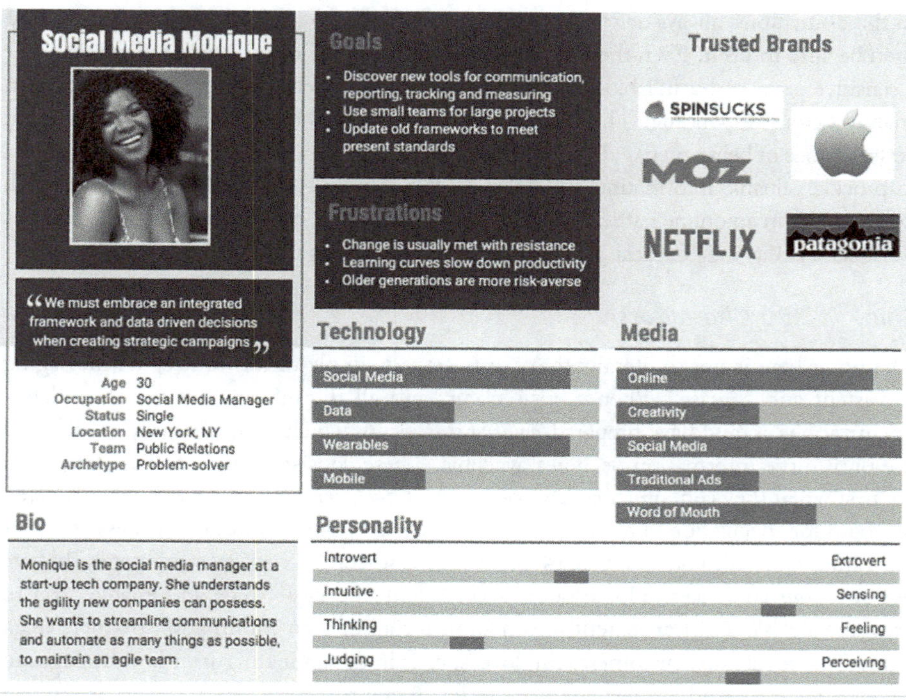

Pictured here is an example of a traditional audience persona.

CRISIS COMMUNICATION PLAN

Crisis Communications for a 24/7 News Cycle

Michael Meath (principal, Fallingbrook Associates, LLC) advises that crises are not a matter of if, but when.

Today, every organization operates in a complicated and interconnected world. The chances of something going wrong and needing a carefully worded and positioned response are inevitable. Meath suggests that to help prepare for this eventuality, organization leaders consider the following five key factors to successfully navigate crises and sensitive issues.

Take the "Critical 10"

Answering any inquiry in haste during a crisis may exacerbate the problem. Being on the receiving end of a phone call or urgent message always puts you at a disadvantage as you may not only be unprepared but also are operating on someone else's timetable.

In these situations, always defer your availability and offer to call back in ten minutes. **And then be sure to do it**. Even these few minutes can make the difference between managing a sensitive issue and a full-blown crisis. Always give yourself time to digest, reflect, and analyze before responding. Then, when you get back to the inquirer, you have a much better chance of being prepared and in control of the conversation and you are better suited to provide valuable information and answers. When negative digital media is employed, don't engage in an online battle. Try to get the person into a conversation offline as soon as possible. Taking the "Critical 10" can keep you from firing back and later regretting it.

Think in 280 Characters

The point here is not to literally think in tweets. It simply means to keep all messaging consistent and concise. When a crisis occurs and all the information is not available, organizations should have prepared *holding statements*, which they can easily modify and use until more information becomes available. These consistent and concise statements are best when they contain three key components: *fact*, *empathy*, and *what's next*. There's no room for speculation. The same process is necessary when crafting key messages later on. Limit yourself to one page of 14-point font, and craft five to seven messages that are useful for *all* audiences. This ensures a consistent and clear voice and enables you to provide valuable and transparent information for all of your information partners (e.g., journalists, regulators, customers, employees, etc.) in disseminating your key messages to larger audiences. And even as you prepare for digital first responses (or even on-camera responses), prepare your key messages in writing first. Too many situations have gone poorly when messages weren't committed to writing for everyone to use and reference.

Who Speaks and Who Is the Designated Backup?

While one person should be designated as the primary spokesperson for your organization (often the CEO or other executive), be sure you train and prepare a backup spokesperson as well as specific subject matter experts to step in as needed. Training can be effectively done by both in-house and outside staff—but be sure you are objective about the training you are getting. Sometimes the CEO wants to be the spokesperson, but this doesn't automatically make him or her the best choice. In this instance, an outside consultant can help with an objective opinion.

And remember this: "You can always go up, but you can't go down," says Meath. If you put your senior leadership person out in front of an incident, be sure she stays there until the situation has been resolved. To do otherwise will undermine your organization's credibility.

Bridge With ATM

During a particularly sensitive interview or inquiry by a reporter, a regulator, or even a customer, think about ATM: acknowledge, transition, message. Acknowledging a question or point may be difficult, but it demonstrates a reflective tone and active listening, an attempt to understand, and show empathy. Phrases such as *No comment*, *Look*, *Listen*, or *What you need to know* are dismissive, combative, and demoralizing and can actually hurt your reputation further. Instead, once you've acknowledged the inquiry or concern, begin with the phrase *What I can tell you is* to return to and emphasize your key messages. A gentle approach will better enable you to get back to the important points you need to make during a crisis or sensitive situation.

Always Take Dessert

This seldom-used technique is one of the easies yet is often forgotten or dismissed. At the conclusion of most interviews or inquiries, an opportunity is almost always offered you to provide additional thoughts. Yet people being interviewed seldom take it. The answer to a concluding question of "Is there anything else you would like to add?" should always be an emphatic "Yes!" Use this gift to reiterate one of your key messages and potentially save the interview. Do not use this opportunity to offer new, additional messages. Keep it simple and prepared.

Meath further suggests that when developing a crisis communication plan, organizations should use the following outline:

Plan Purpose. What is the overarching objective of the plan? Take a few paragraphs to outline what the plan seeks to accomplish (e.g., to communicate effectively to employees, customers, and the public during a crisis situation; to ensure continued operation of the business; or to protect the reputation of the organization). Have the CEO of the company sign the statement to demonstrate the highest level of commitment to the plan.

Risk Scenarios and Issues Management. List the most likely situations that the organization will have to deal with in an emergency or crisis. These may include things such as vehicle accidents, hazardous materials spills, public health risks, improper use of social media, or mishandling of company assets. Be realistic and include the highest priority items.

Incident Assessment. Meath advises use of a high-, medium-, and low-level assessment tool to help determine the possible impact of a crisis. For example, a low-level hazardous materials incident would involve a minor spill with no exposure or injuries, while a high-level incident may involve multiple injuries or fatalities. Create an incident assessment tool that works for your organization.

Roles and Responsibilities. Identify those individuals who make up your Emergency Communications Team (ECT)—those critical people in your organization who will be part of responding to any crisis situation. This list likely includes your CEO, chief communications officer (COO), legal counsel, and key operational staff. Keep the number of people on your ECT as small as possible. Supplement this with an advisory team, which will include key resources both inside and outside the company that you can call on in a crisis situation. Finally, prepare a directory that includes the contact information for both your ECT and your advisory team, and keep that information on your smartphone for easy access. Assign someone to review and update this list no less than twice per year.

Coordination With Key Stakeholders. Identify the key stakeholders that may need careful attention from a communications standpoint during a crisis. For example, in a health-care environment, family members of patients and residents are as critical as the patients themselves. Be sure to identify the audiences that are most affected and plan to include them in any communication plan rollout.

Media Response Guidelines. Prepare a generic list of media response guidelines so that your spokespersons and/or subject matter experts can be reminded of best practices for a media interview. Items to be included on the list include the importance of maintaining eye contact and positive body language, avoiding the use of industry jargon, and other useful tips.

Dark/Failover Website Preparation. Work with your web developer to prepare a “dark” or “failover” page that can be quickly mobilized in the event of a crisis. It would allow for key information specific to the crisis situation to be posted and made available to the public. A failover site may also come in handy if your organization website is hijacked or crashes for some reason.

Emergency Communications Action Steps. List out the actual step-by-step actions that need to be taken from a communications standpoint during a crisis situation. This will look different for every organization, but it should include separate step-by-step action items for low-, medium-, and/or high-level situations. It’s meant to serve as a checklist when you are quickly building plans during a crisis event.

Incident Review and Evaluation. Build in a specific timetable for reviewing your response to an incident within 15–30 days of the event. What went well? What needs to be changed in the organization’s response? Formalize this review process to ensure that the organization learns from the communication strategies and tactics used during the crisis.

Finally, Meath suggests that appendices be added that include time-stamped tracking logs (which can be managed electronically), sample holding statements, an organization phone and email directory (including personal cell phones), and other additional resources that may help you respond during an event.

A good crisis communications plan is as different as the organization preparing it, and it is never something that answers all the questions that come up during an incident. However, it provides a much-needed place to start during a crisis—which is no time to begin preparing one.

Appendix

TOPICS

1. Research
   a. Sample Likert Scale Items
   b. Method for Conducting Surveys
   c. Matching the Question With the Method
   d. Example Methods and Research Questions
   e. Focus Group Moderator Tips
   f. Defining Key Audiences, Stakeholders, and Publics
   g. Content Analysis
      i. Media Coverage Analysis
   h. Survey Development
      i. Survey Questions
      ii. Types of Survey Data Collection
      iii. Sampling Versus Census
2. Objectives
   a. How *Not* to Write Objectives
3. Strategies
   a. When *Not* to Use Social Media
   b. Review: Positioning Campaigns for Maximum Impact
      i. Uniqueness
      ii. Audience Focus
      iii. Playing to Your Strengths
4. Tactics
   a. Paid Media
      i. Outdoor
      ii. Print
      iii. Radio

iv. TV
v. Digital Display
vi. Search Engine Marketing (SEM)
vii. Social Media
viii. Event Sponsorship

b. Earned Media
i. Media Advisories
ii. Press Releases/News Releases
iii. Press Conferences and Media-Friendly Events
iv. Bylined Articles and Op-ed Pieces

c. Shared Media
i. Blogs: An Organization's Content Hub
ii. Social Media Networks
iii. Microblogging
iv. Image, Video, and Interest Sharing
v. Community Management

d. Owned Media
i. Website Content Management
ii. Marketing Tactics
iii. Publications
iv. Collateral Materials

RESEARCH

Sample Likert Scale Items

Sample Likert Scale Items for Answering PR Questions

- Awareness
  - I am aware of X.
  - I have heard of X.
- Recall
  - I have seen X.
  - I recall my friends with X.
- Knowledge
  - I know about X.
  - I really don't know much about X.

- Interest
  - I am really interested in X.
  - I am not interested in X.
- Relationship
  - I can relate well to others who have X.
  - X does not really see me with X.
- Preference
  - If I were to consider it, X would be what I want.
  - I like X more than…
- Intent
  - I intend to purchase X.
  - X is not something that I would buy.
- Advocacy
  - X is something I will tell others to purchase.
  - I have been advocating X for quite some time.

Source: From Don W. Stacks, *Primer of Public Relations Research*, 3rd ed. (New York: Guildford Press, 2017), 72.

Method for Conducting Surveys

1. Write a research question (establish what you need to learn).
2. Review the literature and develop a hypothesis (what you think you might find). Example: People who like us on Facebook will have the most positive opinions of our cause.
3. Select the public or sample "universe."
4. Decide on the format—online, phone, mail, in-person, and so on.
5. Plan the arrangement of question topics—nonthreatening questions, threatening questions (items about possibly embarrassing behaviors), and demographic data (age and income questions are sometimes threatening).
6. Write questions.
7. When you write questions about nonthreatening topics, remember the following:
   - Use closed-ended responses (such as Yes/No or 1, 2, or 3) for responses that tabulate quickly.
   - Use open-ended responses to get a range of data and bring up ideas you had overlooked.
   - Make questions and responses specific. Avoid double-barreled answers.
   - Use terms everyone can understand; avoid jargon.

8. When you write questions about threatening topics (things such as drinking, drug use, or gambling, that might embarrass respondents if they talked about them openly), remember the following:
   - Create an environment that lets people comfortably respond.
   - Prefer open-ended items that let people decide how to respond.
   - Include necessary qualifiers and context in questions.
   - Avoid technical terms.
   - Phrase your question in terms of "most people you know." People are usually more willing to talk about others than themselves.
   - Ask about past behavior before you ask about present behavior.
   - Keep questions about deviant behavior in clusters with related items about deviant behavior.
   - Put threatening questions toward the end of the questionnaire.
   - Answers to threatening questions may be lies.
9. When you write questions to test knowledge, remember the following:
   - Ease into items (e.g., Do you happen to know?). Don't make the questionnaire seem like a test.
   - Simplify questions and answers.
   - Leave questions with numerical answers open-ended.
   - If you ask yes/no questions, use related questions later to double-check responses.
   - Do not use mail or online questionnaires to test for knowledge.
10. When you write opinion questions, remember the following:
   - Be very specific.
   - Use close-ended responses.
   - Keep the affective (feeling), cognitive (thinking), and action aspects in separate questions.
   - Gauge the strength of responses by providing a response scale (e.g., How important is this issue to you? Very important, somewhat important, etc.).
   - Start with general questions and then move to specific questions.
   - Group questions with the same underlying values.
   - Start with the least popular proposal.
   - Use neutral terms (e.g., the president, not President Smith).

11. Write questions so answers will be easy to tabulate.
12. Consider question order and possible order bias.
    - Keep like questions together.
    - Start with nonthreatening items.
    - Ask demographic questions last. They can be considered threatening.
    - Diagram questions in a flowchart to see the logic.
    - Don't make your questionnaire too long. (Some topics may require many questions, but dropout rates increase with questionnaire length. Therefore, you may need to ask priority questions near the beginning of a long questionnaire to increase the likelihood of getting responses to those items.)
    - Start with general questions and then go to specifics.
    - Go forward or backward in time, but don't jump around.
    - Reverse scale order in some items to eliminate habitual responses.
13. Format the questionnaire.
14. Pretest the survey with people who know about the study. Adjust questionnaire elements that don't perform the way you expected.
15. Conduct a pilot test by surveying a small number of people from the public you want to check. Adjust survey elements that don't perform the way you expected.
16. Initiate the full-scale survey.

Source: From *APR Study Guide* (University Accreditation Board, 2016), 35, https://www.prsa.org/wp-content/uploads/2016/07/apr-study-guide.pdf.

Matching the Question With the Method

When performing research, practitioners should follow the question at hand to help determine the best research method to apply. Methods can serve exploratory, descriptive, or explanatory purposes. Exploratory approaches often answer open-ended questions, attempting to understand fundamental elements of a particular situation. Descriptive approaches seek to provide additional detail about the factors of a more specific situation or phenomenon. By contrast, explanatory research examines causal factors to better understand what might be motivating individual or group behaviors or opinions.[1]

- **Who?** Questions about publics and audiences can take many forms, including the examination of secondary research on demographic groups or publics, primary research using social listening tools, as well as qualitative and quantitative interviews and surveys.

- **Example:** Who are the opinion leaders in a particular community?
    - **Method:** Secondary research on community leadership, dialogue, and demographic trends
    - **Method:** Interviews with and/or surveys of community members
- **Example:** Who has discussed our company/brand/organization on social media in the past?
    - **Method:** Primary, quantitative, and/or qualitative content analysis, social listening

- **What?** These questions can either be exploratory ("what have we learned from…") or more specific and enumerable (acting in place of "how much…?" or "how many…?").
  - **Example:** What did our organization learn from opening our new branch location?
    - **Method:** Exploratory qualitative interviews and/or surveys with multiple audiences to examine the event from multiple perspectives
    - **Method:** A case study approach (combine the interviews with analysis of internal and external documents, media coverage, and social media conversations)
  - **Example:** What impact has our product made for our customers?
    - **Method:** Interviews or surveys (ideally qualitative and quantitative) to capture the broad range of potential insights and experiences, as well as to provide quantitative data generalizable to all customers
- **Where?** Secondary methods are often the best starting point, although there are increasingly digital tools to track and identify the location of audiences.
  - **Example:** Where do our customers and potential customers live and work?
    - **Method:** Using social listening tools to track the locations of users and potential customers (when possible)
  - **Example:** Where should we focus our resources for expansion?
    - **Method:** Demographic studies can help make the case for entering a specific geographic market (for example, finding a city with similar socioeconomic makeup or similar cluster of industries to expand your organization's outreach)
- **Why and How?** Qualitative approaches are often most effective at providing the holistic, detailed answers needed to begin to answer *why* and *how* research

questions. Quantitative investigation often serves as a secondary step once researchers have initial perspectives and direction.

- **Example:** Why would community members donate to other nonprofit organizations rather than ours?
    - **Method (Step 1):** Qualitative interviews with key informants inside and outside of the organization to assess potential factors
    - **Method (Step 2):** Based on the initial findings, quantitative survey to isolate both demographic factors among these audience groups as well as to gain additional insight into their behaviors

Example Methods and Research Questions

Based on Figure 1.2 "Case Study Methods" by Robert K. Yin.[2]

Primary Research Method	Qualitative or Quantitative?	Advantages	Disadvantages	Example Research Question
Experiments	Quantitative	– Control of the situation – Isolation of variables – Focus on causation	– Expertise needed to design, conduct, and analyze data – Expensive to run	Will our donors and volunteers respond and take action based on emotional appeals or logical appeals about the need for support?
Content Analysis	One or both	– Flexible, based on the size of the data set – Customizable to a wide variety of data and questions	– Drawbacks exist for both human analysis (time consuming) and digital methods (lack of nuance)	How much has trade media coverage reflected key campaign themes and messages?
Focus Groups	Qualitative	– More efficient than in-depth interviewing – Allows observation of group interaction	– Needs skilled moderation – Individuals can be left out or overshadowed (unequal participation) – Much less depth of information for individual participants	Which messages from past campaigns have resonated most with our key stakeholder groups? Why?

In-depth Interviews	Qualitative	- Volume of information collected - Broad, holistic perspective - Brings up unrealized issues/questions	- Time investment for interviewing and analysis - Flexibility in questions can bring uneven results	Why are community members upset about our new facility announcement?
Surveys	One or both	- Efficient data collection - Readily available analysis tools - Multiple data collection methods	- Expertise needed to write questions and implement - Large data collection is expensive - Short participant attention spans	What percentage of voters support the organization's position?
SWOT Analysis	Qualitative	- Relatively quick process - Group process can involve and empower team members	- Not an in-depth, systematic or formal process	

Focus Group Moderator Tips

- Warm up the conversation: A smooth, clear introduction sets a professional tone and lays out the goals for a successful session.
- Order matters: Structure the most important questions in the middle of the session, leaving less critical concepts to the end.
- Be positive but nonpartisan: An impartial, business-like approach is best.
- Get everyone involved: Don't let one or two participants dominate—call on others who look they have something to say.
- Agreement is positive, but avoid groupthink: Encourage participants to build off of each other's ideas but acknowledge outliers and encourage different perspectives.

Defining Key Audiences, Stakeholders, and Publics

Once some of the initial questions have been answered, practitioners must define who will be impacted by the situation at hand. These may be organizational audiences, stakeholders, and publics. Audiences are the direct targets of organizational outreach—individuals and groups who come into contact with organizational campaigns, messages, and spokespersons. Stakeholders can be defined as individuals who can have an impact on the ability of an organization to meet its goals or have an interest in the corporation's success.[3] Organizational audiences include internal stakeholders (such as employees, the board of directors, and stockholders) as well as external stakeholders (such as customers, potential customers, competitors, and vendors). They can also include publics (such as community members). Audiences are defined by the organization, while publics are (as explained by the *Situational Theory of Publics*) self-organizing around issues, based on their recognition of a problem, recognition of constraints to solving the problem, and their degree of involvement.[4] From a marketing or sales perspective, external communication is about targeting audiences to achieve business objectives such as sales goals. From a purely relational perspective, external communication is about strengthening the bonds with important internal and external stakeholders and publics. An integrated communication approach, led by publics relations, takes into account all of these perspectives when researching, developing, and executing campaigns.

Although the task of identifying key groups may seem daunting, this exercise is most useful with a smaller, specific group to whom specific objectives can be designed, strategies directed, tactics implemented, and messages crafted. Campaigns conducted without research and appropriate targeting may accidentally connect with important audiences and stakeholders, but they are more likely to miss the target.[5] Practitioners should remember not to overlook the importance of internal publics, audiences, and stakeholders.

In order to evaluate and pinpoint the relevant audiences or stakeholders, it is important to understand the process for developing a more granular view. The first step can be as simple as working with the leadership team in order to identify the important internal and external stakeholders. The team may then use this information to further distinguish any key characteristics, allowing a deeper profile to emerge. Completing this exercise may result in more, fewer, or the same number of audience groups; however, it does provide a starting point to the larger team for developing a better understanding of the organizational view of its position within the marketplace, as well as its internal and external communication challenges and opportunities.

More importantly, the smaller size and inherent commonality of each subgroup allows an organization to listen more closely to these publics and engage in true, two-way communication. Awareness of any issues or challenges can impact campaign and organizational strategy at the highest levels. Companies often have a strong understanding of *some* key audience groups but are not fully able to see the complete picture. The following are a few common challenges relating to properly defining key audiences, stakeholders, and publics:

- Organizations often focus obsessively on sustaining their current customers, members, or donors, at the expense of seeking and understanding opportunities for expansion and growth in new markets.

- The opposite problem is also common: organizations may direct all of their resources and attention toward acquiring new customers, members, or donors. Current customers may be left without clear, ongoing communication.
- Organizations may not be wholly aware of activist groups or other organized publics who may see the organization, its business, or its structure as a threat.

Even with these same communication strategies at their disposal, far too many PR campaigns are initiated as an attempt to address a perceived need from an organizational perspective: "Our customers are unhappy, so we must communicate with them in a different way," or "These groups don't know about our products. If they did, they would buy them!" While this approach may identify an organizational gap, it does not help to find the root of the problem. What research can provide is a roadmap to the solution, the approach to turn the problem into an opportunity.

Content Analysis

Depending on what is appropriate for the situation at hand, the necessary media materials that require review could range from a complete analysis of all media coverage pertaining to an organization over a particular time period of interest, to a much narrower slice of coverage in trade journals on a specific issue or product. Regarding social media, this could include a review of a content and commentary on a specific social medial channel such as Twitter or event-focused research covering multiple social media channels. Social and earned media can and should be reviewed together to generate a holistic picture of public conversation on a specific topic or issue.

Paine highlights multiple categories that can be valuable to track, including prominence, visibility, tone, sources mention, and messages communicated.[6] As an example, a campaign developed to raise the profile of a specific product could examine the entire portfolio of company media coverage for a specific subset of media (audience targeted) and then evaluate how prominently product-specific messaging was a focus of given articles. Based on this baseline research, the practitioner can establish a measurable objective—increasing the frequency (percentage) of inclusion or its prominence within coverage—and devise strategies to ensure that outgoing paid, earned, owned, and social media messages reflect this shift. Tailoring for specific metrics can ensure that each campaign is measuring the correct combination of channels and variables in order to both create reliable baselines and track success.

Media Coverage Analysis. One of the more valuable places to start when initiating research on a new project is to conduct media analysis on the specific organization, challenge, or industry in question. This specific type of content analysis can be conducted either quantitatively or qualitatively, formally or informally. By using digital tools to help in the analysis, it can be easy to catalog data or trends from the time period of interest. This is important in understanding how a specific issue has been framed and reported, which journalists are interested in the topic, and how much media coverage the topic has historically received.

As an example, consider a technology company interested in launching a new application for serious at-home cooks. In order to understand the relevant opportunities for earned media, paid media, and social media, an organization could research specific recipes, ingredients, and techniques that best fit a desired demographic profile from a variety of food-related websites. They might then select the top five websites / media outlets that support the key factors that they have researched and further investigate all associated articles, authors, and topics that appear most frequently. By following this approach, an organization can compile large amounts of quantitative data that support the subsequent planning stages of objective creation, content and messaging development, and audience demographics. Additional qualitative analysis could help to determine questions of tone, article structure, newsworthiness, and target journalists for media relations outreach.

This type of analysis requires a certain degree of pretesting to develop the appropriate scope. For example, searching publications and periodicals that specifically serve the target audience using a defined set of key terms can provide valuable insights regarding an acceptable approach to outreach. Narrowing the research down to the most relevant terminology (as defined by the publications) and the most relevant publications (as defined by the terminology) ensures that deeper, more time-intensive research is time well spent.

Survey Development

Survey Questions. As part of survey construction, researchers construct scales—sets of questions or *items*—that address a particular concept or attitude. Often, such questions will be constructed on a "strongly agree" to "strongly disagree" continuum known as a Likert-type scale. Likert-type scales always have an odd number of responses to allow for a "neutral" answer.

Additional options include open-ended questions, multiple-choice questions, and ranking answers.[7] Open-ended questions (often including an empty response box, for example) are not conducive to easy quantification but can add depth and nuance to understanding a particular issue. Multiple-choice questions can be valuable for illuminating the potential causes for a particular challenge, the value of certain solutions, or the resonance of particular messages. Including an "other" option is a useful way to gather information that falls outside the researcher's initial conception of the answers.

Finally, ranking answers—asking respondents to order a set of answers in a particular order (best-to-worst, most likely to least likely, etc.)—can be a valuable method for understanding the relative importance or benefits of certain concepts, messages, or potential actions.

Types of Survey Data Collection. There are several methods through which survey data can be collected, dependent on the type of respondent and type of information at hand. For example, a survey looking to capture public opinion on a statewide ballot initiative will be most generalizable, credible, and efficient using a short telephone survey and professional callers. Surveys of existing customers or donors would be least invasive (and most truthful) when done privately and confidentially through a digital survey tool such as SurveyMonkey or Qualtrics. Examinations of specific communities for nonprofit campaigns and outreach—particularly when publics may have limited access to technology—may be accomplished most effectively through personal intercept interviews, where the survey team collects responses in-person. These often work best in high-traffic public places that reflect the survey's purpose, such as malls, libraries, or community centers. Digital and telephone surveys are most effective for collecting large amounts of data quickly, but phone numbers and email addresses can be difficult and expensive to collect.[8] Personal interviews can provide the greatest depth of information and access to difficult-to-reach populations but take significant resources and training to implement. Mail surveys are still used widely but are increasingly being replaced by digital alternatives with higher response rates, significantly faster data collection, and nearly instantaneous analysis tools. That said, mail still may be a reasonable choice for select publics, demographic groups, or geographic locations. With all methods, practitioners should focus on increasing response and completion rates by having concise questions and regular follow-up.

Sampling versus Census. When conducting surveys, researchers must enter the domain of sampling: gathering data from select respondents to represent the whole. By contrast, a census is a universal sample. Practitioners may also, depending on the circumstances, choose a random or probability sample of a given population, or a nonprobability sample.[9] Probability samples allow generalizations to be made about the entire population at hand, while nonprobability samples only have statistical validity within the respondents.[10] There are many advantages to a census approach when available, including procuring specific information, rather than having to extrapolate estimates from smaller sample sizes. However, a true census requires contacting each and every member of the identified group, which is often extremely difficult and a time consuming, expensive, and inefficient approach.[11] Some audiences are easily accessible and conveniently available at the same time. This might include taking advantage of a gathering of company shareholders at an annual meeting, reaching out to employees during a work retreat, or customers at the point-of-purchase.[12]

OBJECTIVES

How *Not* to Write Objectives

There are multiple approaches that we have highlighted to aid in the development of valuable objectives, but it is also valuable to examine what *not* to do through ways objectives can be poorly written.

- **Does the measurement matter? (Problem: Output-based rather than outcome-based):**
  - A variety of metrics have been used in the history of PR to keep pace with a data-driven business world and to gain leadership buy-in relative to the marketing and advertising functions. Unfortunately, many of them have been based less on impact and more on measurement methods including ad value equivalency (AVE), or counting the number of media clips rather than looking at their value.[13] The 2010 adoption and subsequent 2015 and 2020 revisions of the Barcelona Principles for PR Measurement explain that AVE and clip counting are not valuable objectives as they do not directly relate to organizational goals.[14]
  - Examples:
    - Original (output) objective: Place seven media stories in targeted industry publications prior to a January event.
      - This objective is easily measurable but not based on an audience outcome.
    - Revised (outcome) objective: Drive web traffic (1,500 visitors) to the registration page for a January event among key industry audiences.
      - This objective is both easily measurable *and* clearly focused toward the organizational goal of event attendance.
      - Strategies for executing this objective may include media relations outreach with stories including a link directly to the registration page.
- **Is the objective primarily communication driven? (Problem: Metrics are not tied to public relations efforts):**
  - Public relations objectives can be sidetracked with shared objectives, specifically those relying on the outputs from another department. This can happen with sales and marketing, human resources, events, membership, fundraising, and many other functions within the organization. Organizational goals and objectives at the highest level can often only be

achieved when departments work together. The development of appropriate public relations objectives improves the outcome and cohesiveness.

- Examples:
  - Original (multidepartmental) objective: Increase employee retention by 15 percent over the next year.
    - This objective relies on multiple factors outside of communication efforts. The human resources department may not be supportive of the initiative or have any resources that support or justify communication efforts on behalf of this objective.
  - Revised (communication-specific) objective: Increase employee awareness of a new benefits package from 30 to 60 percent over the next six months.
    - This objective focuses on awareness and information distribution within the scope of what communication can accomplish.
    - While the revised objective may not solve the entire organizational challenge, it does tackle a communication-specific piece of the retention puzzle. Continued cross-functional cooperation during the planning, implementation, and evaluation phases of the campaign would ensure a coordinated effort toward the larger objectives.
    - Additional communication objectives working toward a similar organizational objective may include those related to a change of opinion about the employer, development of new internal communication tools, or even new channels to improve the flow of information within the organization.

- **How much impact will come from achieving the objective? (Problem: Metrics are not closely related to organizational goals):**
  - Objectives can be extremely well written, clear, and measurable, but not relate closely enough to organizational priorities. This may include a media relations effort that does not result in on-message coverage, campaigns that do not adequately prioritize the audiences they target, as well as disconnections between short-term and long-term objectives.
  - Examples:
    - Original objective: Increase awareness of consulting services for existing clients from 50 to 75 percent over the next six months.
      - If the organizational priority is to target *new* clients with consulting services, rather than existing clients, it doesn't matter how effective they are at exposing existing clients to this information.

        - Revised objective: Capture contact information from twenty potential clients interested in consulting services over the next three months.
            - The revised objective measures an opt-in behavior on the part of the potential client, rather than awareness, as well as focusing on new clients rather than existing clients.
            - Strategies for this approach could include internal and external research as needed to define the ideal new client; targeted awareness efforts using paid, earned, shared, and owned media; as well as a lead-capture strategy such as a dedicated landing page as part of a website or blog.

- **Is it organizationally feasible? (Problem: Not enough enthusiasm, time, or resources to complete the effort):**
    - Some objectives may be ideal from the perspective of the public relations team but not the best approach for other areas of the organization. This situation can cause significant internal conflict and divert the resources and energy needed to accomplish the goal. Of course, the more organizational clout the public relations department or agency carries (usually earned through prior success), the better chance that they have of bringing other departments and executive leadership around to their position.
    - Examples:
        - Original objective: Increase awareness of a new type of mortgage loan product among targeted prior customers from 15 to 30 percent in the next three months.
            - Unfortunately, the objective starts at the same time as a new regulatory measure comes into effect, taking up significant time for the loan officers who would have spearheaded the outreach.
        - Revised objective: Increase awareness of a new type of mortgage loan product among targeted prior customers from 15 to 30 percent in the next six months.
            - As the new mortgage loan product was not revolutionary, simply new to the company, communicators may recommend that the campaign could either begin later or be spaced over a longer period of time to ensure key internal stakeholders were able to fully participate.
            - The objective can also be revised to lower the measured change, assuming that loan officers would not be able to participate.

When Not to Use Social Media

While the overwhelming narrative is that organizations must use social media constantly, it is easy to find examples of when *not* to use social media as part of strategic campaigns. In 2013, communicators at JPMorgan Chase, the largest bank in the US, used the @JPMorgan handle to tweet, "What career advice would you ask a leading exec at a Global firm? Tweet a Q using #askJPM. On 11/14 a $JPM leader takes over @JPMorgan." The strategic transparency backfired when JPMorgan Chase, a company that had been heavily implicated in the 2008 financial crisis and had recently suffered criticism for significant losses due to exceptionally risky stock market trades, received an avalanche of negative tweets from hundreds including disgruntled consumers and opportunistic reporters. A *New Yorker* article recapping the incident put it succinctly: "This is Twitter's very purpose: to allow any individual to share the same space with, for example, a hugely powerful bank.... Unlike at JPMorgan's Park Avenue headquarters, there are no security guards keeping undesirable elements out of Twitter."[15]

While organizations may control the initial message, any response is out of their hands. In this way, social media strategies carry inherent risk. The rewards of a successful campaign often clearly outweigh such risks, but it is a calculation that communication team members should make based on thorough analysis and understanding of the organization and the publics involved. Practitioners should ask themselves and their colleagues, "What is the worst thing that could happen?" before undertaking strategies on potentially challenging subjects.

Review: Positioning Campaigns for Maximum Impact

Uniqueness

Whether it's a channel, a message, or the strategy itself, finding a way to make it new or distinctive will always add value. A story can become more newsworthy, an event can become more attractive for potential attendees, and a member donation can be made more impactful. Uniqueness is often found when organizations act the opposite way from how their audiences expect them to.

That said, content, programming, or campaigns need not be wholly new to reap the benefits. It can be new for a region, new to an industry, or new to a company. It's the degree of difference from expectation or from competitors that defines its value for a given audience. This holds both for the impact to a reporter (news value) as well as the impact on an organizational stakeholder.

Audience Focus

If a strategy is not right for the audience, it doesn't matter how big the budget, how bold the message, or how well-timed a campaign might be.[16] At the strategic level, practitioners should consider how the audience perceives the organization or the issue at hand, how that perception must change to achieve the goal, and what the best avenue might be to facilitate that change. What does your audience need to hear to move the needle toward completing an objective? Where are they listening? When are they most likely to hear and understand your message? If a strategy clearly addresses all three of these questions, it is well on its way to being effective.

Playing to Your Strengths (and Competitor's Weaknesses)

It is a truism in advertising, marketing, and sales: trumpet your advantages over competitors. Once areas of distinction have been pinpointed, often through SWOT analysis, it allows communicators to choose strategies and messages that effectively reinforce them. These differences could be communication-related, such as expertise and resources devoted to managing and monitoring social media channels, or it could be company-, product-, or service-related, such as having a highly regarded industry expert on staff. This knowledge could inform strategies across a variety of channels impacting the campaign, such as content creation and distribution (expert white papers or bylined articles), media relations (expert source for reporters), or events (expert speaking opportunities). Even channel-specific advantages can support multiple strategies. A superior social media team can strengthen real-time customer interactions during an event, while improving the impact of earned media placements through additional sharing and promotion.

TACTICS

Paid Media

Outdoor. Outdoor advertising, traditionally dominated by print billboards that are located on or near highly trafficked roads, provides cost-effective advertising options for organizations. Both standard, highway-sized billboards and smaller *junior* billboards are generally purchased for a defined period of time (by the week or month), allowing for effective audience repetition and awareness for organizations and their events, products, or announcements. As some communities see billboards as unsightly, there are many local restrictions on their size and placement, making it difficult to blanket a community in the way that broadcast advertising can. Billboards are often purchased through national firms with availability in all major markets.[17] Beyond traditional billboards, *transit advertising* (such as on buses and trains), building signage, and digital billboards can all offer additional flexibility and target different audiences.

Print. Traditional newspaper, trade publication, or magazine advertising focuses on specific audiences bound by geography, profession, or interest much more clearly than broadcast media. There are multiple types of newspaper advertisements. *Display advertising* includes large, often image-driven ads scattered throughout the publication.

By contrast, *classified ads* are smaller, organized by content, text-heavy, and contained in a specific section.[18] Print ads are generally measured in inches and priced by size, color, location, and audience. As a prime location, the back cover of a magazine, for example, is often much more expensive than inside pages. Overall, rates are often driven by the type of audience as much as its size: a publication that targets high-income consumers or business executives will often charge more for the same advertisement than one that has a lower-income or less influential readership.

Radio. Similar to television, traditional broadcast radio stations often carry a mix of local and national content based on their format (news/talk, music, community/public radio, etc.). As commuters are the primary radio listeners, the most expensive periods for advertising are during *drive time*: the morning and evening commutes of local residents. Listeners often tune in daily to the same radio personality or channel, creating a more reliable audience than other media.[19] While alternative distribution channels such as satellite radio, digital live streaming, and podcasts continue to grow, the majority of advertising opportunities are still found within traditional over-the-air broadcasts.

TV. Television advertising starts with the relatively high cost of both creative production (the ads themselves) and air-time (the duration, frequency, and location where they appear). With that in mind, there is significant variance between relatively inexpensive local network affiliate advertising, regional or national cable advertising, and national network advertising. Ads within a program are called participating program announcements, or participations. Longer-form ads that resemble programming are called infomercials.[20] When purchasing TV ads, discounts are available given quantity and frequency. Airtime during primetime evening programs is the most expensive.

Digital Display. Digital display ads come in a variety of formats, from the ubiquitous pop-ups to website banners, each with continuously evolving targeting and richness. Such ads can be directed based on a combination of the context of the content, user behavior, geography, time of day, and numerous other factors.[21] Advertisers are working to balance the robust capability of these ads to include attention-grabbing animation, sound, and other features, with the potential for intrusion and annoyance of the audience.

Search Engine Marketing (SEM). Paid advertising directly to search engines, such as Google or Bing, allows organizations to have ads served to potential customers, members, donors, or supporters based on specific search terms, demographics, and geographic factors. It is the most popular form of digital advertising.[22] Distinct from organic search and search engine optimization (SEO), paid SEM results in advertisements set apart from the organic results. Tools such as Google Ads allow organizations to create highly customized, flexible, and scalable SEM campaigns for targeting their audiences. Rather than a negotiation method to purchase ads, used in most other formats, SEM uses a bid format based on the popularity and competitiveness of the keywords.[23] Such functionality makes SEM complicated to execute effectively, which can be a barrier for many small organizations.

Social Media. Paid social media outreach or advertising is another growing area available to even the smallest organizations. The detailed information available for each individual user allows for very specific targeting and efficient paid outreach. There are a variety of paid options available on many different social media channels, ranging from boosting existing content—paying for additional reach on organizational posts or events—to display and banner advertising. While Facebook and other platforms reward conciseness and visually compelling ads (rather than text-heavy content), research has shown that "informativeness" and creativity are critical drivers of consumer action for advertising on social networking sites.[24] To be informative, ads must give audiences the relevant information they need and expect. Creativity in this context captures attention both through the approach as well as the design and structure of the advertisement itself. Tactics can range from a variety of message strategies (e.g., functional appeals, emotional appeals, or comparative appeals) to promotions (e.g., sweepstakes, discounts, and special events), and user-generated content (e.g., submission contests, engaging surveys, or other brand engagement activities).[25]

Event Sponsorship. An opportunity to connect with professional networks or large community groups fuels investment in event sponsorship. There may be large discrepancies in pricing between becoming the named sponsor for an entire regional music festival or sponsoring snacks at the mid-afternoon break of a local professional conference. Organizations should tailor event-related opportunities to their budget and, as much as possible, to the themes and messages they are trying to convey. Event coordinators often have broad flexibility to customize sponsorship opportunities based on budget and organizational needs. That said, companies can be competitive in jockeying for position at key events, so locking in sponsorships early is always recommended.

Earned Media

Media Advisories. Media advisories are invitations for media to cover a specific event scheduled for a defined date, time, and location. Any advisory should include (in a list rather than paragraph format) what the event is, who will be taking part, when it will take place, where it will take place (either geographically or digitally), and why it is newsworthy. Leveraging media advisories can be particularly useful for campaign events where a broad range of journalists may be invited. They should be concise but clearly outline why a reporter would want to attend. The hook is often about the experience that can be captured as much as the news value of the information being shared.

Press Releases/News Releases. The ubiquitous press release or news release, while often considered out-of-touch in a world of increasingly customized media outreach, can still serve as a highly effective outreach tool. Howard and Matthews describe the press release as "a for-your-information memorandum to an editor."[26] Like a memo, the information contained within a press release should be concise, while also answering the major questions a journalist might have about the announcement. It should provide a basic grounding from which a reporter can further research and gather information for a story. Most importantly, such an announcement must contain genuine news. A press release without news value is as appetizing for reporters as being offered a sandwich and receiving two pieces of dry bread. Practitioners should understand the value in a release before they send it out and only share it with reporters who would appreciate that news value for their beat and their readers.

Press Conferences and Media-Friendly Events. Despite the reduction in media resources to cover news stories, media-focused events can still be a useful tactic to gain coverage and support other strategic objectives. Events cultivate relationships with key audiences, provide information, and can be much more engaging and immersive than a press release. That said, the days of holding a press conference for every major corporate announcement are long gone. Practitioners should always ask themselves what an event would add to the story for a reporter. Why would it be more effective than a traditional announcement? Would the event still be a success if no reporters attended? What content (images, video social media posts, narratives, etc.) could be captured during the event for future use? Do I have the budget to achieve the event's goals?

When planning events with the media in mind, it is important to consider what would make it convenient and valuable to cover, such as timing, visuals, and community relevance. In some cases, these questions may point to a staged media event with relevant speakers. If the news value is high enough, a full-scale event may be the best fit. If not, a media conference call with key parties may be able to address the same media needs and be more efficient for everyone involved. Reporters should be sent invitations to such events well in advance, as well as reminded as the date of the event approaches.[27] A media advisory (see description above) is designed specifically for this purpose.

Bylined Articles and Op-ed Pieces. Many practitioners underestimate media outlets' willingness to accept and publish submitted content. When organizations have something to say, be it a clear position on a topic, an insight to share, or a point to drive home, opportunities such as op-ed pieces and bylined articles become a useful tool. An op-ed, short for *opposite of the editorial page*, is a focused, single-issue perspective piece designed for a general audience.[28] Bylined articles, often accepted by industry trade publications, can provide a look inside the successful strategies, unique decisions, or innovative technologies. The most effective bylines for both journalists and a publication's audience are educational and informative rather than self-serving for the author's organization.

For example, a company opposed to a piece of state legislation may gain added publicity and credibility, as well as influencing the debate at hand, with a thoughtful 500-word essay from the CEO explaining the potential challenges of such new laws. Hundreds of local and national op-eds are published in the US every day. Alternatively, trade publications appreciate bylined articles that provide insight into processes, innovations, trends, or controversies within that industry. With a new technology, product, or process, it may make the most sense to have an article with the VP of engineering's byline, while a story focused on the organization itself may have more value coming from the CEO. It is particularly important to find the right degree of technical language for an industry audience, particularly as an outside agency practitioner. Often, the slow process of reading multiple industry publications and asking many deliberate questions about terminology can bring communicators up to speed.

Shared Media

Blogs: An Organization's Content Hub. The center of social media outreach is the idea of blogging, individuals sharing their ideas with anyone else in the world who stumbles upon them. Organizations should consider one central point of information for their digital presence and organize around it.[29] Often, this job is done by a blog or blog-like part of the organization's website. The ability to post original or curated content and solicit public feedback through comments and discussion are the foundation of Web 2.0, or the *social web*. This major advance made interactivity accessible to those without knowledge of programming languages and made the Internet a significantly more potent force for (and sometimes against) public relations practitioners.

Many different types of blogs exist, both in form and function. The most traditional (such as many hosted on sites such as Blogger and WordPress) feature a single author or core group of authors, a key topic or theme, and a regular posting schedule. The blogger owns and controls the main content on the site, although he or she usually allows and encourages interactivity. At the other end of the spectrum are the microblogging sites such as Twitter, where content length is limited, and the conversational space is shared among the user base. Social media sites such as Facebook and LinkedIn are found somewhere in between and include different forms of blogging within their functionality, as well as channels such as YouTube and Vimeo that allow the creation and sharing of (among other types of multimedia) video blogs or vlogs.

Organizations can use blog tactics as the centerpiece of a content creation strategy: a content hub. It could include traditional press room content (company news and press releases, executive bios, and photographs, as well as basic company background and content information) but also feature a variety of voices, such as employee and customer posts, and perspectives from different geographic or departmental areas. The audience includes both internal and external publics, including potential employees, customers, and community members.

Social Media Networks. Social networking allows organizations to connect, share information, and listen alongside potentially millions of customers, fans, or supporters. It gives organizations the privilege of speaking directly to this audience and audience members the opportunity to speak back. Safko notes that, because of this delicate relationship, social network content should not be a place for selling but for building brand loyalty through sharing useful and interesting information.[30]

While many networks exist, four in particular have added significant value for many organizations: Facebook, Instagram, LinkedIn, and Twitter. As the largest consumer social networks in the US, Facebook, Instagram, and Twitter have significant reach to both broad and highly targeted groups of individuals. Organizations can manage their *pages* to share content, create events, capture contact information, point users toward a website, and develop a base of followers resulting from *page likes*. Both organic and paid tactics are useful for increasing exposure to key audiences and drive engagement as part of campaigns. Successful outreach requires a long-term content strategy, including multimedia, and an understanding of what your organization's audience will find both readable and shareable. As Facebook is considered a personal social network, its content tends to focus less on business-to-business and more on consumer products and services. Instagram (owned by Facebook) is a more highly curated and visually dominated platform, which has developed an important niche as a hub for influencers, particularly for fashion, fitness, and other related industries.

LinkedIn, by contrast, functions for many users like a Rolodex, a listing of individuals and their job histories. Many organizations have also taken advantage of the network's underutilized sharing and connectivity functions. As part of campaigns, LinkedIn can be a valuable place to share content. As a professional network, LinkedIn provides an avenue for conducting business-to-business conversations and networking, improving job skills, or advancing careers. While LinkedIn may not necessarily be a fit for every campaign, many could benefit from its reach.

Microblogging. Twitter is the clear microblogging leader with more than 320 million monthly users as of March 2016.[31] Microblogging can be particularly effective for expanding coverage, engagement, and digital participation in campaign events, as well as to connect with key influencers or constituencies. Organizations can feature a variety of relevant content, including retweeting important information, starting public conversations about issues, and linking to organizational content, including blog posts. Since Twitter is largely public and searchable, it can serve as a useful listening tool as well. One downside of engagement is that it requires organizations to post content consistently in order to be impactful. Organizations must evaluate whether the investment required to create and manage the content will be sustainable for the length of the campaign.

Hashtags allow organizations to enter or create conversations around events, campaigns, and other interest areas.[32] By considering relevant, concise hashtags, practitioners can more easily drive conversations among those interested in specific topical content.

Image, Video, and Interest Sharing. A variety of image- and video-driven social networks have evolved and added unique functionality to the social sphere. YouTube and Vimeo are the largest long-form video sharing services. As the algorithms for Facebook, Instagram, and other channels continue to prioritize video sharing, these channels will only grow in importance. While the quality of video for shared media does not necessarily need to match broadcast media standards or budgets, practitioners should focus on the quality of their message. As Safko points out, the most important element is "quality content, not quality production."[33] If a cellphone video communicates the message to viewers and captures a shareable, authentic moment, it may be more effective than spending tens of thousands of dollars on professional video production. It is all about the context, message, and, of course, the audience at hand.

Additionally, a wide variety of niche networks have evolved for sharing specific types of content. Each has its own set of customs and should only be used organizationally when the content is a very clear fit with its functionality. For example, many fashion and lifestyle brands have embraced Instagram's and Pinterest's cultures of high-quality images, while location-driven brands can take advantage of Snapchat's geofilters or the light-hearted nature of TikTok's platform. Live video streaming using Facebook Live and other apps may also be a useful way to share important campaign events with those who may not be able to attend in person. The evolving possibilities of social media mean that practitioners must constantly investigate and evaluate new channels and possible tactics relevant to their organization or clients.

With any social network, establishing an audience is a significant investment of time, effort, creativity, and oftentimes, financial resources. As campaigns are time-bound and budgeted, practitioners must prioritize the channels for interaction based on where audiences already exist. Put simply, an organization would be better served to focus additional campaign resources to support its strong, active Facebook following, rather than branching out into new networks, even if the content may be a strong fit for Instagram or Pinterest. With that being said, campaigns can also be an opportunity to expand an organization's social media presence, particularly when it is done logically and with a long-term focus.

Community Management. Social media community management should be an ongoing activity for organizational communication, but it can also be integrated into campaigns as a tactical approach. AudienceBloom founder and CEO Jayson DeMers defined community management, distinct from social media channel management, as "the process of creating or altering an existing community in an effort to make the community stronger."[34] Communities, whether based on organizations or interest, can be extremely valuable groups to tap or empower as part of campaign tactics. Such tactics must be managed carefully to ensure that information shared is valuable to the community and not just to the organization. Communities have specific rules, and campaign tactics should only include them if the organization or its members, staff, or other stakeholders are already active, contributing participants.

Whether sharing content or managing communities for a campaign, being able to listen is also of immense importance. It goes beyond simply turning on and responding to notifications about an organization's existing channels. Listening comes in the form of following both the broad trends and discussions that happen on relevant social media channels, as well as the evaluation of specific posts, content types, channels, communities, and strategies. Even if sharing content with such communities is not an appropriate step, being a part of the conversation can lead to valuable insights about their conventions, the style and tone of discussions, and the types of messages that resonate.

Owned Media

Website Content Management. Organizational websites are nonnegotiable in today's business world. They are a foundational piece of credibility and are one of the first places any new stakeholder goes to learn about the organization and to take actions, such as purchasing products, downloading content, or renewing a membership. Campaigns often seek a form of conversion, an action such as buying an event ticket or signing up for an email list, as an objective; and websites are often where such tactics occur.

Organizational websites exist prior to, during, and after campaigns, and integration should support the businesses' overarching purposes and messages. Campaigns often need a temporary online home as part of this digital presence. This could present itself in the form of a dedicated page or section of the website or a separate microsite that integrates all campaign information and functions, often serving as a place to drive traffic from other digital and traditional channels. Organizational websites also provide opportunities for rotating, newsworthy content as part of their homepage, and campaigns should see this as one significant opportunity to draw in users who are interested in the organization but not necessarily the campaign. Similarly, they can point interested users to dedicated campaign information.

Marketing Tactics. PRSA defines marketing as "the management function that identifies human needs and wants, offers products and services to satisfy those demands, and causes transactions that deliver products and services in exchange for something of value to the provider."[35] Many public relation activities are closely connected to marketing activities and are often underused toward marketing ends. For example, positive earned media coverage should be shared with key organizational publics. This could include integrating the media coverage into paid/boosted content shared via social media channels, e-newsletters, or even traditional printed brochures.

Publications. Organizations develop a wide variety of print and digital publications that serve both to distribute content and provide audiences the chance to browse a wider breadth of stories that they may otherwise not be exposed to. The bar for content creation in such outlets is high since the information must be both valuable and interesting to readers. Publications come in several varieties, including recurring *serial publications* like newsletters (print and digital), organizational magazines, and annual reports.[36] Newsletters and magazines, even in print form, are still a popular form of organizational communication and represent an accessible way to share information both within and outside of a campaign structure. While design and production costs vary greatly, particularly when printing and mailing are involved, many organizations still see the value for member/donor outreach, sales and marketing, and event promotion. Many organizations adapt the content produced for such publications for digital purposes. Digital versions of publications, often distributed via email distribution services such as MailChimp, have the advantage of metrics that track clicks on stories and links. Practitioners can use this information to improve story selection, multimedia content, and writing for future issues. The effectiveness of these publications is dependent on having an up-to-date mailing or email distribution list.

Stand-alone (nonrecurring or nonscheduled) publications include e-blasts, reprints, reports, and whitepapers, as well as brochures and flyers. E-blasts are often used to alert specific audiences about more immediately newsworthy content and are timed around the specific event rather than on a weekly, monthly, or quarterly schedule. Reprints are designed versions of media articles that can be repurposed for print or digital use.[37] Copyright law's fair-use provisions provide for some internal and educational use of reprints, but public dissemination generally must be approved and paid for by the media outlet itself. Reports encompass a variety of documents from public-facing research whitepapers (which can be written and disseminated on campaign-specific topics) to customer or member-focused reports on key organizational issues. Generally, the purpose of such reports is to inform the audience in detail on a specific topic or provide information tailored for a specific time, event, or campaign. Similarly, fewer organizations have a comprehensive brochure about their work, but many have maintained product- or program-specific brochures. Brochures are made up of folding panels, in contrast to flyers or sales sheets, which often accomplish the same narrowly focused purpose but on a flat piece of paper.[38] One advantage to flyers and sales sheets is that they can be printed easily in-house, although the quality, particularly with color images and photos, often suffers.

Collateral Materials. Additional materials can be developed for both digital and traditional uses, either as stand-alone pieces or as part of a broader event or campaign. These can range from a variety of branded logo items to the trade show booths that will represent the business focus. Organizations often use their own space as a type of collateral, including decorations inside and outside of the building for special events. This can expand to a variety of posters and banners ranging from small easel-mounted foam core pieces to specialty printed banners that take up an entire side of a building. The design should reflect the scope and importance of the campaign itself, always representing the larger brand.

Glossary

Advertising. Paid communication: Controlled information placed in a channel by an identified sponsor, often for a specific time period, in a specific physical space, or for a specific demographic group.

Agenda Building Theory. The process through which organizations and publics advocate for bringing issues to public attention, often using earned media and journalist relationships.

Agenda Setting Theory. Widely accepted view of how mass media interacts with society, positing that mass media do not tell us what to think but what to think about. In this way media set the public agenda.

Associated Press. AP is a nonprofit news-gathering organization that provides global reporting services to many member news outlets, allowing them to pool resources and provide coverage of events and issues otherwise beyond their capability.

Audience. The immediate listeners/viewers or targets of a particular campaign or message. Audiences are distinct from publics in that they are created or made distinct by the organization, rather than being self-selecting.

Blog. Short for weblog, a blog provides a central point for organizations or individuals to create, curate, and share content they see as being potentially valuable to readers or publics. They are generally organized chronologically and reflect a narrow topical perspective or purpose.

Boosted Content. A paid social media strategy that allows organizations to expand the reach of their organically created or curated content; specifically targeting audiences by interest, geography, demographics, and other factors depending on the platform.

Brand. A distinct organizational identity represented through language and imagery as well as an organization's actions and behaviors. Brands are also constructed in part by an organization's publics and their conversations about its actions and identity.

Branding. The process of an organization actively engaged in creating, maintaining, adjusting, or sharing its public identity or brand.

Budget. An estimate of income and expenditure for a set period of time or particular project.

Budget, Administration. Campaign expenditures for office-related needs, travel, and other incidental activities.

Budget, Infrastructure. Costs for upgraded items such as equipment, facilities, and software that are often wholly or partially integrated into campaign budgets.

Budget, Materials. Tactic-specific outlays such as printing, video production, or newswire distribution.

Budget, Media. Advertising and marketing costs such as print, broadcast, or digital ad buys.

Budget, Personnel. Professional time costs for the research, planning, development, execution, and evaluation of campaigns.

C-Suite. A corporation's senior executive team. Titles include chief executive officer (CEO), chief financial officer (CFO), or chief technology officer (CTO).

Channel. The medium through which messages are sent, such as the elements within the PESO model (e.g., paid print advertising, earned trade media placements, organizational social media channels, or an organization's website).

Codebook. Used in the coding process for content analysis, a guide to the units of measurement (words, phrases, themes, symbols, etc.). Codebooks are particularly necessary when multiple individuals are coding the same set of data.

Coding. The process of identifying words, phrases, tones, themes, or other symbols in a variety of materials to look for frequency and patterns during content analysis.

Communication Audit. A full investigation of an organization's communication practices in order to evaluate whether they are meeting the needs of the organization as well as stakeholders and publics. An audit should examine the form and function of all existing (and potential) channels to look for areas of strength and improvement.

Communication Goal. See **Public Relations Goal**.

Communication Theory. The branch of knowledge dealing with the principles and methods by which information is conveyed.

Community Relations. The public relations responsibility for building and strengthening relationships with an organization's communities, including both the publics within close geographic proximity as well as digital and industry-specific stakeholders.

Competitive Objectives. In a given marketplace or industry, particular objectives may be based on success relative to the results of competitors. These could be the share of voice objectives in social media or earned media coverage, as well as organizational fundraising or sales goals.

Content Amplification. The convergence process that brings together content (often owned and earned media) with paid tactics. Content amplification allows marketers to use paid tactics to increase the reach of messages to publics across multiple channels, including websites, and social media sites.

Content Analysis. The process of analyzing data (often narrative data such as media articles, social media posts, or web content) to look for critical themes, the frequency of particular words, phrases, or symbols, as well as collecting relevant metadata. Content analysis can be performed from a purely quantitative perspective using digital tools (such as counting the occurrence of specific words), or from a qualitative perspective (such as coding a set of articles for a negative, neutral, or positive tone).

Content Creation. The generation of a variety of different written and visual communication on behalf of an organization, which may be used in multiple formats as part of paid, earned, shared, owned, and converged channels.

Content Hub. A centralized digital location (part of an owned media property such as an organization's website) to house differing types of written and multimedia content that can be repurposed, shared, and linked to through a variety of channels, including social media, digital newsletters, or earned media opportunities. Excellent content hub management includes tracking the popularity, reach, and effectiveness of each piece, as well as creating a browsable environment encouraging visitors to take in additional content.

Contingency Theory. Rather than falling into rigid categories, most organizations practice a variety of models of strategic communication (on a continuum from advocacy to accommodation) based on multiple internal and external factors.

Control Group. In a scientific experiment, the group that is not acted on by the variable being studied.

Controlled Media. Primarily paid and owned media channels where the organization has full control of the design, content, timing, and reach of the messages.

Converged Media. Within the PESO model, media that overlaps several categories, such as boosted posts through social media that maintain qualities of both paid and shared content.

Conversion. Often used as a metric to track campaign success: a member of a target group completing a desired action such as donating to a fundraiser, buying a product, or signing up for an e-newsletter.

Corporate Social Responsibility. Also referred to as CSR, an organizational philosophy that emphasizes an organization's obligation to society beyond profit.

Counseling. Advising management or organizational leaders concerning policies, strategy, public relations, and communication.

Crisis Communication. Communicating on behalf of organizations facing a significant threat to their reputation and/or their legitimacy. It involves investigating and understanding how publics and stakeholders view the situation and devising appropriate communication approaches to rebuild relationships with these groups.

Crowdfunding. The practice of funding a project or venture by raising small donations from a large number of people, typically through digital channels.

Data. The content analyzed through research. Data can take many forms, from interview transcripts and media articles to social media posts and experiment results.

Diagnosis. The process of identifying the core problem or opportunity for communication and public relations efforts. It should be based on information gleaned from internal and external research, balancing the organization's goals, immediate environmental circumstances, and resources to identify where the greatest positive impact can be made.

Diffusion Theory. Diffusion Theory describes the process of a community or society adopting technology (including both physical devices and ideas) from early adopters through laggards. While individuals have different degrees of desire and enthusiasm for this process, they all must go through the same steps of being exposed to the technology and testing it before choosing to adopt it. Those at the front end often become trend setters or opinion leaders helping to popularize or inform others about new developments.

Diversity. Differences among individuals within a group, including both potentially visible factors (age, gender, ethnicity, disability, etc.) and potentially invisible factors (sexual orientation, gender identity, religion, health status, and socioeconomic status, etc.). Diversity is valued among public relations practitioners due to the wide variety of individuals and publics with which organizations communicate.

Earned Media. When practitioners use media relations to provide information subsidies to and build relationships with journalists, bloggers, and others, increasing the probability that they include an organization's ideas and perspective as part of media coverage.

Employee Relations. Communication between organizational leadership and employees. Effective employee relations improves employees' understanding of their role and value within the organization as well as increases management's knowledge of employee needs.

Evaluation. The analysis of completed or ongoing activities that determine or support a public relations campaign.

Excellence Theory. Specifies how excellent public relations makes organizations more effective. It presents a strategic framework for PR departments to understand their organizations' environments, make contributions to leadership and decision making, as well as measure the value of public relations.

Financial Communication. Public relations efforts that focus on financial issues with organizations (often public companies), such as attracting new investors, maintaining and improving relationships with current investors, and disseminating information used by those active in the financial markets. It includes the work of investor relations or shareholder relations.

Framing Theory. By focusing attention on certain events, issues, or themes, a communicator places them within a field of meaning for their audience and points them toward what information is most critical.

Gantt Chart. A campaign planning and execution tool that visually represents a variety of campaign activities and the timeline during which they will each be implemented.

Generalizability. Formal research using a comprehensive or representative sample makes the results applicable to a larger group than the study itself.

Global Public Relations. Cross-national public relations, involving either an organization communicating to publics in a different country from where it is based or to publics in multiple countries at the same time.

Government Relations. Communication and relationship building between organizations and government officials, including elected officials and regulators. Often, it involves advocacy to influence policy and regulatory decisions that impact an organization or industry.

Hard Costs. Fixed expenditures that cannot change during the course of the campaign, such as production of collateral materials, event costs, and broadcast ad buys.

Hashtag. Originating on Twitter, a symbol (#) preceding a word or phrase to allow for its categorization or search within a social media channel or channels.

Hierarchy of Needs Theory. As human beings, we prioritize our needs from the most essential (such as air, food, water, and shelter) to self-fulfillment. PR practitioners must understand whether publics are in need of information about their basic survival (as in a natural disaster), major household or societal needs (such as hiring or layoff announcements), or personal identity (including sales of consumer products and services).

I.M.P.A.C.T. Acronym for media content analysis categories: Influence or tone, Message communicated, Prominence, Audience reached, Consultant/spokesman quoted, and Type of article.

Impact Role for Communication. Communication cannot solve all problems. Like any tool, it has areas where it is more or less effective. An important facet of setting public relations or campaign goals is understanding the circumstances so that efforts are aimed at where communication engagement can make a significant, positive impact.

Implementation. The point in the campaign process where the campaign plan is put into operation.

Influencer. An expert in a specific category with a loyal and engaged following.

Information Subsidy. The value of information provided to a reporter by a source, including public relations professionals.

Integrated Marketing Communications. Coordinated communication activities developed to promote or sell products and services using a variety of paid, earned, shared, and owned channels.

Issues Management. The organizational process of monitoring, evaluating, and (when appropriate) engaging in public conversations about societal issues.

Iterative Planning. Research, goal-setting, and campaign planning are not separate, ordered steps, but part of a continuous cycle of understanding the organization and its environment. Communicating and listening to publics serve both to share information on behalf of the organization, but also to raise new questions and prompt more research.

Lead Capture. A potentially valuable marketing-based objective, gathering contact information for interested potential customers or donors can be a useful outcome of campaign communication and relate very directly to organizational goals and objectives.

Lead Generation. Broadly, public relations generates awareness for organizations, products, and services that open the door to behaviors such as buying products, attending events, or donating to nonprofits. Specifically, public relations campaigns can generate and capture sales/donor leads among specific audiences as part of their objectives.

Likert-type Scale. A popular and established measurement item construction using an odd number of points along a "strongly agree" to "strongly disagree" continuum of answers.

Management by Objectives (MBO). A widely used model developed by Peter Drucker, management by objectives (MBO) outlines a process through which organizational goals are broken down into their component parts to create measurable objectives assigned to different professional units (PR, sales, HR, accounting, etc.). This increases transparency and accountability for accomplishing objectives.

Marketing. Marketing involves the processes for developing, designing, delivering, and tracking strategies for promoting and selling items of value (products and services) to customers or members of businesses and other organizations.

Marketing Research. Research to improve understanding of the publics who may be interested in purchasing products or services, as well as to evaluate existing marketing practices.

Media Ad Value (or Ad Value Equivalency/AVE). A historically popular, but broadly discredited, practice of measuring the impact of earned media coverage by estimating its equivalent advertising value. The Barcelona Principles—the most important statement by top industry measurement experts—specifically call for practitioners to utilize more advanced and relevant metrics, including changes in the awareness, opinion, or behavior of publics.

Media Relations. The public relations function that deals with building and strengthening relationships with journalists. Media relations involves both proactive outreach, such as sending pitches and media alerts, as well as reactive outreach, including responding to reporter inquiries and coordinating media interviews.

Mediated Communication. Communication that is conducted via any information-disseminating medium (e.g., computer, telephone, letters).

Messaging. The process of defining, crafting, integrating, and distributing organizational messages through a variety of communication channels.

Methodology. A framework, process, and perspective that informs the analysis of data or information, such as quantitative or qualitative approaches to research.

Microblogging. The short posts, often including links, images, and videos, that characterize social media content on platforms such as Facebook, LinkedIn, and Twitter.

Native Advertising. Organization-generated content that resembles a media outlet's editorial content but is paid for by the organization and intended to promote it. To be effective, native advertising should be tailored to the media outlet and its audience, but also clearly labeled as paid content.

Newsworthiness. The qualities that make a particular story appealing for journalists to cover, including timeliness, uniqueness, breadth of impact, and relevance to the media outlet's audience.

Nonmediated Communication. Communication that is conducted face to face and not via an information-disseminating medium (e.g., computer, telephone, letters).

Objectives. Specific, measurable statement of what needs to be achieved as part of reaching a goal.

Observer Bias. Individuals are predisposed to evaluate results to confirm their own opinions and biases.

Online Community Management. Organizational engagement with digital communities, best conducted in mutually beneficial ways that include information sharing and organizational listening.

Organizational Goal. Significant, stable, long-term aspirations defined by the management and leadership of organizations.

Outcome Objectives. Measurable changes in the behavior of publics that contribute directly to organizational goals through action, such as increased website traffic, sales, event attendance, or, for advocacy campaigns, public opinion shifts.

Output Objectives. Measurable process objectives that support reaching more important outcome objectives but do not by themselves meet organizational goals. This may include earned media outreach and media tracking or basic social media outreach.

Outtake Objectives. Measurable objectives that support reaching more important outcome objectives but do not by themselves meet organizational goals. This may include awareness of organizational messages or social media engagement metrics.

Owned Media. The editorial and messages produced by an organization and distributed across its numerous owned, controlled communication channels.

Paid Media. The channels for which money is paid to place the message and control its distribution.

Persuasion. An attempt to influence a person's actions or beliefs. Persuasion can take many forms, including appeals to his or her self-interest; techniques such as logical, credibility-based, or emotionally driven arguments (logos/ethos/pathos); or using power, influence, or other compliance-gaining tactics.

PESO. An acronym for paid, earned, shared, and owned media. In the PESO model, each channel delivers unique importance and can be used together in a wide variety of combinations during campaigns.

Press Agentry Model. Creating newsworthy stories and events to attract media attention and gain public notice, although not all attention may be positive. Categorized as one-way communication, this model may use persuasion, half-truths, and manipulation to influence an audience to behave as the organization desires.

Press Room. A website page or group of pages that provide reporters and other outside entities with materials necessary for research on the organization, including traditional press releases and media kit items (e.g., fact sheets, executive bios, backgrounders, and high-resolution images), as well as videos, informational links, and prior media coverage.

Proactive Public Relations. Outreach centering on content creation and distribution through PESO channels to share organizational perspectives and drive change in awareness, opinions, and behaviors of key publics.

Programmatic Media Buying (sometimes called Programmatic Buying). Traditional paid media is purchased strategically by advertising, marketing, or public relations professionals in consultation with sales specialists at media outlets or other channels, but programmatic buying uses algorithmic approaches so that ads are continually optimized toward specific goals for awareness or activation.

Promotion. Activities and tactics designed to win publicity or attention. Promotional activities often generate interest in a person, product, organization, or cause, and often focus on the needs of journalists in order to make the most of potential media coverage.

Propaganda. Persuasive messages and strategies designed to be in the best interests of an organization without consideration for the needs or preferences of publics. The term carries a strong negative connotation, having been associated with harmful political messages and the use of tactics such as lying and misinformation.

Public. Any group of people tied together by some common factor or interest. Demographics, psychographics, motivating self-interests, status of current relationships with an organization, location or other characteristics define these publics.

Public Information Model. Practitioners act as journalists-in-residence, providing newsworthy information flowing one way from an organization to its stakeholders. It is factual and logical information rather than persuasive or promotional.

Public Relations. Public relations is a strategic communication process that builds mutually beneficial relationships between organizations and their publics.

Public Relations Campaign. A public relations campaign is a strategic approach to achieving organizational and communication goals through researching, planning, implementing, and evaluating a series of objectives, strategies, and tactics.

Public Relations Goal. Informed by organizational goals, PR/communication goals should reflect the most effective use of campaign outreach (impact role) to support the achievement of organizational goals.

Publicity. In media relations, the process of sharing information with journalists with the aim of publishing it for a wider audience.

R.A.C.E.. A four-step communication planning model. R.A.C.E.: Research and planning, Action, Communication, Evaluation.

R.O.P.E.. A four-step communication planning model. R.O.P.E.: Research, Objectives, Programming, Evaluation.

Raw Volume. Simple media evaluation and reporting based solely on the number of "clips"—organizational or campaign mentions in relevant media coverage.

Reactive Public Relations. PR practices that prioritize responding to journalist inquiries and external actors rather than proactively working to reach out and influence discourse or set media/public agendas.

Relationship. Considered by many scholars and practitioners to be the core unit of public relations success; relationships between organizations and publics are measured by factors including trust, satisfaction, commitment, and the degree of mutual control.

Relative Volume. Comparing the amount of media coverage between, for example, different organizational messages/objectives, or among competing organizations in the same publications or channels.

Reputation Management. Strategic communication efforts designed to build or rebuild an organization's perceived legitimacy by organizational publics and stakeholders. It may involve many coordinated PESO strategies and tactics; interpersonal, traditional media and digital media channels; as well as concrete changes to organizational policies and actions.

Research. The systematic collection and explanation of data used to increase understanding of particular phenomena.

Research, Developmental. Formative research is done as part of the campaign planning process. Often, it's done to better understand an organization's environment or audiences and publics.

Research, Evaluative. Research to understand a campaign's impact and better inform future campaigns. This should be related to objectives (did the campaign achieve what it set out to achieve?) as well as beyond them (what unexpected results occurred due to the campaign?).

Research, Experimental. Scientific research designed to establish whether one variable (independent) is influencing a second variable (dependent).

Research, Formal. Research done using standardized, systematic techniques and accepted practices for social science research, including large-scale surveys, quantitative content analysis, and experimental research.

Research, Informal. Useful knowledge-gathering practices engaged in by public relations practitioners through conversations with multiple publics (inside and outside the organization) as well as maintaining a general knowledge of key issues and trends in the media. These processes might include maintaining relationships with leadership and stakeholders, consuming mainstream and trade media, following influencers on social media, and attending relevant community events.

Research, Primary. Research of many forms conducted by practitioners to inform their understanding of the organization, external situation, or a specific campaign.

Research, Qualitative. Research utilizing primarily nonquantitative, language-based approaches, providing a holistic and broad perspective on the data or phenomena being examined.

Research, Quantitative. Research grounded in numeric approaches to understanding specific phenomena, generally focused on narrowing the scope to one or several key elements (variables) to determine their importance and impact.

Research, Refinement. Research done in the middle stages of the campaign to ensure strategies and tactics are reaching audiences, having the desired impacts, and balancing channels and resources efficiently.

Research, Secondary. Often an early step in the research process, secondary research includes the gathering of insights from research conducted by others, often involving the collection and analysis of a significant number of existing reports, studies, or other primary research sources.

Scope. The boundaries of a particular project or campaign. This can be difficult to envision, particularly in the early planning stages, but practitioners must be aware of and do their best to define them for a campaign to effectively prioritize its efforts.

Share of Voice. A useful metric or objective comparing one organization, message, or campaign with competitors in a given space. It can be used to measure success on social media, earned media, or other venues.

Shared Media. Social media channels characterized by the opportunities for all participants to engage with content, including commenting and sharing.

Situational Crisis Communication Theory (SCCT). SCCT suggests that, to best protect an organization's reputation, crisis communication managers should base crisis responses on the level of crisis responsibility publics perceive, the type of crisis, and the degree of the reputational threat.

Situational Theory of Publics. Publics can be identified and classified by problem recognition, level of involvement, and constraint recognition: the degree to which they are aware of a problem, the degree to which a problem has an impact on them, and the extent to which they feel capable of doing something about the problem.

Social Listening. Systematic approaches to monitoring digital conversations to better understand publics, communities, and an organization's environment.

Social Media. Digital communication networks that allow users (both individuals and organizations) to connect with others as well as share information, opinions, and other content (images, videos, etc.) through both public and private channels.

Social Media Analytics. The systematic collection of data about the usage of and interaction with social media channels to improve strategic decision making both narrowly within the channel (optimizing content) and broadly (informing understanding of customer, member, or community opinion and behavior).

Social Media Monitoring. Continuous tracking of social media activities, conversations, influencers, issues, and trends to evaluate outreach and to identify upcoming challenges and opportunities.

Social Sphere. The broad network of interactive digital and social media channels that collectively create a new form of public sphere.

Soft Costs. Flexible outlays that can be responsive to environmental changes during a campaign, including professional time and some digital ad buys.

Stakeholder. Those with a concrete interest in a particular organization, including internal groups such as employees and board members as well as external groups such as customers/donors, vendors, and community members.

Strategic Communication. The deliberate use of communication and public relations by organizations to meet their goals and objectives.

Strategies. Public-specific communication approaches (often specifying the channel) used to send a message to achieve objectives.

SWOT Analysis. A process to help organizations define their strengths, weaknesses, opportunities, and threats. Generally, SWOT analyses are considered a qualitative research method that brings together a variety of secondary research about an organization and its competitors/industry peers, combined with primary research to organize and synthesize the input and perspective of organizational leaders.

Systems Theory. Systems theory explains that any system tends toward maintaining equilibrium. For an organization, this means constant and careful management of internal and external relationships, as well as continual awareness of the economic, political, and social conditions within communities that may impact an organization's publics and stakeholders.

Tactics. Strategy-specific communication products that carry messages to key publics. Tactics are tangible items such as a press release, social media post, or a website.

Theory. Explanations of interrelated concepts to better understand and predict events and behaviors.

Triangulation. The use of multiple methods and/or data sources to reinforce the credibility of research findings.

Two-step Flow of Communication. Suggests that mass media influence society's opinion leaders, who, in turn, influence society.

Two-way Asymmetrical Model. Organizations use organizational listening, research, and scientific methods to persuade stakeholders to adopt organizational perspectives or opinions.

Two-way Symmetrical Model of Public Relations. Two-way symmetrical communication prioritizes mutually beneficial communication and decision making among organizations and their publics.

Uncontrolled Media. Refers to outreach methods (such as media relations) that are not under direct control of the company, organization, or sender of messages. These channels include newspapers and magazines, radio and television, external websites, externally produced blogs and social media commentary, and externally developed news stories. Positive media outreach cannot guarantee that the public-facing content will be favorable to the organization.

Uses and Gratifications. People select particular media to satisfy their needs or to be entertained.

Validity. Whether a specific research program or individual question/scale is measuring what it is intended to measure.

Vlogs. Video blogs, largely YouTube-based.

Weighted Volume. Quantitative reporting of media coverage using formulas to adjust the value of individual news stories based on factors such as prominence, outlet quality, and campaign message inclusion, providing a richer reporting perspective.

References

Preface

1. "Occupational Outlook Handbook: Public Relations Specialists," U.S. Bureau of Labor Statistics, last modified, Sept. 1, 2020, https://www.bls.gov/ooh/media-and-communication/public-relations-specialists.htm.
2. "The Relevance Report 2020," USC Annenberg Center for Public Relations, accessed Oct., 22, 2020, http://assets.uscannenberg.org/docs/relevance-report-2020.pdf.

Introduction

1. Marianne Dainton and Elaine D. Zelley, *Applying Communication Theory for Professional Life: A Practical Introduction* (Thousand Oaks, CA: SAGE Publications, 2015).
2. Merriam-Webster Dictionary, "Theory," https://www.merriam-webster.com/dictionary/theory.
3. Yunna Rhee, "The Employee-Public-Organization Chain in Relationship Management: A Case Study of a Government Organization" (Unpublished doctoral dissertation, College Park: University of Maryland, 2004).
4. James E. Grunig, "Excellence Theory in Public Relations," in *The International Encyclopedia of Communication*, ed. W. Donsbach, vol. 4 (Oxford and Malden, MA: Wiley-Blackwell, 2008), 1620–22.
5. James E. Grunig and Larissa A. Grunig, "Excellence Theory in Public Relations: Past, Present, and Future," in *Public Relations Research: European and International Perspectives and Innovations*, ed. A. Zerfass, B. V. Ruler, and K. Sriramesh (Wiesbaden: VS Verlag, 2008), 327–47.
6. Grunig, "Excellence Theory in Public Relations."
7. David Dozier, Larissa A. Grunig, and James E. Grunig, *The Manager's Guide to Excellence in Public Relations and Communication Management* (Mahwah, NJ: Lawrence Erlbaum Associates, Inc., 1995), 48.
8. Scott M. Cutlip, Allen H. Center, and Glen M. Broom, *Effective Public Relations*, 9th ed. (Upper Saddle River, NJ: Pearson Prentice Hall, 2006).
9. Everett Rogers, *Diffusion of Innovations*, 5th ed. (New York: Simon and Schuster, 2003).
10. Herbert F. Lionberger, *Adoption of New Ideas and Practices* (Ames: Iowa State University Press, 1960), 32.
11. Lynn M. Zoch and Juan-Carlos Molleda, "Building a Theoretical Model of Media Relations Using Framing, Information Subsidies, and Agenda-Building," in *Public Relations Theory II*, Carl H. Botan and Vincent Hazleton (Mahwah, NJ: Lawrence Erlbaum Associates, 2006).
12. Ibid.
13. Ibid., 281.
14. Kirk Hallahan, "Seven Models of Framing: Implications for Public Relations," *Journal of Public Relations Research* 11, no. 3 (1999): 205–42.
15. Ibid.
16. Maxwell McCombs, "Agenda Setting Function of Mass Media," *Public Relations Review* 3 (1977): 89–95, https://doi.org/10.1086/267990.
17. Zoch and Molleda, Public Relations Theory II.
18. Matthew C. Nisbet, "Agenda Building," in *The International Encyclopedia of Communication*, ed. W. Donsbach (New York: Blackwell, 2008), https://doi.org/10.1111/b.9781405131995.2008.x.

19. Ron Smith, "Agenda Setting, Priming & Framing," updated Summer 2011, http://faculty.buffalostate.edu/smithrd/PR/Framing.htm.

20. Sun Young Lee, "Agenda-Building Theory," in *The SAGE Encyclopedia of Corporate Reputation*, ed. Craig E. Carroll (Thousand Oaks, CA: SAGE Publications, 2016), http://dx.doi.org/10.4135/9781483376493.n16.

21. W. Timothy Coombs, *The Handbook of Crisis Communication* (Chichester: Wiley-Blackwell, 2012).

22. W. Timothy Coombs, *Crisis Communication* (Thousand Oaks, CA: SAGE Publications, 2014).

23. Cutlip, Allen, and Broom, *Effective Public Relations*.

24. Ibid.

25. Lynn M. Zoch and Juan-Carlos Molleda, "Building a Theoretical Model of Media Relations Using Framing, Information Subsidies and Agenda Building," in *Public Relations Theory II*, ed. Carl H. Botan and Vincent Hazleton (Mahwah, NJ: Lawrence Erlbaum, 2006), 279–309.

26. James E. Grunig and Todd Hunt, *Managing Public Relations* (Belmont, CA: Thompson Wadsworth, 1984).

27. Cutlip, Allen, and Broom, *Effective Public Relations*.

28. Dozier, Grunig, and Grunig, *The Manager's Guide*.

29. Grunig and Hunt, *Managing Public Relations*.

30. Ron Smith, "Public Relations, History," 2011, http://faculty.buffalostate.edu/smithrd/pr/history.htm.

31. Sheila Clough-Crifasi, "Everything's Coming Up Rosie," *Public Relations Tactics* 7, no. 9 (2000): 22.

32. Michael Turney, "Acronyms for the Public Relations Process," On-line Readings in Public Relations by Michael Turney, April 1, 2011, https://www.nku.edu/~turney/prclass/readings/process_acronyms.html.

33. Nisbet, "Agenda Building."

34. James G. Hutton, "The Definition, Dimensions, and Domain of Public Relations," *Public Relations Review* 25, no. 2 (1999): 199–214.

35. Nisbet, "Agenda Building."

36. Gilmore Girls' Early Ratings: Revival Ranks as One of Most-Watched Netflix Originals," *Ad Age*, December 01, 2016, http://adage.com/article/media/gilmore-girls-ratings-revival-ranks-watched-netflix-originals/306977.

Chapter 1

1. Marlene S. Neill and Erin Schauster, "Gaps in Advertising and Public Relations Education: Perspectives of Agency Leaders," *Journal of Advertising Education* 19, no. 2 (2015): 5–17.

2. Regina Luttrell, "Social Networking Sites in the Public Relations Classroom: A Mixed Methods Analysis of Undergraduate Learning Outcomes Using WordPress, Facebook, and Twitter" (PhD diss., California Institute of Integral Studies, 2012).

3. CEPR: The Global Standard in Public Relations Education," PRSA, 2019, last modified 2019, https://prssa.prsa.org/wp-content/uploads/2018/09/CEPRguidelines-2019.pdf.

4. Darrell Etherington, "People Now Watch 1 Billion Hours of YouTube Per Day," TechCrunch, February 28, 2017, https://techcrunch.com/2017/02/28/people-now-watch-1-billion-hours-of-youtube-per-day.

5. University of Michigan, "Michigan Athletics Diversity, Equity and Inclusion," Athletics, last modified January 21, 2019, https://mgoblue.com/sports/2017/6/16/diversity-equity-and-inclusion.aspx.

6. *Diversity and Inclusion Tool Kit*, 5th ed. (New York: Public Relations Society of America, 2016), last modified 2016, accessed October 13, 2019,

https://www.prsa.org/docs/default-source/about/diversity/prsa-diversity-and-inclusion-tool-kit-2016.pdf?sfvrsn=7fe7113e_4.

7. Itamar Goldminz, "The 4 Layers of Diversity [Gardenswartz & Rowe]," Medium, Org Hacking, December 17, 2019, https://medium.com/org-hacking/the-4-layers-of-diversity-gardenswartz-rowe-47013e42070f.
8. Lee Gardenswartz and Anita Rowe, "Who We Are," EIDI, accessed January 27, 2020, https://www.eidi-results.org/who-we-are-1.
9. Lynn Perry Wooten, "Guest Editors Note: Breaking Barriers in Organizations for the Purpose of Inclusiveness," *Human Resource Management* 47, no. 2 (2008): 191–97, https://doi.org/10.1002/hrm.20207.
10. Adapted for use by the Program on Intergroup Relations and the Spectrum Center, University of Michigan. Resource hosted by LSA Inclusive Teaching Initiative, University of Michigan, http://sites.lsa.umich.edu/inclusive-teaching/.
11. Ibid.
12. Regina M. Luttrell and Adrienne A. Wallace, "Improving Student Awareness of Diversity, Equity, and Inclusion Efforts Through Public Relations Campaigns," *Journal of Public Relations Education* 7 (forthcoming).
13. Frank Dobbin and Alexandra Kalev, "The Architecture of Inclusion: Evidence From Corporate Diversity Programs," *Harvard Journal of Law & Gender* 30 (2007): 279.
14. Wooten, "Guest Editors Note."
15. Regina M. Luttrell and Natalia Flores, "7 Steps to Adopting a D&I-First Approach to PR," *PR Daily* (blog), entry posted September 25, 2019, https://www.prdaily.com/7-steps-to-adopting-a-di-first-approach-to-pr/.
16. Harvard University, About Us, Project Implicit, https://implicit.harvard.edu/implicit/aboutus.html.
17. Alcohol Justice, "Report on How the Organization Alcohol Justice Believes That Big Alcohol Twists 'Drink Responsibly' to Market Its Products," May, 2012.
18. Produção," Ambev, accessed October 16, 2019, https://www.ambev.com.br/sobre/producao/.
19. Edilaine Moraes, Marcio Mariano Moreira, and Geraldo Mendes de Campo. "Costs of Drinking and Driving in Brazil," *Sleep Medicine and Disorders: International Journal* 1, no. 6 (December 28, 2017): 124–26, https://doi.org/10.15406/smdij.2017.01.00026.
20. Center for Disease Control (CDC), "Impaired Driving: Get the Facts," Center for Disease Control and Prevention, accessed January 15, 2020, https://www.cdc.gov/motorvehiclesafety/impaired_driving/impaired-drv_factsheet.html.
21. National Highway Traffic Safety Administration, Traffic Safety Facts 2016 Data: Alcohol-Impaired Driving, U.S. Department of Transportation, Washington, DC, 2017, https://crashstats.nhtsa.dot.gov/Api/Public/ViewPublication/812450.
22. J. Mendoza, "Beer Consumption in Brazil From 2017 to 2021," Statista, last modified January 10, 2020, https://www.statista.com/statistics/727090/beer-consumption-brazil/.
23. Eric Duncan, "Topic: Alcoholic Beverages in Brazil," Statista, accessed October 16, 2019, https://www.statista.com/topics/4673/alcoholic-beverages-in-brazil/.
24. Smart Drinking Goals," AB InBev, accessed January 16, 2020, https://www.ab-inbev.com/what-we-do/smart-drinking/smart-drinking-goals.html.
25. Press Release, "Anheuser-Busch InBev Launches Global Smart Drinking Goals," Brewbound, December 11, 2015, https://www.brewbound.com/news/anheuser-busch-inbev-launches-global-smartdrinking-goals.
26. Smart Drinking Goals."

27. Contagious, "AmBev, Dirnk Repsnosilby," *Contagious*, June 3, 2019, https://www.contagious.com/news-and-views/ambev.

28. Ibid.

29. Brahma Oficial (@brahmaoficial), Facebook, 2019, https://www.facebook.com/brahmaoficial/.

30. AmBev, "Dirnk Repsnosilby," *Contagious*, June 3, 2019, https://www.contagious.com/news-and-views/ambev.

31. Danilo Macielx, Twitter Post, April 28, 2019, 5:21 p.m., https://twitter.com/CervejariaAmbev/status/1122660088362229761.

32. CervejariaAmbev, Twitter Post, April 28, 2019, 8:23 p.m., https://twitter.com/CervejariaAmbev/status/1122660088362229761.

33. Contagious, "AmBev, Dirnk Repsnosilby."

34. Press Release, "Anheuser-Busch InBev Launches Global Smart Drinking Goals."

35. "Dirnk Repsnosilby," Wave Festival, accessed October 16, 2019, http://www.wavefestival.com.br/premiados2019-social-change/dirnk-repsnosilby-846/.

36. Contagious, "AmBev, Dirnk Repsnosilby."

37. Castilho Leite and Jade Gonçalves, "Cabify e Ambev Criam Campanha De Conscientização No Trânsito," Consumidor Moderno, May 7, 2019, https://www.consumidormoderno.com.br/2019/05/07/cabify-ambev-campanha-transito/.

38. Contagious, "AmBev, Dirnk Repsnosilby."

39. Ibid.

40. Norman R. Nager and T. Harrell Allen, *Public Relations: Management by Objectives* (Lanham, MD: University Press of America, 1991).

41. "Smart Drinking Goals."

Chapter 2

1. Aaron Huey, "We Believe Art Has the Power to Wake People Up," Kickstarter, last modified February 2017, https://www.kickstarter.com/projects/amplifierfoundation/we-the-people-public-art-for-the-inauguration-and?token=43200cc2.

2. Ibid.

3. Cara Egan, "Bill & Melinda Gates Foundation Discovery Center Presents 'We the Future: Young Leaders of Social Change' Exhibition," Bill & Melinda Gates Discovery Center, last modified October 3, 2019, https://www.discovergates.org/press-release-we-the-future-exhibit/.

4. Aleena Gardezi, "The Amplifier Foundation: 'An Art Machine for Social Change.'" *Diverge* (blog), entry posted January 18, 2017, http://divergenow.com/news/2017/01/amplifier-foundation-art-machine-social-change/.

5. Gabriel Min, "Campaigns," Amplifier, last modified 2019, https://amplifier.org/campaigns/.

6. Tom Hagley, *Writing Winning Proposals: PR Cases* (Boston, MA: Pearson Allyn and Bacon, 2006).

7. Katie Place, "Listening as the Driver of Public Relations Practice and Communications Strategy Within a Global Public Relations Agency," *Public Relations Journal* 12, no. 3 (May 2019): 1–18, accessed May 2019, https://prjournal.instituteforpr.org/wp-content/uploads/katieplace_listening.pdf.

8. James Macnamara, "Organizational Listening: Addressing a Major Gap in Public Relations Theory and Practice," *Journal of Public Relations Research* 28 (2016): 146–69.

9. What Is Strategic Communications?," IDEA, March 16, 2011, http://www.idea.org/blog/2011/03/16/what-is-strategic-communications.

10. Linda Childers Hon, "Demonstrating Effectiveness in Public Relations: Goals, Objectives, and Evaluation," *Journal of Public Relations Research* 10, no. 2 (1998): 103–35.

11. Norman R. Nager and T. Harrell Allen, *Public Relations: Management by Objectives* (Lanham, MD: University Press of America, 1991).

12. John E. Marston, *Modern Public Relations* (New York: McGraw-Hill, 1979).

13. Jerry A. Hendrix and Darrell C. Hayes, *Public Relations Cases*, 7th ed. (Belmont, CA: Thomson/Wadsworth, 2007).

14. Dictionary.com, "Diagnose," accessed October 24, 2015, http://www.dictionary.com/browse/diagnose.

15. Nager and Allen, *Public Relations*.

16. Nysha King, "Making the Case for Diversity in Marketing and PR," *Forbes* (blog), entry posted February 15, 2019, https://www.forbes.com/sites/forbescommunicationscouncil/2019/02/15/making-the-case-for-diversity-in-marketing-and-pr/#4007d073424d.

17. Ibid.

18. Ibid.

19. Kalina Nedelcheva, "The 2019 Microsoft Super Bowl Commercial Aims at Inclusion," *Trend Hunter* (blog), entry posted February 1, 2019, https://www.trendhunter.com/trends/microsoft-super-bowl.

20. John V. Pavlik, *Public Relations: What Research Tells Us* (Newbury Park, CA: SAGE Publications, 1987).

21. Glen M. Broom and Bey-Ling Sha, *Cutlip and Center's Effective Public Relations*, 11th ed. (Boston, MA: Pearson, 2013).

22. Ibid., 272.

23. Patricia Swann, *Cases in Public Relations Management*, 2nd ed. (Boston, MA: McGraw Hill, 2014).

24. Dennis L. Wilcox, *Think Public Relations*, 2nd ed. (Boston, MA: Pearson, 2013).

25. Broom and Sha, *Cutlip and Center's Effective Public Relations*.

26. Huey, "We Believe Art Has the Power to Wake People Up."

27. Amplifier," Similar Web, accessed December 2, 2019, https://www.similarweb.com/website/amplifier.org#websiteMobileApps.

28. The Coca-Cola Company, "How Coca-Cola Fosters an Inclusive LGBTQ Employee Community," News release, March 27, 2019, https://www.coca-colacompany.com/news/coca-cola-fosters-inclusive-lgbtq-community.

29. Human Rights Campaign, "HRC Story," Human Rights Campaign, https://www.hrc.org/hrc-story.

30. Human Rights Campaign, "Rating Workplaces on LGBTQ Equality," Corporate Equality Index, https://www.hrc.org/campaigns/corporate-equality-index.

31. DoSomething Strategic, "DoSomething Strategic Finds Most Brands' Support of Cause Platforms Are Not Breaking Through to Gen Z," News release, May 8, 2019, https://www.prnewswire.com/news-releases/dosomething-strategic-finds-most-brands-support-of-cause-platforms-are-not-breaking-through-to-gen-z-300845935.html.

32. Peter Adams, "Diet Coke Debuts Label-Free Cans in Challenge to Stereotypes," *MarketingDive* (blog), entry posted June 27, 2019, https://www.marketingdive.com/news/diet-coke-debuts-label-free-cans-in-challenge-to-stereotypes/557783/.

33. The Coca-Cola Company, "Coca-Cola Supports Marriage Equality in Australia With Limited Edition Cans," News release, September 20, 2017, https://www.coca-colacompany.com/news/coke-supports-marriage-equality-in-australia.

34. Adams, "Diet Coke Debuts Label-Free Cans in Challenge to Stereotypes."

35. Eric Schultz, "These Unlabeled Diet Coke Cans May Hit the Store Shelves Next Year," *AdAge* (blog), entry posted July 15, 2019, https://adage.com/creativity/work/diet-coke-label-free-cans/2183876.

36. The Coca-Cola Company, "Diet Coke Takes on Complex Topic of Labels by Taking Off Its Own." Diet Coke Removes Labels – News & Articles,

July 15, 2019, https://www.coca-colacompany.com/news/diet-coke-removes-labels.

37. The Coca Cola Company, "[unlabeled]™," Diet Coke, last modified July 2019, https://www.dietcoke.com/unlabeled/.

38. Ibid.

39. Schultz, "These Unlabeled Diet Coke Cans May Hit the Store Shelves Next Year."

40. About, Civic Dinners, last modified 2010, https://about.civicdinners.com/.

41. The Coca Cola Company, "[unlabeled]™."

42. Sarah Kim, "Diet Coke Promotes Diversity and Inclusion by Removing Labels From Cans," *Forbes*, accessed July 26, 2019, https://www.forbes.com/sites/sarahkim/2019/07/26/diet-coke-unlabeled/#557ac4451f7c.

43. Ibid.

44. The Coca-Cola Company, "Diet Coke Takes on Complex Topic of Labels by Taking Off Its Own."

45. Maxwell E. McCombs Donald Lewis Shaw, David Hugh Weaver, and Maxwell Mc Combs, *Communication and Democracy: Exploring the Intellectual Frontiers in Agenda-Setting Theory* (Mahwah, NJ: Psychology Press, 1997).

Chapter 3

1. Mark Thabit, "How PESO Makes Sense in Influencer Marketing," *PRWeek*, June 8, 2015, http://www.prweek.com/article/1350303/peso-makes-sense-influencer-marketing.

2. Gini Dietrich, "PR Pros Must Embrace the PESO Model," Spin Sucks, March 23, 2015, http://spinsucks.com/communication/pr-pros-must-embrace-the-peso-model.

3. Lee Odden, "Paid, Earned, Owned and Shared Media," TopRank Marketing, online marketing blog, 2011, accessed July 19, 2016, http://www.toprankblog.com/2011/07/online-marketing-media-mix.

4. Sabine Raabe, "AVE – Does Anyone Actually Still Use This?," Prowly, https://prowly.com/magazine/2017/06/01/peso-instead-of_ave/.

5. Odden, "Paid, Earned, Owned and Shared Media."

6. Brian Solis, *X: The Experience When Business Meets Design* (Hoboken, NJ: John Wiley & Sons, 2015).

7. Scott Guthrie, "The 7 Rs of Influencer Relations." *Ketchum* (blog), March 16, 2016, https://www.ketchum.com/7-rs-influencer-relations.

8. Odden, "Paid, Earned, Owned and Shared Media."

9. Ibid.

10. Jim Macnamara et al., "'PESO' Media Strategy Shifts to 'SOEP': Opportunities and Ethical Dilemmas," *Public Relations Review* 42, no. 3 (2016): 377–85.

11. Marlene S. Neill and Erin Schauster, "Playing Nice in the Sandbox: Is Collaboration Among Advertising and Public Relations Agencies the Same as Integration?," *Journal of Current Issues & Research in Advertising* 39, no. 2 (2018): 140–59.

12. "PR and The Social Whirl: The Peso Model," PRA Public Relations, 2014, http://www.prapublicrelations.com/peso-media-model.

13. Ibid.

14. Influencer Marketing Hub, "Top 13 Employee Advocacy Programs to Increase Your Brand Reach," June, 25, 2019, https://influencermarketinghub.com/top-10-employee-advocacy-programs/.

15. John McKelvey, "Cannes Lions Case Study: Under Armour Kicks Its Way to the Top: Digital Marketing Industry Case Study Library," Digital Training Academy, accessed January 5, 2018, http://www.digitaltrainingacademy.com/case-studies/2015/07/cannes_lions_case_study_under_armour_kicks_its_way_to_the_top.php.

16. E. J. Schultz, "Ad Age's 2014 Marketer of the Year: Under Armour," *AdAge*, December 8, 2014, http://adage.com/article/news/marketer-year-armour/296088.
17. "Cannes Lions Case Study: Under Armour Kicks Its Way to the Top," Digital Training Academy, accessed July 22, 2016, http://www.digital-trainingacademy.com/casestudies/2015/07/cannes_lions_case_study_under_armour_kicks_its_way_to_the_top.php.
18. Schultz, "Ad Ages's 2014 Marketer of the Year."
19. "Cannes Lions Case Study."
20. "Inspiring Young Girls to Be Amazing," March, 5, 2020, https://about.underarmour.com/news/2020/02/international-womens-day-2020-and-curry-7-bamazing-colorway.
21. IBM Research, "5 in 5," https://www.research.ibm.com/5-in-5/.
22. Ragan's PR Daily, "IBM whips up significant media coverage for its 2019 '5 in 5' tech predictions," 2019, https://www.prdaily.com/awards/digital-pr-social-media-awards/2019/winners/media-relations-campaign/.
23. PRSA, "2019 Bronze Anvil Results," https://www.prsa.org/docs/default-source/conference-and-awards/anvil-awards-documents/2019-bronze-anvil-winners.pdf?sfvrsn=1b35bcd0_0.
24. Lee Bell, "Sustainability Tech: The Top 5 Innovations Set to Transform Our Lives Over the Next Five Years," *Forbes*, February 25, 2019, https://www.forbes.com/sites/leebelltech/2019/02/25/sustainability-tech-the-top-5-innovations-set-to-transform-our-lives-over-the-next-five-years/#6a97aac04886.
25. Sean Captain, "Is This Olive Oil Fake? IBM Will Let You Check Using Blockchain," *Fast Company*, January 15, 2020. https://www.fastcompany.com/90451960/is-this-olive-oil-fake-soon-ibm-will-let-you-double-check-using-blockchain.
26. Emma Woollacott, "How Do You Know Where Your Olive Oil Really Comes From?" BBC News, March 22, 2019, https://www.bbc.com/news/business-47553054.
27. Anna Lingeris, Rachel Brueno, and Gail Dent, "Reese's Tips-Off NCAA® March Madness® and Continues NCAA Partnership by Celebrating College Basketball Fandom," *BusinessWire*. https://www.businesswire.com/news/home/20160314006107/en/Reese%E2%80%99s-Tips-Off-NCAA%C2%AE-March-Madness%C2%AE-Continues-NCAA.
28. Jose Angelo Gallegos, "The Best Social Media Marketing Campaigns of 2016," *TINT Blog*, August 21, 2017, https://www.tintup.com/blog/best-social-media-marketing-campaigns.
29. Walt Disney Word Parks and Resorts, "Disneyland® Resort and Make-A-Wish® Celebrate the Success of Worldwide 'Share Your Ears' Campaign," News release, *CISION PR Newswire*, March 14, 2016, https://www.prnewswire.com/news-releases/disneyland-resort-and-make-a-wish-celebrate-the- success-of-worldwide-share-your-ears-campaign-300235681.html.
30. Gallegos, "The Best Social Media Marketing Campaigns of 2016."
31. Ann Dwyer, "Gini Dietrich: Owned vs. Earned Media—Measuring the ROI," *Crain's Chicago Business*, September 30, 2011, http://www.chicagobusiness.com/article/20110930/BLOGS06/309309996/gini-dietrich-owned-vs-earned-media-measuring-the-roi.
32. Tanya Gazdik, "Jared Offers Virtual Weddings," *MediaPost*, May 5, 2020, https://www.media-post.com/publications/article/351041/jared-offers-virtual-weddings.html.
33. Rebecca Lieb and Jeremiah Owyang, "The Converged Media Imperative," Report, Altimeter Group, July 19, 2012, https://www.slideshare.net/Altimeter/the-converged-media-imperative.

34. Nina Dias Da Silva, "Organic Tampons From The Female Company," *Stadt Kind* (blog), entry posted March 8, 2018, https://www.stadtkind-stuttgart.de/bio-tampons-von-the-female-company/.

35. Samantha Guff, "Women Protested the UK's 'Tampon Tax' by Bleeding in White Pants," *Huffpost*, accessed November 9, 2015, https://www.huffpost.com/entry/women-protest-tampon-tax-in-white-pants_n_5640bf35e4b0411d3071a92e.

36. Abbey Marshall, "Protesters Rally Outside Capitol on First National Period Day," *Politico*, accessed October 19, 2019, https://www.politico.com/news/2019/10/19/national-period-day-protesters-tampon-tax-051506.

37. The Female Company and Scholz and Friends Group, "Why German Feminists Hide Tampons in a Book," News release, April 16, 2019.

38. Alison Flood, "No Luxury: Book Containing Tampons Is Runaway Hit," *The Guardian*, accessed June 21, 2019, https://www.theguardian.com/books/2019/jun/21/no-luxury-book-containing-tampons-is-runaway-hit.

39. Ibid.

40. The Female Company and Scholz and Friends Group, "Why German Feminists Hide Tampons in a Book."

41. Ibid.

42. Brand Buffet, "The Tampon Book – Cannes Lions 2019 Winners," YouTube, June 19, 2019, https://www.youtube.com/watch?v=vapeqkHtiFA.

43. Ibid.

44. Ibid.

45. Scholtz and Friends, "Huge Triumph for the Tampon Book at CLIO Awards 2019," Scholtz and Friends, last modified April 9, 2019, https://s-f.com/en/huge-triumph-for-the-tampon-book-at-clio-awards-2019/.

46. Contagious, "Cannes Lions: PR Winners 2019: Female Hygiene Brand Wins PR Grand Prix for Hiding Tampons in Books," *Contagious* (blog), entry posted June 19, 2019, https://www.contagious.com/news-and-views/cannes-lions-pr-winners-2019.

47. Patricia Swann, *Cases in Public Relations Management: The Rise of Social Media and Activism* (New York and London: Routledge and Taylor & Francis Group, 2020).

Chapter 4

1. Don W. Stacks, *Primer of Public Relations Research*, 3rd ed. (New York: Guildford Press, 2017), 5.

2. Donald Jugenheimer, Larry D. Kelley, Jerry Hudson, and Samuel D. Bradley, *Advertising and Public Relations Research*, 2nd ed. (London: Routledge, 2014), 11.

3. Donnalyn Pompper, "Public Relations' Role as Diversity Advocate: Avoiding Microaggressions and Nurturing Microaffirmations in Organizations," *Public Relations Journal* 13, no. 2 (2020): 1–21.

4. Stacks, *Primer of Public Relations Research*, 23.

5. Ibid.

6. Dennis Wilcox and Bryan H. Reber, *Public Relations Writing and Media Techniques* (Boston, MA: Pearson, 2016).

7. Ibid., 322.

8. Glen Broom and David M. Dozer, *Using Research in Public Relations* (Englewood Cliffs, NJ: Prentice Hall, 1990), 24.

9. Glen Broom and Bey-Ling Sha, *Cutlip and Center's Effective Public Relations*, 11th ed. (Boston, MA: Pearson, 2013), 244–45.

10. Stacks, 360.

11. Stacks, *Primer of Public Relations Research*, 59.

12. Linda Childers Hon and James E. Grunig, *Guidelines for Measuring Relationships in Public Relations* (Gainesville, FL: Institute for Public Relations, 1999).

13. Sarah J. Tracy, *Qualitative Research Methods: Collecting Evidence, Crafting Analysis, Communicating Impact* (Malden, MA: Wiley-Blackwell, 2013), 40.

14. Ibid, 230.

15. Pompper, "Public Relations' Role as Diversity Advocate," 1.

16. Ibid., 10.

17. National Association of Manufacturers, "Top Twenty Facts About Manufacturing," 2017, **http://www.nam.org/Newsroom/Facts-About-Manufacturing**.

18. American Medical Association, "AMA Releases Analyses on Potential Anthem-Cigna and Aetna-Humana Mergers," 2015.

19. **http://www.ama-assn.org/ama/pub/news/news/2015/2015-09-08-analysis-anthem-cigna-aetna-humana-mergers.page**.

20. Stacks, *Primer of Public Relations Research*, 143.

21. Katie Delahaye Paine, *Measure What Matters* (Hoboken, NJ: John Wiley & Sons, 2011), 49.

22. Stacks, *Primer of Public Relations Research*, 271.

23. Stacks, *Primer of Public Relations Research*, 275.

24. Broom and Sha, *Cutlip and Center's Effective Public Relations*.

25. Thomas R. Lindloff and Brian C. Taylor, *Qualitative Communication Research Methods*, 3rd ed. (Thousand Oaks, CA: SAGE Publications, 2011).

26. Mattel, "To Inspire the Limitless Potential in Every Girl," Barbie, 2020, **https://barbie.mattel.com/en-us/about.html?icid=all_header_top-nav_our-purpose_p2**.

27. Ibid.

28. Eliana Dockterman, "Barbie's New Body: How to Buy the Four New Dolls Now," *Time*, January 28, 2016, **https://time.com/4194206/new-barbies-how-to-buy-them/**.

29. Mattel, "Barbie Toys, Dolls, Playsets, Vehicles and Dollhouses," Barbie, 2020, **https://barbie.mattel.com/shop**.

30. Carolyn Cox, "Mattel Revamps Barbie, Releases Dolls With Three New Body Types as Part of Massive 'Project Dawn' Overhaul," Mattel Releases Barbies with New Body Types, The Mary Sue, January 28, 2016, **https://www.themarysue.com/new-barbie-bodies/**.

31. Sarah E. McComb and Jennifer S. Mills, "A Systematic Review on the Effects of Media Disclaimers on Young Women's Body Image and Mood," *Body Image* 32 (2020): 34–52.

32. Tonje Sanderlien Troen, "A Study of the Effects on Women's Body Image of Exposure to Ideal Female Body Images in Advertising," Master's Thesis, Hawaii Pacific University, 2009.

33. Galia Slayen, "The Scary Reality of A Real-Life Barbie Doll," *HuffPost*, December 7, 2017, **https://www.huffpost.com/entry/the-scary-reality-of-a-re_b_845239**.

34. Royal Television Society, "Rethinking Barbie: New Documentary Takes a Fresh Look at the Icon," Royal Television Society, November 2018, **https://rts.org.uk/article/rethinking-barbie-new-documentary-takes-fresh-look-icon**.

35. Sophie Gilbert, "Can Barbie Really Have It All?," *The Atlantic*, May 1, 2018, **https://www.theatlantic.com/entertainment/archive/2018/05/tiny-shoulders-review-hulu/559277/**.

36. Ibid.

37. Royal Television Society, "Rethinking Barbie."

38. Ibid.

39. Mattel, "To Inspire the Limitless Potential in Every Girl," Barbie, accessed February 10, 2020, **https://barbie.mattel.com/en-us/about.html**.

40. U.S. Labor Force Change, "A Century of Change: The U.S. Labor Force, 1950–2050,"

May 2002, https://www.bls.gov/opub/mlr/2002/05/art2full.pdf.

41. Mattel, "To Inspire the Limitless Potential in Every Girl."

42. Nick Schager, "Film Review: 'Tiny Shoulders: Rethinking Barbie'," Variety, October 22, 2018, https://variety.com/2018/film/reviews/tiny-shoulders-rethinking-barbie-review-1202788880/.

43. Lorraine Ali, "The Creators of 'Tiny Shoulders: Rethinking Barbie' on Remaking America's Doll Just Before #MeToo," *Los Angeles Times*, April 27, 2018, https://www.latimes.com/entertainment/tv/la-et-st-barbie-documentary-20180427-story.html.

44. Eliana Doktorman, "Barbie Has a New Body Cover Story," *Time*, accessed February 10, 2020, https://time.com/barbie-new-body-cover-story/.

45. Gilbert, "Can Barbie Really Have It All?"

46. Doktorman, "Barbie Has a New Body Cover Story."

47. Entertainment One, "Bringing the Best Content to the World," Entertainment One, accessed February 10, 2020, https://www.entertainmen-tone.com/.

48. Tribeca, "Never Miss a Beat!," Tribeca, accessed February 10, 2020, https://www.tribecafilm.com/festival.

49. Mattel, "Barbie® Wellness," Barbie Wellness, Barbie Shop, Mattel, accessed February 10, 2020, https://barbie.mattel.com/shop/en-us/ba/barbie-wellness#facet:&productBeginIndex:0&orderBy:&pageView:grid&minPrice:&maxPrice:&pageSize:&contentPageSize:&.

50. Robert Mitchell, "Entertainment One Takes International Rights to Hulu's Barbie Documentary," Variety, May 10, 2018, https://variety.com/2018/film/news/eone-takes-international-distribution-hulu-doc-tiny-shoulders-rethinking-barbie-1202804816/.

51. Joan Verdon, "It's Barbie to the Rescue as the 60-Year-Old Brand Leads Mattel's Turnaround," *Forbes*, April 26, 2018, https://www.forbes.com/sites/joanverdon/2019/04/26/its-barbie-to-the-rescue-as-60-year-old-brand-leads-mattel-turn-around/#203449957af0.

52. Mattel, "What Is the Dream Gap?," The Barbie Dream Gap Project, Mattel, 2020, https://barbie.mattel.com/en-us/about/dream-gap.html.

53. Channel Signal, "As Barbie Turns 60, Mattel Aims to Stay on Trend With Consumers," Channel Signal, April 20, 2019, https://channelsignal.com/blog/as-barbie-turns-60-mattel-aims-to-stay-on-trend-with-consumers/.

54. Andrea Nevins, "Tiny Shoulders: Rethinking Barbie," Hulu Press Site, April 27, 2018, https://www.hulu.com/press/show/tiny-shoulders-rethinking-barbie/?temp=synopses.

55. Channel Signal, "As Barbie Turns 60."

56. Elena Selevko, "CCY 2019 Chamberlain Lecture Film Screening of Tiny Shoulders Rethinking Barbie Nevins 2018 Comments," Quick Links Menus, Faculty of Liberal Arts Professional Studies, November 30, 2018, https://ccy.huma.laps.yorku.ca/2018/11/ccy-2019-chamberlain-lecture-film-screening-of-tiny-shoulders-rethinking-barbie-nevins-2018/.

57. Margaret Abrams, "You Can Now Buy a 'Wellness' Self-Care Barbie Which Comes With Gym Clothes and a Protein Bar," Business Insider, February 4, 2020, https://www.businessinsider.com/wellness-self-care-barbie-gym-wear-spa-products-pajamas-launch-2020-2.

58. Ibid.

59. Emma Day, "'What Makes Us Different Makes Us Beautiful': Barbie Introduces Dolls With Vitiligo and Alopecia," *The National*, January 29, 2020,

https://www.thenational.ae/lifestyle/family/what-makes-us-different-makes-us-beautiful-barbie-introduces-dolls-with-vitiligo-and-alopecia-1.971486.

60. Ibid.
61. Ibid.
62. Sarah Young, "Barbie Manufacturer Launches New Dolls With No Hair and Vitiligo," *The Independent*, January 28, 2020, https://www.independent.co.uk/life-style/barbie-mattel-hair-loss-vitiligo-prosthetic-limb-diversity-childrens-dolls-toys-a9305206.html.
63. University of Twente, "Communication Studies Theories: Overview by Category: University of Twente," Universiteit Twente, 2019, https://www.utwente.nl/en/bms/communication-theories/.

Chapter 5

1. Glen Broom and Bey-Ling Sha, *Cutlip and Center's Effective Public Relations*, 11th ed. (Boston, MA: Pearson, 2013), 265.
2. Donald W. Stacks, *Primer of Public Relations Research*, 3rd ed. (New York: Guildford Press, 2017).
3. Laurie J. Wilson and Joseph D. Ogden, *Strategic Communications Planning*, 5th ed. (Dubuque, IA: Kendall/Hunt, 2008), 75.
4. Otto Lerbinger, *Corporate Public Affairs: Interacting With Interest Groups, Media, and Government* (Mawah, NJ: Lawrence Erlbaum, 2006).
5. Jeffrey S. Harrison, Robert A. Phillips, and R. Edward Freeman, "On the 2019 Business Roundtable" Statement on the Purpose of a Corporation,'" *Journal of Management* 46 (2019): 1223–37.
6. Katie Delahaye Paine, *Measure What Matters* (Hoboken, NJ: John Wiley & Sons, 2011), 34–35.
7. Ronald D. Smith, *Strategic Planning for Public Relations*, 3rd ed. (New York: Routledge, 2009), 261.
8. Broom and Sha, *Cutlip and Center's Effective Public Relations*.
9. Dan Lattimore, Otis Baskin, Suzette T. Heiman, and Elizabeth L. Toth, *Public Relations: The Profession and the Practice*, 4th ed. (New York: McGraw-Hill, 2012), 122.
10. Betteke Van Ruler, "Agile Public Relations Planning: The Reflective Communication Scrum," *Public Relations Review* 41, no. 2 (2015): 187–94.
11. Laurie J. Wilson, and Joseph D. Ogden. *Strategic Communications Planning: For Effective Public Relations and Marketing* (Dubuque, IA: Kendall Hunt Publishing Company, 2008).
12. Norman Nager and Harrell T. Allen, *Public Relations Management by Objectives* (Lanham, MD: University Press of America, 1984).
13. Kirk Hallahan, "Organizational Goals and Communication Objectives," in *The Routledge Handbook of Strategic Communication*, ed. D. Holtzhausen and A. Zerfass (New York: Routledge, 2015).
14. Maureen Morrison, "Burger King Launches New Tagline: 'Be Your Way,'" May 19, 2014, http://adage.com/article/news/burger-king-launches-tagline/293283.
15. Erik Oster, "Ad of the Day: Burger King Makes the Most Fabulous Whopper Ever for LGBTQ Pride: Sandwich Has Limited Reach but a Big Heart,"*Adweek*, July 2, 2014, http://www.adweek.com/news/advertising-branding/ad-day-burger-king-makes-most-fabulous-whopper-ever-lgbt-pride-158724.
16. Kathy Steinmetz, "Burger King Debuts Gay Pride Whopper," *Time*, July 1, 2014, http://time.com/2947156/burger-king-debuts-gay-pride-whopper.
17. Bruce Horovitz, "Burger King Sells Gay Pride Whopper," *USA Today*, July 1, 2014, http://www.usatoday.com/story/money/business/2014/gay-rights/11903861.
18. Steinmetz, "Burger King Debuts Gay Pride Whopper."

19. Brendan Snyder, "How Brands Are Taking a Stance (and Winning) With LGBT Advertising," Netimperative, April 13, 2015, http://www.netimperative.com/2015/04/how-brands-are-taking-a-stance-and-winning-fans-with-lgbt-advertising.

20. Jenn Harris, "Burger King Selling a Proud Whopper for Gay Pride," *LA Times*, July 2, 2014, http://www.latimes.com/food/dailydish/la-dd-burger-king-sells-a-proud-whopper-for-gay-pride-20140702-story.html

21. Anna Brand, "Burger King Reveals Special Gay Pride Whopper," *MSNBC*, July 2, 2014, http://www.msnbc.com/msnbc/burger-king-proud-whopper-gay-pride-san-francisco.

22. Steinmetz, "Burger King Debuts Gay Pride Whopper."

23. Horovitz, "Burger King Sells Gay Pride Whopper."

24. Steven Overly, "What Burger King's Proud Whopper Tells Us About Marketing to LGBT Consumers," *Washington Post*, July 3, 2014, https://www.washingtonpost.com/news/business/wp/2014/07/03/what-burger-kings-proud-whopper-tells-us-about-marketing-to-lgbt-consumers/?utm_term=.7bcdac 66fb4b.

25. Sauus, "Burger King Sells 'Proud Whopper' in San Francisco to Change Views on LGBT," n.d., accessed March 12, 2016, http://sauus.com/b/Burger-King-sells-Proud-Whopper-in-San-Francisco-to-change-views-on-LGBT.

26. Eleftheria Parpis, "How Fernando Machado Is Bringing Burger King 'Back to Greatness,'" May 23, 2016, http://www.campaignlive.com/article/fernandomachado-bringing-burger-king-back-greatness/1395717.

27. Joe Morgan, "Burger King Transforms a Whopper Into Diamonds for a Gay Couple's Wedding," *GSN* (blog), entry posted June 28, 2019, https://www.queerty.com/burger-kings-new-pride-ad-features-f-bomb-burger-diamond-2-super-cute-hus-bears-2 0190628.

28. Alex Bollinger, "Burger King Turned a Whopper Into a Gay Couple's Diamond Wedding Rings to Celebrate Pride," *LGBTQ Nation* (blog), entry posted June 2019, https://www.lgbtqnation.com/2019/06/burger-king-turned-whopper-gay-couples-diamond-wedding-rings-celebrate-pride/.

29. Patricia Swann, *Cases in Public Relations Management* (New York: Routledge, 2014).

30. James F. Grunig and Fred C. Repper, "Strategic Management, Publics, and Issues," in *Excellence in Public Relations and Communication Management*, ed. James E. Grunig (New York: Routledge, 1992), 117–57.

31. Steinmetz, "Burger King Debuts Gay Pride Whopper."

32. Burger King – Diversity, accessed February 3, 2020, https://company.bk.com/diversity.

Chapter 6

1. Peter F. Drucker, *The Practice of Management: A Study of the Most Important Function in America Society* (New York: Harper & Brothers, 1954).

2. Ibid., 129.

3. Ibid., 121.

4. *APR Study Guide* (Universal Accreditation Board, 2017), 37.

5. Walter K. Lindenmann, "An 'Effectiveness Yardstick' to Measure Public Relations Success," *Public Relations Quarterly* 38 (1993): 7.

6. Matthew W. Ragas and Ron Culp, *Business Essentials for Strategic Communicators: Creating Shared Value for the Organization and Its Stakeholders* (New York: Palgrave Macmillan, 2014), 147.

7. Ibid., 148.

8. George T. Doran, "There's a S.M.A.R.T. Way to Write Management's Goals and Objectives,"

Management Review (AMA FORUM) 70, no. 11 (1981): 35–36.

9. Ibid., 145.
10. Glen M. Broom and David M. Dozier, *Using Research in Public Relations: Applications to Program Management* (Englewood Cliffs, NJ: Prentice Hall, 1990), 13.
11. Ronald E. Rice and Charles K. Atkin, *Public Communication Campaigns*, 4th ed. (Los Angeles: SAGE Publications, 2013), 14.
12. Robert C. Hornik, "Why Can't We Sell Human Rights Like We Sell Soap?," in *Public Communication Campaigns*, ed. R. E. Rice and C. K. Atkin, 4th ed. (Los Angeles: SAGE Publications, 2013), 35–49.
13. Ibid, 42.
14. Drucker, The Practice of Management.
15. Glen M. Broom and Bey-Ling Sha, *Cutlip and Center's Effective Public Relations* (Boston, MA: Pearson, 2013).
16. *APR Study Guide* (Universal Accreditation Board, 2010).
17. Don W. Stacks and David Michaelson, *A Practitioner's Guide to Public Relations Research, Measurement and Evaluation* (New York: Business Expert Press, 2010).
18. David M. Dozier, Larissa A. Grunig, and James E. Grunig, *Manager's Guide to Excellence in Public Relations and Communication Management* (Mahwah, NJ: Lawrence Erlbaum, 2013), 14.
19. Ibid., 73.
20. Ibid., 50.
21. Broom and Dozier, *Using Research in Public Relations*, 43.
22. The United Nations, "United Nations Global Solidarity Movement For Gender Equality," HeForShe, The United Nations, 2020, **https://www.heforshe.org/en/movement**.
23. Abigail Somma, "New Report Puts Spotlight on Gender Equality in Universities," United Nations, September 2016, **https://www.un.org/sustainabledevelopment/blog/2016/09/new-heforshe-report-puts-spotlight-on-gender-equality-in-global-universities/**.
24. Ibid.
25. Stony Brook University, "About HeForShe: HeForShe: Movement for Gender Equality," Stony Brook University, accessed February 14, 2020, **https://www.stonybrook.edu/commcms/heforshe/about/**.
26. HeForShe, "#HeForShe on Instagram: 'On Today's International Day of Women and Girls in Science We Share the Mentorship Story of Kerris Moore from the #HeForShe #ImpactReport…,'" Instagram, February 11, 2020, **https://www.instagram.com/p/B8bXEULIQcd/?utm_source=ig_web_copy_link**.
27. The United Nations, FleishmanHillard, and Public Relations Society of America, "Case Study: More Powerful Together," 2019.
28. United Nations. "Why Solidarity and Allyship Matter: UN Women HeForShe Global Gender Equality Champions Release Annual IMPACT Report," September 24, 2019, **https://www.prnewswire.com/news-releases/why-solidarity-and-allyship-matter-un-women-heforshe-global-gender-equality-champions-release-annual-impact-report-300923722.html**.
29. The United Nations, FleishmanHillard, and Public Relations Society of America, "Case Study."
30. Alley Pascoe, "Marking 5 Years Of The #HeForShe Movement," Marie Claire, September 18, 2019, **https://www.marieclaire.com.au/heforshe-un-women-emma-watson-gender-equality**.
31. Emma Herman, "Emma Watson's UN Gender Equality Campaign Invites Men Too | Emma Herman," *The Guardian*, October 3, 2014, **https://www.theguardian.com/global-development/poverty**

-matters/2014/oct/03/emma-watsons-un-gender-equality-campaign-is-an-invitation-to-men-too.

32. Council of Europe, "HeforShe Campaign," Council of Europe, April 10, 2015, https://www.coe.int/en/web/portal/news-2015/-/asset_publisher/9k8wkRrYhB8C/content/heforshe-campaign?_101_INSTANCE_9k8wkRrYhB8C_languageId=en_GB.
33. The United Nations, FleishmanHillard, and Public Relations Society of America, "Case Study."
34. Ibid.
35. Ibid.
36. Ibid.
37. Ibid.
38. Hayley Leibson, "HeForShe's Emerging Solutions for Gender Equality," *Forbes*, September 26, 2018, https://www.forbes.com/sites/hayleyleibson/2018/09/26/heforshes-emerging-solutions-for-gender-equality/#285a0a2d234e.
39. Bob Fine, "Behind The Hashtag: #HeForShe," *The Social Media Monthly*, March 27, 2017, https://thesocialmediamonthly.com/behind-the-hashtag-heforshe/.
40. The United Nations, "Global Solidarity Movement."
41. United Nations Women, "Donate: HeForShe," HeForShe, United Nations Women, 2020, https://donate.unwomen.org/en/give/heforshe.
42. The United Nations, FleishmanHillard, and Public Relations Society of America, "Case Study."
43. Ibid.
44. Ibid.
45. The United Nations and Publicis, Ogilvy, Weber Shandwick, Hootsuite, "UN Women's #HeForShe Solidarity Movement for Gender Equality – The Shorty Awards," 2019, https://shortyawards.com/7th/un-womens-heforshe-solidarity-movement-for-gender-equality.
46. Ibid.
47. The United Nations, FleishmanHillard, and Public Relations Society of America, "Case Study."
48. Ibid.
49. The United Nations, "Your Personal Invitation," HeForShe, The United Nations, 2020, https://www.heforshe.org/en.
50. Ibid.
51. The United Nations, "UN Women Announces United Nations Police Adviser Luís Carrilho as HeForShe Advocate for Gender Equality," HeForShe, The United Nations, November 25, 2019, https://www.heforshe.org/en/un-women-announces-united-nations-police-adviser-luis-carrilho-heforshe-advocate-gender-equality.

Chapter 7

1. Glen M. Broom and Bey-Ling Sha, *Cutlip and Center's Effective Public Relations*, 11th ed. (Boston, MA: Pearson, 2013).
2. Ibid., 273.
3. Ibid., 170.
4. Gini Dietrich, *Spin Sucks: Communication and Reputation Management in the Digital Age* (Indianapolis, IN: Que, 2014).
5. Ganga S. Dhanesh and Gaelle Duthler, "Relationship Management Through Social Media Influencers: Effects of Followers' Awareness of Paid Endorsement," *Public Relations Review* 45, no. 3 (2019): 101765.
6. Andrew T. Stephen and Joseph Galak, "The Effects of Traditional and Social Earned Media on Sales: A Study of a Microlending Marketplace," *Journal of Marketing Research* 49, no. 5 (2012): 624–39.
7. Broom and Sha, *Cutlip and Center's Effective Public Relations*.
8. Ibid., 209.

9. Dietrich, *Spin Sucks*.

10. Ibid., 40.

11. Dietrich, *Spin Sucks*.

12. Guy Kawasaki and Peg Fitzpatrick, *The Art of Social Media: Power Tips for Power Users* (New York: Portfolio, 2014).

13. Donald K. Wright and Michelle Drifka Hinson, "An Updated Examination of Social and Emerging Media Use in Public Relations Practice: A Longitudinal Analysis Between 2006 and 2013," *Public Relations Journal* 7, no. 3 (2013): 1–39.

14. Angelica Evans, Jane Twomey, and Scott Talan, "Twitter as a Public Relations Tool," *Public Relations Journal* 5, no. 1 (2011): 1–20.

15. Karen Freberg et al, "Who Are the Social Media Influencers? A Study of Public Perceptions of Personality," *Public Relations Review* 37, no. 1 (2011): 90–92.

16. Michael L. Kent and Chaoyuan Li, "Toward a Normative Social Media Theory for Public Relations," *Public Relations Review* 46, no. 1 (2019): 101857.

17. Ibid., 44.

18. Mikal Belicove, "Five Reasons Why Websites Still Matter," *Entrepreneur*, September 13, 2011, **http://www.entrepreneur.com/article/220307**.

19. Charlene Li and Josh Bernoff, *Groundswell: Winning in a World Transformed by Social Technologies* (Boston, MA: Harvard Business Press, 2008).

20. Dennis Yu, "Does Facebook's 'Boost Post' Button Work?," *Adweek*, June 30, 2014, **http://www.adweek.com/socialtimes/does-facebooks-boost-post-button-work/299859**.

21. Brian Sheehan, "More Effective Native Advertising Is a Solution to Ad Blockers," *Ad Age*, February 3, 2016, **http://adage.com/article/digitalnext/effectivenative-ads-a-solution-ad-blockers/302476**.

22. Brenda Dervin and Lois Foreman-Wernet, "Sense-Making Methodology as an Approach to Understanding and Designing for Campaign Audiences," in *Public Communication Campaigns*, ed. Ronald E. Rice and Charles K. Atkin (Thousand Oaks, CA: SAGE Publications, 2012), 147–62.

23. Laurie J. Wilson and Joseph D. Ogden, *Strategic Communications Planning for Effective Public Relations and Marketing*, 5th ed. (Dubuque, IA: Kendall-Hunt, 2008), 102.

24. Ibid., 103.

25. James E. Grunig and Fred C. Repper, "Strategic Management, Publics, and Issues," in *Excellence in Public Relations and Communication Management*, ed. James E. Grunig, David M. Dozier, and W. P. Ehling (Hillsdale, NJ: Lawrence Erlbaum Associates, 1992), 117–57.

26. Broom and Sha, *Cutlip and Center's Effective Public Relations*, 269.

27. John Vernon Pavlik, *Public Relations: What Research Tells Us* (Newbury Park, CA: SAGE Publications, 1987), 56.

28. Roger D. Wimmer and Joseph R. Dominick, *Mass Media Research: An Introduction*, 9th ed. (Boston, MA: Cengage-Wadsworth, 2011), 335–36.

29. Kirk Hallahan, "Inactive Publics: The Forgotten Publics in Public Relations," *Public Relations Review* 26 (2001): 499–515.

30. Dave Chaffey, "Mobile Marketing Statistics Compilation," Smart Insights, March 1, 2017, **http://www.smartinsights.com/mobile-marketing/mobile-marketing-analytics/mobile-marketing-statistics**.

31. Greg Sterling, "Mobile Makes Up 21 pct. of Online Spending in Q4, as Digital Commerce Reaches $109 Billion," Marketing Land, February 14,

2017, http://marketingland.com/m-commerce-21-percent-online-spending-q4-digital-commerce-reaches-109-billion-206591.

32. Dean Kruckeberg and Marina Vujnovic, "The Death of the Concept of Publics (Plural) in 21st Century Public Relations," *International Journal of Strategic Communication* 4, no. 2 (2010): 117–25.

33. Natalie Tindall and Jennifer Vardeman-Winter, "Complications in Segmenting Campaign Publics: Women of Color Explain Their Problems, Involvement, and Constraints in Reading Heart Disease Communication," *Howard Journal of Communications* 22, no. 3 (2011): 280–301.

34. Ibid., 299.

35. Jennifer Vardeman-Winter, Natalie Tindall, and Hua Jiang, "Intersectionality and Publics: How Exploring Publics' Multiple Identities Questions Basic Public Relations Concepts," *Public Relations Inquiry* 2, no. 3 (2013): 279–304.

36. Jennifer Vardeman-Winter, "Confronting Whiteness in Public Relations Campaigns and Research With Women," *Journal of Public Relations Research* 23, no. 4 (2011): 412–41.

37. Matthew W. Ragas and Ron Culp, *Business Essentials for Strategic Communicators: Creating Shared Value for the Organization and Its Stakeholders* (New York: Palgrave Macmillan, 2014), 85–91.

38. Jack Healy, "Ferguson, Still Tense, Grows Calmer," *New York Times*, November 26, 2014.

39. Jason Purnell, Gabriela Camberos, and Robert Fields, "For the Sake of All: A Report on the Health and Well-Being of African Americans in St. Louis and Why It Matters for Everyone," (report, Washington University in St. Louis/Saint Louis University, 2015), http://www.forthesakeofall.org.

40. Brentin Mock and CityLab, "What New Research Says About Race and Police Shootings," CityLab, August 7, 2019, https://www.citylab.com/equity/2019/08/police-officer-shootings-gun-violence-racial-bias-crime-data/595528/.

41. The In St. Louis Project," https://instlouis.wustl.edu/.

42. The ACLU's Work in Focus: Reflections from an Internship," University Libraries, May 14, 2019, https://library.wustl.edu/aclu-work-in-focus/.

43. Monica Anderson, "History of the Hashtag #BlackLivesMatter: Social Activism on Twitter," Pew Research Center: Internet, Science and Tech, December 31, 2019, https://www.pewresearch.org/internet/2016/08/15/the-hashtag-blacklivesmatter-emerges-social-activism-on-twitter/.

44. Communication Theories," Universiteit Twente, http://www.utwente.nl/communication-theories.

45. Kirk Hallahan, "Seven Models of Framing: Implications for Public Relations," *Journal of Public Relations Research* 11, no. 3 (1999): 205–42.

46. Patricia Swann, *Cases in Public Relations Management*, 2nd ed. (Boston, MA: McGraw Hill, 2014).

Chapter 8

1. Mary Jo Hatch and Ann L. Cunliffe, *Organization Theory: Modern, Symbolic and Postmodern Perspectives* (Oxford: Oxford University Press, 2013).

2. Larry Kelley, Kim Sheehan, and Donald W. Jugenheimer, *Advertising Media Planning: A Brand Management Approach* (New York: Routledge, 2015), 149.

3. Andrew McStay, *Digital Advertising* (New York: Palgrave Macmillan, 2009).

4. Kelley, Sheehan, and Jugenheimer, *Advertising Media Planning*.

5. Lynn M. Zoch and Juan-Carlos Molleda, "Building a Theoretical Model of Media Relations

Using Framing, Information Subsidies and Agenda Building," in *Public Relations Theory II*, ed. Carl H. Botan and Vincent Hazleton (Mahwah, NJ: Lawrence Erlbaum, 2006), 279–309.

6. *APR Study Guide* (Universal Accreditation Board, 2010), 18.
7. Carole Howard and Wilma Mathews, *On Deadline: Managing Media Relations* (Long Grove, IL: Waveland Press, 2013), 129–30.
8. Glen M. Broom and Bey-Ling Sha, *Cutlip and Center's Effective Public Relations*, 11th ed. (Boston, MA: Pearson, 2013), 7.
9. Zoch and Molleda, "Building a Theoretical Model of Media Relations."
10. Lon Safko, *The Social Media Bible: Tactics, Tools and Strategies for Business Success*, 3rd ed. (Hoboken, NJ: Wiley, 2012).
11. Daniel Jacobson, "COPE: Create Once, Publish Everywhere," ProgrammableWeb, 2009, **https://www.programmableweb.com/news/cope-create-once-publish-everywhere/2009/10/13**.
12. Ann Handley and Charles C. Chapman, *Content Rules: How to Create Killer Blogs, Podcasts, Videos, e-books, Webinars (and More) That Engage Customers and Ignite Your Business*, vol. 13 (New York: John Wiley & Sons, 2012).
13. *APR Study Guide.*
14. Ron Smith, *Strategic Planning for Public Relations* (Mahwah, NJ: Lawrence Erlbaum, 2005), 201.
15. Ibid., 202.
16. Ibid., 201.
17. Dean Mundy, "From Principle to Policy to Practice? Diversity as a Driver of Multicultural, Stakeholder Engagement in Public Relations," *Public Relations Journal* 9, no. 1 (2015): 1–20, 12.
18. Dean Mundy, "Bridging the Divide: A Multidisciplinary Analysis of Diversity Research and the Implications for Public Relations," *Research Journal of the Institute for Public Relations* 3, no. 1 (2016): 1–28.
19. Tiphané P. Turpin, "Unintended Consequences of a Segmentation Strategy: Exploring Constraint Recognition Among Black Women Targeted in HIV/AIDS Campaigns," *Public Relations Journal* 7, no. 2 (2013): 96–127.
20. PEEPS, Coyne Public Relations, and Public Relations Society of America, "Case Study: PEEPS Counts Down to a Sweet New Year," 2019.
21. Gael Fashingbauer Cooper, "A Pennsylvania Town Will Ring in the New Year by Dropping a 400-Pound Marshmallow Peep," Insider, December 31, 2018, **https://www.insider.com/400-pound-marshmallow-peep-drop-new-years-eve-pennsylvania-2018-12**.
22. Ibid.
23. PEEPS, Coyne Public Relations, and Public Relations Society of America, "Case Study."
24. Just Born Quality Confections, "PEEPS® Invites Fans Inside the Factory for the First Time," PR Newswire: press release distribution, targeting, monitoring and marketing, January 8, 2019, **https://www.prnewswire.com/news-releases/peeps-invites-fans-inside-the-factory-for-the-first-time-300774155.html**.
25. Ibid.
26. Ibid.
27. PEEPS, Coyne Public Relations, and Public Relations Society of America, "Case Study."
28. Just Born Quality Confections, "PEEPS® Invites Fans."
29. Ibid.
30. Ibid.
31. Ibid.
32. Ibid.

33. Just Born Quality Confections, "PEEPS® Invites Fans Inside the Factory for the First Time," Just Born, May 31, 2019, https://www.justborn.com/news-and-media/2019/peeps-invites-fans-inside-factory-first-time/.

34. PEEPS, Coyne Public Relations, and Public Relations Society of America, "Case Study."

35. Ibid.

36. Ibid.

37. Ibid.

38. Ibid.

Chapter 9

1. Glen M. Broom and Bey-Ling Sha, *Cutlip and Center's Effective Public Relations*, 11th ed. (Boston, MA: Pearson, 2013), 287.

2. Peter Morris and Jeffrey K. Pinto, *The Wiley Guide to Project Organization and Project Management Competencies* (Hoboken, NJ: John Wiley & Sons, 2011), x–xi.

3. Dennis P. Slevin and Jeffrey K. Pinto, "An Overview of Behavioral Issues in Project Management." in *The Wiley Guide to Project Organization and Project Management Competencies*, ed. Peter Morris and Jeffrey K. Pinto (Hoboken, NJ: John Wiley & Sons, 2011), 1–19.

4. These categories are based on those developed in the following text: Ronald Smith, *Strategic Planning for Public Relations*, 3rd ed. (London: Routledge, 2009), 261.

5. Ibid., 261.

6. Connie Delisle, "Contemporary Views on Shaping, Developing, and Managing Teams," in *The Wiley Guide to Project Organization and Project Management Competencies*, ed. Peter Morris and Jeffrey K. Pinto (Hoboken, NJ: John Wiley & Sons, 2011), 36–69.

7. Ken James, *Escoffier: The King of Chefs* (London: Hambledon and London, 2002).

8. Smith, *Strategic Planning for Public Relations*, 257–59.

9. For more on project team leadership, see Thomas and Kerwin's chapter: Peg Thomas and John J. Kerwin, "Leadership of Project Teams," in *The Wiley Guide to Project Organization and Project Management Competencies*, ed. Peter Morris and Jeffrey K. Pinto (Hoboken, NJ: John Wiley & Sons, 2011), 70–88.

10. Ibid., 80.

11. Doug Newsom, Judy VanSlyke Turk, and Dean Kruckeberg, *This Is PR: The Realities of Public Relations*, 7th ed. (Belmont, CA: Wadsworth, 2000), 329.

12. See Alvin C. Croft, *Managing a Public Relations Firm for Growth and Profit* (New York: Haworth Press, 1996), 160.

13. Broom and Sha, *Cutlip and Center's Effective Public Relations*, 293.

14. Carole Howard and Wilma Mathews, *On Deadline: Managing Media Relations* (Long Grove, IL: Waveland Press, 2013).

15. Ibid., 65.

16. Ibid., 66.

17. Ibid., 75.

18. Ed Zitron, *This Is How You Pitch* (Muskegeon, MI: Sunflower Press, 2013), 30.

19. Ibid., 71.

20. Betteke van Ruler, "Agile Public Relations Planning: The Reflective Communication Scrum," *Public Relations Review* 41, no. 2 (2015): 187–94.

21. James E. Grunig and Fred C. Repper, "Strategic Management, Publics, and Issues," in *Excellence in Public Relations and Communication Management*, ed. J. E. Grunig (Hillsdale, NJ: Lawrence Erlbaum, 1992), 118.

22. Augustine Pang, Yan Jin, and Glen T. Cameron, "Contingency Theory of Strategic Conflict

Management: Directions for Practice of Crisis Communication from a Decade of Theory Development, Discovery, and Dialogue." in *The Handbook of Crisis Communication*, ed. W. T. Coombs and S. Holladay (Malden, MA: Wiley-Blackwell, 2010), 527–49.

23. Ibid., 533.
24. Girl Scouts of Greater New York, "Who Are We?," Girl Scouts of Greater New York, 2020, https://www.girlscoutsnyc.org/en/about-girl-scouts/who-we-are.html.
25. Ibid.
26. Justin Tasolides, "Homeless NYC Girl Scouts Hold 1st Cookie Sale With Some Snap, Crackle and Pop," *ABC News*, April 11, 2018, https://abcnews.go.com/GMA/Family/homeless-nyc-girl-scouts-hold-1st-cookie-sale/story?id=54390922.
27. Dana Rosenwasser, "Girl Scout Troop 6000™ Empowers Girls at Domestic Violence Shelters," Safe Horizon, April 1, 2019, https://www.safehorizon.org/programs/girl-scout-troop-6000-domestic-violence-shelters/.
28. Bethany Braun-Silva, "NYC Girl Scout Troop Comprised of Girls Living in Shelters Hold First Cookie Sale," NY Metro Parents, April 12, 2018, https://www.nymetroparents.com/article/troop-6000-homeless-girl-scout-troop-first-cookie-sale.
29. Ibid.
30. Girl Scouts of Greater New York, "Troop 6000," Girl Scouts of Greater New York, accessed February 26, 2020, https://www.girlscoutsnyc.org/en/whatgirlsdo/gs-troop-6000.html.
31. Tasolides, "Homeless NYC Girl Scouts."
32. Ashley Serianni, "First-Ever Homeless Girl Scout Troop in NYC Smashes Cookie Sales Goal," *NBC New York*, April 24, 2018, https://www.nbcnewyork.com/news/local/girl-scout-troop-for-nyc-homeless-girls-sells-more-than-32k-boxes-of-cookies-at-their-first-cookie-sale/491851/.
33. Ibid.
34. Ibid.
35. Girl Scouts of Greater New York," Bringing the Girl Scout Experience to Girls in the NYC Shelter System," 2019, https://www.girlscoutsnyc.org/en/whatgirlsdo/gs-troop-6000.html.
36. Growing the Girl Scout Sisterhood: Troop 6000," Youtube, Girl Scouts of Greater New York, 2018, https://www.youtube.com/watch?v=yzbl1LuaUKY.
37. Ibid.
38. Kellogg's, Girl Scouts of Greater New York, Reilly Connect, and Anthem Worldwide, "Case Study: Kellogg's Sweetens First Ever Cookie Sale Event for Girl Scouts Living in NYC Homeless Shelters," 2019.
39. Ibid.
40. Ibid.
41. Ibid.
42. Girl Scouts of America, "G.I.R.L. Agenda Powered by Girl Scouts," Girl Scouts of the USA, accessed March 2, 2020, https://www.girlscouts.org/en/g-i-r-l-agenda.html.

Chapter 10

1. Tom Watson and Paul Noble, *Evaluating Public Relations: A Guide to Planning, Research and Measurement* (London: Kogan Page, 2014), 22.
2. Dan Lattimore, Otis Baskin, Susan T. Heiman, and Elizabeth Toth, *Public Relations: The Profession and the Practice*, 4th ed. (New York: McGraw-Hill, 2011).
3. Watson and Noble, *Evaluating Public Relations*, 17.
4. Watson and Noble, *Evaluating Public Relations*.
5. Ibid., 36.

6. Ibid., 76.
7. Ibid., 79.
8. Ibid., 76.
9. Ibid., 99.
10. Katie Delahaye Paine, *Measure What Matters* (Hoboken, NJ: John Wiley & Sons, 2011).
11. Watson and Noble, *Evaluating Public Relations*, 147.
12. Marianne Eisenmann, "Speak Their Language: Communicating Results to the C-Suite," *Public Relations Tactics* (PRSA, 2011).
13. Ibid.
14. Larry Kelley, Kim Sheehan, and Donald W. Jugenheimer, *Advertising Media Planning: A Brand Management Approach* (New York: Routledge, 2015), 323.
15. Watson and Noble, *Evaluating Public Relations*, 98.
16. Kartikay Kashyap, "Global Wellness Challenge: Hewlett Packard Enterprise' Mini Olympics," HR Katha, March 20, 2019, https://www.hrkatha.com/special/employee-benefits-and-engagement/global-wellness-challenge-hewlett-packards-mini-olympics/.
17. Ibid.
18. RSW, "Employee Wellness: Reducing Costs and Increasing Engagement," RSW Creative, January 29, 2018, https://rswcreative.com/employee-wellness-reducing-costs-increasing-engagement/.
19. Ibid.
20. Ibid.
21. Ibid.
22. RSW, "Power of Prevention," RSW Creative, January 12, 2019, https://rswcreative.com/work/power-of-prevention/.
23. Ibid.
24. Kashyap, "Global Wellness Challenge."
25. Ibid.
26. The Fuller Life, "Corporate Health Summit – 2018 Recap," The Fuller Life, September 14, 2018, https://thefullerlife.com/2018/09/14/corporate-health-summit-2018-recap/.
27. Ibid.
28. Kashyap, "Global Wellness Challenge."
29. Joe Dixon, "How Samanntha DuBridge Helps Others Discuss Mental Health at HPE," American Healthcare Leader, February 18, 2019, https://americanhealthcareleader.com/2019/dubridge-hpe-mental-health/.
30. Ibid.
31. Ibid.
32. Ibid.
33. Ibid.
34. Albert Bandura, "Social Cognitive Theory," in *Handbook of Theories of Social Psychology*, ed. P. A. M. Van Lange, A. W. Kruglanski, and E. T. Higgins (Thousand Oaks, CA: SAGE Publications, 2011), 349–73.
35. Albert Bandura, "Social Cognitive Theory: An Agentic Perspective," *Annual Review of Psychology* 52, no. 1 (2001): 1–26.
36. Patricia Swann, *Cases in Public Relations Management*, 2nd ed. (Boston, MA: McGraw Hill, 2014).

Chapter 11

1. Women in PR, "12 Steps to a Successful PR Campaign," Women in PR, January 12, 2012, accessed March 4, 2017, https://womeninpr.wordpress.com/2012/01/10/12-steps-to-a-successful-pr-campaign/.
2. L. J. Wilson and J. Ogden, *Strategic Communications Planning for Public Relations and Marketing* (Dubuque, IA: Kendall Hunt, 2016).
3. D. C. Hayes, J. A. Hendrix, and P. D. Kumar, *Public Relations Cases* (Independence, KY: Cengage, 2013).

4. C. R. Christensen, K. R. Andrews, and J. L. Bower, *Ideas for Instructors on the Use and Content of Business Policy, Text and Cases* (Homewood, IL: R. D. Irwin, 1978).

5. K. Beamish and R. Ashford, *Marketing Planning, 2005–2006* (Oxford: Elsevier Butterworth-Heinemann, 2005).

6. KPI Examples, Klipfolio, n.d., accessed March 4, 2017, https://www.klipfolio.com/resources/kpi-examples.

7. G. Nelissen, "Four PR Metrics You Can Start Using Today," Spin Sucks, December 3, 2014, accessed March 4, 2017, http://spinsucks.com/communication/four-pr-metrics-you-can-use-today/.

8. S.Elson, "PR Planning 101: Defining Objectives, Strategies and Tactics," CommuniquePR, April 8, 2016, accessed December 18, 2017, http://www.communiquepr.com/blog/?p=8422.

9. G. Dietrich, "PR Pros Must Embrace the PESO Model," Spin Sucks, March 23, 2015, accessed February 3, 2016, http://spinsucks.com/communication/pr-pros-must-embrace-the-peso-model/.

10. What Is a Gantt chart?," Gantt.com, 2017, accessed March 4, 2017, http://www.gantt.com/index2.htm?utm_expid=11664174-46.EjGD5xWgTOia25IJzkiv2w.2&utm_referrer=https%3A%2F%2Fwww.google .com%2F.

11. R. Luttrell, *Social Media: How to Engage, Share, and Connect* (Lanham, MD: Rowman & Littlefield, 2016).

12. T. Biderbeck, "The Creative Brief: 10 Things It Must Include," Felt and Wire, February 8, 2011, accessed August 11, 2017, https://www.mohawkconnects.com/feltandwire/2011/02/08/the-creative-brief-10-things-it-must-include/.

13. Dietrich, "PR Pros Must Embrace the PESO Model."

14. Christina Newberry, "How to Build a Buyer Persona," *Hootsuite* (blog), entry posted November 21, 2018, https://blog.hootsuite.com/buyer-persona/.

15. Kane Jamison, "10 Customer Persona Tools and Templates," *Content Harmony* (blog), entry posted March 5, 2017, https://www.contentharmony.com/blog/customer-persona-tools/.

Appendix

1. Robert K. Yin, *Case Study Research: Design and Methods*, 5th ed. (Thousand Oaks, CA: SAGE Publications, 2013), 10–11.

2. Ibid., 9.

3. Brad L. Rawlins, *Prioritizing Stakeholders for Public Relations* (Gainesville, FL: Institute for Public Relations, 2006), http://www.instituteforpr.org/wp-content/uploads/2006_stakeholders-1.pdf.

4. Linda Aldoory and Bey-Ling Sha, "The Situational Theory of Publics: Practical Applications, Methodological Challenges, and Theoretical Horizons," in *The Future of Excellence in Public Relations and Communication Management: Challenges for the Next Generation*, ed. E. L. Toth (Mahwah, NJ: Lawrence Erlbaum Associates, 2007), 339–55.

5. James E. Grunig and Fred C. Repper, "Strategic Management, Publics, and Issues," in *Excellence in Public Relations and Communication Management*, ed. J. E. Grunig (Hillsdale, NJ: Lawrence Erlbaum Associates, 1992), 118.

6. Katie Delahaye Paine and William T. Paarlberg, *Measure What Matters: Online Tools for Understanding Customers, Social Media, Engagement, and Key Relationships* (Hoboken, NJ: Wiley, 2011).

7. *APR Study Guide* (University Accreditation Board, 2017), 35.

8. Ibid., 35.

9. Don W. Stacks and David Michaelson, *A Practitioner's Guide to Public Relations Research, Measurement, and Evaluation* (New York: Business Expert Press, 2010), 115.

10. Glen Broom and David M. Dozer, *Using Research in Public Relations* (Englewood Cliffs, NJ: Prentice Hall, 1990), 119.

11. Ibid., 118.

12. Broom and Dozer, *Using Research in Public Relations*, 117.

13. Tom Watson, "Advertising Value Equivalence—PR's Illegitimate Offspring" (Paper presented at 15th International Public Relations Research Conference (IPRRC), Miami, FL, March, 2012).

14. Andre Manning and David B. Rockland, "Understanding the Barcelona Principles," The Public Relations Strategist, March, 2011, http://www.prsa.org/Intelligence/TheStrategist.

15. Emily Greenhouse, "JPMorgan's Twitter Mistake," *The New Yorker*, November 16, 2013, http://www.newyorker.com/business/currency/jpmorgans-twitter-mistake.

16. Charles K. Atkin and Vicki Freimuth, "Guidelines for Formative Evaluation Research in Campaign Design," in *Public Communication Campaigns*, ed. Ronald E. Rice and Charles K.Atkin (Thousand Oaks, CA: SAGE Publications, 2013), 53–68.

17. Larry D. Kelley, Donald W. Jugenheimer, and Kim Sheehan, *Advertising Media Planning: A Brand Management Approach*, 4th ed. (New York: Routledge, 2015).

18. Ibid., 171.

19. Ibid., 168.

20. Ibid., 158.

21. Andrew McStay, *Digital Advertising* (Basingstoke: Palgrave Macmillan, 2010).

22. Ibid., 49.

23. Kelley, Jugenheimer, and Sheehan, *Advertising Media Planning*, 192.

24. Jieunn Lee and Ilyoo B. Hong, "Predicting Positive User Responses to Social Media Advertising: The Roles of Emotional Appeal, Informativeness, and Creativity," *International Journal of Information Management* 36, no. 3 (2016): 360–73.

25. Christy Ashley and Tracy Tuten, "Creative Strategies in Social Media Marketing: An Exploratory Study of Branded Social Content and Consumer Engagement," *Psychology & Marketing* 32, no. 1 (2015): 15–27.

26. Carole Howard and Wilma Mathews, *On Deadline: Managing Media Relations* (Long Grove, IL: Waveland Press, 2013), 44.

27. Ibid., 128.

28. Ibid., 52.

29. Andrew Rohm and Michael Weiss, *Herding Cats: A Strategic Approach to Social Media Marketing* (New York: Business Expert Press, 2014).

30. Lon Safko, *The Social Media Bible: Tactics, Tools, and Strategies for Business Success* (Hoboken, NJ: John Wiley & Sons, 2012).

31. Here's How Many People Are on Facebook, Instgram, Twitter and Other Big Social Networks," *AdWeek*, April 4, 2016, http://www.adweek.com/digital/heres-how-many-people-are-on-facebook-instagram-twitter-other-big-social-networks/#/

32. Regina Luttrell, *Social Media: How to Engage, Share, and Connect* (Lanham, MD: Rowman & Littlefield, 2016).

33. Safko, *The Social Media Bible*, 567.

34. Jayson DeMers, "Why Community Management Is Different Than Social Media Marketing," *Forbes*, February 12, 2015, https://www.forbes.com/sites/jaysondemers/2015/02/12/why-community-management-is-different-from-social-media-marketing/#63fe1f8567d9.

35. *APR Study Guid*e, 18.

36. Ronald D. Smith, *Strategic Planning for Public Relations* (New York: Routledge, 2017).

37. Ibid., 202.

38. Ibid., 201.

Index